Network Security in a Mixed Environment

Dan Blacharski

IDG Books Worldwide, Inc.
An International Data Group Company

Foster City, CA ◆ Chicago, IL ◆ Indianapolis, IN ◆ Southlake, TX

Network Security in a Mixed Environment

Published by
IDG Books Worldwide, Inc.
An International Data Group Company
919 E. Hillsdale Blvd., Suite 400
Foster City, CA 94404
www.idgbooks.com (IDG Books Worldwide Web site)

Library of Congress Catalog Card No.: 97-077800

ISBN: 0-7645-3152-2

Printed in the United States of America

10 9 8 7 6 5 4 3 2 1

1DD/QS/QS/ZY/FC

Distributed in the United States by IDG Books Worldwide, Inc.

Distributed by Macmillan Canada for Canada; by Transworld Publishers Limited in the United Kingdom; by IDG Norge Books for Norway; by IDG Sweden Books for Sweden; by Woodslane Pty. Ltd. for Australia; by Woodslane Enterprises Ltd. for New Zealand; by Longman Singapore Publishers Ltd. for Singapore, Malaysia, Thailand, and Indonesia; by Simron Pty. Ltd. for South Africa; by Toppan Company Ltd. for Japan; by Distribuidora Cuspide for Argentina; by Livraria Cultura for Brazil; by Ediciencia S.A. for Ecuador; by Addison-Wesley Publishing Company for Korea; by Ediciones ZETA S.C.R. Ltda. for Peru; by WS Computer Publishing Corporation, Inc., for the Philippines; by Unalis Corporation for Taiwan; by Contemporanea de Ediciones for Venezuela; by Computer Book & Magazine Store for Puerto Rico; by Express Computer Distributors for the Caribbean and West Indies. Authorized Sales Agent: Anthony Rudkin Associates for the Middle East and North Africa.

For general information on IDG Books Worldwide's books in the U.S., please call our Consumer Customer Service department at 800-762-2974. For reseller information, including discounts and premium sales, please call our Reseller Customer Service department at 800-434-3422.

For information on where to purchase IDG Books Worldwide's books outside the U.S., please contact our International Sales department at 650-655-3200 or fax 650-655-3295.

For information on foreign language translations, please contact our Foreign & Subsidiary Rights department at 650-655-3021 or fax 650-655-3281.

For sales inquiries and special prices for bulk quantities, please contact our Sales department at 650-655-3200 or write to the address above.

For information on using IDG Books Worldwide's books in the classroom or for ordering examination copies, please contact our Educational Sales department at 800-434-2086 or fax 817-251-8174.

For press review copies, author interviews, or other publicity information, please contact our Public Relations department at 650-655-3000 or fax 650-655-3299.

For authorization to photocopy items for corporate, personal, or educational use, please contact Copyright Clearance Center, 222 Rosewood Drive, Danvers, MA 01923, or fax 978-750-4470.

ABOUT IDG BOOKS WORLDWIDE

Welcome to the world of IDG Books Worldwide.

IDG Books Worldwide, Inc., is a subsidiary of International Data Group, the world's largest publisher of computer-related information and the leading global provider of information services on information technology. IDG was founded more than 25 years ago and now employs more than 8,500 people worldwide. IDG publishes more than 275 computer publications in over 75 countries (see listing below). More than 60 million people read one or more IDG publications each month.

Launched in 1990, IDG Books Worldwide is today the #1 publisher of best-selling computer books in the United States. We are proud to have received eight awards from the Computer Press Association in recognition of editorial excellence and three from *Computer Currents'* First Annual Readers' Choice Awards. Our best-selling *...For Dummies®* series has more than 30 million copies in print with translations in 30 languages. IDG Books Worldwide, through a joint venture with IDG's Hi-Tech Beijing, became the first U.S. publisher to publish a computer book in the People's Republic of China. In record time, IDG Books Worldwide has become the first choice for millions of readers around the world who want to learn how to better manage their businesses.

Our mission is simple: Every one of our books is designed to bring extra value and skill-building instructions to the reader. Our books are written by experts who understand and care about our readers. The knowledge base of our editorial staff comes from years of experience in publishing, education, and journalism — experience we use to produce books for the '90s. In short, we care about books, so we attract the best people. We devote special attention to details such as audience, interior design, use of icons, and illustrations. And because we use an efficient process of authoring, editing, and desktop publishing our books electronically, we can spend more time ensuring superior content and spend less time on the technicalities of making books.

You can count on our commitment to deliver high-quality books at competitive prices on topics you want to read about. At IDG Books Worldwide, we continue in the IDG tradition of delivering quality for more than 25 years. You'll find no better book on a subject than one from IDG Books Worldwide.

John Kilcullen
CEO
IDG Books Worldwide, Inc.

Steven Berkowitz
President and Publisher
IDG Books Worldwide, Inc.

Eighth Annual
Computer Press
Awards ≥1992

Ninth Annual
Computer Press
Awards ≥1993

Tenth Annual
Computer Press
Awards ≥1994

Eleventh Annual
Computer Press
Awards ≥1995

Credits

ACQUISITIONS EDITOR
Anne Hamilton

DEVELOPMENT EDITORS
Kerrie Klein
Jennifer Rowe

TECHNICAL EDITOR
Larry Van Der Jagt

COPY EDITOR
Michael D. Welch

PRODUCTION COORDINATOR
Tom Debolski

BOOK DESIGNER
Jim Donohue

**GRAPHICS AND
PRODUCTION SPECIALISTS**
Maureen Moore
E. A. Pauw
Andreas F. Schueller
Trevor Wilson

QUALITY CONTROL SPECIALISTS
Mick Arellano
Mark Schumann

ILLUSTRATOR
Joan Carol

PROOFREADER
Mary C. Barnack

INDEXER
Carol Burbo

About the Author

Dan Blacharski is a technology and business writer, novelist, and satirist with several years' experience. He has written numerous magazine articles and books, and works out of his home in Santa Cruz, California.

To my son, Shanti

Preface

Securing the network used to be easy when it consisted of a mainframe in a locked room and several dumb terminals. But as we embrace distributed client/server computing, corporate networks become more complex than ever. A typical network may encompass a wide geographic region, connect dozens of branch offices to headquarters, and incorporate PC LANs, mainframes, and minicomputers. It may run multiple protocols and network operating systems, contain gigabytes or even terabytes of data, and run hundreds of programs. As such, it is important to implement a company-wide security plan that takes into account the needs of every location, every department, and every machine and user within the enterprise, regardless of what type of system they may be using.

The goals of network security will depend on the enterprise, but generally include the following:

♦ Control access to the network

♦ Control access to specific files and applications

♦ Protect information being transmitted

♦ Detect any breaches in security, and take appropriate action

♦ Prevent accidental damage from occurring

♦ Institute a recovery plan in case of system failure

♦ Protect against physical theft and tampering

♦ Plan for disasters

Network security is often an unpopular subject because it is unhandy, restricts what we can and cannot do, and offers no immediate payoff or reward. Its implementers may ultimately get a pat on the back, but only after disaster strikes. More frequently, security policies and the people who implement them are cursed. Nonetheless, security is absolutely essential to a network's survival.

This Book's Organization

Having a secure network entails much more than running antivirus software and doing backups. I've attempted to cover this broad field as thoroughly as possible, with a goal to explore all of the many different elements you must address before you have a truly secure network. I've arranged these elements into the following divisions.

PART I: POLICIES AND THEORY

In Part I, I discuss policy and theory. Before implementing any type of hardware or software solution, it is extremely important that a solidly defined policy be put in place. Security goals are not always obvious, and may differ greatly between companies. A comprehensive policy document will be detailed and far-reaching, and will outline procedures, responses to disasters and network intrusions, and how to handle intruders once they've been caught.

Surprisingly, network attacks and other security breaches often come from within the company — and sometimes it is unintentional. Of course, the best way to respond to this type of breach is with education, and by making system files and other vulnerable areas unavailable to those who have no reason to access them. Intentional attacks, on the other hand, require more drastic measures. Guarding against intentional network attack may require an investment in software and hardware, but also most assuredly requires a great deal more than that. Protecting the network against harm requires a precisely defined policy that outlines your goals, identifies your physical and knowledge-based assets, and places strict controls over who can access what. Your policy document, once completed, will guide your decisions regarding what types of security software and hardware to purchase.

Part I also looks at disaster planning, which should be considered part of the overall network security plan. In planning for network security, you must guard not only against intruders, but also against disasters such as earthquakes, fires, riots, or hurricanes. Any of these events can be just as devastating, or in some cases even more devastating than having an intruder break into your network.

PART II: SOFTWARE

After you have created a policy document, you can go on to purchase your software and hardware. Part II addresses the software issue, discussing network management systems, monitoring software, encryption issues, and the security features of network operating systems. This part covers NetWare, Windows NT, and UNIX, and specifically discusses security products such as Legato Systems' NetWorker, which works on all three systems. Our goal is to secure a mixed environment; therefore, products such as NetWorker are ideal for our purpose because they can secure a heterogeneous network with a single interface.

Software used to make networks secure is varied and far-reaching. The network operating system itself usually offers some native security features, but these features usually come disabled as the default. It is up to you to decide which ones to use, and to enable them. Network and systems management software, too, offer some security features. Last, specialized security software can fill the gaps and offer specialized security services to your network. These software products may include antivirus packages, network monitors, or programs such as the notorious SATAN, used to detect network vulnerabilities.

PART III: HARDWARE AND NETWORK DESIGN

Part III looks at hardware and network design, and the advantages of such configurations as Virtual LANs, Virtual Private Networks, and segmentation. Firewalls and routers are commonly deployed as part of an overall security strategy. Although the firewall itself does not make up a complete security environment, it can certainly be a large part of your security plan.

Network computers, a newer trend in network computing, may also have applications in security. These small, inexpensive devices may lend themselves to a secure environment. They are ideal for task-oriented users with little systems knowledge, simply because less opportunity exists for unintentional security breaches caused by an unskilled worker attempting to install software or edit a systems file. Because network computers often lack a floppy or fixed disk, no opportunity exists for a worker to introduce a virus by loading the latest version of a favorite computer game. In addition, network computers lend themselves to centralized control.

PART IV: THE INTERNET

Part IV takes a look at the Internet and electronic commerce. In the future, the Internet will become a viable marketplace for all types of financial transactions. At present, the number of financial transactions that take place over the Internet is relatively minimal, but as people become more comfortable with it and it becomes more secure, this number is destined to grow.

PART V: RESOURCES

To round out this book, I've included a number of network security resources. These include appendixes on the following topics: service port numbers, security standards and protocols, the Secure Shell program, a sample security policy, a list of products and vendors mentioned in this book, and information about the accompanying CD-ROM. I also include a glossary of network security terms.

Trusted Network Security

Over the years, I've seen security at its best and at its worst, and I'll give such examples throughout this book. The key to successful network security planning and disaster anticipation is to imagine the worst—because the worst could happen.

If network security is your responsibility, it helps if you're a little paranoid. You have to consider every possible risk that could befall your company. You must consider everyone a potential threat. Anyone can be a network intruder; it could come from inside, outside, or from a vendor's or partner's company. Perhaps the best philosophy to adopt in terms of network security is to *eliminate opportunities for attack whenever possible.* Although everyone who needs network access should get it, it is still necessary to take every security precaution.

With the information you glean in these pages, and through the resources this book highlights, I trust that your organization will soon be on the road to trusted network security.

Acknowledgments

I would like to thank the many hard-working editors at IDG Books Worldwide who stood by me through the numerous delays I experienced in creating this book, including Kerrie Klein, Anne Hamilton, Jennifer Rowe, Jim Sumser, and Michael Welch.

Also thanks go out to the many vendors, consultants, and experts who provided me with information, including Dan Farmer and Charles Cresson Wood, the folks at Haystack Labs (Trusted Information Systems), Cheyenne Software (Computer Associates), and all the other companies mentioned in this book.

Thanks also go to my son Shanti, my parents, and friends who kept me going through an exceptionally difficult summer.

Contents at a Glance

Contents

Part 1
Policies and Theory

Chapter 1

What Have You Got to Lose?

IN THIS CHAPTER

◆ When is security appropriate?

◆ What are the risks?

◆ The three different types of security (Internet, network, and physical)

◆ Government policies

NEARLY ALL ORGANIZATIONS WORK hard to create information or products of great monetary or strategic value. Most likely your organization would suffer a great loss if network security breaches robbed you of proprietary data. Even small security slip-ups are unacceptable. In either extreme, you need network security. After all, you've got a lot to lose.

In this book you'll learn how to create and customize network security for your organization. This chapter looks at the different security methods as well as regulations and legislation. We'll start by assessing your needs.

Assessing Your Security Needs

Security goals in your company may differ greatly from those in other companies. Your goals will influence which specific security products you use and how you use them. Depending on your goals, a given product may be a magic bullet or a white elephant. Security needs will vary, depending on the context. For example, the security needs of a contractor working with the U.S. Department of Defense will be significantly greater than the security needs of a university's biology department. Thus it is critical to outline your goals before deploying a security infrastructure.

In the early days of computing, the greatest risk was that a clerk would get the cardboard punch cards out of order and foul up the program. Computers were huge and typically kept in specially controlled, locked rooms. Networking was minimal, and most connections to the central computer took place through dumb terminals.

Computing has changed significantly, however, and connectivity has expanded far and wide. The centralized model has become less popular as distributed computing takes advantage of far-flung resources.

With distributed computing, however, vulnerabilities can come from many different areas. A system with multiple access points is more vulnerable. Network-to-network links may permit access to the organization from anyone connected to the external network. A dial-up link, on the other hand, may be configured to enable access to a single system's login port and may be less vulnerable – that is, unless the dial-up line is connected to a terminal server, in which case the dial-up line can be used to access the entire system. Unfortunately, terminal servers often do not require authentication, and an intruder may use the terminal server to great advantage. For example, an intruder can use the Telnet application to gain access to the network, and then use it to go back out of the network, thereby making it very difficult to track the intruder.

Each organization should have someone in charge of network security. That person, whether it is the systems administrator, designated security officer, or Chief Information Officer (CIO), must have full authority to implement security precautions and to act on infractions when they occur. In addition, this individual must also have the authority to gather and analyze network information in order to determine security needs. The individual also needs to be able to monitor policy compliance and have the authority to take action against those who violate procedures. The individual must also be able to work with development staff to make security an essential part of applications development and network design.

Larger enterprises may want to organize a separate security department, with expert individuals able to analyze threats and design countermeasures against them.

The staff, or individual in charge of security, should have the following responsibilities:

◆ Reports to management about the reliability and security of existing systems

◆ Evaluates every incident of compromised security

◆ Periodically reviews all practices pertaining to data-handling

◆ Guarantees that all procedures and the systems on which they run have a level of security appropriate to the particular procedure

The security budget must be taken seriously by top management. The security officer needs to be able to effectively lobby management to provide an adequate security budget.

Although most managers agree that security is important, nearly half of all American businesses do not have a written security policy to deal with information security problems. The policy document, however, is what drives the purchasing decisions; without policy, security-related hardware and software purchases will have no cohesiveness and no overall strategy. Indeed, planning and policy form the very foundation of security. Without this foundation, all the world's software, firewalls, and other security gizmos are nearly useless.

Policy is especially important as a means of taking into consideration the "people" side of security. While firewalls and other tools are useful, how people use them and what they are allowed to do on the network must be explicitly stated and enforced.

A Policy Document

The first step in securing your network does not involve deploying any software, buying any hardware, or getting bids from vendors. The first step is, instead, to generate a comprehensive policy document. This document, a sample of which you can find in Appendix D, outlines your security goals, needs, and details. Individual products are not even considered yet in this step; the technical details of security are considered later.

To make the policy document as comprehensive as possible, several different individuals need to have input. Besides your security officer and network administrator, top management must be involved, if for no other reason than to gain their support. Without management support, your security project may not get adequate funding. Perhaps even more importantly, midlevel managers, supervisors, and power users should have input, because they have a greater understanding of the realities of who needs to look at what. Your security committee should be made up of representatives from every department, no matter how insignificant that department may seem. Security policies, even when created to accommodate a single department or business unit, may have an impact on the entire enterprise; it is therefore important that the entire enterprise be involved in the policy's creation.

The security committee should also be balanced so it does not favor any one group, whether that group be management, technical staff, or end users. Each group will have its own take on what should or should not be done, but each group has a lot to contribute. Committee representation from the technical staff is, of course, essential. These members will help govern the policy from a technical standpoint and inform other members of technical limitations. Management support is equally important to fund the implementation and to put the force of authority behind it. End-user input is also critical; they will tell everyone else what is reasonable to expect of them and what will be an undue burden.

Your policy document's goals should be all-encompassing to protect the network from any type of accidental or deliberate threat, real or imagined. But in addition to preventing security breaches, the security policy should also address the issue of how to deal with breaches if they do occur. Goals of the security policy may include the following:

- ◆ Guaranteeing that authorized users have access to files and other resources

- ◆ Preventing unauthorized use

- ◆ Maintaining data integrity

- ◆ Limiting access to sensitive data

- ◆ Preventing accidental damage to hardware, software, and other resources

- ◆ Preventing intentional damage to hardware, software, and other resources

The policy should further outline the rights and responsibilities of individual users, including "ownership" of data, accountability, and responsibility for security-related tasks. The document should state specifically which users are allowed to use and access which data and equipment, what they are allowed to do with it, and include a list of acceptable and unacceptable uses.

The policy document needs to explicitly state who is authorized to use which equipment in great detail. It also must outline proper use of resources. For example, it should include guidelines for personal use of equipment and guidelines for copying material.

A hierarchy of authority must be designated. Specifically, the policy must state which person is authorized to grant or deny access to others. Systems administrator privileges are wide-reaching, and the person who has them needs to be trustworthy. When an end user requests a special privilege, it is often essential to carrying out a business-related task and needs to be granted. However, the request should be carefully recorded and granted only for the length of time necessary to complete the task.

The rights of the end user must also be explicitly stated. The policy document should state how often the user should change passwords, it should spell out specifically what constitutes abuse of the system, and should state whether or not users are allowed to share accounts or passwords with others and under what circumstances. End-user rights and responsibilities should also include explicit policy statements on e-mail privacy.

The policy must also address storage of sensitive data. Storing sensitive data on an unsecured PC is probably unacceptable; the policy needs to state specifically where and how sensitive data should be stored and whether or not it can be copied.

When a policy item has been violated, the policy statement must also outline prewritten actions that are to be taken. An investigation should be held to determine how and why the policy was violated. A policy might be violated unknowingly or by accident, or it may have been violated intentionally. The consequences of the violation may depend on the results of this investigation.

The security policy is typically divided into separate areas, including prevention, maintenance, and actions taken if security breaches do occur. Furthermore, the security policy must be written to comply with existing corporate policies and business rules. The impact of a security policy on the business in general must be considered as well. Will a particular security policy cause more problems than it fixes? Will it alienate employees? Gaining the support of both management and staff is essential before a security policy can be effective.

One example of an unpopular security policy concerns e-mail privacy and "employee monitoring" programs. Software programs have become available that can give the administrator a full report on each employee's Web browsing expeditions. Some companies have also held to the belief, in the past, that any e-mail sent or received on company machines is company property, and can therefore be monitored at will. In some highly sensitive environments e-mail monitoring may be necessary, but most often monitoring will be seen as an intrusion into privacy, and could even cause legal problems. Monitoring an employee's Web browsing habits may also help management keep tabs on who is wasting company time, but again, used to an extreme browser monitoring is also intrusive and often a waste of management's time.

A particularly good example of an ineffective security policy can be seen in offices all around the country. Most companies use some sort of password mechanism for access to the network, and those companies that have written security policies include use of passwords in this document. However, merely stating "all employees are to use passwords to gain access to the network" is inadequate. This policy statement lacks details and enforcement. Employees could, according to this policy, use simple passwords that can be easily broken, or could even go so far as to write their passwords on sticky notes and place them on their computer monitors. A more effective policy statement would be:

- ◆ All employees, contractors and other personnel accessing the corporate network shall be required to enter a password before gaining access.

- ◆ Passwords shall not be shared under any circumstances.

- ◆ Passwords shall not be written or posted in a conspicuous place.

- ◆ Passwords shall not be any word in the dictionary or any proper name. Passwords shall be at least eight characters, at least two of which shall be nonalphabetic characters.

- ◆ Temporary passwords issued to contractors or employees working on special projects shall be revoked by the administrator as soon as they are no longer required.

- ◆ Violation of these procedures may result in disciplinary action.

Communication is perhaps one of the most important elements of a good security policy. A quarterly security newsletter or bulletin can communicate to the staff what the risks are, why specific policies have been implemented, and answer any questions that have been posed to the security staff. Don't let the security officer be perceived as the "bad guy" who makes life difficult for everyone. Security policies need to be out in the open, discussed frequently, and explained in full. And management must also be flexible enough to retract a bad security policy.

The contents of the policy document may also be influenced by a risk assessment. Although a formal risk assessment may be in order, even an informal risk assessment can yield a great deal of information. A risk analysis takes a closer look at what is being protected, what the potential dangers are, and who may be posing a risk. Surprisingly, although the Internet has created a huge security threat, a large percentage of risks come from inside an organization. The risk analysis should list all potential risks and rank them according to their severity. This ranking can be particularly useful when allocating funds. Besides identifying potential threats, the risk analysis should also identify all assets, including physical hardware, software, and data that require protection. After making such a list, it is then possible to make a corresponding list of potential threats to each asset.

A policy document that lacks thoroughness, or worse yet, lacks the "teeth" of enforcement, may lull your organization into a false sense of security. Having a weak security policy document is perhaps even worse than having none at all, and may well result in some very significant problems and confusion.

Risks and Horror Stories

The Internet, and connecting your corporate enterprise network to it, brings tremendous advantages as well as big risks. But the Internet is not the only place from which a threat can originate – thus, it is absolutely essential to protect your network from many different types of harm. Even a network that is not connected to the Internet can be subject to viruses, as employees bring in floppy disks of their favorite computer games, tinker with configurations, or even try to steal corporate secrets.

A computer system can become vulnerable through any number of weaknesses. For example, a vulnerability may be exposed when users unintentionally violate security procedures by giving out their passwords or writing them down on a notepad. Another vulnerability exists when users choose obvious passwords that can be easily guessed; for example, a birth date, middle name, or even any word in the dictionary.

Those intent on doing harm may unleash a computer virus, install a rogue software program designed to damage information, or trigger a future attack. According to the U.S. Department of Defense, the three most common methods for attacking a computer system include the following:

◆ **Sendmail.** This common type of Internet-based e-mail can hold malicious code. When the message is received, the attacker's code will be executed. Sendmail executes at the system's root level and therefore possesses all system privileges. It could, for example, even enter a new password into the system's password file, giving the attacker total control over the system.

- ◆ **Password Cracking and Theft.** Password cracking involves guessing a password, which can then be used to gain access to the system. Although an attacker with some personal knowledge of the user may be able to guess the password outright, the technique has been highly automated with computer programs that systematically go through the dictionary and attempt all possibilities. An obvious way to prevent the dictionary attack is to use passwords that are not dictionary words, preferably combinations of numbers and letters.

- ◆ **Packet Sniffing.** This technique involves placing a rogue computer program in a host computer or in a network switch. The program will then monitor all information packets as they go through the network. By looking at these packets, an attacker can easily learn passwords and user identifications.

After gaining access to the system, an attacker can function as a legitimate user, steal information, deny service to authorized users, or bring down the system by flooding it with packets.

What is the motive behind attacking a computer system? If you think there's nothing anybody could possibly want on your network, think again. Even if your network contains no sensitive information, attackers may break in just for the challenge itself. In the process of doing so, damage may occur, even inadvertently.

Motives may go far beyond amusement and curiosity, however. An attacker may want to do harm to a particular organization for political or personal reasons. An attacker may be working for the competition, and may want to steal company secrets, client lists, and other sensitive information.

The attacker has a virtual arsenal of tools that can be used to wreak havoc on any system. Unfortunately, many of these software tools are so easy to operate, it is no longer necessary to be an evil genius to break into a computer network. Information on breaking into networks can easily be found on the Internet and through informal hacker groups such as the Legions of Doom or Phrackers Inc.

Password Tricks and Traps

The Computer Emergency Response Team (CERT) reports that network intruders commonly use the following method: An end user receives an e-mail message, ostensibly from the systems administrator. In reality, however, the message is from an intruder. The message states that the user is required to change passwords for security reasons, and then proceeds to instruct the unsuspecting user to change passwords to a new password that the "systems administrator" has provided. Of course, once this has been done, the intruder knows the password and can attack the system. A security-conscious administrator would never make such a request, and a security-conscious user would report it immediately.

Security threats can come from anywhere, and can be directed at almost anything. Threats may be directed at any of the following:

- ◆ **Hardware.** The most obvious threat to hardware is theft, although other threats may come from tampering with settings, cutting cables, or unauthorized use of the hardware.

- ◆ **Software.** Software threats may come from many places. Software can be deleted, either accidentally or on purpose. Another all-too-common threat is the theft of software programs, or piracy. Software or files can be corrupted, either by a user inputting incorrect settings, introducing a virus, or by improper use.

- ◆ **Operation.** Threats to the operation of the network may exist when a connection is severed or if some type of interference is introduced. Electrical interference can cause a disruption in network transmissions; this type of interference may be either accidental or may be part of a deliberate attempt to subvert the network. Another common threat to network operation is a simple traffic bottleneck, which is often inadvertent, but may be the result of a self-replicating virus.

UNINTENTIONAL HARM
The most glamorous aspect of computer security may be keeping out corporate spies, hackers, and secret agents, but equally important is preventing unintentional harm. Allowing users to install their own software, for example, may seem like a good way to off-load some of the burden from IS, but a policy against this may prevent an accidental network crash because someone unintentionally changed the network configuration.

Under the category of unintentional harm, areas such as power protection, fault tolerance, redundant cabling, and data backups may fall in the jurisdiction of the security officer. The lowly uninterruptible power supply (UPS) is an often-ignored little device, sitting by itself in a dusty corner and never mentioned until the power fails. Nonetheless, the UPS represents a critical component of security in the area of power protection. A power surge or power failure can result in serious harm to the network and may result in corrupted data. For further information on UPSs and other backup strategies, refer to Chapter 14.

Fault tolerance involves redundant components, which enable a secondary device to take over in case the primary device fails through an error, act of sabotage, or natural disaster. Fault tolerance may extend to cabling, where a second set of connections runs parallel to the first. In a fault-tolerant cabling system, each node would have two network interface cards.

Data backup is also a critical part of an overall security policy. When data is compromised (whatever the reason), if a separate backup is available, some level of restoration can be made. The most effective backup method is to maintain the backup media in a separate physical location, preferably in a separate building. Backup may also involve a redundant array of inexpensive disks (RAID) system, where multiple copies of information are stored.

Unintentional misconfiguration represents a significant security risk. Network operating systems may be quite complex; an untrained administrator may easily leave open a security gap without knowing it. In addition to misconfiguration, software bugs may also represent a security problem. Part of the security policy to resolve this problem involves installing regular updates of all software, including bug patches and fixes.

INTENTIONAL HARM – ESPIONAGE!

Intentional harm to the network can come from inside the company as well as over the Internet.

In the late '80s, I was unfortunate enough to see the effects of network mischief firsthand, when a trusted employee single-handedly brought down a major financial services firm by pilfering and falsifying information. With no internal security in place, this individual was able to download all the files he wanted, concoct a story designed to force clients to cancel their contracts, and even use the company fax machine to send out his bogus documents.

Regrettably, this was the *second* incident of internal harm within two years. The first one involved another trusted employee downloading a full list of clients and information on the services they purchased, contract and pricing information, and internal operational procedures – and peddling them directly to the competition.

Both of these incidents occurred in part because of the lack of an overall security policy document, and because no individual had been placed in charge of network and computer security. What security there was fell under the domain of the systems administrator, and merely became one of a thousand duties already allocated to this overworked individual.

Even if every single person in your organization has earned your trust, you still must implement protective measures. Most incidents of intentional harm come from trusted individuals – people with pictures of their families on their desks, people who have helped you out in a pinch, and people with whom you've gone out for drinks after hours.

Although external break-ins receive a great deal of attention, perhaps because of the excitement and exotic nature of the subculture involved, insiders can also represent a major threat to a company's computer security. An insider may have more knowledge of the computer system and the data contained in it, and may have easy access to equipment. It's far easier for an insider, with previous knowledge of the system, to wreak havoc than it is for an outsider with no knowledge of the company. An employee about to be "downsized," or one that has been passed over for promotion, may carry a grudge and decide to steal information and sell it to the competition.

Could you be the victim of espionage? It's more common than you might think. Competitors looking for an advantage, vendors or potential vendors looking for inside information, spies, private investigators, "intelligence consultants," or even others from inside the company could all have reasons to perpetrate acts of espionage.

You may think of espionage as the domain of arms traders and drug smugglers, but it happens to everyday corporations as well. Whether your company makes nuclear bombs or cardboard boxes, you may be susceptible. Espionage, like any other sort of intrusion, is also preventable, if you take the proper precautions. The "Data Remanence" section that appears later in this chapter details how spies can take vital information from discarded or unsecured storage media that has been erased, and ways you can prevent this common security slip-up from happening to you. Actually, taking waste is legal, according to the U.S. Supreme Court. Once it's thrown away, it's fair game!

Bugs and wiretaps are also perhaps more common than anyone realizes. These are difficult to detect and may require professional services. However, if you think you may be vulnerable, you can easily purchase devices to prevent or limit this type of intrusion. An area such as a corporate boardroom or the CEO's office, where corporate secrets are openly discussed, should be extremely secure, and as impenetrable as possible. But to protect against the possibility of an intruder planting a surveillance device in the room, a bug detector should be deployed or a professional surveillance sweep should be arranged periodically. Telephone tap analyzers and tap alerts can also be used to inform you if someone is listening in on your phone calls.

The Economic Espionage and Protection of Proprietary Economic Information Act of 1996 applies the force of the U.S. federal government to the problem of industrial and corporate espionage. The law puts the FBI on your side – allowing the agency to investigate cases in which a foreign intelligence service attacks American firms to gather proprietary information to benefit companies in their own countries. A surprising number of foreign countries are engaged in this type of espionage against American companies. According to a Congressional report, at least 12 foreign countries are actively involved in gathering proprietary information from U.S. companies. According to the report, the high technology and defense industries are the primary targets. The Act also redefines the definition of stolen property to include proprietary economic information.

While the economic impact of industrial espionage is not fully known, victims have reported losses in the hundreds of millions of dollars.

According to the bill's cosponsor, Senator Herb Kohl, "It would not be unfair to say that America has become a full-service shopping mall for foreign governments and companies who want to jump-start their business with stolen trade secrets."

A government report, prepared by the National Counterintelligence Center (NACIC), highlights the significance of this threat, stating that in the post-Cold War environment, economic and technical information is as much in demand by foreign intelligence agents as military or political information.

The report further states that "In today's world in which a country's power and stature are often measured by its economic/industrial capability, foreign government ministries – such as those dealing with finance and trade – and major industrial sectors are increasingly looked upon to play a more prominent role in their respective country's [economic] collection efforts. While a military rival steals documents for a state-of-the-art weapon or defense system, an economic competitor steals a US company's proprietary business information or government trade strategies. Just as a foreign country's defense establishment is the main recipient of US defense-related information, foreign companies and commercially oriented government ministries are the main beneficiaries of US economic information. The aggregate losses that can mount as a result of such efforts can reach billions of dollars per year, constituting a serious national security concern."

According to the bill's cosponsors, Senators Herb Kohl and Arlen Specter, espionage has become a pervasive problem. For example, the senators claim that foreign intelligence agents have been known to recruit midlevel managers and scientists as spies. These "moles" accept money from the foreign governments in exchange for providing them with trade secrets, formulas, and other information that could give foreign corporations an unfair advantage.

The following episode appeared in a report issued by the National Counterintelligence Agency (reprinted with permission of the United States National Counterintelligence Agency). It shows just how common espionage can be, and highlights some particularly effective methods of preventing it.

Spy Hobbled by Northrop Security

The Man, His Motive

Thomas Cavanagh had secrets to sell, and his motive was money. "Before our relationship ends, I want to be independently wealthy," he told the prospective buyers. He knew espionage was a serious crime: he was aware of the recent FBI arrest of several people now in jail. To clear up mounting debts, and make himself rich, the Northrop engineer was still willing to take some chances.

The First Meeting

At the first meeting on 10 December 1984, Cavanagh introduced himself to his contacts as "Mr. Peters." Two topics dominated his conversation: his financial problems and worries about getting caught. "They're real security conscious [at Northrop] . . ." he remarked, "So somehow we have to come to an agreement on money." He added that he needed several thousand dollars, "Just to get the bill collectors off my back." He thought he could bypass the document controls and random searches at the plant.

Hampered by Tight Security

He did not want to talk about his contacts on the telephone "because it's constantly being bugged; they bug it with microwaves." His biggest source of anxiety, however, was the security program at Northrop. He was extremely concerned about his accountability for documents. He refused to turn them over to the KGB agents because he wanted to get them back to the plant as quickly as possible. "I can't give you the documents and have them back in time. They have audits. A guy just came by today and asked me how many secret documents I have." He was afraid that Security might open his safe and check his documents at any time. By sheer coincidence, Cavanagh had a surprise audit of his classified documents on the very day he first met with the KGB. It was strictly a random check by a company security representative – who had no suspicion that the material he reviewed was about to be sold to the Soviets. The security officer found everything in order, but Cavanagh was visibly shaken, according to coworkers interviewed after the arrest.

Reproduction controls at Northrop hampered Cavanagh. "You can't run your own copies in the plant. They got that regulated too." Northrop Advanced Systems Division controlled document reproduction through a system of "fully controlled machines." There is no self-service because special operators handle all copying machines under the oversight of security. These operators guarantee that all requirements meet authorization, marking, and accountability regulations. The KGB agents had to obtain a camera and a portable copier to make copies in the motel room.

Northrop employees were subject to random searches of anything carried in or out of the plant. Cavanagh worried about that as well. "I had to stick it in my shirt and walk out with it." He could not always fit things under his shirt, but he thought he could get through exit searches without detection because they were sufficiently infrequent and predictable.

Subsequent Meetings

When he arrived for a second meeting on 12 December, his "friends" greeted him warmly. He again mentioned the difficulty of getting documents out. He pressed anxiously for quick payment and wanted several thousand dollars in two days, but the Russians would not make any promises. Concerned because his background investigation was due to begin, Cavanagh wanted to cover his debts.

The third and final meeting with the KGB agents occurred on 18 December. When Cavanagh arrived, he asked about the money. Cavanagh showed them the documents. He spoke of his financial bind and displayed bitterness that he could not get a business loan for his Amway distribution, although foreign immigrants easily got them.

The agents suggested that future meetings be held outside the United States. Cavanagh refused by saying that he did not want to keep his documents out that long. Besides, he said that unexplained foreign travel might flag his activities with security.

Nabbed by the FBI

After copying the documents, the agents handed Cavanagh the payment in small bills. He counted it eagerly. He wanted to have monthly meetings with substantial payment each time. After they finished their business, there was a knock on the door. When they opened the door, FBI agents entered the room and arrested Cavanagh. Charged and convicted on two counts of espionage, he was sentenced on 23 May 1985 to concurrent life terms in prison.

Important Lessons

The FBI caught Cavanagh before he reached the Soviets. Northrop security did its job in curbing the range of his activities through document accountability and control, and effective enforcement of need-to-know. Particularly notable is the taming of the "Xerox" machine. Many people felt that ready access to photo reproduction made document control obsolete. Northrop effectively controlled its copiers, which forced Cavanagh to use original documents that were under accountability. This exposed him to detection through random audits, and it limited the number of documents he could compromise and the length of time he was willing to keep them outside the plant.

Greed and indebtedness were the major motivations for Cavanagh, but he showed some traits seen before in other spy cases. Job and career dissatisfaction are big ones, especially when it involves a sense of resentment toward the organization. In addition, Cavanagh showed some tendency to violent or disruptive behavior, some instances of dishonesty, and a general lack of respect for authority and procedural process.

Still, none of this rose to the level where supervisors considered reporting it for security purposes. Cavanagh was not a model citizen, but his behavior was well within tolerable limits. He went over the edge, quite suddenly by all indications, and tried to sell out the country to make himself rich.

How do we distinguish the Cavanaghs, before the fact, from the many other cleared people who are simply having difficulties with life's normal trials and tribulations? Unfortunately, we do not often distinguish them, until after the fact, and we cannot — until and unless we know a lot more about human psychology.

We can protect the documents and the information, as Northrop did, by applying the proper measures for accountability and control, as well as physical safeguards. None of that will completely prevent espionage. A clearance, like any other kind of trust, always carries the potential for betrayal. Controls, however, can make spying a lot tougher, a lot more expensive, and a lot more risky.

As the marketplace becomes more competitive, more companies are relying on competitive intelligence (which is legal) or even espionage (which is illegal) to gain a competitive edge. *Competitive intelligence* is quite common, and even arguably ethical and definitely legal. It involves gathering public information, going through waste, or even posting a sentinel outside a competitor's shop to count how many customers go in.

Types of Security

A single product won't protect your company from security threats; simply too much ground has to be covered. Besides securing your internal network from unintentional or intentional harm from within, you must also protect yourself against harm that may come from outside — over the Internet. The last area of security is one that is often overlooked — physical security. By physical security, I don't mean monitoring the supply closet for pilfered pencils. Physical security entails keeping track of computer hardware through a rigorous inventory system, using a check-out policy to keep track of who is taking equipment home, and generally making sure hardware and software stays where it is supposed to be.

In general, the purpose of security is to protect the confidentiality of documents, to provide for the availability of files and services to all authorized users, and to maintain the integrity of information by preventing destruction, theft, or corruption.

Internet Security

To stay competitive, companies have to get online. Customers need to send you e-mail, check your price list on the Web, or even conduct financial transactions with you electronically. Eschewing the Internet because of security concerns may keep the hackers at bay, but it will keep your customers at bay as well.

You can, however, open your enterprise to the Internet while still protecting it. Firewall technology, passwords, and virtual private networks are all techniques you can use to great advantage.

In 1988, the Computer Emergency Response Team (CERT) Coordination Center was organized to serve as a central focal point for security concerns over the Internet. Founded by the Defense Advanced Research Projects Agency (DARPA), the need for CERT was made evident after the notorious Internet Worm Incident. The agency offers a variety of services and products, including 24-hour technical assistance for responding to serious security incidents. The organization issues advisories and posts security-related documents on its Web site at `http://www.cert.org`. In addition to CERT advisories, the agency also posts vendor-initiated bulletins, which contain text from vendors relating to specific security problems. Lastly, the CERT Summary serves as a useful overview of the different types of attacks being reported to the center.

The Internet Worm

A worm is a program designed to replicate itself. It may perform any number of tasks and, in fact, was first designed to perform useful network management functions. At Xerox PARC in 1982, researchers attempted to use worms as a method of performing tasks in a distributed environment and to improve performance of network management tasks. The biggest problem, however, was worm management, or controlling the number of copies of the worm program that were executing at any given time. A worm does not require a host, is activated by creating a process, and in the case of a network worm, replication occurs across communication links. Malicious worms, however, can take advantage of flaws in the operating system or poor systems management to replicate themselves. Unchecked, a worm can shut down an entire network.

The first malicious use of a worm occurred in 1987, when a program known as the Christmas Tree Exec attacked IBM mainframes and brought down the global IBM network and BITNET. This was not a true worm, however, but actually a Trojan horse with a replicating mechanism (more on Trojan horses later in this chapter). In this program, a user received an e-mail Christmas card with executable REXX code. Once executed, the program would draw a Christmas tree in the recipient's terminal, and would then send a copy of the program to everyone on the recipient's address list.

The Internet Worm incident brought ten percent of all Internet systems to a halt in November 1988 — at the time, about 6,000 computers. Prior to this incident, nearly no security existed on the Internet. The Internet Worm was a true worm. It attacked Sun and DEC UNIX systems attached to the Internet, and had two sets of binaries, one for each type of system. It took advantage of TCP/IP protocols, operating system flaws, and system administration flaws to replicate itself.

In its early stages, the World Wide Web posed no great threats and, in fact, little reason existed to break into a Web site. However, in recent years, an entire subculture of ne'er-do-wells and electronic vandals has emerged, whose sole purpose in life is to break into other people's computers for fun or profit.

Although simply viewing content can be harmless, the Web has become a dangerous place due to the emergence of downloadable plug-ins and Java applets. Java, ActiveX, and the like have brought tremendous capabilities to the Web and have made it a much more productive and exciting place to be. Unfortunately, it is also more exciting for those whose intentions are less than honorable as well. A downloadable applet can theoretically alter local software or hardware. The most popular Web browsers include Java support, and a Java applet will run as soon as the page is downloaded. The only way to avoid risk is to turn off the Java support. End users who want to see all the little dancing bears and scrolling marquees on the screen will balk, but nobody will download any destructive programs.

As an alternative to blocking Java at the firewall, the security administrator may instead decide to rely on the digital signature feature built into Java. This lets the client decide, based on the digital signature, whether to allow a particular Java applet to execute certain tasks or gain access to resources that would not otherwise be available to that applet.

A new type of virus, called a *macro virus*, poses another big challenge. Simply downloading a word-processing file can open the system to harm. Once the macro virus is unknowingly triggered, it can inflict untold damage on the system. This type of virus passes through the firewall with ease, because it is usually passed on as either an e-mail message or simply downloaded as a text document.

The macro virus represents a significant threat because it is difficult to detect. Previously, viruses were limited to attaching themselves to executable files; a macro virus can attach itself to a word-processing document. A few of the leading antivirus products now include features for detecting macro viruses. Prohibiting e-mail attachments is perhaps the most drastic, and most inconvenient approach; short of that, routine checks of your word processing program's macro list are in order. For more information about macro viruses, refer to Chapter 17.

In many cases, companies may spend a great deal of money on developing a Web site that effectively promotes a positive corporate image. *Spoofing* is a technique that can be used by hackers to gain control over a Web site and alter it. Intruders can also use other techniques to gather critical corporate information and enter protected sites. Spoofing involves changing network packets so that the recipient or a host device believes the packet originated from somewhere other than where it really originated. It's like putting a phony return address on an envelope. For example, a spoofed packet may be altered to appear as if it came from within the firewall instead of outside, and therefore gain access to privileges that would not otherwise be available.

Network monitors are the first line of defense against spoofing. Preventing spoofs can also be done by configuring a filtering router so that packets are not allowed through if they have a source address from the internal network.

Watch Out for Disabled Security Features

Software applications often come with the security features disabled. Vendors ship their products this way to make installation easier. The downside to this practice is that users opting for the automatic setup may not even be aware that security has not been enabled. This serious omission can lead to a large, gaping hole in an otherwise sound security practice.

Network Security

Regardless of whether your company is on the Internet, some security measures must be applied to the network. These measures may be as simple as requiring users to change passwords regularly or may involve using the network operating system and third-party utilities to enforce policies and restrict access.

In creating your policy document, consider what areas of the network should be open to everyone, and what areas could be restricted. Is it really necessary to allow the file clerks to access critical information about a company takeover? If steps have not been taken to deny that access, then, by default, it has been allowed. It is never appropriate to assume that nobody would look at it—even if nobody knows of the document's existence, a curious employee may decide to "browse through the files" and stumble across it.

Regardless of whether the network is connected to the Internet or not, data backup is an important part of security. If security is breached and data is corrupted, availability of a recent backup or parallel data source may save days of frustration, and thousands of dollars. Backup procedures need to be written into the policy document and communicated to each individual involved. Besides providing a source of duplicate data, a backup may also be useful in tracking and documenting an intruder's activities.

Two types of backup are available: full and incremental. A *full backup* copies the entire system to tape or to another type of storage medium. A partial, or *incremental*, backup, is done more frequently (weekly or daily). The latter type of backup only copies the files or portions of files that have changed since the previous backup, and it takes a lot less time to execute. The media that holds the backed-up data should be kept physically separate from the original data, preferably in a separate building. If backups are kept in the same location as the original data, a fire or a natural disaster such as an earthquake will destroy both sets of data.

The 1989 Loma Prieta earthquake shut down San Francisco's financial district for days. Some companies never recovered, but those with good backup plans and disaster recovery policies were back in business within a very short period of time. The same financial services company discussed in the "Risks and Horror Stories" section may not have had a good security plan, but they did have an effective disaster plan. When the earthquake completely destroyed their offices at 5:04 p.m. on August 17, 1989, the firm's CEO was on the phone hours later implementing a backup plan. An alternative operating site had been selected well ahead of time. Seventy-two hours after the earthquake, the company was back in full operation in one of San Francisco's most prestigious hotel ballrooms. The company was able to set up operations immediately, with 30 phone lines, three fax lines, 13 PCs, and a mainframe computer, all of which had been prearranged in a detailed contingency plan.

PASSWORDS

One of the biggest and first lines of defense in network security is the password. Unfortunately, it is also the most frequently abused. Workgroup leaders, supervisors, and managers must be responsible for enforcing password policies and ensuring that all individuals in their areas are adhering to password procedures outlined in the policy document.

A successful password system depends on all passwords being kept secret. Yet, passwords are inherently vulnerable in several ways. When first entered into the system, a new user must be initially assigned a password. The time between when the first password has been assigned and the new user changes the password could present a possibility for intrusion. Immediately after password assignment, the systems administrator and the new user both know the password; because the password should be totally secret—not even the systems administrator should know it—it must be changed immediately. Another vulnerability is the necessity for users to remember their passwords; that is, if it is not easily remembered, users may be tempted to write them down. Writing down passwords presents the potential for password theft. However, passwords that are too easily remembered may also be too easily guessed.

Some simple guidelines for users to follow include:

- ◆ Do not write down your password.
- ◆ Do not give out your password.
- ◆ Do not choose a password that is the same as a user name or account name.
- ◆ Do not choose a password that comes from personal information, such as the name of a child or spouse.
- ◆ Do not use any word in the dictionary as a password. A hacker can use a special program that tries every word in the dictionary in order to gain access to an account.
- ◆ Do choose a password that contains a combination of alphabetical and nonalphabetical characters.
- ◆ When it is time to change passwords, do not change it incrementally by altering only one character.
- ◆ Change passwords at least every 90 days; more often if you are a user with access to sensitive information.

A favorite trick of intruders is to call an individual and claim to be so-and-so "from the computer center," or from some computer vendor's office. The tricky intruder will then ask the victim for his or her password, saying that it is necessary for some type of "system check." Never believe this line! Ask for verification or ask for a phone number so you can call back.

A final area of vulnerability is the password database contained within the network system. The password database must be afforded the greatest extent of security possible.

Several software applications and operating systems come equipped with default user IDs or passwords. The administrator must change these default passwords immediately.

If two or more people know the password for one user ID, this should be considered a security violation (except in the temporary case stated earlier, where the systems administrator has just assigned a password to a new user).

Whenever an employee leaves the company or is terminated, that employee's password should be disabled by the systems administrator immediately. A procedure should be in place so the administrator gets prompt notification of any personnel departures.

Many security applications include a feature that enables the administrator to regulate how many login attempts can be made before access is denied; setting this parameter at three is usually adequate.

Further, the security system should include the capability to create an audit trail of password use and changes. The audit trail should not, of course, include the actual passwords given, but should include a record of all successful logins and unsuccessful logins. Furthermore, the system should provide for an immediate, real-time notification to be given to the systems administrator if several consecutive, unsuccessful login attempts have been made.

Another simple, common security measure is to configure the system so that, when a user logs in, the date and time of the most recent login is given, as well as all unsuccessful login attempts made since the previous successful login. This simple configuration lets the user know at a glance whether or not someone has attempted to use his or her account.

REMOTE ACCESS

An increasingly mobile workforce often demands remote network access. Remote access can be a blessing; it can help sales staff gain immediate access to a product database, it can facilitate a telecommuting system, and it can help traveling executives stay in close contact with headquarters. However, this type of access should be granted cautiously and judiciously, and only to those who require it. For remote users who call in from a fixed location, a *dialback modem* offers an excellent security precaution. When using a dialback modem, the remote user calls into headquarters and the main system calls back the remote user at a predefined phone number to make the connection. However, this precaution will not work for users who call in from various locations. Ports used for modem access can be further protected with frequently-changed passwords.

Most modern operating systems provide at least some measure of control over file access; these features should be fully exploited to prevent unauthorized access to sensitive files. Additional protection can be applied by the database management system or other application, which can further control access to specific data within the file.

Again, network equipment such as hubs or routers should always be in a protected place, whenever possible. Regardless of their location, however, additional precautions can be taken. An Ethernet hub with an unused port can be set to "dead," which would prevent an intruder from gaining access. An intruder may attempt to establish a connection by disconnecting a live port, but doing so may lead to detection if the person being disconnected is currently logged on and working.

DATA REMANENCE

Another area of security that is seldom considered is the possibility that spies will scavenge discarded magnetic media to gain access to data.

It's not as easy as simply issuing an "unerase" command. *Data remanence*, or the residual data that still exists after storage media has been erased, may permit some data to be reconstructed. A discarded or unsecured machine that is no longer in use may be a target for a scavenging data thief.

Storage media, especially media that has held strategic or classified documents, must be treated with caution if it is to be destroyed, reused, or sold. Sensitive information could be compromised if proper care is not taken. Very few security policies even take this into account; As early as 1960, however, the military has been aware of the retentive properties of storage media and has had policies regarding its destruction. Some typical methods of ensuring that residual data is not accessible include degaussing, overwriting, data encryption, and physical destruction of the media.

The method used to eliminate residual data may depend on what the final disposition of the media will be. If a storage media, such as a hard disk drive, is going to be reused within the same secure office, simple clearing of the information may be adequate. If it is going to be discarded, sold, or stored in an unsecure location, a more thorough purging is in order. Clearing ensures that the erased data cannot be reconstructed through normal means; purging goes a step further to eliminate the possibility that residual data can be reconstructed through extraordinary means. Clearing may involve overwriting unassigned system storage space.

No procedures should be considered adequate to thoroughly purge CD-ROM, WORM, or magneto-optical discs; the options are either destruction or to simply not use this type of media for highly sensitive information.

Degaussing, more commonly known as demagnetizing, is appropriate in some circumstances (as I discuss momentarily), if used properly and judiciously. But first let's look at what it does.

Coercivity is a property, measured in oersteds (Oe), of magnetic material that measures the amount of applied magnetic field of an opposite polarity that is required to reduce the magnetic induction to zero from its remanent state. Manufacturers will be able to provide coercivity values for their products.

A degausser generates a magnetic field for degaussing a magnetic storage media. Two types of degaussers exist, Type I and Type II, each of which apply to Type I and Type II storage media, respectively. Type I storage media has a lower coercivity rate than Type II. A Type II degausser can purge both Type I and Type II tapes.

When data is stored on magnetic media, magnetic domains on the media change their magnetic alignment to reflect a given pattern. Degaussing causes these domains to take on random patterns, rendering data unrecoverable. However, some of the domains may not become randomized; the information held in these domains is what is called the magnetic remanence. A thorough degaussing, however, will generally be adequate enough to guarantee that not enough remanence is available to reconstruct any data.

The degausser should be periodically tested to ensure its functionality. A test of the degausser's effectiveness may be executed using a gaussmeter.

In what circumstances would it be appropriate to use each method? Using overwrite as a technique to clear sensitive data may be inadequate. An unusable or "bad" track in a disk drive cannot be overwritten. However, sensitive data may have been previously written to the bad track.

Proper degaussing techniques should be taught to any staff member who will be carrying out the degaussing procedure. Although degaussing is adequate for purging most media, if used improperly, it can leave data on the disk. The media, for example, could be removed from the degaussing device before the cycle has been completed. Or, if the degausser is not tested regularly, it may not be functioning to full capacity. Another danger is trying to purge a Type II tape with a Type I degausser. To avoid the latter possibility, all magnetic tapes should be labeled with their coercivity level.

When destruction of the media is in order, the U.S. Department of Defense recommends three possible methods, each of which is preceded by a purge:

- Destruction at a metal destruction facility

- Incineration

- Application of an abrasive substance, such as a disk sander, to the disk or recording surface

Physical Security

Here's where you can literally batten down the hatches. Computers, besides being subject to electronic attack, can also be subject to physical attack or theft. Notebook computers taken on the road by traveling users are particularly vulnerable.

A stolen computer can translate into a much bigger loss than the actual cost of the hardware. The data inside the computer may be invaluable to the user, and what's more, it may also be valuable to the thief. Private records, company information, or even passwords and phone numbers can be gleaned by a clever thief.

Fortunately, several products have emerged to address the issue of physical security. Encryption software products can make it impossible for anyone other than the authorized user to read any of the data on a computer. For stationary computer equipment, a wide range of security devices and locks are available. Disk drive locks, screw mounts, and other physical devices are inexpensive, and make it nearly impossible for anyone to walk away with equipment.

Your security policy should certainly include a provision for check-out of hardware and other equipment. A simple sign-out process can go a long way toward alleviating the problem of forgotten hardware.

The policy statement should address the issue of physical security. Keeping unused hardware on a shelf in the supply closet next to the boxes of pens and stacks of letterhead may be convenient, but it is also an invitation to theft. It may make little difference if an employee pockets a couple of pens or a notepad, but keeping equipment out in the open this way makes it all too easy to simply drape a jacket over a computer printer and walk out the door with it.

Unused equipment should be kept in a locked room. Furthermore, an inventory should be kept, not only of active equipment but also of this unused inventory. Very often, equipment gets stored away and forgotten; thousands of dollars worth of hardware collecting dust and serving no purpose loses its value very quickly. If it's unlikely to ever be used again, sell it, or donate it to a charity and take a tax write-off.

The level of physical security depends on the size and scope of the organization, amount of equipment and sensitive information, and other related issues. Physical security can be seen as a control issue, and if not properly implemented, may cause employees to feel like they are not trusted. Some years ago, I signed on as managing editor of a publishing company. The publisher believed in security merely for its own sake; he used it as a control tool. I held the job for three days, until a sign-out sheet policy was instituted that required every employee, including management, to sign out before leaving the office – even to go to the bathroom down the hall. In all but the most sensitive of sites, such a policy is overkill, and a sure-fire way to alienate employees.

Physical security is perhaps one of the most important aspects of a secure system. If an intruder can gain physical access to machines, untold havoc can be perpetrated. Critical equipment such as servers, communications links, and key machines should be located in a physically secure area.

Laptops are especially vulnerable to theft; and a surprisingly large number of them are stolen in airports. Thieves are on the lookout for well-dressed travelers; the moment you set down that little carrying case you are putting yourself at risk. Set it down to make a phone call, check your ticket, or buy an overpriced burrito – and it could be gone in less than a minute. Outside of handcuffing it to your wrist, the only solution here is simple caution and vigilance.

Protect Your Notebook Data

Here's a simple, obvious, and often-overlooked tip: When a traveling business person becomes a victim of a notebook thief, the notebook computer itself is usually not as great a loss as the data the computer contained. Take a brief inventory of what is inside your notebook—contact addresses and phone numbers, client information, presentations, perhaps years of accumulated data or research. Is it valuable? Probably. Is it worth more than the value of the computer itself? Sure.

Back it up before you travel. In fact, back it up on a regular basis. Our networked computers are usually backed up by the systems administrator; the more conscientious among us buy a tape drive and back up our freestanding desktop PCs as well. But the laptop is sometimes left out of the backup strategy, simply because it's not wired to the network, and you can't stick a tape drive in it. One of the easiest solutions, then, is to use a data synchronization program, such as LapLink, that establishes a direct connection between the laptop and desktop machine. These programs usually come with the cable you need to plug into both machines; some offer the convenience of an infrared connection if your hardware supports that option. With this program, all the information on the laptop can easily be ported to the desktop machine, which is then backed up on a regular basis.

Despite the existence of physical restraints, PCs—especially notebook computers—still get stolen. CompuTrace, an innovative service from Absolute Software (Vancouver, British Columbia), places an undetectable software program on the PC. The software periodically calls in to the CompuTrace monitoring center. If a computer is stolen, the customer contacts one of the CompuTrace theft recovery officers, who are available 24 hours a day. Once alerted, the stolen computer can then be traced the next time the automatic call-in is made. CompuTrace automatically shuts off the speaker for the duration of the call, so the thief will not know that the call is being placed. The CompuTrace intelligent software agent then tells the monitoring center the number from which it is calling (even if caller ID blocking has been enabled). The unusual software uses a "stealth" technology that prevents it from being detected or erased, even after a hard drive format. Absolute Software works with law enforcement agencies; with the information provided by CompuTrace, police are usually able to get a search warrant and attempt to look for the stolen computer.

Unfortunately, all too many organizations devote all their security resources to network security while completely ignoring physical security. Yet physical security is essential; and theft of equipment constitutes a major risk factor. Although some companies may institute elaborate protection measures to ensure against electronic attack, there may still be no safeguards to prevent anyone from walking out with a floppy disk full of data, or indeed, with an entire computer. How easy is it for an outsider to walk into your corporate office? How accessible is your wiring closet? Here's an area that's often neglected. We assume that nobody would want to get in there other than the systems administrator, but would it be possible for a disgruntled employee to simply open the door and yank out a handful of wires? A simple two-dollar lock will prevent that possibility.

Controlling physical access to workstations can be an important consideration, especially when that workstation may hold valuable data. Don't think that a spy from a competitor won't walk into your marketing department while the secretary's out to lunch and quickly download your customer list from her computer. Another possibility is that an employee, who would not be suspected, may also download valuable data and sell it to a competitor.

Any workstation with valuable information should be protected. Some possible protection measures include the following:

◆ Keep the workstation in a secure location.

◆ Purchase workstations with lockable CPUs.

◆ Store sensitive data only on a removable cartridge or removable hard disk, and keep it in a secure location when the workstation is not in use.

◆ Deploy software that automatically locks up the computer after it has not been used for a preset period of time; the authorized user must enter a password to reactivate it.

Confidential Reports

Another area of critical importance is the handling of confidential or sensitive reports. Again, protecting access to the computer network is the most obvious course of protection, but the issue of printing must also be addressed. Sensitive reports that are printed in the computer center for delivery to an individual outside of the computer center must be handled accordingly, and procedures must be instituted for their handling. Leaving sensitive material in an "out" box outside of the computer room is obviously unacceptable; ideally, the sensitive report should be hand-delivered to its owner.

Client/server computing has also led to printer sharing; which offers a great convenience and cost savings. However, when sensitive reports are printed, sending them to a remote printer also causes a security problem. Any individual who regularly prints sensitive reports should have a dedicated printer next to his or her desk.

The wiring closet and the central computer room that holds servers, hubs, and other critical equipment should be considered restricted areas. An electronic system of authorized entry should be used; in the absence of that, at least a paper log-in sheet should be enforced. In addition, any access codes that must be entered to gain access to the computer room should be changed periodically. Lastly, the computer room's location should not be widely advertised. If possible, its location should be out of the way, and no sign should be placed on the door.

Government Policies and Regulations

The organization that is perhaps most concerned with security is the United States Department of Defense. Defense Department policies, procedures, and decisions sometimes have a major impact on how everyone else operates, so it makes sense to take a look at how they operate.

The Defense Department has policies for computer network security, Internet security, encryption regulations, and more. Defense's restrictions and proposed restrictions on encryption software are hotly debated, and the Pentagon has concerned itself with what it calls the threat of "electronic warfare." The Defense Science Board on Information Warfare deems the threat significant, and even goes so far as to propose a role for Defense in protecting the security of both military and civilian information systems.

A 1996 General Accounting Office (GAO) report calls attacks on defense-related computers a "serious and growing threat," and the Defense Information Systems Agency (DISA) claims that as many as 250,000 attacks may have taken place over the past year. Even more worrisome is DISA's contention that the attacks are successful 65 percent of the time. In the past, attackers have taken over entire Defense systems that support critical functions, including weapons systems research, logistics, and finance. According to these reports, the Pentagon worries about terrorists using electronic warfare to do harm to its command and control systems.

The report's recommendations include the following:

◆ Improve security policies and procedures.

◆ Increase user awareness and accountability.

◆ Set minimum standards to ensure that system and network security personnel have enough time and adequate training to perform their jobs.

◆ Implement proactive technical protection and monitoring systems.

◆ Evaluate Defense's incident-response capability.

These recommendations can also be applied to civilian organizations, and should be incorporated into every policy document. The last one, in particular, is often ignored. Although companies may spend a great deal of energy trying to prevent incidents, too often they do not put a policy in place to deal with what to do if an incident does occur. An incident-response policy may include such tasks as auditing in order to try to track down the attacker, and attempting to determine how the attack occurred to help prevent it from occurring again.

DISA's Vulnerability and Assessment Program also contains some useful information from which civilians can learn. Under this program, DISA itself attempted to penetrate several military and Defense computer systems via the Internet. By attempting to break into its own computers, DISA has been able to learn a great deal about Defense's own vulnerabilities, and has tested the effectiveness of preventative measures. DISA's own "hackers" were successful a surprising 65 percent of the time; out of these successful attacks, only about four percent of the attacks were detected by the target agencies.

Attacks on Defense computer systems have been costly and damaging. In the past, attackers have stolen, modified, and destroyed data, installed back doors to allow attackers to gain access in the future, and have completely shut down entire systems.

The well-known attack on the Rome Laboratory in New York serves as a shocking example of how quickly a small group of attackers can take over a Defense network.

The Rome Laboratory, an Air Force command and control research facility, studies artificial intelligence, radar guidance, and target detection and tracking. The lab works with a variety of academic institutions, commercial research labs, and Defense contractors, and makes heavy use of the Internet for communications. In 1994, a small group of hackers used Trojan horses and sniffers to take over Rome's operational network. (A *Trojan horse* is a malicious program that secretly attaches itself to another legitimate program for the purpose of infiltrating a system. A *sniffer* is a device or computer that sits between a user and a host. The sniffer, which is undetectable, examines every packet that passes by, collecting information such as origin, destination, and other data from the packet header.) The group prevented their attacks from being traced by creating a complex path through various phone switches in South America, various commercial sites on both United States coasts, and then to the Rome Laboratory. The attackers controlled Rome's support systems for several days, copied critical information, and attacked systems at other government agencies and Defense contractors. Only one of the attackers was ever caught, and investigators still do not know what was done with the copied information.

The attack cost the government over $500,000 for the Rome Laboratory alone. However, millions of dollars worth of research was compromised as a result.

The GAO acknowledges that support from top management is essential in crafting an effective security program. Top management must not only understand the risks inherent in network computing, but they must also be willing to commit the resources to address security issues.

The report indicates that every single agency, department, or unit must adhere to the same standards; indeed, an organization's security is only as strong as the weakest link. A policy needs to set minimum standards and requirements, and must clearly delineate responsibilities and accountabilities to ensure that the policies are carried out. Lastly, the GAO suggests that security policy dictate that adequate personnel and training be devoted to implementing the policies. A policy statement, with no staff to implement it, is useless. The GAO report puts forth a list of nine security activities that are most important:

◆ Clear and consistent information security policies and procedures

◆ Vulnerability assessments to identify security weaknesses at individual divisions or agencies

◆ Mandatory correction of identified network/system security weaknesses

◆ Mandatory reporting of attacks to help better identify and communicate vulnerabilities and needed corrective actions

◆ Damage assessments to reestablish the integrity of the information compromised by an attacker

◆ Awareness training to ensure that computer users practice good security and understand the security risks associated with networked computers

◆ Assurance that network managers and systems administrators have sufficient time and training to do their jobs

◆ Prudent use of firewalls, "smart cards," and other technical solutions

◆ An incident-response capability to aggressively detect and react to attacks and to track and prosecute attackers

DISA has taken several steps to implement its security plan, including the establishment of a Global Control Center at DISA headquarters. The center is responsible for detecting and responding to computer attacks and also for providing the equipment and personnel to implement the plan.

Some of the technologies being used or considered by DISA include a smart card called Fortezza, which was developed at the National Security Agency (NSA). The card is designed around the Personal Computer Memory Card International Association (PCMCIA) standard, and like other PCMCIA cards, is about the size of a credit card. It stores digital information that can be recognized by a separate reader, and will be used by government agencies to provide for both encryption and authentication services.

Other technologies being used by the Department of Defense include firewalls. Firewalls are usually combinations of hardware and software that protect a network from attack by blocking and filtering all incoming traffic. For more information about firewalls and their potential benefits, see Part III.

Other technologies in use or under investigation by DISA and the military include automated biometrics systems, which identify an individual by his or her physiological traits, such as fingerprints, retina patterns, or voice patterns. Another technology under development is known as location-based authentication, and it can be used to determine the precise geographic location of a user who is attempting to access the system.

Government Security Classes

The Orange Book, a Department of Defense publication known formally as the *Trusted Computer System Evaluation Criteria*, defines four security classes:

◆ Class D (minimal security)

◆ Class C (discretionary protection)

◆ Class B (mandatory protection)

◆ Class A (verified protection)

These categories are of special interest to government agencies, and to anyone wanting to do business with the government.

Class D systems are not considered secure. A Class D system may be a PC-based operating system, such as MS-DOS or System 7.

Class C security consists of two subcategories, C1 and C2. UNIX and other network operating systems with password protection usually fall under class C. C1 features include use of passwords, file-access restrictions, and the capability to prevent accidental harm such as destruction of system files. C2 systems are more secure, and include capabilities to audit user activity and restrict individual user activity.

Class B consists of three subcategories, which are generally required to provide security documentation, actively prevent threats to security, and maintain security during a system failure. B1 systems include all of the same features as a C2 system, and must also separate out security-related system components from nonsecurity-related system components. B2 systems also add a mathematical description of the security system, offer a secure method for managing configuration changes, and ensure that new applications do not have any unusual "back doors" through which an outsider may gain entrance into the system. B3 systems go a step further, and require a systems administrator to be in charge of security, and require security to be maintained in the event of a system failure.

Class A security represents the highest level. A Class A system must verify mathematically that the security system and policy is compliant with the security design specifications.

There has been significant debate over government regulation and export of encryption software, primarily because the government considers it a munition and heavily regulates its export. A November 15, 1996 U.S. Executive Order transferred jurisdiction of commercial encryption exports from the State Department to the Commerce Department. However, many Commerce Department policies will still not be applicable to encryption products, so this shift actually does little to address the encryption issue.

Most encryption customers are requesting longer key lengths of 128 bits for Internet applications, especially applications for electronic commerce. United States export law prohibits the export of encryption products of that length. The result, however, is widely recognized as giving U.S.-based companies a distinct disadvantage in the global marketplace. It should be noted here that only one other country, France, regulates the export of encryption products. The new policy does allow export of 56-bit products, but only if vendors can demonstrate a commitment to key recovery systems, such as the Clipper chip key escrow scheme. Key escrow places the United States government in the position of holding users' private encryption keys. The Clipper system has an 80-bit key, but includes a mandatory escrow feature that many users find objectionable and an invasion of privacy.

The 56-bit encryption type is inadequate for U.S. companies wanting to participate in the global electronic marketplace; 128-bit products are absolutely essential for Internet-based electronic commerce.

Key recovery, as opposed to key escrow, is a more market-driven solution that still allows users to keep a spare private encryption key in a safe place. Key escrow, however, requires the key to be maintained by the U.S. government.

The bottom line of the encryption issue is that foreign companies are now able to provide software products with strong encryption, and U.S. companies are not. In the long run, this could make a serious competitive dent in U.S.-based companies' profits and position in the global marketplace.

The Business Software Alliance (BSA), a consortium of software vendors, outlines what it believes are five key principles that are essential for U.S. policy to be effective and acceptable to U.S.-based technology companies. In a letter to Vice President Al Gore, the alliance outlines these principles, as follows:

(1) VOLUNTARY AND MARKET DRIVEN: To be successful, any key recovery initiative must be voluntary and market-driven. Our companies cannot sell what consumers do not want. As BSA CEOs have discussed with numerous Administration officials, the U.S. software industry is operating in a very competitive, international market—hundreds of strong encryption products are presently available around the world, many easily downloaded from the Internet. Consumers are demanding strong encryption and it is key to the success of the Internet. Unless users find value in a key recovery function, they will not buy products with this function. The result: American companies lose sales and the government will have failed in its efforts to have such products widely deployed.

(2) UNLIMITED KEY LENGTH FOR KEY RECOVERY PRODUCTS: "Key recovery" products should be exportable without key length limit if they include features making the recovery of plain text stored information accessible without the assistance of the individual who has encrypted the information.

As we have explained to the Working Group, there may well be commercial demand for products that enable the recovery of stored encrypted data, but there is little, if any, commercial demand for a key recovery function in real-time communications. Accordingly, there should be no such requirement for exportable encryption communications products (or products which do both communications and stored data as long as there are key recovery features for stored data).

Furthermore, key recovery is not key escrow. A purchaser or user of a product being able to recover his data is different than, and separate from, the decision as to whether to voluntarily empower a trusted third party to be able to recover the data.

(3) NO INDUSTRIAL POLICY: The government should not dictate "milestones" for company-specific plans regarding key recovery products as a condition for interim export control relief. Companies have already announced plans to develop such key recovery products; for example, 35 companies have joined IBM in a key recovery alliance. Numerous other companies already have key recovery products on the market today. There is no need for the government to go down the road of industrial policy by insisting upon becoming a partner with each company. We urge the Administration to adopt the simplest possible process.

(4) EASY EXPORT OF 56-BIT PRODUCTS AS PROMISED: Interim export control relief must permit the export of 56-bit nonkey recovery encryption products under Department of Commerce General License procedures that represent actual liberalization. The mere transfer of licensing jurisdiction to Commerce is of little significance unless accompanied with expedited product reviews and realistic licensing requirements. Yet, the recent Executive Order states that products which already have export licenses will have to undergo new reviews—only this time with FBI scrutiny. There is also an urgent need to permit the export of 128-bit encryption for financial applications (when done with appropriate safeguards).

(5) MEETING MARKET DEMANDS NOW AND IN THE FUTURE: Any interim export control relief will be only a mirage unless it meets business needs after two years. Quite simply, there must be interoperability between key-recovery and nonkey-recovery products. It also must be possible for American companies to service and support the installed base of 56-bit nonkey-recovery products.

The American software industry needs immediate relief. It is a matter of jobs and international competitiveness. For the Administration's policy to be successful, the government must accept and work with the market, not try to supplant it. It is clear that many in Congress understand the urgency and importance of this issue and the need for strong protection for Internet users. We thought that the October 1 announcement showed that the Administration was also coming to grips with these issues. But now, only a few weeks later, we wonder.

Specific Legislation

H.R. 695, sponsored by Representative Robert W. Goodlatte, known as the SAFE Act, would allow the United States software industry to provide the data security features that consumers want, according to the BSA. According to Microsoft senior counsel Ira Rubinstein, who testified on behalf of the BSA before the House Subcommittee on Courts and Intellectual Property, computer users in the U.S. and abroad are demanding stronger encryption in order to protect their privacy, and the security of their electronic information. According to Rubinstein, "Not only are these government restrictions hindering consumers, they also dampen the continued growth and success of the U.S. computer software industry." Rubinstein's position is that "Unless there is a change in current U.S. export controls, one study estimates that the computing industry stands to lose more than $60 billion annually by the year 2000."

The SAFE legislation protects both United States computer users and United States software vendors and promotes the continued growth of the software industry.

While the software industry has lobbied for a voluntary, market-driven encryption scheme, the government continues to promote its strict policies and an unpopular key escrow encryption mechanism, where the government would hold the keys to access confidential information.

SAFE legislation gives American software users the freedom to use software with unlimited encryption strengths, prohibits mandatory key escrow, and allows for export of encryption software.

BSA President Robert Holleyman also testified before the Senate Commerce Committee, in support of S.377, the Promotion of Commerce On-Line in the Digital Era (Pro-Code) Act, introduced by Senator Conrad Burns; and S.376, the Encryption Communications Privacy Act (ECPA), introduced by Senator Patrick Leahy. Both proposals significantly liberalize export restrictions on software with strong encryption, and seek to protect both privacy and security on the Internet. Both bills give software users the freedom to use data security software with no government "back door."

Summary

In this chapter, you learned the following:

◆ The first part of implementing a successful security environment is to create a security policy document. This is a high-level document; it details all of an organization's major security-related goals, outlines a hierarchy of authority and details who is authorized to access what, and details responses to be taken in case of attack.

◆ Harm to the network can be intentional or unintentional; that is, it can come from either a skilled hacker intent on stealing information, or from an employee who simply doesn't know any better.

◆ Corporate espionage or business intelligence gathering can be directed against your company. It is much more common than most people believe, and many intelligence practices are legal.

◆ In addition to protecting data, it is also important to consider physical security. Implement safeguards against theft or destruction of equipment.

Chapter 2

Implementing a Security Policy

IN THIS CHAPTER

- ◆ Establishing a security policy
- ◆ Restricting access
- ◆ Responding to violations
- ◆ The concept of the "survivable system"

IN THIS CHAPTER, WE look closely at your security policy document. Your security policy document does not outline the specifics of how each policy item is implemented. Rather, it is a higher-level document that details what needs to be done, and by whom. Drafting the security policy comes first; only after you have a complete policy in place do you consider how to implement it with specific products and procedures.

Planning Your Security Policy

When developing a security policy, the administrator must take several issues into account. The first step, and perhaps the most important, is to determine who should be involved in the policy-making process. As we discussed in Chapter 1, the policy committee should consist of a broad cross-section of the enterprise, including:

- ◆ Top management
- ◆ Midlevel management
- ◆ Supervisory employees
- ◆ Power users
- ◆ Front-line users
- ◆ Technical staff

A selection of delegates from every department should be included; not just IS. While it may be IS's role to implement the policy, it will be those other individuals just listed, in all areas of the company, who will know best from an operational viewpoint what policies will be necessary and reasonable.

Once you figure out who should be involved in your policy committee, you need to assess the overall situation before actually writing down specific policy items. This involves the following process:

1. **Identify what you need to protect.** This includes data, messaging systems, physical equipment, cabling, and the building itself. You should take a full inventory, not only of the obvious systems on desktops and in the IS department, but of all computers in employees' homes, remote offices, or stored in closets.

2. **Determine who may do harm to any of the items listed in Step 1.** By "harm," I mean both unintentional and intentional harm. An employee with too little knowledge and too much access can cause hours of extra work for the administrator, if not irreparable damage, even if the employee means no harm. Intentional harm can come from inside as well as outside your organization. Nearly half of all computer thefts are perpetrated by employees. A disgruntled employee with easy access can also cause a great deal of electronic mischief. And of course, unknown hackers from the outside also represent a considerable threat, especially if your network is connected to the Internet.

3. **Determine what types of threats exist.** An assessment of potential risks and hazards should outline any potential threat, no matter how insignificant. All threats should then be ranked according to potential damage and importance. This type of ranking is especially important when you're dealing with a limited budget, and will help you spend your money more wisely on those areas of security that pose the greatest threat of significant loss.

4. **Determine your priorities.** Of your property that must be protected, which is the most important? It is essential to have a good grasp on priorities, especially with a limited budget. If you have only so many dollars to spread around, you have to decide how best to spend them. Protect the most important systems and data first.

After making this assessment, you will find it much easier to actually sit down and write the specifics of your policy document. Once you write the security policy, you need to revisit it periodically. Networks grow, and as time goes on, new threats that were previously unknown may develop. The policy itself should receive at least an annual reevaluation. These security audits should review not only the policies that have been put in place but the procedures used to carry them out.

Implementing Your Security Policy

Once you have assessed your needs, you must consider how to implement your security policy. To do this, you need to do the following:

♦ Automate the security process for ease of use.

♦ Limit user access.

♦ Publish your policy for external and internal employees.

♦ Avoid dangerous situations.

♦ Schedule security drills.

Your ultimate goal, of course, is to protect you network, and implementing an effective plan will help you achieve that goal.

Automate the Security Process

When implementing the security policy, try to use as much automation as possible. It's a fact of life that end users don't like to back up their systems. Also, end users often see security as little more than a nuisance, and management sees it as a budget drain. Because nobody likes to deal with security, a high level of automation will ensure that it still gets done. Most backup software, for example, permits you to schedule periodic backups to be executed automatically at a predetermined time.

The National Institute for Standards and Technology (NIST) offers a useful guideline known as the "Minimal Security Functional Requirements for Multi-User Operational Systems." This document presents the following as the major functions that should be present in any security system. Keep these in mind when drawing up your policy, and in considering what types of security tools to purchase:

♦ **Identification and authentication.** Using passwords or other mechanisms to check a user's authorization status.

♦ **Access control.** Preventing users from accessing material they are not authorized to see. Most major operating systems have some type of access control mechanism that enables you to set access parameters for different files or subdirectories.

♦ **Accountability.** Linking all network activity to a user identity. This is done through a tracking utility or by using an activity log. These logs can be useful when going back to analyze an intrusion.

♦ **Audit trails.** Determining when a security breach has occurred and what was damaged or lost.

◆ **Object reuse.** Securing any data or other resource that will be accessed by multiple users.

◆ **Accuracy.** Protecting against errors that may cause inadvertent damage.

◆ **Reliability.** Guarding against a single user monopolizing resources.

◆ **Data Exchange.** Securing communications.

Limit Access

It's not always easy to determine who should have access to what. A typical network security system grants rights in a hierarchical manner, with more rights granted to those at the top of the hierarchy and only minimum rights granted to those on the bottom. A proposed hierarchy is as follows:

◆ **Level 1: Systems administrator/network supervisor.** This individual (or group of individuals) has the highest level of access and usually has the privilege of accessing all systems.

◆ **Level 2: Network administrators.** These individuals may be delegated authority by the systems administrator or network supervisor to carry out specific administrative tasks, such as updating software or implementing a network-wide backup.

◆ **Level 3: Power users.** An elite group of trusted users with sophisticated knowledge of computers may require access beyond what would normally be assigned to a person in their position.

◆ **Level 4: Task-oriented users.** Clerks, data-entry personnel, and other low-level employees are likely to need access to only a very limited portion of the network.

You should only grant users access that is necessary for the completion of their work. An individual's trustworthiness may be taken into account, but even a trustworthy file clerk is still a file clerk, and does not need superuser access. Granting the lowest level of access possible should be a general rule when setting these privileges. By doing so, you minimize the possibility of internal attack or accidental user errors that compromise security.

The occasion may arise, however, when an individual needs temporary access to files to which he or she would not ordinarily have access. The need may be completely legitimate; for example, the employee may be assigned to a special task or project. In such a case, the security administrator needs to grant access as required, but it is equally important to revert the employee's access privileges to the previous state once the project has been completed. Consequently, an important part of project management is to notify the security manager when a project requiring special access has been completed.

Publish Your Policy

For security to be effective, you must publish, discuss, and widely publicize your security policies. Furthermore, to guard against the "shove it in the drawer and forget about it" syndrome, you should periodically circulate memos that reiterate an outline of the most important security procedures, particularly if a specific violation has occurred recently.

If your company works with outside suppliers, contractors, or vendors who have access to the internal network, you should require them, by the terms of their contracts, to have secure networks as well.

All users, whether internal or external, should be required to agree explicitly, perhaps in writing, to abide by the rules set forth in the security policy. In addition to including this broad statement, however, a security document signed by the user should also itemize some security basics, such as the following:

1. The user will follow all established password practices set forth in the policy statement (no sharing of passwords, guidelines for creating passwords, and so on).

2. The user agrees not to allow any unauthorized personnel to access systems or data.

3. The user agrees not to gain access or attempt to gain access to any systems or data to which he or she does not have authority to access.

4. The user agrees not to copy software or data without authorization.

5. The user agrees not to introduce any foreign programs into the system without authorization.

6. The user agrees that the company has the right to monitor use of the system.

You should require any guest, outsider, contractor, or other individual who needs temporary access to the system to adhere to the same procedures outlined in the policy document. The practice of giving several occasional users access to a single account should be prohibited, due to the lack of accountability that results from this practice. Even if a person will be using the network only once, that person should still be given a separate, temporary account; which should be promptly deleted after the work has been completed.

Avoid Danger

The introduction of malicious programs represents a major threat to networks. A malicious program could be a virus, a Trojan horse, or a time bomb; the security policy must take steps to prevent the introduction of these notorious little devils. Few countermeasures are available at the operating system level that are meant to prevent a Trojan horse from operating. For example, if an authorized user has permission to access a host and has a Trojan horse at his or her disposal, this user could wreak a great deal of havoc on the network fairly easily.

The policy should, therefore, define the parameters under which new software (whether off-the-shelf or internally developed) may be introduced to the network. All software development that takes place on the network must be monitored; in addition, the introduction of any off-the-shelf program or utility must be carefully regulated. Users are prone to bringing in software from home, or downloading programs off the Internet. This practice must be discouraged. If the user needs a particular utility, the company should spend the extra few dollars to buy its own copy of it and not simply tolerate the installation of the user's copy. One advantage of this procedure is that it guards against the use of bootleg software. This is worth doing not only because bootleg software puts the company in legal jeopardy, but also puts it at risk of unknown viruses that may exist within the bootleg program.

If a program must be downloaded from the Internet, unless it is from a highly reliable source, it should be checked first on a stand-alone system before it is allowed on the network.

Drills and Staged Intrusions

As part of the audit/review process, you may want to schedule a drill from time to time to evaluate preparedness and verify the effectiveness of your response systems. You may also want to orchestrate a staged intrusion periodically. Doing so will determine the effectiveness of detection systems as well as the overall effectiveness of the system's firewalls and other tools used to keep out attackers.

The staged intrusion concept has become more popular in recent years. This process involves having a trusted individual with high-level clearance (or in some cases, an outside contractor) attempt (with the blessings of the company) to break into the system. Tools such as SATAN have popularized this method. (For more information about SATAN, refer to Chapter 8.) Although giving any individual carte blanche to break into your computer network may be risky business, the benefits can be tremendous. The process can yield valuable information about the network's vulnerabilities and tell you exactly what holes need to be plugged to achieve a higher level of security.

If a formal drill is too time-consuming and disruptive to operations, you or your administrator should at least test individual procedures to make sure that they are functioning properly.

Performing Background Checks

Having an effective security plan in place is not enough if you don't know your users. A common misconception is that security is primarily a technical issue that can be addressed with firewalls and antivirus programs. While these devices are important, security goes beyond technology. It is also a "people" problem. Computer crimes are carried out by people who only use computers as a tool with which to carry out their misdeeds. Making the tools more secure is one important avenue of security, but dealing with the perpetrators themselves is another.

Remember, the biggest threat to any organization comes from within. That's why it's important to perform employee background checks. Any individual who will occupy a position of trust should undergo a background check before being offered a position. This can be as simple as talking with a former employer, or can be as rigorous as hiring a private security firm to do a full investigation. Some companies run a credit check on every prospective employee, although in most cases this will be of little value and may be seen as an intrusion of privacy. In some limited situations it may be warranted, such as if the employee will be handling large sums of money.

Not performing background checks can be costly to you in the long run. The one individual who brought down my former employer, a financial institution handling $5 billion a year in client funds, had a decidedly checkered background. In retrospect, had we known this in advance, he surely would not have been hired. We discovered too late that he had given the personnel department a phony Social Security number and had a two-year gap in his resume that could not be accounted for.

A New Type of Criminal

Technology has given us a new type of criminal – the computer criminal. Long ago, when books were kept with a mechanical adding machine and paper ledgers, embezzlement was difficult to carry out, and could more easily be detected through regular audits. Computers have made it easier for your employees to steal from you, and in larger amounts, too. In a matter of seconds, a skilled computer criminal could transfer thousands of dollars into a phony account.

The computer can be used as a tool to carry out a fraudulent activity or theft, but it can also be used for many other types of mayhem. For example, the computer may be employed as a tool to carry out acts of revenge. A terminated employee may go for one last "hurrah" by deleting a hard drive or two before being escorted out the door. The computer can also be used for espionage – stealing your trade secrets, customer lists, or other critical information; or it can be used to invade someone else's privacy. Background checks won't stop every mischievous lance, but by not doing these checks, your organization perpetuates a vulnerable chink in its armor.

Warning Signs

What do you look for when conducting a background check? Some common areas to look out for are:

♦ Large, unexplainable gaps in career history

♦ A spotty employment record – several jobs of short duration

♦ A degree from a college you have never heard of

Here's another tricky one: When you call to check references, do you get nothing but answering machines? That's a red flag. A job-seeker with no good references may "manufacture" a reference by paying $10 or $15 to a voice-mail service, recording a greeting for a phony company, and taking your message. The job-seeker's confederate later returns your call, and gives you a glowing recommendation. You've just hired yourself a criminal.

What about personality traits? What type of person is likely to conduct a computer crime? Although by no means universal, here are a few clues: look for individuals in low-level jobs with an unusually strong interest in technology. The individual may have a strong interest in games of strategy, such as chess. It may be a college graduate with a low-level degree, or someone with serious money problems. Of course, individuals with interests in firearms, paramilitary organizations, and the like may be suspect as well. Very often, a computer criminal is a solitary individual with few friends, considered a loner by coworkers.

Striking a Balance Between Security and Privacy

When a system has been violated numerous times, it may be tempting to impose draconian restrictions upon system users. Policies such as reading employee e-mail, checking backpacks and purses, and locking supply closets may address some security concerns, but they also may create an atmosphere of mistrust and employee dissatisfaction. Many of us have become accustomed to having to use a security card to get into the office building, but it is not likely that we would stand for such extreme invasions of privacy as purse or backpack searches. I personally left a management job after three days when a policy was implemented that required all staff to sign in and out before going down the hall to use the bathroom.

What are the most important areas of security? A major part of assessing your security environment is to establish priorities. Losing data and valuable equipment are probably very close to the top. Security officers who put energy into locking up the office supply closets could do much better by spending their time elsewhere. You may save a few dollars by preventing pencil pilferage – but while you're counting message pads, somebody's breaking into your network and taking your customer list! Which is more important, the message pad . . . or the message?

An additional drawback of locked supply closets is the resentment it fosters because of the level of mistrust. If you keep anything of significant value in the supply closet, by all means, take it out and keep it in a safe, locked place. But otherwise, keep the pencils and pens out in the open.

A common but regrettable security practice is to require a terminated employee to leave immediately and under guard. This practice is extreme and may seem heartless, but unfortunately it may be needed in some environments. A terminated employee may be angry and resentful over the termination, and could easily delete data or cause other damage within a few minutes, simply out of revenge. In conjunction with this policy, the terminated employee's network access privileges should be revoked before they receive notice of termination. Ten seconds of Delete commands on the part of an unhappy soon-to-be ex-employee could wind up costing the company millions of dollars.

Responding to Violations

Now you have a complete security policy document. It has been debated, discussed, written down on paper, and finally, distributed to everyone in the company. Soon afterward, somebody violates it. It's inevitable. It's going to happen, so you need to figure out ahead of time what to do about it.

Is It a Real Threat?

Some types of events may lead a user to believe that a virus is present or a break-in is underway. However, the problem may merely be the result of a software bug or a flaw in network design. As the first part of the response procedure, it is important to determine that a true security incident has in fact occurred.

Suspect events, which may or may not be the result of a security breach, may include the following:

◆ System crash

◆ Unfamiliar user accounts

◆ Appearance of new files

◆ Altered, deleted, or relocated files

◆ Attempts to write to system files

Although none of these events provides any absolute proof that a break-in has occurred, they are all certainly cause for concern and should be thoroughly investigated.

Set Up an Action Plan

Your policy should include a section devoted to incident response, allowing for quick action and to minimize damage once you determine a violation has occurred. A response plan will reduce the possibility of hastily made decisions and panic.

The Old "I'm from IS" Ploy

"Hi, Bob, this is Jack, from IS down the hall. We're working on an incident response to last week's break-in. We want to make sure nothing like that ever happens again, so we're going to beef up our systems. I need to get some configuration information from you about your workstation."

Be aware of such calls. IS may not even employ a person named Jack; this may be a "social engineer" trying to gather valuable information to prepare for another break-in. Policy should include strict procedures for responding to calls requesting sensitive security-related information, such as passwords or configuration information. Only one or two individuals on the security team should be authorized to make such calls, and everyone in the company should be made aware of that fact. So, when "Jack" calls, the recipient of the call will be clued in to the fact that "Jack" is an intruder.

But what if the person authorized to request information, "Joe," calls, but it's really "Jack" masquerading as "Joe?" A policy that requires an employee to call back Joe at a prespecified number will take care of that trick quite handily.

The first part of response is notification. Many monitoring tools include facilities for automatic notification, through e-mail, pager, or other method. After confirming that an incident has occurred or is underway, notification must be imminent. Besides technical staff, several others may also need to be notified, depending on the nature and scope of the incident. Management and other staff may need to become aware of the incident, as well as law enforcement agencies, legal counsel, vendors whose data could be affected, contractors, and service providers. The individual who is the first point of contact, usually the systems administrator, is responsible for contacting others if necessary.

When appropriate, the system can be configured to also issue a notification to the perpetrator that he has violated your security policy. In some cases, this may be enough to scare the perpetrator away; or in the case of unintentional breach, make the perpetrator aware of a violation and inform him or her of proper system use.

If you are on the receiving end of a notification, it is important to verify that an individual calling for information is legitimate. Callers may be masquerading as law enforcement officers or other persons of authority, and may trick someone into giving out sensitive information about the incident. Policy must lay out specifically how an individual should respond to a request for information about an incident or other security information.

A single "point man" should be designated to respond to intrusions; this person may or may not be the individual who is the first point of contact. The point man is responsible for coordinating efforts and avoiding confusion, interpreting policy, and making decisions relevant to the incident. The point man should have technical expertise as well as management expertise.

When responding to an incident such as network intrusion, the first order of business is to determine what has been compromised, or could have been, and then undertake the following actions:

- Guarantee the integrity of any mission-critical systems.

- Attempt to stop any further attack.

- Determine where the attack originated.

- Determine how the attack occurred.

- Restore normal operations.

- Involve law enforcement and take legal action, if appropriate.

- Take legal or other punitive action against the attackers.

- Avoid negative publicity.

The latter can be especially important from a marketing perspective. We always hear that most incidents go unreported, and this is why: news of a break-in can cause clients or potential clients to worry about their own sensitive information that may be contained on your system.

As a follow-up, a more long-term item in your response list should be to fix the system so that a similar attack cannot happen again in the future. You never *want* a break-in, but if one does occur you can at least learn more about your system and improve its security.

The response to any given violation will be determined by the nature and scope of the violation. It should be determined what the potential damage is or could be for any given violation; this potential will in part determine the response. Before determining response, examine the potential seriousness of the infraction by examining the following issues:

- Are multiple sites (branches, divisions, servers) involved?

- How many computers are affected?

- Is sensitive data at risk?

The seriousness of the attack impacts how quickly the response must be executed and who should be involved. For example, if the break-in was more of an obvious "joyride" than an attempt to steal corporate secrets, and the only files that were hacked were a few word-processing documents, it's probably not necessary to call in the national guard. In such an event, while it may be wise to inform the executive staff of the incident, their immediate response is not necessary. Their involvement will come later, when you conduct a post-incident analysis in an attempt to close up the hole through which the attacker entered.

After the incident has occurred, the damage has been contained, the vulnerability sealed, and the perpetrators punished, you should conduct a post-incident analysis. The purpose of this analysis is to look over how the incident was handled and determine whether any procedures need to be changed for the future. The analysis should include a detailed log of events — which can be useful both internally and for legal reasons.

The post-incident analysis is a fairly high-level undertaking. Unlike the creation of the policy itself, which is undertaken by individuals from all levels, the post-incident analysis should be carried out by the following people:

1. The technical staff involved in responding to the incident

2. Midlevel management personnel from the affected department or business unit

3. Top-level management

Establish Policies for Different Types of Violators

The security policy itself should include a section that lays out specifically what action will be taken against different violators. One factor you should take into consideration is where the violation occurred. A violator can be either an insider (employee, contractor, partner) or an outsider (hacker, corporate spy, thief).

When an insider violates security policy, your actions could include the following, depending on the severity of the infraction and the frequency with which it occurs:

◆ **Verbal warning.** The least severe response, issued for first-time minor offenses and unintentional security breaches.

◆ **Written warning.** Issued when an employee repeatedly violates policy for minor infractions.

◆ **Reassignment of duties or demotion.** Action taken for more serious infractions, such as habitual misuse or attempting to gain access to unauthorized files.

◆ **Firing.** Action taken for the most serious infractions, such as causing intentional damage to the system or for stealing information.

◆ **Filing legal charges.** Action taken as a follow-up to dismissal when warranted.

When an outsider infringes on your network, your response is not quite as cut and dry. Although you may be able to take legal action, the most difficult part of responding to an outside violator is tracking down the perpetrator. Whether it is appropriate to pursue the violator depends on the severity of the violation. For the most part, however, your response to outside violation will involve finding out how the outsider gained access and then plugging up that vulnerability with a technological solution.

When a violation, security breach, or other unwanted event occurs, it is important to be prepared to respond to it. Although security policies often pay a great deal of attention to implementing protective systems and monitoring software, they often devote less attention to the procedures involved once you detect an attack. Nonetheless, this is an important part of policy that you need to consider when creating the policy document. The policy document should outline appropriate responses to different types of violations and the relevant priorities in protecting the system.

Non-Technology Security Policy

Your security policy need not be strictly technological in nature; some of it may be procedural. While the end result may be to protect data that exists electronically, procedural policies can significantly enhance your overall security environment.

DUMPSTER DIVING

Corporate spies intent on stealing secrets can gain a significant amount of knowledge just by going through your trash. In Chapter 1's "Data Remanence" section, we saw how a thief could take a discarded hard drive or other storage device and retrieve information from it even if it had been erased. Be careful about what you put into the trash!

It may surprise you to learn that taking trash is actually legal, according to the United States Supreme Court. According to a 1988 ruling, no expectation of privacy exists for any item that has been discarded.

Discarded computer printouts can contain valuable information. Shredders should be strategically located throughout the office; smaller, personal desk-side shredders should be provided for anyone who consistently works with sensitive documents.

PHOTOCOPIER REGULATIONS

In the "Risks and Horror Stories" section of Chapter 1, we saw how tight control over office photocopy machines foiled a corporate spy.

While instituting check-in and check-out procedures to keep track of corporate documents is wise and necessary, this procedure is rendered useless if a spy can merely check out a document, make a photocopy of it, and then return it to the document storage facility. Besides being convenient for accounting purposes, regulating who uses the copy machine and for what will go a long way toward preventing its use in copying sensitive documents.

PHONY WORKMEN

When we see a guy wearing a white coat and carrying a clipboard, we tend to assume that he is engaged in some sort of legitimate business. We may not even question him as he walks into our office, and then walks back out with an armload of corporate documents or computer equipment.

Anybody attempting to enter the office claiming to be a repair person, delivery person, or outside technician should be asked to show a work order. The receptionist should verify that the work has, in fact, been requested before allowing entry.

THE SECRETARY'S DESK

A good spy doesn't go to the president's office to look for documents. That's usually kept locked. He will instead go straight to the secretary's desk, which is probably out in the open and full of sensitive data.

Make sure the secretary has a locking drawer on the desk, and that it is used consistently. Dictation tapes may be left out on top of the desk while the secretary goes to lunch; these may contain information valuable to a spy. If anyone in the company needs a secure area to work, it's the executive secretary. This individual often holds the keys to all of the company's secrets. The secretary's desk may contain floppy disks full of sensitive letters, and other secret information for which a competitor would pay dearly. Keep this area as secure as possible!

MEETINGS AND TRADE SHOWS

Large, off-site meetings are a particularly rich source of information for someone engaged in industrial espionage. It is often much too easy for a spy to put on business clothes, carry a briefcase and put on a name tag, and just walk right into these types of meetings.

When attending off-site meetings or conventions, refrain from discussing business in public areas if at all possible. Furthermore, you should be aware of friendly strangers. If a spy wants to know all he can find out about your company, all he needs to do is read name tags until he finds his mark. And most importantly, do not leave your briefcase or laptop computer unattended. We are often lulled into a false sense of security while at these meetings. After all, these are all your colleagues, what do you have do worry about? The answer is—plenty.

Survivable Systems

The Computer Emergency Response Team (CERT) Coordination Center has created a new paradigm in security known as *survivable systems*. System survivability refers to the capability of a system to complete its task in a timely manner, even if parts of the system have been attacked. This is a recent (1997) study, but it encompasses several traditional areas of software engineering, including reliability, testing, dependability, fault tolerance, verification, performance, and information systems security.

Currently, most security setups rely on encryption and isolation. Isolation is carried out largely through segmentation and firewalls, but as networks become more widely distributed and unbounded, firewalls will become less effective.

CERT predicts that future systems will be more unbounded; that is, they will shift from a customer-controlled model to an unbounded network model, where computing resources are contained within a larger, unbounded network infrastructure and controlled by multiple service providers. The Internet is a prime example of an unbounded network.

The survivability model acknowledges that no matter how many preventive measures you put in place, network attacks will continue to occur. Consequently, the concept of systems security needs to be expanded to focus on building systems that can survive after an attack occurs.

Presently, the concept of a survivable system is mostly theoretical, and the nuts and bolts of building a survivable system still have yet to be determined. But it presents a great deal of potential and may ultimately become the most important part of security policy. CERT recommends taking an architecture-based approach to achieving survivability. That is, you should take an approach where design issues, rather than specific hardware or software products, are key to creating such a system.

According to CERT, you must address four basic problems before you can create a survivable system:

◆ The concept of system survivability is generally misunderstood. Further research is required to identify the basic concepts and techniques used to design a survivable system.

◆ When they are initially designed, computer networks rarely are built with an eye toward security. Consequently, security is relegated to being an afterthought, something added on later when budget permits or after an attack has already occurred. Security and survivability, however, must be part of the initial design to achieve the greatest level of effectiveness.

◆ When software quality is being assessed, several areas should be considered, including performance, ease of use, extensibility, and interoperability. However, system security must also be a consideration when making this assessment.

◆ Security and survivability research has been based on a bounded system, which assumes that control over all resources is possible.

The proposed survivability-based system would, to a large degree, depend on intelligent agents that share information and facilitate replication to increase the possibility of survival. In addition, agents could be used to detect specific types of threats and even take action against them without any user intervention.

The current state of network security takes a decidedly narrow view, focusing on "hardening" the system to prevent break-ins. Survivability goes a step further and presents a network that may still have the same firewalls and other security measures, but has also been designed to survive after an attack has occurred.

Summary

In this chapter, you learned the following:

- You need to identify what needs to be protected, who you are protecting it against, and what types of threats may exist.

- Nobody likes to do the grunt work, so automate as much of the security implementation as possible.

- Restrict access to the network, equipment, and individual files with a four-level hierarchy: level 1 (the highest level) includes the systems administrator/network supervisor; level 2 includes network administrators who are delegated assignments by the systems administrator; level 3 is power users and other trusted users; and level 4 is task-oriented users.

- Responses to all violations need to be clearly documented and carried out without exception. Responses may include written warning, reassignment of duties, firing, and legal action.

- A "survivable system" is a new concept that goes beyond preventive measures to attempt to create a system that can survive even if an attack occurs.

In the next chapter, we look beyond network security and examine planning for and responding to disasters.

Chapter 3

Disaster Planning

IN THIS CHAPTER

- ◆ Disaster planning strategies
- ◆ Recovering from a disaster
- ◆ Hot sites
- ◆ Data backup strategies
- ◆ Maintaining vital records

WHAT WILL YOU DO when the big one hits? An earthquake, flood, or fire can cause untold destruction to your computer systems. If your company goes through a major disaster, it has about a one in three chance of surviving. With a little planning and forethought however, your company could be the one that survives. An effective disaster plan can help take some of the pressure off when the unthinkable happens.

Your preparedness plan depends to some degree on your geographic location. If your office is in San Francisco, plan for earthquakes. If it's next to the Mississippi River, plan for floods. And if it's in the Midwest, anticipate tornadoes. Unfortunately, that's not all you should worry about. Dozens of different types of disasters can befall a company, including hurricanes, fires, civil unrest, terrorism, or even vermin infestation. To ensure the complete security of your network, it is important to prepare for each disaster's possible impact. In addition, you should keep a list of relevant telephone numbers handy in case of natural disaster.

A disaster-planning committee should address your company's specific needs in response to any number of disasters that may occur. This committee may be made up of the same members as the security policy committee; and the policy committee may even undertake disaster planning as an ancillary function of its original goals.

Planning for the Worst

A disaster plan consists of multiple parts. It should include a section that lists provisions for recovery after a disaster – which requires a lot of planning but little in the way of immediate action. The other part of the disaster plan requires proactive action, and includes tasks such as installing environmental monitoring equipment where computer equipment is located. The proactive disaster plan also includes deploying uninterruptible power supplies (UPSs), which facilitate an orderly shutdown of equipment in case of a power outage.

Other proactive measures include making sure that water shut-off valves and fire extinguishers are easy to spot, and that instructions on how to use them are posted near each device. In addition, a written set of procedures outlining how to respond to various emergencies should be posted in every department.

A comprehensive disaster recovery plan (which is separate from but complementary to the security policy document) may include the following components:

♦ Information concerning staffing and staff responsibilities under emergency conditions, such as line of authority

♦ Procedures and plans for moving to an alternate site

♦ Procedures and plans for restoring and returning to the original site after the disaster

♦ Detailed assignments, showing what actions need to be taken and who is authorized to take action in case of emergency

♦ Procedures for recovering lost data

♦ Procedures for retrieving equipment, supplies, files, and other material from a damaged site

♦ Plans for notifying staff, clients, vendors, and others who may be affected by the disaster

♦ A "Vital Records" list (which I discuss in a later section)

1989 Loma Prieta Earthquake, Disaster Response

When the Loma Prieta earthquake hit the company I was working for in 1989, the first order of business was to telephone each and every employee at home to determine that they were safe. The response plan was then rapidly implemented. First of all, we had an alternate location. Part of the disaster preparedness plan was to arrange for alternate, temporary headquarters; this involved arranging with a local hotel to have the privilege of taking over their grand ballroom in case of emergency. Because our facility had been declared unsafe to enter, this contingency saved the day. Because we had considered the possibility of an earthquake, we had long before planned out what our response would be. This advance planning enabled the company to be up and running in a makeshift office within 24 hours, with 30 phone lines, an AS/400, and readily available staff.

Company-wide coordination of disaster and contingency planning is essential for its success. Every individual within the enterprise may have a crucial role in the process of recovering from a disaster; every staff member's cooperation is essential. Everyone, starting with the clerical level, should have at least some familiarity with disaster procedures.

Having a written disaster plan minimizes the pressure to make decisions quickly after the disaster has occurred. Decisions made under these circumstances may not be well thought-out, or may even be impossible to make if communications have been affected by the disaster.

The major focus of disaster planning is getting operations up and running as quickly and efficiently as possible. The immediate goal is to restore at least partial operations, perhaps at an alternate site, within 24 to 48 hours. The larger goal is to restore operations to a predisaster state as quickly as possible.

Such advanced planning explicitly defines a maximum period of time that is acceptable before partial and full operations are restored. This time window may be different for separate areas within an enterprise, and this time window determines what sorts of measures you take to restore each given system. For example, a payroll tax management company would want to restore the system that makes tax payments on behalf of clients within 24 hours. A larger window may be accorded to a less critical function, such as the generation of marketing analysis data.

Form a Disaster-Planning Committee

The entire disaster-planning process may require more than time and a committee; it may require funds. As is the case with any business process that requires a budget allocation, support from top management is necessary. Without resources, the disaster plan may not be possible to implement, and may be useless. The disaster-planning committee should enlist management's active participation in the planning process in an attempt to achieve its full cooperation.

Another effective way to get the cooperation of the executive staff is through education. No CEO wants his or her company to fail, but many companies without disaster plans never recover after a major disaster. Make a report on the company's reliance on technology and what the potential impact would be on that technology if specific disasters occurred. The executives are very likely to take notice if you point out how essential this type of planning really is to the business.

After you get a commitment from the executive staff, you should form a planning committee to create the disaster plan. This committee should include a member of the executive staff, as well as members of the technology staff and representatives from any division or area that is engaged in a critical function. The committee could be the same as the security policy committee.

One of the primary functions of the committee is to assess the company's existing ability to recover from a disaster. This assessment determines any existing strong points, as well as weaknesses that must be overcome. The assessment should paint a picture of how well the company would be able to operate, if at all, after a disaster.

Afterwards, a risk analysis should be undertaken to determine what areas are vulnerable, what potential damage could occur, and what steps are necessary to re-establish services to each area within the company. As part of the risk analysis, you must take an inventory of assets, including physical assets, such as computers, and knowledge-based assets, such as data.

In addition, when considering what sorts of damage can happen, consider the likelihood of each, and the consequences of each. This helps determine how much of a limited budget to allocate to each area of the disaster plan, and also helps determine priorities during the emergency. When setting the budget and priorities for restoring services, be sure to consider the following questions:

- What resources must be expended to restore each service?

- What impact will the loss of a particular service have on the operation? For example, losing your dedicated private line that links different regional offices could be devastating. An alternate link should be considered. An encrypted Internet link may be significantly slower, but as an alternate means of communication, it could prove very valuable.

- What public relations and marketing issues need addressing in the event of a service disruption? Your public relations people should be on top of the disaster immediately. Press releases should be written to put a positive spin on the event, highlighting, for example, how your company responded to the event successfully.

- What costs are involved in restoring service? Budgetary considerations must be taken into account. Make sure you have enough discretionary funds to handle it. Make sure that management is on hand to make these budgetary decisions.

In addition to planning for the disaster, the review itself may bring to light some procedures that simply must be changed in order to mitigate the disaster's effects. As such, the disaster-planning document may have far-reaching implications, not only for the future, but for the present as well. As a result of the disaster review, the committee may decide to recommend several actions that change the way the company presently operates. Such recommendations may include purchasing redundant equipment, implementing a more rigorous data backup plan, and con-tracting with off-site service providers.

The committee must consider several issues. Besides creating an asset inventory list, the committee should also obtain, for inclusion in the disaster-planning docu-ment, a logical and physical diagram of the computer system, a description of the system architecture, and an identification of any single point of failure that may exist. While the system administrator may know all this information by heart, he or she may be inaccessible; thus it is important to have this information docu-mented and readily accessible.

In addition, every company operation can be classified into one of three categories:

1. Must continue on schedule

2. Restore as resources become available

3. Can be delayed

Further, if any operation requires the cooperation of an outside contractor, other branch or division, or input from clients, the other entity should be made aware of emergency procedures.

The task of resuming full service with any given operation may be very detailed; often, more tasks may be involved than you realize. When a function is running smoothly, we tend not to notice how much is really going on behind the scenes. When planning for service restoration, however, make plans for everything, including the following:

◆ Hardware and software

◆ Any communications that are necessary to complete corporate functions

◆ The cooperation of any other divisions, branches, vendors, or contractors essential to task completion

◆ Funding

◆ Staff required to complete each task

The plan must also identify any office equipment or backup data necessary to complete each task.

Transportation can be a problem after a disaster. Staff, delivery persons, and others may have difficulty getting to your site after the emergency. In metropolitan areas in particular, headquarters may be located in the center of the city, while most staff live in the suburbs. Public transportation and major arteries may be inaccessible after a natural disaster, and the transportation logistics will need to be addressed. If roadways are passable, this may mean arranging for rides between the office and outlying areas for staff members.

Immediately after the disaster has occurred, a preliminary damage assessment is in order. Based on the findings, the individual in charge of the disaster committee will decide whether to activate the disaster recovery plan.

A cache of disaster supplies should be kept on-site at all times. Such supplies can be essential in many circumstances; for example, a blizzard or other crisis may cause personnel to have to stay in the facility for several days. Disaster supplies might include the following:

- Batteries
- Blankets
- Bull horn
- Cash
- Cellular telephone
- Crow bar
- Drinking water
- Flashlights
- Battery-operated radio
- First-aid kits
- Food
- Hard hats
- Laptop PC
- Telephone lists
- Tools

In addition to having supplies on hand, you may want to have an alternative meeting site.

Pick an Alternate Work Site

The availability of an alternate work site can be of tremendous benefit in recovering operation within the specified time frame. You can take either of two approaches to this challenge: the cold site approach and the hot site approach.

A *cold site* is merely an available space, such as a hotel ballroom, warehouse, or empty office space, that your company contracts to use in case of emergency. Plans are implemented to move equipment and furnishings into this space as quickly as possible, and to get up and running in the shortest time possible. Along with the cold site plan, arrangements with equipment vendors should be in place to acquire additional computers and other equipment on short notice in case of emergency.

A *hot site*, on the other hand, is an alternate site that already has furnishings, equipment, and computers up and running. This is obviously one of the most expensive options, but also one of the most effective. One way to minimize the expense at least somewhat is to distribute the cost among several companies or divisions. A company with several divisions or offices may well afford the deployment of one hot site for use by all divisions after an emergency.

The alternate site approach you take may depend in part on the type of disaster involved. In a disaster such as an earthquake, some buildings may be completely destroyed while others just blocks away remain intact. Consequently, planning an alternative site may include the following options:

- Contracting with other office building operators for hot site services; that is, they agree to give you first refusal of any available office space in the event of an emergency

- Making reciprocal agreements with other companies

- Making reciprocal arrangements with other divisions or branches within your own company

◆ Implementing a separate "recovery center" to be used by all divisions of a company in case of emergency

Whether you operate from your office or an alternate site, you will probably need additional resources – our next topic.

Plan for Additional Resources

The financial impact of a disaster, especially one that takes out the computer system, can be tremendous; in fact, it can easily cause a company to go bankrupt. Unfortunately, many companies have not committed the financial resources necessary to develop a disaster plan to protect against this possibility. A disaster as basic as a prolonged power outage could deal a devastating blow to any business, especially if it relies heavily on automation and technology. Because more and more companies rely on computers for their day-to-day operations, a disruption of the ability to use the computer system can be devastating.

This factor, perhaps, makes businesses even more vulnerable than ever to disaster. In many cases, the great losses that accrue as a result of a disaster are not directly related to the disaster itself (whether it be earthquake, fire, flood, or civil unrest), but because of the lack of utilities that may result as a side effect of the disaster.

According to the California Office of Emergency Services, the average company that suffers from a computer outage longer than ten days will never completely recover, and 50 percent of those businesses will be out of business after five years. Smaller businesses without the same financial resources as major corporations are especially vulnerable. A smaller business is more likely to close permanently after a disaster, especially if it works on a small margin, or because its business drops off temporarily as a result of the disaster.

Even if your business is not directly affected, and even if you are able to maintain utility services, the effects the disaster has on the rest of the community may have an impact. Other businesses on which your company depends may have suffered, or the disaster may trigger civil unrest and violence. Your disaster plan should take this into account, and lay out procedures for getting services and supplies from alternate sources. Further, the plan should specify a procedure for getting in additional security personnel (such as a private security firm).

Automated Data Backups

You can avoid complete disaster by protecting your files before it's too late. All data should be backed up to a portable medium on a regular basis. You should have a backup schedule written and implemented that clearly delineates responsibility for the backup task. Use of backup strategies goes beyond being part of the disaster plan, although it is particularly relevant here. When disaster strikes, it is clearly advantageous to have backed-up data at an off-site location.

For servers, minicomputers, or mainframes that are frequently used, a weekly full backup plus a daily incremental backup may be in order. Two sets of backup tapes are recommended: one stored locally for easy access for routine file restoration, and a separate set stored off-site to be used in case of physical disaster.

For individual PCs or workstations, two backup options exist: making each user responsible for backing up his or her own PC, or centralizing the task. Because individual PC users tend to be lax in this area, it is recommended that the task be centralized and carried out by the systems administrator (or an individual to whom the administrator has delegated this authority). This task should also be automated as much as possible.

Use of an automated tape library to store and recover data, as opposed to a manually-operated system, is not only more time-efficient but also safer. Manually moving tape cartridges is an inherently risk-prone procedure. Labels may get lost, incorrect cartridges can be mounted, and errors can be made in the process.

Automated systems are widely available, from companies such as ADIC (Redmond, Washington). These solutions help minimize the potential for error and speed up the backup/restore process as well. These devices (see Figure 3-1) typically use robotic mechanisms to manipulate multiple tape cartridges simultaneously. Because all cartridges can be mounted in the library, the need for a staff member to physically mount and dismount the cartridges is removed – thereby eliminating a possible source of error. The operator merely provides the backup software with scheduling information, and the entire procedure is automated.

Figure 3-1: ADIC's automated tape library backup procedure eliminates the possibility of human error.

A stacker is one type of tape library that arranges tapes in sequential order. The disadvantage of this approach is that if tape number one is loaded and tape number four is being requested, the stacker must move through three other tapes before getting to the one that is needed. However, for environments that require only a few tapes, the stacker is an ideal solution because of its low price.

A jukebox, as opposed to a stacker, is randomly accessible. Tapes can be loaded in any order, without having to cycle through all of the intervening tapes. For environments with a large number of tapes, the jukebox is the obvious choice, although it is the more costly option. Another advantage of the jukebox is the availability of multiple tape drives in the same device. The availability of dual tape drives in the same jukebox can allow for redundancy, as well as the capability to back up and retrieve at the same time.

One viable backup option is to use a *remote backup service*. These services enable you to ship your files to them every night, via modem, for storage in an off-site facility. The benefits of this approach are many: it relieves staff from a task that is often ignored or done in haste, and it also provides the advantage of storing backup data off-site. The latter advantage is especially important in the event of fire or other disaster that may damage your facility. An off-site backup service should offer a high degree of automation, and should offer you a secure, encrypted method for transferring your data.

Data Backup in a Mixed Environment

The distributed computing paradigm represents a dramatic shift in the computer industry. It brings numerous advantages and empowers more users, but at the same time, it also has the potential to cause confusion and result in lost control over systems. But control does not need to be sacrificed in order to embrace distributed systems.

Data backup, if it exists at all, is often a patchwork of unconnected tape drives, boxes of floppy disks, and stacks of cartridges. Software tools such as Legato's NetWorker offer an enterprise approach, applying storage management techniques to mixed environments with Windows NT, NetWare, and UNIX. Enterprise storage management restores some of the lost control IS once had over storage management, way back in the days of glass houses and mainframes. Although a return to completely centralized computing is not desirable and would be highly inefficient, certain things should retain some level of centralization. Storage management is one of them.

Although centralization in storage management is desirable, the old model of closed systems and proprietary technology is not. Consequently, the new trend in storage management is to offer centralization, but to accommodate multiple operating systems and place a Web-based, open interface on the software to enable it to be accessed from any authorized client system on any network operating system.

Another advantage of the centralized model is that it enforces a standard operating procedure. Again, when every department, branch, or division takes charge over its own separate backup, not only does IS lose control, but overall, backup policy becomes a confusing mix of nonstandard policies, products, and procedures.

Legato's GEMS (Global Enterprise Management of Storage) system includes an open, Web-based management software application. With it, standard operating procedures can be enforced, and because of its open nature, existing storage management structures can be preserved.

The Legato system accommodates Windows NT, UNIX, and NetWare (see Figure 3-2). Tapes can be exchanged among servers on all three platforms, and the product is capable of protecting a mixed environment through the use of additional ClientPaks. The system's OpenTape format facilitates full platform interoperability and tape interchangeability between NetWorker servers hosted on all three platforms. The architecture is based on the uncoupling of managed systems (the *data zone*) from the management infrastructure (the *control zone*). This uncoupling enables the data protection process to be separate from the management control process. As a result, storage needs can be met with a system that is capable of adapting to the organization.

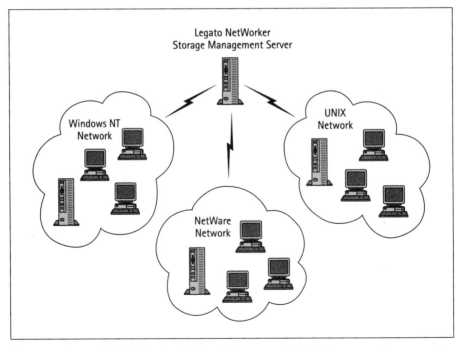

Figure 3-2: Legato's NetWorker for Windows NT manages data backup across three separate environments.

The data zone is the boundary of customer servers and desktops that is managed by a single NetWorker server. The data zone is composed of customer data, the metadata that describes it, tape devices that store it, and an administrative function to control the data protection process within the data zone.

The control zone is the collection of data zones that are managed by a Legato GEMS control station. This enables most storage management administrative functions to be performed at a central point in the organization via the company's intranet infrastructure, as well as locally. Control processes can be redefined centrally without disrupting any data zone.

GEMS also provides the tools needed to manage tasks across multiple data zones, including policy-based administration, software distribution, software licensing across data zones, and management of all tape media whether inside or outside a tape library, which may be shared across applications.

UNIX-Based Backup

UNIX administrators often rely on the *dump* and *tar* commands for backup and recovery. These are especially convenient because they come free with the operating system. However, their unwieldy and limited nature leads to a higher cost of administration.

The *dump* and *tar* commands are provided for the purpose of copying data from disk to tape and were not meant to be an enterprise data-management tool. With *dump*, for example, a separate command must be issued for each file system. In a large system, maintaining backup with the *dump* utility can be a daunting task indeed.

In addition, because *dump* and *tar* are not directly integrated with the applications running on the system, the data structure and locking rules of these applications may not be supported by *dump* and *tar*. This lack of support makes it impossible to back up live applications, a highly desirable feature offered by several other utilities.

Unfortunately, when *dump* encounters a tape write error or reaches the end of a tape in the middle of a backup, the entire dump is aborted. If it is not possible to complete the backup on another new tape, the entire backup must be rerun. Another major consideration is cross-compatibility. Although *dump* and *tar* are UNIX commands, they are not portable across all UNIX platforms.

A separate graphical utility may ultimately be the most economical option. Systems such as those offered by Legato provide a major advantage over these native UNIX utilities because they can accommodate multiple implementations of UNIX. In addition, a third-party system may also be able to back up live files and offer parallel data streaming, and will be easier to operate because of the graphical interface. And third-party utilities can often better handle tape write errors or end-of-tape situations. Third-party backup management tools such as NetWorker also offer a greater degree of automation and transparency, as well as scheduling facilities.

Hierarchical Storage Management

Automated backup systems can also facilitate a hierarchical storage management (HSM) solution. An HSM system automates the process of migrating infrequently used files to a hierarchy of less expensive, off-line storage media.

HSM is policy-based; that is, data management is driven by a set of policies that dictate the movement of data from one storage medium to another. Those files that have been migrated still appear to be local to the end user, and when the user attempts to access them, they are automatically retrieved from their location. In most cases, the minimal delay experienced in retrieving files from a tape, optical disk, or other storage bank is well worth the money saved and convenience in the overall storage strategy.

Storage media in an HSM system is organized in levels, which are based on access speed and cost. The first layer of the hierarchy consists of the most expensive media with the fastest access time, typically magnetic disk. Tape, which is least expensive and slowest, is the last stage in the hierarchy (see Figure 3-3).

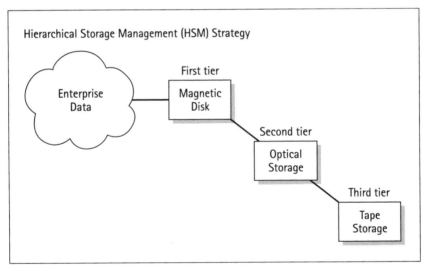

Figure 3-3: Hierarchical storage management stores data in a hierarchy of progressively less expensive media.

Typically, the migration operation can be either automatic or on-demand. The automatic model executes a migration whenever a certain threshold is reached. With the on-demand model, the systems administrator initiates the migration procedure through a direct command. Whenever possible, the migration should be automatic.

HSM is not, however, a replacement for a regular backup routine and archiving, but is instead a complementary system. A backup system executes a full backup on a regular basis, perhaps once a week, and an incremental backup on a more frequent basis, perhaps daily. Data archiving takes a snapshot of a file or series of files at one given point in time. HSM is highly complementary to both of these procedures. It is a very useful procedure for managing data, by moving older, less frequently used data to less expensive media and making room for new files on the primary storage media.

An HSM strategy is based on archiving. Archiving manages the task of organizing files prior to executing long-term, off-site storage. Once the files have been archived, they can then be deleted if desired, to free up disk space.

Data backup, data archiving, and HSM differ from each other in significant ways. Data backup merely stores redundant copies of files, usually copying them from a hard disk to some sort of removable media. These redundant copies are used as part of a recovery process, which takes place if the original file, which exists on the hard disk, becomes damaged or is inaccessible. Data archiving, on the other hand, takes a snapshot of a group of related files that reside on primary media at a specific point in time. This snapshot is stored on a removable medium. Once this snapshot has been stored on a removable medium, files can be deleted from primary storage as desired. While data backup is typically centrally controlled, data archiving is usually controlled by the end user, and is usually associated with files relating to a specific project. Lastly, HSM is a policy-driven strategy that migrates data from one storage medium to another, based on a set of rules, including how often the file is accessed. HSM creates the illusion of infinite storage by establishing a series of three or more storage mechanisms that can be added onto as needed. The HSM solution you choose should support all platforms in the network to encompass the entire enterprise. Unfortunately, not all operating system vendors support file migration, which may require a third-party application that modifies the file system. NetWare 4.1 has an HSM-ready file system; in addition, the Data Management Interface Group (DMIG) standard for UNIX establishes a common interface to enable all operating system vendors to make their file systems HSM-ready. In keeping with the spirit and intent of open systems, the HSM system should also work with any storage media and should not require a vendor-specific storage device.

In addition, the HSM system should enable the preservation of specific files. This lets the administrator flag a file so it will never be migrated, no matter how infrequently it is accessed. Files that should not be migrated include, of course, system and configuration files, or files with sensitive information that may best be retained in a secure location.

Vital Records

A vital records plan can be instituted to help identify a company's most important records – specifically, those that are essential to continued operation. Such a program identifies these records and makes every effort to afford them extra protection in case of emergency or disaster. In addition, records identified as vital should be duplicated and stored both on-site and off-site, in case the premises are destroyed or inaccessible.

The vital records plan starts out by identifying those records that are vital to continued operation and then takes extra measures to ensure their appropriate storage and periodic updating. An inventory of vital records may include the following:

- ◆ Information necessary for disaster or emergency response
- ◆ Operating procedures documents
- ◆ Names and contact information of critical personnel, clients, and vendors
- ◆ Information regarding the physical location of off-site data storage sites
- ◆ Building plans and other physical plant data
- ◆ Equipment inventories
- ◆ Systems documentation
- ◆ Accounting records
- ◆ Social Security and personnel records
- ◆ Insurance records

A written plan for recovering both the vital data and other operational data should be in place. This plan should include the following:

- ◆ Details about whom to notify
- ◆ Procedures for recovering data, including information about the data's location and who is authorized to recover it
- ◆ Information about contractors and disaster recovery services

Summary

Disasters can wreak havoc on security; as such, it is important to have a good disaster plan in place. This chapter showed you how to do just that by teaching you the following:

- ◆ A good network security plan should be implemented in conjunction with a disaster plan. While network security plans may focus on accidental network problems and intentional attacks, disaster plans address the needs of the systems and network after a major disaster.

◆ A great many disasters can befall a company, including fire, flood, earthquake, riot, or even terrorism, depending on your location and the nature of your business. A good disaster plan will make a contingency plan for each.

◆ A disaster plan is both proactive and reactive. It attempts to prevent disasters from causing harm by deploying equipment such as uninterruptible power supplies; at the same time, it also plans out careful strategies for dealing with the results of the disaster.

◆ Make a contingency plan to move to an alternate site in case your existing facility is inaccessible.

◆ All company operations can be classified into one of three categories for the purpose of disaster planning: must restore immediately, restore as resources become available, or restoration can be delayed.

◆ A fully automated data backup system with off-site redundancy is the most effective and safest approach to making sure critical data is available after an emergency.

◆ An alternative location should be planned for in case your primary location is destroyed or inaccessible. This can be a *cold site*, which is merely any available space to which equipment and computers can be moved in case of emergency, or a *hot site*, which is already furnished with equipment, technology, and backup data.

◆ Hierarchical storage management (HSM) is complementary to, and not a replacement for a good data backup plan.

◆ A *vital records* program compiles a set of vital information, including telephone numbers, location of vital data, building plans, equipment inventories, and procedures for recovering data.

Chapter 4

Security Levels

IN THIS CHAPTER

- ◆ Department of Defense Guidelines
- ◆ A look at the C2 security level
- ◆ Various operating systems' C2 designations
- ◆ Discretionary access control

THE NATIONAL COMPUTER SECURITY CENTER (NCSC) is the United States government agency responsible for performing software product security evaluations. These evaluations are carried out against a set of requirements outlined in the NCSC's Department of Defense Guidelines. This chapter reviews these and other guidelines, as well as security designations.

Department of Defense Guidelines

Perhaps the one organization most concerned with security is the U.S. Department of Defense. Consequently, the department has published a great many documents, manuals, and guidelines having to do with security, many of which you may find useful for your organization. We'll take a look at what are called the Orange, Red, and Brown books.

The Orange Book

The Department of Defense *Trusted Computer System Evaluation Criteria*, also known as the Orange Book, is often quoted when making or implementing a security policy. You don't have to be part of the military to take some lessons from the Orange Book. This nearly 100-page document breaks out security into four broad categories and provides a method for evaluating security control effectiveness in any type of data-processing system.

The Orange Book addresses three major objectives:

- ◆ To give users a measure for assessing the degree of trust that can be placed in any given computer system

◆ To provide manufacturers with guidelines on what features to build into trusted commercial products

◆ To provide guidelines that can be used when specifying security requirements for a given acquisition

The Orange Book sets out six basic requirements; four deal with controlling access to information, and two deal with assurances that the computer system is indeed trusted. The six requirements are as follows:

1. **Security policy.** The system must enforce a well-defined security policy. A system must therefore contain a set of rules used to determine whether any given subject can gain access to any given object.

2. **Marking.** Every object stored in a computer must be able to be marked, in order to identify the object's security level.

3. **Identification.** All individual objects must be identified. Every time an object is accessed, the access attempt must be mediated based on who is attempting to access it, and what authorization level they possess.

4. **Accountability.** Audit data must be kept and protected, so that any actions taken that impact security can be traced. A trusted system records all occurrences of events relevant to security in an audit log.

5. **Assurance.** The system must contain a mechanism that can be independently evaluated, so as to provide assurance that the system enforces requirements one through four.

6. **Continuous protection.** The mechanisms in place that enforce requirements one through four must be continuously protected against tampering or unauthorized changes.

The Red Book

The Red Book, formally known as the *Trusted Network Interpretation Environments Guideline*, gives users some more insight into issues specific to maintaining a trusted computer network. The Red Book identifies minimum security requirements for different types of network environments.

According to the Red Book, every network should have a "Network Security Architecture and Design" (NSAD). What this proposes, and what has been suggested earlier in this book as well, is that a network should be built from the ground up with security in mind. Your NSAD, or whatever you choose to call your security design document, should encompass all types of security, including communications security, physical security, personnel security, and information security. Furthermore, the security policy should be written to apply to all components or subsystems of the network.

The Brown Book

The Guide to Understanding Trusted Facility Management, or the Brown Book, is another Defense guide that looks at the issues involved in creating a trusted facility. Having a trusted facility is a critical part of security; implementing network security and other precautions may be useless if the facility itself is vulnerable.

According to the Brown Book, weak facility management can result from unclear or unenforced administrative roles. Specifically, three weaknesses pointed out are as follows:

- Unauthorized modification of hardware or software configuration
- Penetration of administrative roles by nonadministrative users
- Misuse of authority

Again, as mentioned before, allowing unauthorized or unskilled individuals to attempt to configure software or hardware can result in serious security hazards. Although they may be unintentional, these hazards can still be quite disruptive. Security policy should explicitly prohibit unauthorized configuration of either hardware or software, and should clearly delineate roles and levels of authority for these types of tasks.

C2 Security

Your security measures may involve more than following the government guidelines. You may also want to take advantage of the features of a government certified security system.

Of all the government-specified security levels, C2 is perhaps the most high-profile and most important, because almost all government contracts require C2 security. This fact makes C2 an important consideration not only for government agencies, but for any company wishing to sell products or services to the government. Microsoft raised a few eyebrows in 1996 when it won a government contract that called for an operating system with C2-level security. In the past, although it wasn't explicitly stated, it was assumed that UNIX was the only operating system that could qualify; and some cried "foul" when Microsoft's Windows NT operating system was installed. Most government contracts involving purchases require C2 security. But even if you're not dealing with the government, you may still want to take advantage of the security features of a C2-certified system.

The major elements of C2 security are as follows:

- An individual who owns a resource or file must have the capability to control access to that resource.

◆ The operating system must be able to prevent objects from being randomly reused by other processes. For example, the system must protect memory such that its contents cannot be read after a process frees it.

◆ All users are required to enter a unique logon name and password before accessing the system. In addition, the system must be able to use this information to track any user's activities.

◆ Authorized administrative users must have access to audit data to audit security-related events.

◆ The system must be able to protect itself from external tampering and other types of interference, such as modification of system files.

C2 and other security levels do not dictate an individual security policy, they only guarantee that the operating system can enforce it. It is up to you to determine your company's requirements, what your needs are, and what level of access you will allow. In other words, specific protective measures are up to you; the C2 evaluation is merely a mechanism for planning them or evaluating them once they are in place.

The C2 rating is important to many government agencies and private businesses that do business with the government. It is also critical to banks and other financial institutions because they often require a C2-evaluated operating system and database. For those enterprises that require C2 compliance for both the operating system and database, the only available option is OS/400.

The difference between Orange Book compliance and Red Book compliance is significant, so claiming Orange Book compliance does little for a networked environment. In fact, until Microsoft earns Red Book certification (which it surely will) for Windows NT, the moment a C2-certified NT box is connected to the network, it loses its security clearance. The major difference between the Orange Book and the Red Book is that the Orange Book evaluates an individual component for its trustworthiness, and the Red Book evaluates the product as it relates to a general-purpose network. The Red Book builds on the Orange Book specifications to define how each component interacts in a distributed networked environment.

Microsoft Windows NT and C2 Security

Microsoft Windows NT does indeed qualify for the C2 security designation. The National Computer Security Center, mentioned previously, performs security evaluations to determine whether a software product complies with the rigorous Orange Book requirements. Furthermore, NT is also evaluated by the NCSC for its networking security facilities to determine whether it complies with the organization's Red Book, which is more specific to network security.

Until Microsoft's Windows NT operating system has been Red Book-certi-
fied, its C2 clearance applies to stand-alone systems only. NT's networking
services were not included as part of the NCSC C2 evaluation. When you run
Microsoft's C2Config application and you are on a network, you get the following message: "C2 compliance requires that no networking software be
installed on your system. One or more network services have been detected
on your system. Select OK to use the Network Control Panel Applet to
remove these services." Doing so, however, disconnects your PC from the
network.

Windows NT 4.0 has been evaluated by the NCSC at the Orange Book's C2 security level, which covers the base operating system. Furthermore, NT is in the
process of being evaluated by the NCSC for its networking component, in compliance with the Red Book. The Red Book interprets the Orange Book as it applies to
network security. The Orange Book applies to security as it relates to a stand-alone
system. If NT is your operating system of choice, you will need the C2Config application, which is part of the Windows NT 4.0 Resource Kit. With this application
you can select from the settings used in evaluating Windows NT for C2 security
and implement the settings you want to use in your installation.

Both Microsoft and Novell have addressed the C2 issue, somewhat leveling out
the playing field among Windows NT, NetWare/IntranetWare, and UNIX – and
making significant progress toward ending UNIX's monopoly on secure systems.

Novell IntranetWare and C2 Security

Novell promotes IntranetWare, and the NetWare 4.11 network operating system
that is part of it, as C2-compliant. In addition, however, Novell also claims Red
Book compliance, giving it at least a temporary edge over Windows NT.
IntranetWare has the advantage of being the first general-purpose network operating system to obtain the C2 rating resulting from the evaluation of a server component, client component, and a complete network.

While Microsoft's current implementation focuses on C2 security for stand-alone
systems only, Novell goes a step further by accommodating the network as a whole.
C2-related features of IntranetWare include:

◆ An enhanced AUDITCON utility, which permits users, acting
   independently of network supervisors, to audit network transactions.

◆ Automatic secure configuration is enabled through the Enable
   SECURE.NCF SET parameter. This parameter lets you specify that a server
   be configured automatically during system boot as an Enhanced Security
   Server.

◆ Audit log files are presented as directory objects. Presenting these files as directory objects facilitates strict control over access to them, by using the directory rights assignments.

Novell's Open Security Architecture enables not only the server, but each workstation and the network as a whole to be trusted. Novell includes SISTEX's Cordant Assure EC product to meet the NCSC requirements of the trusted LAN model. The product provides the security features necessary for the workstation to control access to the network, local memory, and peripherals. Because of the open security architecture, however, other third-party security products can also be used to meet user requirements.

IBM OS/400 and C2 Security

AS/400 users also enjoy C2 security. In fact, the AS/400 is the first system to receive C2 certification for both the operating system and database operating as a unit. AS/400 includes the integrated DB2 database.

If you're an AS/400 administrator, you can configure each AS/400 with one of several security levels to meet different requirements. These levels are similar to the ones offered by Microsoft Windows NT, and include:

◆ **Minimal security.** No passwords; users can perform any function.

◆ **Password security.** Passwords are required, but users can still perform any function.

◆ **Resource security.** Passwords are required, and object usage can be controlled. Users can be limited to specific functions.

◆ **Resource security and operating system integrity.** Passwords are required, and object usage can be controlled. Users can be limited to specific functions. Use of unsupported interfaces is restricted.

In addition, a feature exists for logging and preventing attempted usage of unsupported interfaces and machine interfaces; also, a security journal logs all security violations and changes to security definitions. The security journal cannot be altered, and forms the basis of problem resolution and research into security problems on an AS/400 system.

Discretionary Access Control

One of the most important parts of a C2-certified operating system is *discretionary access control (DAC)*. The NCSC defines DAC as "a means of restricting access to objects based on the identity of subjects and/or groups to which they belong."

DAC has one big limitation, however. Under this type of control, if a user or process has discretionary access to information, that user could pass the data along to someone else.

DAC deals with the concept of *control objectives*, or control over individual aspects of an enterprise's processes or resources. Specifically, any system is secure only with respect to enforcing a specific policy; that is, before any system can be secure, an explicit policy must be put in place. This is one of the biggest reasons why creating your policy document, without regard to specific software or hardware, is the first step in implementing a secure network. Once your policies are in place, only then can you decide how to enforce them.

Discretionary control is a common type of access control, perhaps the most common in all modern computer systems. Discretionary control enables one user, typically the network or systems administrator, to specify what levels of access other users are allowed to have. Discretionary controls are based completely on the identities of the users and of the objects they want to access. Mandatory control, on the other hand, does not implement the decisions of any one supervisory user; instead, it makes decisions based solely on each user's security clearance or trust level, and the particular sensitivity designation of each file. In other words, in a mandatory control system, the owner of the file or object has no discretion as to who can access it.

While discretionary control affords a finer level of granularity in the access control process, both types of controls can be used effectively and can be seen as complementary. Mandatory controls can be used to control access to broad categories of information; for example, financial information could be restricted to the accounting office, personnel information could be restricted to the human resources office, and so forth. Discretionary controls can be used to fine-tune those broad controls, override mandatory restrictions as needed, and accommodate special circumstances.

As an example, consider a situation in which the operations department has broad (mandatory) access to a transactional database, but no access to the marketing department's records. But, one individual in operations is working with marketing on a client newsletter – so that individual could be granted discretionary access to the marketing department's files.

Access Control Matrix

The process of identifying users and objects is key to discretionary access control. You may want to use an *access control matrix*, which places the names of users in each row and the names of objects in each column. Table 4-1 shows a sample access control matrix.

TABLE 4-1 Network Access Control Matrix

| Users: | Objects (Files or Applications) | | |
	Larry.doc	Moe.doc	Curly.doc
Larry	rw	r	r
Moe	r	rw	r
Curly	r	r	rw

Note: r indicates read-only access; *w* indicates write-only access; and *rw* indicates read and write access.

Entries in each cell of the matrix describe what type of access every user has to every object. Different operating systems may implement this matrix in one of five different ways:

♦ Capabilities

♦ Profiles

♦ Access control lists (ACLs)

♦ Protection bits

♦ Passwords

Capabilities and profiles are used to represent the access control matrix data by row, and connect accessible objects to the user. An ACL and protection bit-based system, on the other hand, represents the data by column, connecting a list of users to an object.

The ACL is the most useful and flexible type of implementation of an access control matrix. The ACL permits any given user to be allowed or disallowed access to any object. The columns of an ACL show a list of users attached to protected objects. Groups and wildcards can be used to represent objects and users to minimize the size of the ACL.

When files are organized in a tree structure, such as in Novell Directory Services (NDS), you can use any of three methods to control access to the directories and their associated files:

♦ Access controls can be placed on individual files, but not on the directories.

♦ Access controls can be placed on the directories, but not on individual files.

♦ Access controls can be placed on both directories and individual files.

Controlling only the directories gives users the same access rights to all files under the directory and requires users to group files according to access type. Placing access controls on every individual file, without regard to directory, may impose a high level of granularity over control – but without access controls over the directory as well, users could still browse through the entire directory to see at least the names of files that they cannot access. Therefore, the third option is the most secure and offers the greatest degree of control.

For example, consider a user in the human resources department that needs to have access to most of the files in the human resources subdirectory. However, if that individual is not directly involved in the payroll function, he or she does not need to know how much money everybody makes. That user may, out of idle curiosity, decide to browse through the payroll file to see how much a coworker makes – a big human resources no-no. This problem can be prevented by simply granting the individual access to the directory, but placing a restriction on that one file.

Audit Capacity

You should implement additional security in the form of *audit capability*. The DAC mechanism should be auditable; that is, any operation that changes the control structure of the DAC should be recorded in an audit log. Furthermore, any attempt to access a protected object should also be recorded, as should changes to group definitions. The audit log should include a timestamp, user's identity, object's identity, and type of action taken.

An audit log system logs file accesses, and audits the file access logs against the user-specified security policy. This is done in a manner that is transparent to the end user. In Windows NT, for example, an object's security descriptor contains a field auditor as well as the ACL. The field auditor refers to the security system's audit capability. For example, while the system administrator can audit system directory changes, if a user tries to change files in the directory, NT makes an entry in the audit log. Regularly reviewing the audit log can help reduce the risk of computer tampering.

Because the DAC system restricts access based on identity, it carries with it an inherent flaw that makes it vulnerable to Trojan horse attacks. Most programs that run on behalf of a user inherit the DAC rights of that user.

Suppose, for example, that two users, Marian and Pawel, are governed by the DAC. Lotus maintains a data file with sensitive information. Pawel, who is actually a double-agent for a competing organization, does not have access to that file but would like to see it. Marian has configured the access control list to reflect that she is the only one who can read the file, and no one else is authorized to access it.

Pawel will get a big bonus if he is able to steal Marian's file, and so he makes use of his existing, legitimate access to the system. Pawel has legitimate access to a particular program, but within that program, he embeds a covert function (Trojan horse) that will read Marian's file and copy it into a separate file, which he titles "Stolen Data.doc" in his own address space. Pawel has an ACL associated with Stolen Data.doc that permits any process executing on behalf of Marian to write to it. Therefore, if Marian unknowingly executes the file and releases the Trojan horse, the covert function will steal Marian's data, write it to Pawel's file, and enable Pawel to read it.

So, Pawel tells Marian about how wonderful the program is and how she might enjoy the beautiful graphic in the introductory screen. Then Marian executes the program and sets the whole process in motion. Minutes later, Marian's secret data is in Pawel's Stolen Data.doc file.

Although the DAC system does afford some level of assurance, it is still possible that an attack could get through. Although software programs produced by commercial manufacturers are unlikely to have Trojan horses, unevaluated software from other sources may contain this type of threat. Therefore, in an environment where sensitive data exists, the policy should state that no user be allowed to load any unauthorized software onto his or her machine. Furthermore, it should state that discretionary access control not be the sole method of protection.

A complementary mandatory access control mechanism would prevent the Trojan horse attack by preventing the Trojan horse from giving sensitive information to any user who is not explicitly authorized to access it.

While mandatory access controls are simpler to administer (that is, they can be used to grant broad access to large sets of files), discretionary access controls are also necessary to add a finer level of granularity to control. Thus the best approach is to use mandatory access controls supplemented by discretionary access controls to regulate control over individual sensitive files.

Summary

In this chapter, you learned the following:

- ◆ Most government contracts require C2-level security. However, civilian enterprises can also benefit from using products that comply with this designation.

- ◆ Microsoft's Windows NT, NetWare/IntranetWare, and UNIX comply with C2 specifications.

- ◆ The C2 specification does not impose any specific security policy; rather, it is used to enforce your own policy.

- ◆ Discretionary access controls (DACs) are used to restrict access to objects, based on the identity of the object and of the user attempting to access the object. Access is controlled at the discretion of a supervisory user.

- ◆ A discretionary access control system, when not used in conjunction with mandatory controls, may be vulnerable to a Trojan horse attack.

Chapter 5

Encryption

IN THIS CHAPTER

- ◆ A look at various encryption mechanisms
- ◆ Digital certificates
- ◆ Making Internet content safe
- ◆ The U.S. Postal Service strikes back
- ◆ Current encryption legislation

YOU CAN DEPLOY LOTS of different security methods to try to keep attackers out of your network. But no matter how thorough you are, it is likely that someone will still get through. When that happens, encryption ensures they cannot read whatever they take.

Most of the major network operating systems have some sort of encryption mechanism. This mechanism is often minimal, however, largely because of federal regulation and a desire to make the software easy to operate. Although the native functions will not deter a determined attacker, they will still prove valuable in deterring the more casual snoop.

 In addition to the built-in encryption utilities included in the major network operating systems, several third-party encryption programs are available. See Appendix E for more details.

Encryption takes a data file and transforms it, through use of a special algorithm, into an unreadable mishmash of letters and characters. An encrypted file is completely unreadable without the password or key, and therefore, so long as the encryption mechanism cannot be broken, you have no need to physically secure the data. Encryption is based on a password, which is used by the encryption software to scramble the file, and a decryptor, which again uses the password to restore the file to its original state. As with any other type of password, an encryption password must be carefully chosen and closely guarded.

Electric Commerce

Nowhere is encryption more important than in electronic commerce. But is it safe to conduct financial transactions over the Internet? In a word, *no*. However, this is a qualified "no." The industry uses a number of technologies that are reasonably secure, but not absolutely, positively, 100 percent secure.

Internet-based electronic commerce is in the same category. We send faxes with critical information to a fax machine located in an office's copy room. The fax may then be picked up by an underpaid copy clerk and walked over to the recipient. But until that underpaid copy clerk comes in from his or her cigarette break and picks it up, anybody could walk by and see it, or even take it.

We give out our credit card numbers over the telephone, but is the telephone secure? Absolutely not. It's a simple matter to tap a phone and retrieve information; furthermore, the person on the other end of the phone could be merely another underpaid employee (who has probably not even undergone a background check).

Even when we sign a credit card slip at the gas station, the attendant will take the carbon paper and toss it in the trash. Again, anybody could pick that up and steal your credit card number.

Although these things could happen, and indeed have happened, they *usually* don't. Reasonable precautions are often taken. Maybe the gas station attendant keeps the trash can behind the counter, or maybe the owner has even had the foresight to use carbonless sheets.

The fact is, probably more precautions are being taken for Internet-based electronic transactions than nearly any other type of transaction. No, it's still not absolutely secure, and a lot of work still needs to be done. You may still not trust some transactions to the Internet, although you can take reasonable precautions (we get into those in Chapter 18).

Public and Private Keys

Once data is encrypted, nobody can read it without a decryption key. Encryption not only keeps the information private, but also provides a mechanism for authentication, where the recipient can be assured of the identity of the sender and the integrity of the message. Authentication protocols are based on either a private key cryptosystem (such as DES, discussed later), or a public key system (such as RSA, also discussed later). Public key systems use *digital signatures* for authentication.

It is possible to break an encryption code. Because of this possibility, it is best to use the strongest encryption possible. The 56-bit Data Encryption Standard (DES), developed by IBM in the 1970s, for example, is widely used by financial institutions and other companies handling secure data. Recently, a group of programmers broke this code — not for criminal activity, but just to show that it could be done and to win a $10,000 prize — using an ordinary Pentium-based desktop computer.

Authentication is a security method that uses digital signatures. A digital signature serves the same purpose as a handwritten signature; that is, it places a unique mark on a document or letter that verifies the identity of the sender.

Public key technology is used in creating digital signatures. When a sender adds a redundancy to a message and applies a secret key to that redundancy, a recipient who knows the sender's public key can easily verify that the message was indeed sent by the owner of the public key, simply by verifying the redundancy.

Several digital signature mechanisms have been proposed or are already available, although the RSA cryptosystem is the only one that can currently be used for both encryption and digital signature creation. A digital signature provides for nonrepudiation of origin. *Nonrepudiation*, or the inability of the sender to deny that he or she sent the message, can be a very important feature in some circumstances because a third party can obtain the sender's public key to verify the validity of the signature.

A simpler alternative to a digital signature is a *hash* function, where the message is indexed to a digest (hashes are discussed later in this chapter in a section on digital certificates). This alternative is only appropriate in situations where both parties trust one another, however, and is therefore of limited use because it does not provide for nonrepudiation of origin.

Private key (symmetric) cryptography is based on the sender and recipient knowing the same secret key. The limitation of private key cryptography is that both sender and recipient must agree on, and exchange, a secret key. That same key is used for both encryption and decryption. If the two parties are in separate physical locations, the key must be transmitted somehow. If the information is transmitted via e-mail or telephone, or even snail mail, an opportunity exists for the key to be intercepted.

Public key (asymmetric) cryptography, on the other hand, addresses this issue of key management. This method, invented in 1976 by Whitfield Diffie and Martin Hellman, gives each individual a public key and a private key. The public key is published, and the private key is kept a secret by its holder. As a result, the sender and recipient do not need to transfer a secret key between them. Communications involve the public key only; the private key is never transmitted. The public key model is thus much more secure.

In the public key model, each user generates a key pair. It is more secure to allow each individual to generate his or her own key pair, as opposed to having an administrator generate them and distribute them as requested; the latter solution may be more convenient, but carries with it a security risk because it involves transmitting the key between two parties. The public key must be registered with a Certificate Authority (CA), which issues a certificate. The key itself is nothing more than a long jumble of alphanumeric characters.

Another advantage of a public key system is that it offers a facility for digital signatures. Private key authentication again requires that a secret be shared, and is therefore not fully secure. Kerberos, for example, is a private key authentication system that uses a central database to keep a copy of all users' private keys. If that one database were to be attacked, the entire system would be compromised. Kerberos is used to centrally manage access rights, encryption keys, and permissions.

In the public key model, no central database of private keys exists. Each user must protect his or her own private key. The only disadvantage public key methods have is that they are much slower than private methods. The public key mechanism is illustrated in Figure 5-1. In this figure, we see how public key encryption works. When Alice wants to send a private letter to Bob, she encrypts it with Bob's public key. Bob can choose to make his public key available through any number of means; including posting it on his Web site, or publishing it in a corporate directory. The encrypted letter is then mailed. When Bob receives the encrypted letter, he decrypts it using his own private key.

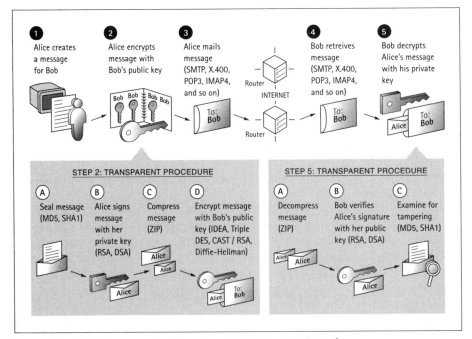

Figure 5-1: Public key encryption (courtesy of Pretty Good Software)

Ideally, both systems can be combined to reap the advantages of security and speed. For example, the public key system can be used to encrypt a private key, which is in turn used to encrypt the larger message.

Encryption Mechanisms

Several public key algorithms can be used for encryption and authentication, as follows:

◆ **RSA (Rivest/Shamir/Adelman)** is the most common public key algorithm, and you can use it for encryption and authentication. It is considered secure, provided you use a long enough key. A secure key is considered to be at least 512 bits, but ideally it should be more than 768 bits. Several commercial and freeware implementations of RSA are available.

◆ **Diffie-Hellman** is another common public key algorithm used for key exchange. Like RSA, it is considered secure if you use a long enough key. Diffie-Hellman is used in Sun Microsystems' secure Remote Procedure Call (RPC) and secure Network File System (NFS). It works by taking a commonly known constant, and raising it to the power of a key that generates a 192-bit number.

◆ **DES (Data Encryption Standard)** was originally published by the U.S. government in the 1970s. It works with a 56-bit key and is widely used. It operates quickly (nearly 1,000 times faster than RSA) and is usually implemented in hardware. These 56-bit keys, however, can be broken with enough brute force. As mentioned previously, a group of programmers with a point to make broke this key simply by sending millions of sets of keys at an encrypted message. The programmers had to find one key out of a possible 72 quadrillion possibilities.

◆ **IDEA (International Data Encryption Algorithm)**, developed in Switzerland, uses a 128-bit key and is more secure than DES.

RSA and DES

The most popular public key algorithm is RSA. RSA Data Security, Inc.'s encryption and authentication technology is used by more than 75 million users worldwide. RSA technology is embedded in hundreds of high-profile products, including Microsoft Windows, Netscape Navigator, Intuit Quicken, and Lotus Notes.

In RSA, both encryption and authentication take place without the sharing of private keys. That is, each person uses his or her own private key, and the other person's public key to encrypt and decrypt messages. The RSA scheme is based on factorization and the fact that while it is simple to generate two large prime numbers and to multiply them, it can be incredibly difficult to take the sum and find the two original primes.

Despite its power when compared with DES, RSA's performance is significantly slower. RSA specifies key ranges from 512 to 1,001 bits in length (150 to 301 decimal points). The ability to break the RSA algorithm and derive a private key is nearly impossible. RSA Inc. has entered into numerous software licensing agreements with other software vendors as a way to promote the RSA algorithm. For example, Novell uses the RSA algorithm in NetWare; and Motorola uses it to support its secure voice communications products. In addition, Lotus Development uses RSA in its Notes groupware product.

RSA is not meant as a replacement for DES, but as a supplement. It provides two functions not offered by DES: secure key exchange without having to exchange secrets, and digital signatures. RSA and DES are used in concert as follows:

♦ The message is encrypted with a random DES key

♦ The DES key is encrypted with RSA before being sent over an insecure channel

♦ The DES-encrypted message and the RSA-encrypted DES key are both sent (this is known as an RSA digital envelope)

DES is typically used to encrypt the message because it is significantly faster than RSA. Users may prefer to use only RSA without DES to send smaller messages, for the sake of convenience.

Several commercial hardware implementations of RSA are available, and they are becoming faster all the time. Currently, the fastest RSA chip has a throughput of more than 600 Kbps, enabling it to perform more than 1,000 private-key operations per second. Within a year, speeds will probably reach 1 Mbps.

DES in software is generally at least 100 times faster than RSA, and up to 10,000 times as fast in hardware, which is why DES is usually used for the message itself.

PGP

PGP (Pretty Good Privacy) is a public key system for encrypting e-mail using RSA. It encrypts the e-mail message using the IDEA cipher with a randomly generated key, then encrypts the key using the recipient's public key. The recipient then uses his or her private RSA key to decrypt the IDEA key, and then uses the IDEA key to decrypt the message. This two-step process is significantly more secure than straight-on encryption.

IDEA, developed in Switzerland, was created in the 1990s as a replacement for DES. It is a *symmetric* mechanism – that is, it uses the same key for encryption and decryption, and uses a 128-bit key. This length makes it virtually impossible to break through brute force alone.

Privacy Enhanced Mail

RSA is used in the Privacy Enhanced Mail (PEM) application, developed by Trusted Information Systems under contract from the federal government. PEM is used as a framework for protecting information communicated via e-mail, and is built on top of the Simple Mail Transfer Protocol (SMTP). While PEM is based on RSA, other encryption algorithms can also be used to generate keys.

PEM can provide authentication, message integrity, and confidentiality for e-mail messages. Message integrity is an important feature, particularly in a distributed system. PEM relies on Message Integrity Checks (MICs) such as Message Digest 4 (MD4), developed by RSA, to guarantee that messages are not tampered with en route.

PEM encrypts the contents of the e-mail message; only an individual with the RSA algorithm and the right key can decrypt the message. When sending a message using PEM, the message itself is put through four separate steps. First, the message is created internally; second, it is translated into an SMTP-compatible format. The third step is when the authentication and encryption services are added to the message contents. Fourth, an MIC is created for the message. Padding is then added to the message to give it a consistent length — because the encryption process itself requires the message to be an integral number of 8-byte amounts.

The PGP security cryptographic package, a product of Phil's Pretty Good Software, is available for DOS, UNIX, VAX/VMS and other platforms. PGP generates a public/private key pair with a key length specified by the user.

PGP enjoys a strong reputation as a secure encryption mechanism; and creator Phil Zimmerman was one of the first to incur the wrath of the federal government in regards to its policy on export of encryption software. On PGP's Web site (http://www.pgp.com), the following warning is issued: "Please remember that all cryptographic software is classified as export-controlled by the U.S. Department of Commerce. If you are a citizen of the USA or Canada, or have permanent alien resident status in the U.S., you may legally purchase and download the software."

The key recovery system, or "government back door," has been a controversial issue and a major limitation for companies wishing to implement strong encryption. The government's position has been that, in order for a company to use strong encryption, they must grant the government the right, through a key escrow system, to gain access to encrypted messages. While the government wants this right as a means of law enforcement and investigation against criminal activity, many people see it as an intrusion of privacy and a compromise of security, because a third party would be used to hold all encryption keys in escrow.

In May 1997, however, PGP received the approval of the Department of Commerce to export its PGP encryption software to the overseas offices of some of the largest companies in the United States. This makes PGP the only U.S.-based firm authorized to export strong (128-bit key) encryption to foreign subsidiaries of large American companies. The approval allows PGP to export its 128-bit encryption without the standard requirement that it contain key recovery features or another back door that allows the government to access the keys.

That's the good news. The bad news is that it applies only to Fortune 100 customers using the product. If you're AT&T, Alcoa, Bechtel, or Rockwell International, you get the goodies. The little guys, on the other hand, still can't use it overseas. However, it may be a step in the right direction.

The government places restrictions on all exports of encryption technology that uses a key length greater than 40 bits. The 40-bit encryption scheme, however, is weak and can be broken in a few hours. If a company develops a method for the government to access the key, the government will usually grant an export license for 56-bit encryption. Using 128-bit encryption, however, is 309,485,009,821,341,068,724,781,056 times more difficult to break than a message encrypted with 40-bit technology.

IBM's Common Cryptographic Architecture (CCA)

IBM's Common Cryptographic Architecture supports DES, RSA, and Commercial Data Masking Facility (CDMF) algorithms to provide consistent cryptographic services across all IBM platforms. The latter algorithm, CDMF, is an exportable, IBM-created encryption algorithm used outside North America. CDMF is intended by IBM to be a substitute for DES in environments where a fully functioning DES product cannot be exported outside of the United States due to government restrictions. While CDMF uses a 64-bit key, it provides the equivalent strength of a 40-bit DES key. CDMF is sometimes referred to as "limited DES."

The CCA architecture establishes a set of cryptographic functions, external interfaces, and key management rules. These rules provide for a consistent, end-to-end cryptographic architecture across all IBM platforms. The Common Cryptographic Architecture defines services for the following:

◆ Data integrity

◆ Data confidentiality

◆ Nonrepudiation

◆ Personal authentication

◆ Personal identification number (PIN) management

◆ Key management

IBM's strategy is to provide cryptographic products driven by market requirements that are standards-compliant and open-systems solutions. In a predominately IBM shop, this strategy can be used to encompass PCs and workstations, RS/6000s, AS/400s, and ES/9000s—in other words, everything from the desktop to the mainframe.

CCA provides a unified API (application program interface) for the following services:

◆ Cryptographic key management

◆ Data encryption

◆ Message authentication and verification

◆ Modification detection

◆ PIN management (generation and verification)

◆ Signature generation and verification

The security architecture uses PIN generation and verification to authenticate users and offers data encryption to protect sensitive data. In addition, CCA relies on the RSA public key algorithm for digital signature generation and verification.

Through CCA, IBM offers cryptography across all strategic IBM platforms. The two major components of CCA are the IBM Transaction Security System (TSS) and the IBM Integrated Cryptographic Facility (ICRF). Security is provided for the following platforms:

◆ PS/2—TSS

◆ RISC/6000—TSS

◆ AS/400—2620 and 2628 cryptographic processors (TSS)

◆ ES/9000—TSS or ICRF

The Transaction Security System includes the following products:

◆ **The IBM 4755 Cryptographic Adapter**—available for the PC (ISA-Bus and MCA-BUS), and the RISC/6000

◆ **IBM Personal Security Card ("smart card")**—implements DES or CDMF and includes both memory and communications circuits

◆ **IBM 4754 security interface unit**—offers a personal security card reader and a keypad for use as an input/output device

◆ **IBM 2620 and 2628 cryptographic processors**—AS/400 I/O processors that use the cryptographic adapter

◆ **4753 network security processor** – a channel-connected cryptographic-processing I/O unit that uses the cryptographic adapter; multiple processors can be connected to an MVS (Multiple Virtual Storage) host

The TSS product line offers a secure subsystem that supports DES and RSA public key encryption and uses a tamper-proof mechanical and electrical design with secure access controls. TSS products are supported in all major computing environments.

For those wanting to use VM/ESA (Virtual Machine/Extended System Architecture) and its guest facilities for testing or running an MVS/ESA application, VM/ESA permits guest MVS systems to use the IBM CCA family of host cryptographic products.

The TSS signature verification feature includes a pen attached to the 4754 security interface unit and a coprocessor that is attached to the 4755 cryptographic adapter. When an individual signs his or her name, this feature compares the movements of the signature verification pen with reference data stored on the personal security card.

Digital Certificates

A digital certificate (also known as a digital ID) is a password-protected and encrypted file that contains identification information about its holder. It includes a public key, which is used to verify the sender's digital signature, and a unique private key. Exchanging keys and certificates enables two parties to verify each other's identities before communicating.

The digital certificate is an important part of establishing the level of confidence necessary to guarantee the security of electronic transactions. This certificate binds a user to a digital key, which is then used to conduct secure communications or transactions. This binding takes place through a trusted third party, which also electronically signs the digital certificate, so all parties involved can have a greater level of confidence in it. A digital signature builds on the public/private key paradigm by enabling you to apply your private key to the contents of your message in a preset manner.

Digitally signing a document involves two steps; first, the message is indexed to a digest (hash). The message digest is, in essence, a reduced and encoded form of the message itself. The hash is then encrypted using the sender's private key. When the recipient receives the message, he or she decrypts the message as well as the attached hash, and the algorithm used to generate the hash. This latter algorithm is known as the session key. The recipient first recreates the hash from the decrypted message by applying the session key to it. Then the recipient decrypts the hash that was attached to the message using the public key. Assuming the two hashes are identical, the signature is genuine. If the hashes do not match, the recipient knows that the message has been tampered with after it was signed.

Even more assurance is provided by the fact that a trusted third party (a Certificate Authority) administers digital certificates, and verifies that they do indeed belong with the corresponding public keys.

One drawback of digital certificates is that they do not identify individuals, but only Internet addresses. A different person could use the same machine with evil intent, and be seen as the legitimate owner of the digital certificate. Furthermore, we are expected to rely on the Certificate Authority to perform a valid and thorough check to verify each individual's identity.

Digital certificates are defined by the International Telecommunications Union (ITU) standard X.509. Over the network, this certificate is meant to serve the same purpose as any other type of physical identity card, such as a driver's license or employee badge. A server can be configured to grant access only to individuals with particular certificates; also, clients can be configured to trust servers that have only certain certificates.

The X.509 digital certificate is actually a digital file that contains the following information:

◆ **The subject's distinguished name (DN)** – a name that uniquely identifies the certificate's owner

◆ **The issuer's distinguished name (DN)** – a name that uniquely identifies the Certificate Authority (such as VeriSign) that signed the certificate

◆ **The subject's public key** – the owner's public key

◆ **The issuer's signature** – the Certificate Authority's digital signature

◆ **The validity period** – the dates between which the certificate is valid

◆ **The serial number** – a unique number issued by the Certificate Authority for administrative purposes

Acquiring a digital ID is becoming more commonplace and easier all the time as more companies get involved in the technology. An agreement between Network Solutions, Inc., and VeriSign (a spin-off of RSA Data Security) (http://www.verisign.com) greatly simplifies the process of obtaining a digital certificate. Network Solutions is the current provider of domain names and IP addresses, including the .com, .net, .org, .edu, and .gov domains. VeriSign is one of the best-known and trusted third-party authorities that administers digital certificates. The agreement enables administrators to sign up for VeriSign digital ID certificates when they apply for a domain name from Network Solutions. Although few users are likely to sign up for the certificates at first through Network Solutions, the deal will ultimately help to increase awareness of the need for digital certificates, and perhaps even promote applications that require digital certificates.

VeriSign's deal with Network Solutions and the promotion of the Secure Electronic Transaction (SET) specification aside, users of Microsoft's Internet Explorer Web browser have an opportunity to sign up for a VeriSign digital ID for free when Explorer starts for the first time.

Using VeriSign

The purpose of a Certificate Authority such as VeriSign is to provide a trusted third party that can attest to an organization's right to use specific encryption keys by digitally signing the digital ID after verifying the identity information it contains.

When a connection is made between a client and a secure server, the client software automatically verifies the server by checking the server's digital ID. The key pair associated with the server's digital ID is used to encrypt and verify a session key, which is then sent between the client and server. The session key is used to encrypt the session. Because the session key automatically expires within 24 hours, even if it is intercepted, it cannot be used to attack future sessions.

The connection protocol used for this process is Secure Sockets Layer (SSL). The SSL transport protocol provides the following services:

◆ Mutual authentication

◆ Message privacy

◆ Message integrity

The process is shown in Figure 5-2.

The capability to send and receive secure data over the Internet is a necessary precursor to electronic commerce. Before you buy something over the Internet, you want to know that some teenage hacker sitting in a cluttered basement in the Midwest isn't going to hack into the transaction and steal your credit card number. Digital certificate technology is the industry's response to this need, and will ultimately go a long way toward promoting electronic commerce over the Internet.

Using this technology, your organization can establish a secure session with visitors to your Web site. Visitors can also verify the site's digital ID, and be assured of the company's identity. Why would a visitor want to verify a company's identity? If the Web site says "Welcome to IDG Books Worldwide," shouldn't you assume that you have indeed contacted IDG's Web site? Not necessarily. A Web spoof attack is a particularly notorious type of hack, in which an attacker replicates a company's Web site and diverts attempts to contact the legitimate site. The attacker can then conduct business or disseminate information as if he or she were the legitimate company. For more information on this type of attack, refer to Chapter 20.

You can use a server-based digital ID to secure the authenticity of your site. From the end-user perspective, the process is transparent; most Web browsers perform server authentication automatically.

Using VeriSign technology, you can implement server authentication on your Web site with a digital ID. You need a Web server that supports the Secure Sockets Layer (SSL) transport protocol, and you need a server digital ID from VeriSign. Most secure servers automatically support server authentication and session encryption using digital IDs. To enable these features, you must:

- ◆ Generate an encryption key pair for the server

- ◆ Submit a server digital ID request

- ◆ Install the digital ID

- ◆ Configure and activate security for the server

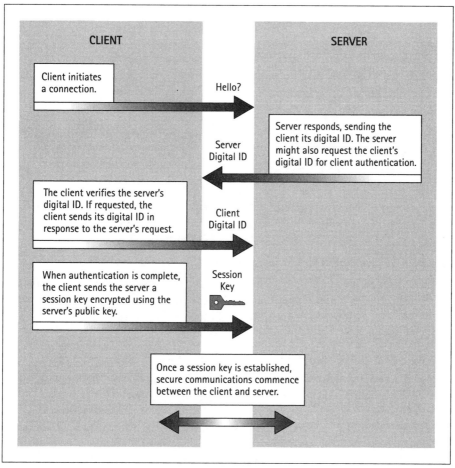

Figure 5–2: Digital certificates help verify a server's identity.

As of yet, very few applications require the presence of a digital certificate. Applications based on the SET specification, developed by the two major credit card companies, do require digital certificates, although applications based on SET are largely still in the developmental stage. Ultimately, digital certificates could form the framework of secure electronic commerce.

VeriSign Class Structure

As a Certificate Authority, VeriSign offers multiple classes of digital IDs that correspond to different levels of assurance and trust. The assurance level varies with the amount of due diligence undertaken by VeriSign (or any other Certificate Authority), as part of its investigation of the applicant's identity.

The three categories of VeriSign digital IDs are for individuals, organizations, and software publishers. Within these three categories are different classes, with Class 1 being the least secure and Class 3 the most.

1. **VeriSign digital IDs for individuals**

   Class 1 digital IDs ensure the uniqueness of a name and e-mail address in VeriSign's database; in issuing a Class 1 digital ID, VeriSign verifies the applicant's e-mail address.

   Class 2 digital IDs provide a higher lever of assurance of the applicant's identity, because VeriSign checks his or her personal identity information against a commercial credit database and performs other validation procedures.

   Class 3 digital IDs from VeriSign require the applicant to personally present appropriate identification documents to a notary public or a VeriSign-approved local registration authority.

2. **VeriSign digital IDs for organizations**

   VeriSign issues Class 3 IDs to businesses. In doing so, VeriSign ensures the applicant's identity and viability with inquiries to databases maintained by Dun & Bradstreet, InterNIC, and other commercial authorities, combined with additional validation procedures.

3. **VeriSign digital IDs for software publishers**

   VeriSign software publisher digital IDs provide Class 2 authentication for individuals and Class 3 authentication for organizations.

It is commonly thought that digital signatures are used to confirm identities of individuals over the Internet. In reality, they do not identify individuals, they identify Internet addresses. In addition, for the consumer class of digital IDs just described, the amount of due diligence put forth by the Certificate Authority may not be seen as sufficient for some purposes, particularly with Class 1 certificates. Class 1 does not require an identity check of any kind.

A version of VeriSign's technology, known as the *Universal ID Card*, recently became available for controlled Web site access and secure messaging. In April 1997, VeriSign rolled out the Universal ID Card, which is basically an enhanced version of its digital ID technology. The IDs support universal Web site login and one-step registration. Digital IDs may ultimately be used to promote electronic commerce by establishing a trusted method of authenticating the identity of each party involved in the transaction.

VeriSign's digital IDs support the following features:

◆ **NetSure protection.** This service offers protection for Class 1 and Class 2 digital ID holders. Class 1 offers coverage up to $1,000 and Class 2 up to $25,000 against economic loss due to theft, impersonation, corruption, or loss of use of a digital ID.

◆ **Secure e-mail.** Digital IDs supporting RSA Data Security's S/MIME (Secure MIME) protocol include encryption and decryption, authentication, and digital enveloping. S/MIME is an open specification for secure electronic messaging. It was created to prevent the interception and forgery of e-mail. S/MIME is integrated into several e-mail and messaging products.

◆ **Universal Web site login.** VeriSign's digital ID uses two-way cryptographic authentication, permitting a Web site to institute a one-step registration process.

Internet Content Certification

Java and ActiveX have advanced far beyond those early dancing logos that appeared in Web pages. These little applets have matured and now can do such useful things as place a stock ticker on your PC, entertain you with games, and calculate your mortgage. Some say that these little components will form the basis for software development in the future. In such a scenario, if you want a word processor, you could make a list of the features you want and download the specific applets from the Internet.

But we also have rogue applets that may be less benevolent, and before this type of development will be widely accepted, the security problems must be overcome. Internet content certification is a way to address security in downloadable applets. Unfortunately, no single standard exists yet that can certify the validity and safety of these applets. Three proposals, however, do address this issue. The three technologies proposed for Internet content certification are:

◆ Microsoft's Authenticode

◆ Netscape Communications' Object Signing

◆ Sun Microsystems' JavaSecurity

The problem with having three proposals is that unless two drop out of the running, developers will have to write three applets – one to fit each proposed standard – instead of one.

These certification APIs guarantee that a particular applet was indeed generated by who you think sent it and that it has been transmitted without modification. Unfortunately, this does not also guarantee that the code is benevolent. It's a good bet that an ActiveX control sent by Microsoft or a Java applet sent by Sun Microsystems is not going to wipe out your hard drive. If an organization has your trust, these APIs will give you reasonable assurance that the applet or control is safe to download. However, if you come across the Web site of *Peter Puke & the Vomits*, unless you know Peter personally, it's probably best not to welcome Pete's Java applet into your computer.

Microsoft Authenticode

Microsoft's Authenticode technology, a feature of the Microsoft Internet Explorer 3.0 Web browser, offers both of the services described in the preceding section. It verifies that the code has not been altered and identifies the publisher of the software through a digital certificate, as shown in Figure 5-3.

Figure 5-3: This digital certificate authenticates the publisher of the executable to be downloaded.

If the software has been tampered with, Internet Explorer will not run the code, provided you have the default safety level set on High. To set this safety level, follow these steps:

1. Open the Internet Explorer View menu and click Options.

2. Click the Security tab.

3. Click Safety Level and then select High.

Explorer will also not download any code that has been unsigned. The certificate itself is issued by VeriSign, a Certificate Authority for digital certificates. Authenticode also lets users deactivate any downloading of active code. Some security managers operating a highly sensitive operation may want to institute a policy to this effect, mandating that no Java applets or ActiveX controls of any type may be downloaded.

Microsoft makes four specific recommendations in regard to downloading software from the Internet:

◆ Keep the safety level on High to make sure that the browser downloads only signed code to the computer.

◆ Before downloading software, make sure that the software publisher is trustworthy. Click on the software publisher hyperlink to go to a Web page with more information about that publisher.

◆ If you have any doubt about downloading active content, turn off the option to allow downloading of active content. From the Internet Explorer View menu, click Options, click the Security tab, and clear the first checkbox. Afterwards, Explorer will not download any active code, whether it is signed or unsigned.

◆ You can also set Explorer to control what types of code run automatically, such as ActiveX controls, Java applets, or plug-ins. You can regulate the type of program from the Internet Explorer View menu by clicking Options, selecting the Security tab, and checking the appropriate boxes in the Active Content section.

The Netscape Object Signing Protocol

The Netscape Object Signing protocol offers the same capabilities as Microsoft's Authenticode, along with support for open standards and cross-platform flexibility. Similar to Authenticode, it offers a function where the user sees a menu that identifies the signed object and its capabilities. The cross-platform technology supports objects on Windows, Macintosh, and UNIX systems, and users can download signed objects on any computer capable of running Netscape Communicator.

Object Signing offers a number of basic features:

♦ **Identification.** Netscape Communicator identifies all signed objects as they are downloaded. The user sees a dialog box that shows who signed the object and what the object can do. The user can then decide whether to allow the object to access the system.

♦ **Capabilities-based Java.** A Java applet written with capabilities can request permission to operate outside of the *sandbox*, or the restricted area on the client system in which a Java applet is normally allowed to operate. With capabilities, the Java applet can request access to the end user's system resources; for example, it can ask permission to write to disk, read from disk, or establish a remote connection. All three of these options represent a potential security breach, and the user has the capability to grant or deny each such request.

♦ **Tamper detection.** A recipient of a signed object can tell whether the object has been altered after signing.

♦ **Capability to sign any object.** Developers can sign any type of object, because it envelopes the signature with the object. Because Object Signing envelopes signatures with objects, the protocol can work with any object format. In other schemes, where the signature is embedded within the object, the signature must be customized for each file format.

♦ **Open standards support.** Object Signing supports the X.509 certificate standard.

♦ **Cross-platform flexibility.** Developers can sign objects on Windows, Macintosh, and UNIX systems. Users can download a signed object on any computer capable of supporting Netscape Communicator.

Netscape also contributed to the development of the Secure Sockets Layer (SSL) transport protocol, which is likely to become an IETF (Internet Engineering Task Force) standard. SSL is a protocol that provides data security between application protocols such as HTTP and FTP and the transmission protocol TCP/IP. SSL includes facilities for data encryption, server authentication, message integrity, and client authentication for a TCP/IP connection. SSL is open and nonproprietary. For more information about SSL, refer to Chapter 16.

Sun Microsystems' Java Security

Sun Microsystems' Java Security API can incorporate both low-level and high-level security into a Java applet. It provides developers with a framework for including security functions in their Java applets and applications. The framework includes cryptography with digital signatures, encryption, and authentication. The Security API is part of the core library, which is the set of APIs present on all Java platforms. The Java Security API, contained in the Java Development Kit (JDK), includes APIs for digital signatures and message digests and interfaces for key management and access control. A future release will also include support for X.509 v3 certificates.

The Java Cryptography Architecture (JCA) establishes a framework for developing cryptographic functions on the Java platform. Besides the JDK 1.1 Java Security API, JCA also encompasses a separate set of conventions. It also introduces a provider-based architecture that enables multiple, interoperable cryptography implementations.

The Java Cryptography Extension (JCE) extends the JCA API with encryption and key exchange facilities. JCE and JCA together offer a complete, platform-independent cryptography API. JCA introduces the concept of a Cryptography Package Provider, which can provide a subset of the Java Security API's cryptographic functions. For example, a Cryptography Package Provider might supply an implementation of the Digital Signature Algorithm or RSA. JDK 1.1 includes a default provider named SUN, which includes an implementation of the Digital Signature Algorithm, and an implementation of the message digest algorithms known as MD5 and SHA-1.

Security is actually an integral part of Java's design. Sun describes the Java security model as a *sandbox*, mentioned earlier. The sandbox is made up of several cooperating system components. These components include security managers that execute as part of the application and other security measures that are part of the Java Virtual Machine or the Java language itself. Generally, the sandbox confines an applet to a virtual "sandbox" after downloading — within a specified area, the applet may do whatever it was meant to do, but it cannot go outside of the sandbox. The result of the sandbox metaphor is that an untrusted applet can execute in a restricted environment to minimize possible damage to the rest of the system. The sandbox concept guarantees that a malicious or untrustworthy applet cannot access system resources.

Another part of the Java security model is the Java Protected Domain, which extends the sandbox into the file system. A Java Protected Domain promotes the use of permissions by the user.

Digital Postmarks

The U.S. Postal Service has jumped into the network security arena by offering an *electronic postmark* that can be used to carry sensitive e-mail across the Internet. The postmark time-stamps e-mail, verifies senders, and guarantees that e-mail arrives at its destination unaltered.

The process starts out when a user submits a message electronically to a Postal Service computer, either over the Internet or a private network. The message is then stamped by the post office with the time and date, hashed, and signed with a private key. The encrypted message is then given a unique tracking number. Recipients are then able to verify that the message has not been tampered with by using the USPS Mail Reader software.

The Post Office's Electronic Postmarking Service does not use any new technology, but it does offer a major convenience and a degree of legal protection. Tampering with the U.S. mail is a federal crime. With the Electronic Postmarking Service, this extends the law beyond mail in paper envelopes to mail sent by the Electronic Postmarking Service. Users of the service send their e-mail to the post office server via the Internet. The messages are then encrypted, digitally signed, and sent to the recipient. Recipients can then view the messages using specialized client software. The service, besides providing authentication, also provides an audit trail and backup copies of messages.

To take advantage of the service, a user needs to have a public/private key pair. The sender would use the recipient's public key to code the message; the recipient would then use his or her private key to decode it. The U.S. Postal Service further plans to issue private and public keys to both individuals and companies, and may also offer e-mail archiving services. The cost of the service will be minimal: 22 cents for an electronic postmark on a file up to 50 kilobytes.

Legal Aspects

Part of the reason it has been difficult to get good encryption is because of federal regulation. Although laws permit domestic sales of the more rigorous encryption implementations, export is forbidden because the military considers it to be a *munition* (material used for wartime activities). This has been a difficult blow for the domestic software industry in terms of competing globally, because domestic firms must compete against foreign products that do offer strong encryption.

The meat of the issue is that the federal government is afraid terrorists will use strong encryption products for the wrong reasons. Although a terrorist could certainly use encryption for illegal activity, encryption is also essential for the advancement of electronic commerce.

Although domestic companies are prohibited from exporting strong encryption products, hundreds of such programs are available on the Internet from foreign sources. Obviously, this puts the domestic software industry at a major disadvantage. A Department of Commerce study demonstrated the availability of foreign encryption programs, and industry studies reveal that 497 foreign programs were available from 28 countries, 193 of which use DES encryption.

Microsoft counsel Ira Rubinstein gave the U.S. Congress some concrete examples of how foreign companies are enjoying success at the expense of domestic firms that are crippled by the current regulations. Rubinstein questioned whether "the genie is out of the bottle" in his address to Congress. He noted that Stronghold, a U.K.-based company, markets a secure version of the popular Apache Server Internet server product that includes a protocol for secure communications at 128 bits. Further, he notes that several foreign software companies have responded to demand for strong encryption by developing add-on products that permit anyone with a Web browser to download a program off the Internet, and upgrade their domestic 40-bit encryption products to 128 bits.

The restriction goes beyond regulation of pure encryption products. For example, Microsoft and other large companies do not include strong encryption products in their software as a result of the regulation. The domestic software industry earns nearly a half of its revenues through exports, and customers are demanding more encryption features. As a result, most commercially-available domestic software and hardware is made to offer the same encryption capabilities both for domestic and foreign markets. The Business Software Alliance reports that the "industry has demonstrated clearly that the easy export of at least 56-bit DES encryption is critical to the future of the Global Information Infrastructure and to the competitiveness of the U.S. software and hardware industries."

In October 1996, the federal government announced a new encryption policy that makes it easier to export 56-bit encryption products. In November 1996, commercial encryption items were transferred from the U.S. Munitions List to the Commerce Control List. However, this shift did not result in simplified export, because the Clinton Administration continued to apply many of the same stringent controls that had been applied to munitions.

Some of the high points of the 1996 regulations include the following:

♦ The regulations permit the export of unlimited key length, key escrow, or key recovery products, but only if they provide the key in advance to a government-approved third party.

♦ These products may be interoperable with other encryption products, but only if data transmitted is still accessible by the government-approved third party.

♦ Communications, including telephone and Internet, are covered in addition to stored data.

♦ The government may approve the export of other recoverable encryption products that allow the government to access unencrypted data and communications (with court authorization), without the knowledge of the user.

♦ Government-approved products can be exported after a one-time review by the Department of Commerce.

♦ Fifty-six-bit nonkey recovery encryption products may be exported up to the end of 1998, but vendors must also produce a government-approved key recovery product, and must submit a business and marketing plan to the government.

♦ Products may be exported if a similar product with comparable security is available from a foreign vendor.

Security and Freedom Through Encryption (SAFE) Act

The SAFE Act, approved in May 1997 by a subcommittee of the U.S. House of Representatives Judiciary Committee, guarantees the right of all citizens and U.S. residents to use or sell any encryption technology. The bill's purpose, according to the text, is "To amend title 18, United States Code, to affirm the rights of Americans to use and sell encryption, and to relax export controls on encryption."

Specifically, the bill makes it legal for any person to use encryption, regardless of encryption algorithm, key length, or implementation technique; makes it legal for any person to sell encryption software, regardless of encryption algorithm, key length, or implementation technique; and prohibits the state and federal governments from requiring anyone to surrender control of an encryption key.

Of course, the bill specifies legal usage, and makes exceptions for using encryption for illegal activities: "Any person who willfully uses encryption in furtherance of the commission of a criminal offense" may be subject to prosecution.

In other words, it's okay to use encryption, just don't use it to send military secrets to whatever foreign country is currently in disfavor. Very few of us could complain about that—for the majority of us, who want to use encryption for safety, security, and privacy reasons, the SAFE bill represents a major breakthrough and a significant turnaround on the part of the federal government. However, the clause that criminalizes use of encryption when used to carry out an unlawful act has been controversial. It could, for example, potentially escalate a minor crime to felony status if the person committing the minor crime used encryption in carrying it out.

Ira Rubinstein, senior corporate attorney for Microsoft, testified before the Courts and Intellectual Property Subcommittee of the Committee on the Judiciary, U.S. House of Representatives, in March of 1997 in support of the SAFE bill. Rubinstein's testimony discussed why strong encryption is absolutely essential:

> Strong encryption is essential to protect the confidentiality and privacy of sensitive personal and confidential business electronic information, as well as to ensure its authenticity and integrity. Without encryption, businesses and individuals will not entrust their valuable proprietary information, creative content, and sensitive personal information to electronic networks and risk unauthorized disclosure, theft or alteration of their information or transactions. The promise and potential of the Global Information Infrastructure simply will not materialize. Companies will hesitate to design new products or work collaboratively from remote locations. A routine visit to the doctor becomes an invasive procedure unless your records can be kept private. Electronic banking and commerce will not happen "on-line" without strong encryption.

Easy exportability of 56-bit encryption products is still unavailable, for the most part, yet the current world benchmark is at a minimum DES with 56-bit keys. This severely limits the extent to which domestic firms offering security-enabled products can participate in the global market. Triple-DES, which uses a 112-bit key, and RC4, which uses a 128-bit key, is becoming more common. Simply put, 40-bit encryption is inadequate and vulnerable to attack.

According to the Business Software Alliance, a trade group that advocates intellectual property protection for legitimate business software, "a plain reading of the new regulations makes clear that the Administration desires to allow the export of only those encryption items that provide the means in advance for a government-approved third party to decrypt a user's information if the government so demands pursuant to court authorization."

BSA president Robert Holleyman agrees that allowing U.S. companies to export 56-bit encryption products is a step in the right direction, "yet further liberalization will be needed as customers will no doubt demand stronger encryption. While the Administration's announcement is welcomed, a number of issues remain unresolved."

Summary

In this chapter, you learned about the following:

- ◆ The encryption mechanisms contained in most major operating systems are only marginally effective at thwarting a determined attacker, largely because federal regulation prohibits the export of effective encryption engines. To sell their products to the global market, operating systems vendors must include weaker types of encryption.

- ◆ IBM's Common Cryptographic Architecture establishes a common framework for cryptography across all IBM platforms.

- ◆ That little dancing cartoon on your screen could be hiding a bomb! Three different security methods exist to ensure that Java applets and ActiveX controls are safe to download.

- ◆ RSA and DES can work together to make a stronger and more secure mechanism for transmitting messages. Although the message itself is encrypted using the faster DES mechanism, the DES key is encrypted using the stronger RSA algorithm. Together, the DES-encrypted message and the RSA-encrypted DES key make up the RSA envelope.

- ◆ PGP (Pretty Good Privacy) is a secure encryption product that uses RSA technology. The strongest version of it, which is illegal to export (unless you're an approved Fortune 100 company), uses 128-bit encryption.

◆ Current laws prohibit the export of strong encryption software. The result of these laws is that it is impractical for domestic software companies to include strong encryption in their products, which puts them at a disadvantage relative to foreign competitors.

Part II

Software

Chapter 6

Security Features of Network Operating Systems

IN THIS CHAPTER

- ◆ Security features of major network operating systems

- ◆ Government research on new operating system security mechanisms

IN MANY INSTANCES, SECURITY has not kept pace with the needs of interconnected, heterogeneous systems and distributed processing. Problems such as multiple logons, multiple copies of data, and overlapping administrative tasks have, in the past, been dealt with manually. Modern operating systems address many of these security needs automatically.

Network operating systems contain native security functions that you can enhance or supplement with third-party programs. However, these features are only effective when used to enforce an overall security policy. The policy document, discussed in Part I of this book, is the first and most important step of implementing network security. Everything else is just tools used in furtherance of enforcing the policy.

Security expert and SATAN creator Dan Farmer says that "a security policy is by far the most important piece of the puzzle, more than everything else put together. Actual adherence to the policy is number two."

The Devil's in the Details — the SATAN Software

Dan Farmer created SATAN (Security Administrator Tool for Analyzing Networks) to give network administrators an easy-to-use tool for finding their network's weak spots. It can find security vulnerabilities in every corner; and offers details on how to plug up the holes. SATAN is also sometimes used by attackers attempting to break into a network. For more information on SATAN, refer to Chapter 8.

Some precautions are fairly universal throughout network operating systems. For example, network operating systems usually have a built-in "Guest" account that casual or temporary users can use. However, this account should be configured so that the guest user cannot write to, or delete files or directories, outside of very specific ones established for the sole use of the guest. In this chapter, we look at some of the differences of the major network operating systems in terms of security features and vulnerabilities.

NetWare

NetWare 4.11 has been combined with other networking products to create IntranetWare, Novell's newest offering that combines the network operating system with other software to create a full-service intranet platform. IntranetWare brings the enterprise all the services necessary to operate an intranet: file, print, directory, security, messaging, Web publishing, wide-area connectivity, and management. IntranetWare includes Web, FTP, and Internet access services that all build on NetWare 4.*x*'s file, print, security, management, and directory services. It also includes GroupWise for messaging, and additional management tools. NetWare 4.11 forms the core of IntranetWare.

Before we look at NetWare security, we must first understand Novell Directory Services (NDS). NDS replaces the Novell Bindery, which was the file structure used in NetWare 3.*x*. NDS adds a hierarchical structure to NetWare 4.*x* files, organizing units, users, groups, and network resources into a *directory tree*. This tree is created by organizing these objects into a multilevel structure. This organization is used to define and restrict access.

NDS is based on the X.500 specification, which establishes a standard method for organizing information so it can be accessed globally and transparently. The directory tree follows a specific set of rules, known as the *directory schema*, which defines how the directory tree is built. The schema defines the following:

- ◆ **Attribute information.** Describes what additional information an object can have associated with it.

- ◆ **Inheritance.** Describes which objects will inherit the rights and properties of other objects.

- ◆ **Naming.** Describes the structure of the directory tree.

- ◆ **Subordination.** Describes the location of objects in the directory tree.

Directory objects all include information categories (properties), along with data included in those properties. This information is stored in the directory database. This database contains three types of objects: the [Root] object, container objects, and leaf objects. Following the tree allegory, the [Root] object exists at the top of the tree. The container objects make up the tree's branches, and the leaves are represented by the leaf objects.

In a mixed environment, NetWare users can enable access to subnets on other network operating systems through Novell's client modules for Windows 95 and NT, Macintosh, and OS/2. IntranetWare's close ties to Windows NT are especially useful in a mixed environment, given the trend toward growing larger, multivendor WANs.

Because NDS is global and standards-based, it can keep information about every resource on the network. NDS brings the entire enterprise network together into a single, consolidated system. It provides a global view of all network resources, which makes a large network significantly easier to manage, even when it is running multiple subnets with different operating systems. Users enjoy a single point of login to all network resources. The IntranetWare client integrates network login with the Windows NT workstation login to further simplify the login process. Users log in through the NetWare 4 GUI login script, enabling them to map network drives, set environment variables, and execute DOS and Windows programs or menuing systems.

The IntranetWare client uses native Windows NT user interfaces for network resource access. NT users are able to access NetWare file and print services through native NT interfaces, and view NetWare resources either through the NDS view, or by logging in as a Bindery user for compatibility with earlier NetWare releases that do not use NDS.

The client extends the NT network interface to enable users to access advanced IntranetWare networking features that are not exposed natively in Windows NT. For example, the client provides extensions to the NT Network Neighborhood that enable users to navigate the NDS-based NetWare network easily. From their NT workstations, users can access NDS and do the following:

- List NDS servers and trees

- Browse NDS trees

- Log in to and out of NDS services and trees

- Control NDS passwords

Windows NT users are able to select resources from the NDS tree through the Explorer or Network Neighborhood. Furthermore, when a user logs into an NT workstation, the IntranetWare client extends the NT login to execute the NetWare 4 RSA public/private key login process. As a result, NT users need only log in once to access both local workstation and network resources, including NetWare resources.

NetWare Security Categories

NetWare offers six categories of security to regulate access to the network. These categories are as follows:

- Login security

- Trustees

- Rights

- Inheritance

- Effective rights

- Attributes

Let's take a look at these security categories individually.

LOGIN SECURITY

NetWare's login security requires a user to enter a valid username and password, and thus controls which users can access the network. The network supervisor is responsible for login security and must create a user object in NDS. (A user object is a leaf object in NDS that represents an individual with network access.)

After creating the user object, the supervisor can then assign it certain object properties that contain information about the user. Among other things, the object properties determine the specific directories and files a user can access, group membership, home directories, account restrictions, time restrictions, network address restrictions, maximum disk space available to the user, and number of workstations that a user can be logged in from at any given time.

TRUSTEES

A *trustee* is a user or group of users who have specific access rights to work with a particular directory, file, or object. The supervisor grants access through a trustee assignment, which can be granted by any object with the RIGHTS, NETADMIN, or NetWare Administrator utility. Every directory, file, and object has a trustee list that specifies who has access rights to it. The trustee list is actually stored in the access control list (ACL), which lists access privileges and other properties of a related object. If several users will have access to a particular directory, file, or object, the supervisor can save a few steps by creating a group object, which contains a group of users, and then grant access rights for the entire group instead of individually. The [Public] trustee can be used to grant open access to everyone. [Public] should be used sparingly and with caution.

You must use caution when assigning rights because of the problem of *inheritance*. Inheritance causes rights to flow down the tree structure. For example, suppose you have a human resources directory. A specific trustee assignment that grants read access to that directory automatically grants the same rights to all of its subdirectories. However, some subdirectories probably exist that you want kept private. If you want to regulate access to subdirectories, you must redefine rights for each one or set the inherited rights filter (IRF) to revoke specific rights. The inherited rights filter is a list of rights that can be created for a file, directory, or object. This list controls which rights a trustee can inherit from a parent directory.

RIGHTS

Rights set out what level of access a given trustee has to a directory, file, or object. This is where the policy document becomes useful – by following this document, the administrator can see where rights should be specifically allowed or disallowed. Careful attention must be paid to every directory, subdirectory, and file, making sure that nothing is forgotten. Inheritance, as discussed previously, makes it even trickier, because rights may be attributed to a subdirectory without the administrator actively doing so. The four different kinds of rights are as follows:

- ◆ **Directory rights** control what a trustee can do with a directory. The rights that a trustee can have include the following:

  - *Supervisor.* Grants all rights to the directory, its files, and subdirectories.

  - *Read.* Grants the right to open files and read their contents.

  - *Write.* Grants the right to change the contents of a file.

  - *Create.* Grants the right to create new files or subdirectories.

  - *Erase.* Grants the right to delete a directory, its files, or subdirectories.

  - *Modify.* Grants the right to change the name or attributes of a directory, its files, or subdirectory.

  - *File Scan.* Grants the right to use the DIR or NDIR command to view the directory and its files.

  - *Access Control.* Grants the right to change trustee assignments and inherited rights filters.

- ◆ **File rights** control what a trustee can do with a file. Rights include the following:

  - *Supervisor.* Grants all rights to the file.

  - *Read.* Grants the right to read the file.

  - *Create.* Grants the right to retrieve a file after it has been deleted.

  - *Write.* Grants the right to modify the contents of an existing file.

  - *Erase.* Grants the right to delete a file.

  - *Modify.* Grants the right to change a file's name and attributes, but not its contents.

  - *File Scan.* Grants the right to see the file with the DIR or NDIR command.

  - *Access Control.* Grants the right to change a file's trustee assignments and inherited rights filter.

♦ **Object rights** control what a trustee can do with an object. These rights include the following:

- *Supervisor.* Grants all access privileges.

- *Browse.* Grants the right to see an object in the directory tree.

- *Create.* Grants the right to create a new object below a given object in the directory tree. This right is available only for container objects.

- *Delete.* Grants the right to delete an object from the directory tree.

- *Rename.* Grants the right to change an object's name.

♦ **Property rights** control a trustee's access to information stored in an object. These rights include the following:

- *Supervisor.* Grants all rights to the property.

- *Compare.* Grants the right to compare any value to one of the property's values.

- *Read.* Grants the right to read the values of a given property.

- *Write.* Grants the right to add, change, or remove the values of a given property.

- *Add or Delete Self.* Grants a trustee the right to add or remove itself as a value of a given property.

INHERITANCE

Inheritance simplifies the task of creating the same trustee assignment for all users, directories, files, and objects. With inheritance, the rights granted via trustee assignment apply to everything below the point of the assignment. For example, a *write* trustee assignment made to the Operations directory flows down to all of the Operations subdirectories.

Although inheritance presents the supervisor with a great convenience, it must also be used with caution to make sure that rights are allocated properly. For example, a subdirectory with sensitive information may need to have additional restrictions. These restrictions can be achieved through the inherited rights filter, which can block inherited rights. The IRF (also called the *inheritance mask*) takes the place of the trustee name in the ACL attribute, and it can be applied to [Entry Rights], [All Attribute Rights], or other specific attribute rights.

In addition, each partition root entry has an inherited ACL attribute, which lists the effective rights that trustees inherit. Unless an IRF is being used, these effective rights are given to any entry within the partition.

EFFECTIVE RIGHTS

Whenever a user takes any action, NetWare calculates the user's *effective rights* to a given directory, file, or object. Effective rights are the rights that the user actually has to the directory, file, or object. A user's effective rights consist of a combination of an object's trustee assignments to the directory or file, inherited rights, trustee assignments of group objects, or trustee assignments of objects contained in a user object's security equivalences list.

ATTRIBUTES

Attributes, or *flags*, describe the characteristics of a particular directory or file. These attributes define what actions are allowed. Attributes apply to files or directories, but not to objects. An attribute cannot be overridden, but it can be changed by a user who has the Modify right.

Attributes are primarily concerned with what can or cannot be done to a directory or file, and are therefore very important to the NetWare security environment.

Table 6-1 shows the IntranetWare attributes available.

TABLE 6-1 IntranetWare Attributes

Attribute	Directory	File	Description
Archive Needed (A)		✔	Indicates that the file has been changed since the previous backup
Can't Compress (Cc)		✔	Indicates that the file cannot be compressed
Compressed (Co)		✔	Indicates that the file is compressed
Copy Inhibit (Ci)		✔	Prevents users from copying the file
Delete Inhibit (Di)	✔	✔	Prevents users from erasing the file
Don't Compress (Dc)	✔	✔	Prevents users from compressing the file
Don't Migrate (Dm)	✔	✔	Prevents the file from being migrated to secondary storage
Don't Suballocate (Ds)		✔	
Execute Only (X)		✔	Prevents users from copying a file
Hidden (H)	✔	✔	Hides a directory from the DOS or OS/2 DIR command

continued

TABLE 6-1 IntranetWare Attributes *(continued)*

Attribute	Directory	File	Description
Immediate Compress (Ic)	✔	✔	Causes all files in a directory to be compressed as soon as the operating system is able to do so
Indexed (I)		✔	Indicates that a file has exceeded a set size, and has been indexed for faster access
Migrate (M)		✔	Indicates that the file has been migrated
Normal (N)	✔	✔	No attributes present
Purge (P)	✔	✔	Causes the directory and its files to be purged when deleted
Read Only (Ro)		✔	Prevents users from writing to the file
Read Write (Rw)		✔	
Rename Inhibit (Ri)	✔	✔	Prevents users from renaming the directory
Shareable (Sh)		✔	Permits a read-only file to be accessed by multiple users simultaneously
System (Sy)	✔	✔	Marks directories used by the operating system only; a system directory cannot be deleted or copied, and is hidden from the DOS and OS/2 DIR command
Transactional (T)		✔	Indicates that the file is protected by the Transaction Tracking System (a NetWare feature that protects data in the event of hardware failure)

Authorization

NDS relies on *access control* to authorize individual users to perform directory operations. Access control places restrictions on different operations, including creating objects, reading or modifying attributes, or comparing attribute values. An entry that has had restrictions placed on it is called a *protected entry*; an entry granted access privileges to that protected entry is called the *trustee* of those privileges.

Access control protects only the entry information stored in the directory. An application can use the directory to store access control data specific to that application, although the directory does not store this information as attributes. Further, the directory does not manage or apply the data on the application's behalf. The directory client application is unable to access the directory without using NDS access control.

NDS uses special entry names that can be used on Access attributes in place of Distinguished Names and Relative Distinguished Names. The following are special entry names used:

DS_ROOT_NAME

DS_PUBLIC_NAME

DS_MASK_NAME

DS_CREATOR_NAME

DS_SELF_NAME

By default, an entry has access privileges to the following:

◆ Every entry in its Distinguished Name, unless one of these objects has an inherited rights filter.

◆ Every special entry name that applies ([Public], [Root], [Creator], [Self], and [Nobody]).

◆ Every entry in its Security Equals attribute, if its object class definition has that attribute.

Access control is determined primarily through the access control list (ACL). The ACL is an attribute that determines what a trustee can do and not do.

The ACL attribute contains these values:

◆ **Protected Attribute ID.** This field contains a reference to the attribute that the Privilege Set field applies to. It could also contain an identifier such as [Entry Rights] or [All Attributes Rights]. If this field contains [Entry Rights], the access privileges apply to the entry that holds this ACL.

◆ **Trustee ID.** This field contains an Entry ID for a specific entry in the directory. However, it could also contain a special entry reference such as [Inherited Rights Filter], [Public], [Root], [Creator], or [Self]. An ACL with [Inherited Rights Filter] as the trustee masks or filters privileges granted to an entry.

◆ **Class ID.** This field can contain a specific object class or [Anything], which includes all object classes.

- ◆ **Privilege Set.** This field lists the privileges that have been granted to the subject. If the subject name is [Inherited Rights Filter], the Privilege Set field lists the rights that can be granted on that entry, although they might not have been granted.

- ◆ **Controls.** Currently the only possible value is Inheritable. If this bit is set, the privilege set being granted is inherited at subordinate objects.

RCONSOLE Vulnerability

An unusual FAQ, known as the "Unofficial Novell Inc. NetWare Hack FAQ," compiled by an anonymous computer security professional known only as Simple Nomad, presents extensive instructions on how to infiltrate a NetWare 3.x or 4.x LAN. As with all security tools and documents, this information can be used for both good and evil. The document lists several common and not-so-common methods of attack and includes countermeasures for many of them.

NetWare's Remote CONSOLE (RCONSOLE) utility gives the supervisor the ability to manage the server from a remote workstation. However, an attacker can misuse this utility to gain access to a NetWare 3.x network. The vulnerability has been closed up in version 4.1, but many sites are still running 3.x servers.

RCONSOLE access is protected only by a single password and simple encryption with RCON.EXE, a program that can be downloaded from the Internet. This program lets an attacker use a sniffer or some type of monitoring device to eavesdrop on the RCONSOLE initialization conversation and break the encryption to get the RCONSOLE password. Once the attacker has this password, he or she can then gain *Supervisor* access and attack the entire file system.

The whole process is done by gaining physical access to the network and capturing packets, which is often appallingly simple. Nomad writes that one simple method to gaining access is dialing into the LAN using pcAnywhere, installing a DOS-based sniffer, and proceeding to capture packets.

Nomad further outlines the attacker's strategy, which involves convincing the Sys Admin to launch RCONSOLE. Nomad outlines the following ploy: The attacker poses as a new employee, and calls the Sys Admin. The attacker then reports to the Sys Admin that when he attempts to log in, he gets the message "The SUPERVISOR has disabled the login function." The Sys Admin then probably launches RCONSOLE to fix the problem, which then gives the attacker his desired packet. The Sys Admin, after launching RCONSOLE, tells the attacker that everything looks okay. The attacker then says that his computer is locked up, which leads the Sys Admin to believe that the problem is in the workstation. The Sys Admin then tells the caller to reboot, and advises him that it should come up okay afterwards. The Sys Admin hangs up, thinking that he just solved an employee's problem. In fact, he has given an attacker a packet.

This type of trickery, or "social engineering," can be prevented only on a policy level, because the root of the ploy is deceit, and not outright breaking and entering.

Of course, a good security policy would have precluded the system administrator from dealing with the caller without first receiving some sort of positive identification. However, the best way to circumvent this type of RCONSOLE attack is to upgrade to NetWare 4.*x*. Many other methods of attack also work best in NetWare 3.*x*; Novell has closed many of these vulnerabilities in version 4.1. However, be sure that your upgrade is a thorough one – even if one or two servers are still running NetWare 3.*x*, the possibility of attack still persists.

Other NetWare Vulnerabilities

As with many other operating systems, NetWare ships with several default accounts, including Supervisor and Guest. In NetWare 4.*x*, it also has Admin and User_Template. In the default state, these accounts have no passwords. A password should be assigned immediately upon installation.

Another common security error is to create special purpose accounts with easy-to-guess names. Examples include a Print account for attaching to a second server for printing, or POST (power-on self-test) for attaching to a second server for e-mail. An attacker may attempt to assign Guest or User_Template a password to gain entrance. To deter this attack, the administrator should regularly check these accounts for tampering, or delete them entirely.

You may have heard rumors about a "secret" method of gaining Supervisor access that Novell used to teach in its CNE classes. A secret method does exist, though Novell does not actually teach it. The method involves using a DOS-based sector editor to edit the entry in the FAT (File Allocation Table) and reset the bindery to the default upon server reboot. The result of this little maneuver is that the attacker then has a Supervisor and Guest account with no password.

In its manual, Novell claims that you have no way to recover if the Supervisor password is lost or the password system is damaged. You must reinstall the server from the most recent backup. Losing the Supervisor password is indeed a major problem. However, you can find an appallingly simple fix to this problem on the Unofficial NetWare Hack FAQ. The fact that such a fix exists, however, raises another problem – an inherent security leak.

The simple fix works with NetWare 2.*x*, 3.*x*, and 4.*x*. This method involves tricking NetWare into believing that the server has just been installed and that no security system has yet been established. The attacker simply deletes the files that contain the security system:

◆ NetWare 2.*x* stores security data in the NET$BIND.SYS and NET$BVAL.SYS files.

◆ NetWare 3.*x* stores security data in the NET$OBJ.SYS, NET$VAL.SYS, and NET$PROP.SYS files.

◆ NetWare 4.*x* stores security data in the PARTITIO.NDS, BLOCK.NDS, ENTRY.NDS, VALUE.NDS, and UNINSTAL.NDS files.

The attacker may attempt to delete these files by first exiting to DOS and running a file maintenance utility. After deleting the files, the attacker attempts to load the NetWare install utility, which prompts the attacker to select an Admin password.

Here are the best ways to secure the server, as outlined by Nomad in the FAQ:

◆ Trust no one.

◆ Physically secure the server – that is, keep it in a secure, protected room with regulated access.

◆ Use the SECURE CONSOLE command to prevent an attacker from loading harmful NetWare Loadable Modules (NLMs) from a floppy drive or a remote location.

◆ Store backups of important files, such as the STARTUP.NCF and AUTOEXEC.NCF files, system login scripts and bindery or NDF files off-site.

◆ Generate a list of NLMs and version numbers and a list of files from the SYS:LOGIN, SYS:PUBLIC, and SYS:SYSTEM directories. Check them against originals periodically to make sure they have not been altered.

◆ Generate a list of users and their access privileges and keep it up to date. Go over this list periodically and make sure a rogue employee does not have access to something they shouldn't have access to.

◆ Run security from the SYS:SYSTEM directory to see who has Supervisor rights. An unusual account, such as Guest or Printer with Supervisor access, should be immediately suspect.

◆ Monitor server console activity through the CONLOG.NLM file.

◆ Turn on the Accounting feature, so that every login and logout attempt can be tracked. While this feature is mainly used to charge back clients or departments for server usage, it can also be used as a security mechanism because it can track reads, writes, time logged in, data stored, and requests serviced.

◆ Do not use the Supervisor account or use it sparingly.

◆ Use NCP (NetWare Core Protocol) Packet Signature to prevent packet spoofing. Packet Signature is a security feature that protects servers and workstations using NCP, by preventing packet forgery. This feature prevents forgery by requiring the server and workstation to sign each packet. Without this feature, an attacker could theoretically gain Supervisor privileges, and gain access to all resources. Add the following line to your AUTOEXEC.NCF file: SET NCP PACKET SIGNATURE OPTION=3. This forces Packet Signature to be employed.

- Do not use RCONSOLE, or use it sparingly.

- Move .NCF files to a secure location. Wanna go fishing? Nomad says you can set a trap by keeping a false AUTOEXEC.NCF file in SYS:SYSTEM with a false RCONSOLE password.

- Use the Lock File Server Console option in Monitor.

- Add EXIT to the end of the System Login script. This addition eliminates the possibility of a Login Script attack.

- Upgrade to NetWare 4.11. Most NetWare hacks work only on NetWare 3.*x*.

- Remove RCONSOLE.EXE from SYS:PUBLIC to prevent everyone from having access to it.

- Remove [Public] from [Root] in NDS.

To avoid many of the preceding hacks, NetWare 3.*x* administrators should enter the SECURE CONSOLE command into the AUTOEXEC.NCF file. Once done, any user who gains access to the server will be unable to load any NLMs, exit to DOS, or change the system time and date. Loading a mischievous NLM is a common way to hack a system. The Internet is full of NLMs whose sole purpose is to gain unauthorized access into a system. Also, many of the workarounds and hacks used by intruders are entered from the DOS command line. Preventing them from exiting to DOS keeps them from issuing many of their commands. In addition, loading MONITOR.NLM and selecting the Lock File Server Console option causes the system to ask for a password before any commands can be entered from the server.

Another common precaution is to prevent access to the network server's floppy drive. In NetWare, remapping the floppy disk drive to a directory on the server causes data to be copied to that server directory instead of to the floppy drive, in the event a user attempts to copy data to the floppy drive. So when the spy in your company who actually works for the competition attempts to download your customer data onto a floppy, it comes up empty. Although the MAP DEL command (used to delete a mapping) can be used by the attacker to get around this precaution, you can still thwart his or her efforts by altering the MAP.EXE program and changing DEL to another three letters, thereby rendering the MAP DEL command useless.

Furthermore, after installing NetWare on the server, be sure to issue the REMOVE DOS command to make sure that any part of MS-DOS (which was used to install NetWare) does not remain on the system. Removing DOS prevents attackers from secretly loading NLMs onto the system. (DOS is used to install NetWare onto the system, but is unnecessary after installation is complete.)

You can prevent users from copying executable files from the server with the FLAG command. The problem here is that although this command prevents the file from being copied, it also prevents it from being backed up.

Despite competition from Windows NT and UNIX, NetWare remains a popular network operating system and enjoys a large installed base. The problem with NetWare is that any attacker who manages to gain access to a supervisor-level ID enjoys broad access to the entire system. Any file on the network can be accessed, the attacker can set up new accounts, or make changes to the privileges of existing accounts. As such, supervisor passwords should be especially closely guarded, changed often, and used by as few people as possible.

In addition, when a user is assigned access to a particular directory, access to all subdirectories is also allowed by default, unless the administrator disables the default. Issuing a quick NDIR command generates a list of access rights, a fast check that should be done periodically to ensure that nobody has rights to more than they should.

Novell's IntranetWare product, which includes NetWare 4.x along with other Internet-related products, also offers some enhanced security features. IntranetWare comes with an IPX-to-IP gateway, which is integrated with NDS and functions as an NLM. This gateway functions as a de facto firewall, because the LAN-based services remain IPX-based and can therefore not be routed over the Internet.

Windows NT

Microsoft has made security a major part of the Windows NT operating system. NT's security subsystem includes four major components:

♦ **Logon Processes.** This component accepts user logon requests, including remote requests.

♦ **Local Security Authority.** This component guarantees that any user who logs on has permission to access that system. The Local Security Authority generates an access token, manages policy, and furnishes user authentication services.

♦ **Security Account Manager (SAM).** The SAM maintains the user accounts database and contains information for all user and group accounts. SAM (sometimes referred to as the *directory database*) also provides user validation services, which are used by the Local Security Authority.

◆ **Security Reference Monitor.** This component checks to see if the user has permission to perform a task or access an object before the user's action is carried out. This serves the purpose of enforcing access validation and audit generation policy (factors that determine whether an audit message is generated), and guarantees that any user or process that is attempting to gain access to an object has permission to do so.

Windows NT was designed to be easy to use and convenient for end users. As such, NT places the username of the last user to log on in the Username field of the Logon dialog box. This convenience may save a few keystrokes for the end user, but it can also be an easy way for an attacker to learn a username.

You can prevent NT from displaying the username, however. Using the Registry Editor, create the following Registry key value:

```
Hive:  HKEY_LOCAL_MACHINE\SOFTWARE
Key:   \Microsoft\Windows NT\Current Version\Winlogon
Name:  DontDisplayLastUserName
Type:  REG_SZ
Value: 1
```

The Windows NT Registry

The Registry establishes a secure database that stores configuration data hierarchically. You can edit the Registry with the Regedt32.exe or REGEDIT.EXE tool. REGEDIT.EXE is the more recent version of Regedt32.exe, and has a Windows NT Explorer interface. You can access either of these tools from the Windows NT Explorer, or by selecting Run from the Start menu, and then entering in REGEDT32 or REGEDIT at the command prompt.

After calling up the Registry, you will see five subtrees:

◆ **HKEY_LOCAL_MACHINE.** This subtree shows information about the local computer system, such as hardware and operating system data.

◆ **HKEY_CLASSES_ROOT.** This subtree holds associations between applications and file types, OLE Registry information, and file-class association data.

◆ **HKEY_CURRENT_CONFIG.** This subtree holds configuration data for the current hardware profile.

◆ HKEY_CURRENT_USER. This subtree holds the user profile for users who are logged on. The profile includes information on environment variables, desktop settings, network connections, printers, and application preferences.

◆ HKEY_USERS. This subtree contains all actively loaded user profiles.

User profiles in the Registry can be protected by restricting access through the Windows NT Explorer. If files are stored on an NTFS (NT File System) volume, the security features of NT Explorer can be used to assign permissions to these files, as well as to the Registry Editors. Access these features by going to the File menu, clicking Properties, and then Security.

Security Access Tokens

Windows NT generates a *security access token* for a user when he or she logs in to the network. This token includes a great deal of information about the user, including the names of the groups to which the user belongs. The token also includes the user's unique security ID. Furthermore, every process that runs on behalf of the user will have a copy of that user's access token.

Whenever a user attempts to access an object, Windows NT looks in the access token for the security ID and compares it with a master list of access permissions to determine whether the user is permitted to access that object.

In addition, the administrator can also assign user rights, or privileges, to specific users. These special rights, such as the capability to back up files, shut down the computer, or change system times, can be assigned through the User Manager tool. The User Manager lets you edit user accounts and policies from a central location. User Manager includes the User Rights Policy Editor and Account Policy Editor utilities. The User Rights Policy Editor is used to define policies for local workstations, and the Account Policy Editor is used to set password restrictions and account lockouts.

Registry Vulnerability

Windows NT contains a potentially damaging vulnerability that could enable someone to read the Registry of a remote computer and gain information such as user lists, shared files, and the Windows NT Registry.

The problem revolves around a built-in but undocumented Windows NT anonymous user. Windows NT uses this user account for machine-to-machine communication. This account was not previously thought to have access to any resources, but it has been demonstrated to be able to access Windows NT resources. As such, take note that the Anonymous user is a member of the Everyone group. This means that an NT machine with NetBIOS bound to the network can have Registry information read or written to, to the same extent that the *Everyone* group has access. It also means that application and system logs can be read, and any file share with access to *Everyone* can be accessed.

A software vendor, Internet Security Systems, Inc. (ISS), has developed a small application that mitigates the threat posed by this undocumented back door. The application, EVERYONE2USERS.EXE, is available free of charge from ISS at their Web site: http://www.iss.net. This utility is intended to replace the Everyone group with the Users group for selected Registry keys. In addition, ISS is planning to incorporate a check for the back door into its own network security assessment product, Internet Scanner, and its real-time attack recognition and response system, RealSecure.

Some other vulnerabilities have been noted in the trade press and on Internet newsgroups:

- Unauthorized access to the password database on Windows NT domain controllers

- Attackers can get access to the password database by accessing backup tapes

- Attackers can get access to the password database from the Repair directory

- An attacker could install an ISAPI DLL that functions as a Trojan horse

- Jobs submitted to the Scheduler (AT command) can be modified by an unauthorized user

All of these vulnerabilities would not exist or would be minimized if a proper security policy were in place. These and other vulnerabilities typically result when an untrusted individual is granted unauthorized access to the Administrator account. These vulnerabilities are not actually flaws in the network operating itself, but merely the result of improperly enforced security policy. As discussed in Part I of this book, the most crucial part of security is not software, but implementation of an appropriate security policy.

Security Levels

Windows NT can accommodate a broad range of security, from none at all to the C2 level specified by the Department of Defense. For computers with no sensitive data, you can make the system fully accessible, with no protections enabled. Depending on the data contained in the machine, you may decide to enable additional security, such as establishing user accounts and passwords. In Windows NT, you can manage user accounts with the User Manager tool, which is found in the Administrative Tools program group. To implement the greatest level of security on your Windows NT machines, you can create a C2-compliant system with Microsoft's C2Config application.

Although the administrator can configure security to meet the company's specific requirements, Microsoft has established recommendations for three separate levels: minimal, standard, and high-level.

MINIMAL SECURITY SETTING

A minimal security setting may be more appropriate for machines that do not contain sensitive data, or machines that are stored in secure locations. The system can be configured with no protections at all; this may be the most appropriate setting if, for example, the computer is used by a single individual in a home office.

Even in a minimal security configuration, however, you must take certain precautions. These precautions may include the following:

♦ Use of a surge protector to protect the machine and peripheral devices from power spikes and subsequent data loss

♦ Physical security to guard against theft

♦ Defragmentation and regular disk scans to ensure the highest level of performance

♦ Use of antivirus software to protect the system against the introduction of viruses

STANDARD SECURITY SETTING

The standard setting accommodates the majority of NT installations and strikes a balance between accessibility and security. In addition to the recommendations stated for minimal security, Microsoft recommends the following for a standard installation:

♦ Establishing and enforcing a policy that outlines procedures such as not writing down passwords and logging off at the end of every day.

♦ Configuring Windows NT so that it displays a legal notice before a user is allowed to log on. The absence of a legal notice, or the presence of a generic Welcome screen, may be construed as an invitation to enter the system. The warning screen should notify any user attempting to log in that he or she may be held legally responsible if attempting to use the system without proper authorization.

♦ Requiring usernames (accounts) and passwords. These can be administered through the User Manager. This means requiring administrative users to have two accounts, one for administrative tasks and one for general activities. Further, the built-in Administrator account should be renamed to make it less easy for an attacker to guess.

♦ Pressing Ctrl-Alt-Del before logging on. Doing so causes any mischievous programs designed to collect passwords to fail.

♦ Using the NTFS file system instead of the FAT system.

◆ Taking steps to protect the Registry, which contains all initialization and configuration information used by the operating system. The Registry can be backed up with Windows NT's backup utility.

NTFS offers better performance on larger volumes, and includes some security-related features not included in FAT. While FAT can be used with multiple operating systems, NTFS still holds the advantage in most circumstances. It is possible, for example, to assign permissions to individual files and folders, and more permission settings are available.

In addition, NTFS includes a recoverability feature that eliminates the need for disk repair programs. If a system crash occurs, NTFS uses its log file and checkpoint information to automatically restore the file system's consistency.

HIGH-LEVEL SECURITY SETTING

A high-level security setting should be used for environments that contain especially sensitive data (such as a military installation, or an environment that processes financial information), or are at high risk for attack (such as a politically unpopular organization). This setting includes everything specified in the standard setting, as well as additional considerations, including the following:

◆ Controlling physical access to sensitive computers by disabling the floppy-based boot, using a CPU with a case that must be opened by a key, and removing the network card if the computer does not require network access. Setting the BOOT.INI time-out to zero disables an existing floppy drive on startup.

◆ Using regular user rights and changing default permissions as appropriate.

◆ Using the ACL editor to set restrictions to access of system files and directories.

◆ Setting additional protections on some Registry keys.

◆ Restricting guest access to the EventLog.

◆ Restricting which users can add printer drivers using the Print folder.

◆ Not using the Schedule service (AT command). This command is used to schedule tasks to run automatically at a preset time.

◆ Windows NT includes the FTP Internet service. The default anonymous user account for FTP is Guest. Change Guest to a different name, and give it a password. Do not give the Guest account access to any privileged groups. Do not allow the Guest account to have the Logon on Locally user right; the latter restriction minimizes the possibility of an insider attack. Furthermore, be aware that FTP can export entire disk partitions. Configure which partitions are accessible via FTP; ideally, a full disk partition should be dedicated exclusively to FTP services.

◆ Limiting the boot process to prevent someone from starting the machine with another operating system, thus bypassing Windows NT's security mechanisms.

◆ Permitting only logged-on users to shut down the computer.

◆ Enabling system auditing. This keeps the administrator up to date on any potential security risks or security breaches.

UNIX

UNIX is often criticized for its lack of security. Many implementations of UNIX have taken the extra step of adding additional security features. And you can get additional security by using third-party programs.

Built-In Features

Even without third-party programs, a few built-in commands can be used for security purposes.

The UNIX encryption system, known as *crypt*, is based on a software implementation of the German Enigma cipher, created in World War II. This cipher was broken by cryptographers during the war more than 50 years ago, and is fairly useless for anything other than hiding information from casual browsers.

If you suspect that an intruder is attacking your system, the first thing you want to do is try to find out who it is and what he or she is doing. You can accomplish this with the *w*, *finger*, and *who* commands.

If you do think an attack is underway, here's how these commands work. The *w* command provides an overview of all users on the system, and what programs they have active. The *w* display gives you an opportunity to determine that all users are valid and that no suspicious software is being run. The *finger* command shows who is on the system and from where they have logged on. *Who* presents the same information.

The problem with these commands is that they are only useful for catching the intruder in the act — they cannot provide you with any information after the fact. Also, the output from all three of these commands can be manipulated by a skilled attacker intent on hiding his or her presence.

After the attacker has left, he or she may have left processes running to gather information. You can see all active processes with the *ps* command. Examine the *ps* output to see if any processes have started at unusual times, if a high percentage of CPU is being consumed, or if a process shows a question mark in the TT column. To double-check the *ps* command, you can execute the *crash* command to show the same information.

After the intruder has gone, it may still be possible to detect his or her footprints through the *last*, *lastcomm*, or *netstat* commands, or by examining the /var/log/syslog file. The *last* command is used to show information about logins and logouts. The *lastcomm* command shows the last command executed. Process accounting must be enabled to use this command. The *netstat* command displays all listening and connected devices.

The /var/log/syslog file is long and difficult to derive any value from; nonetheless, it can provide some useful information. It shows the status of messages sent and received by the system, so you can look through it to try to find any messages sent to suspicious hosts.

Sniffers are a common method of deriving information; the *ifconfig* command can help spot this type of attack. *Ifconfig* displays the current configuration of the network interface. Ethernet adapters are usually configured to accept messages only intended for that particular adapter. If, however, an attacker has reconfigured it to *promiscuous* mode, all activity on that segment can be seen by the attacker. The output from the *ifconfig* command will show whether the adapter is in promiscuous mode or not.

Solaris

Sun Microsystems' Solaris operating system is highly secure and can be used with an Internet server, application server, PC administration server, or on a high-performance workstation. Versions of Solaris are available for the SPARC and UltraSPARC platform, as well as Intel x86, Pentium, Pentium Pro, and PowerPC.

Solaris supports several critical security standards, including the Department of Defense Orange Book specifications for C2 computer security systems. In addition, Solaris supports the POSIX (Portable Operating System Interface for computing environments) specification for access control lists, and a compartmented mode workstation version, Trusted Solaris, has also been released.

Some features of Trusted Solaris have found their way into the standard Solaris release, including a security profiles feature, which enables administrators to limit user access to specific UNIX commands and tools.

Solaris offers three layers of security features:

◆ Level 1 has features and tools that let administrators control who can log into the system.

◆ Level 2 incorporates tools that enable administrators to set the overall security state of the system and regulate access to system resources.

◆ Level 3 encompasses Secure Distributed services and Developers Platforms, describing how Solaris supports different authentication and encryption mechanisms. This level encompasses secure distributed file and directory services.

IMPLEMENTING LEVEL 1 SECURITY

The first level gives the administrator tight control over who can and cannot log into the system, primarily through a password mechanism. However, as with any password system, you have no way to prove that a user employing a password is indeed the user to whom the password was assigned. Therefore, it is important to rigorously enforce a policy that requires all users to diligently protect their passwords. Solaris includes a set of password management features to help protect passwords:

◆ **Password validation.** This feature compares the password entered by the user to one stored for that user in the shadow password file before allowing the user to log in.

◆ **Password aging.** The administrator can set an expiration date for all passwords. Each user is warned when the password is ready to expire, and is requested to set a new one.

◆ **Disallow old password.** This feature prevents a user from reusing a previously used password.

◆ **Password qualification.** This feature enforces a level of difficulty for the password; in other words, it makes sure that the password is difficult for an attacker to guess.

◆ **Shadow password file.** This is a hidden file that stores all users' passwords and is readable only by root.

◆ **Account expiration.** This feature lets an administrator set an expiration date for an account. This feature is especially useful in granting temporary accounts to visitors or temporary workers.

In addition, third-party products offer more password security features that may restrict the hours of access, disable the login screen after a certain number of invalid attempts, or automatically lock the screen or log out after a period of idle time.

A common path used by attackers is the remote dial-up line. Solaris enables you to password-protect modem ports, so any user who dials from a remote location will be asked for the modem port password. This mechanism can be further enhanced with third-party token systems, which generate a one-time only password through a hand-held device.

IMPLEMENTING LEVEL 2 SECURITY

In level 2 of Solaris security, administrators control which resources can be accessed by valid users. This level also provides auditing capability, which can be used to track unauthorized attempts at access.

Solaris' Automated Security Access Tool (ASET) automatically assesses the overall security state of the system and places it into one of three predetermined security states: low, medium, or high. ASET alerts the administrator when any potential security breach has happened.

In the low setting, ASET ensures that file attributes are set at standard values, performs standard checks, and reports any potential vulnerabilities. In the medium security setting, ASET modifies the permission setting for some sensitive system files, and performs additional checks. This setting is adequate for most environments. For a highly secure environment, the high setting allows only minimal access to most system files.

Solaris' file protection mechanism uses both traditional UNIX permission settings and access control lists. With the UNIX settings, the administrator can set the read, write, and execute parameters for a file's owner or a selected group. However, this approach is limited, in that access can be restricted by group only — restrictions cannot be set for one individual. The ACL offers further restriction over file access. This list contains authorization data for every file, thereby enabling the administrator to set a much finer granularity for control over access. This feature permits restrictions to be set for individual users.

Solaris also includes two auditing methods: UNIX System Logs and C2 auditing. UNIX System Logs track login events, resource usage, and other data. C2 auditing (Controlled Access Protection) offers a more thorough audit report. This type of auditing, which is compliant with the Defense Department's Orange Book (see Chapter 4) can generate an audit log by user, event, or class. Furthermore, a C2-compliant auditing system can log any event specified by the administrator.

IMPLEMENTING LEVEL 3 SECURITY

In level 3, Solaris takes advantage of the Open Network Computing (ONC+) network architecture's security features. ONC+ can be configured with additional security features, including the Secure NIS+ distributed naming service, Secure NFS distributed file service, and Secure Transport Independent Remote Procedure Call (TI-RPC) platform. The latter platform, also known as Secure RPC, enhances the basic RPC mechanism with additional security to verify the identity of each RPC user. RPC by itself provides a set of routines that programs use to communicate with each other over the network.

Authentication is an essential part of security in any environment. Solaris is flexible enough to accommodate multiple authentication mechanisms, including Kerberos, Diffie-Hellman and UNIX-based authentication, through the Secure TI-RPC interface.

Sun Microsystems' SunSoft division is developing a new authentication architecture, based on Internet Standard RFC 1508, the Generic Security Services API (GSSAPI). This API combines multiple authentication mechanisms under a single API. Sun's implementation of GSSAPI, known as GSSRPC, integrates TI-RPC with GSSAPI on Solaris. GSSRPC gives RPC-based applications access to multiple authentication options.

SunSoft's Pluggable Authentication Module (PAM) has been adopted by the Open Software Foundation (OSF) for inclusion in the Common Desktop Environment (CDE). PAM establishes a pluggable model for authentication mechanisms, passwords, and other security services. Several of these security mechanisms can be accessed through PAM as dynamically loadable, shared modules. The administrator can install these modules transparently into applications. Authentication can be configured on a per-application basis.

GSSAPI has rapidly become a de facto standard for handling security services in a generic manner. With this API, applications can operate independently of the underlying security mechanisms. PAM and GSSAPI are complementary. Where PAM supports user authentication by system entry servers, GSSAPI is used for network-based client/server authentication. Users on a client/server system would, therefore, first be authenticated by PAM, and then through GSSAPI to communicate to server systems.

Where authentication verifies a user's identity, authorization ensures that the user has permission to access a specific file. Sun's Network File System (NFS), which has also become accepted as a de facto industry standard, provides two separate methods of authorization: file permission indicators, and POSIX-compliant ACLs.

An important consideration in multivendor environments, and a major convenience to end users, is the single sign-on. Typically, each host requires a user to provide a separate password. But in a large environment, the number of passwords required to gain access to all the necessary resources may be unwieldy. Single sign-on provides the user with a single password that is entered just once to gain access to all hosts in the distributed environment.

In its level 4 security mechanisms, Sun addresses physical access to the network. This level includes Sun's Solstice Firewall-1 and Solstice SunScreen.

Solstice Firewall-1 is used to carry out the security policies previously established by the administrator. Firewall-1 combines hardware and software, and functions by either allowing or disallowing packets from entering the internal network. Each packet is granted or denied access based on the previously established security policy. Besides packet filtering, Firewall-1 offers logging and alerting features, and an intuitive interface for management.

Solstice SunScreen combines the firewall features with network-level authentication. SunScreen is network-independent, protocol-independent, and application-independent. With SunScreen, it is possible to establish a virtual secure private network across the public Internet. SunScreen is completely undetectable by intruders, because packets pass through it without it recording any indication of its presence. SunScreen includes a central hardware device, the SunScreen SPF-100, and a secure Administration Station that is used to specify security rules.

Single Sign-On

Sun is focusing on providing the convenience of a secure single sign-on through the Solstice Security Manager line. Under single sign-on, a user can authenticate once to gain access to multiple applications that have been previously defined in the security system.

The advantage of single sign-on goes beyond convenience. Previously, each application had its own security process or used the hosting system's authentication procedure. This process required a lot of redundant development, gave security staff another point of failure, and more areas where security had to be managed. In addition, it is certainly less likely that an end user will memorize ten passwords, which may lead to the unfortunate security breach of having a sheet of passwords written down near the user's workstation.

In Fortune 500 companies, users can have an average of 39 sign-ons per person. With this many points of authentication, management becomes difficult, and security may start to break down. Every time an employee is terminated, the security manager must deactivate all of the employee's passwords. Not only is this time-consuming, but it may also cause the security staff to occasionally miss one, thereby leaving open a vulnerability.

The PAM interface discussed earlier facilitates single sign-on due to its capability to integrate several authentication mechanisms. SunSoft is developing a single sign-on to support multiple environments. Meanwhile, some third-party products are available to integrate Solaris with Windows, MVS (Multiple Virtual Storage), VMS (Virtual Management System) and other environments.

The Open Group is working on a standard, which Sun plans to include in Solaris 2.6. The single sign-on standard (XSSO) offers a guideline for this process by defining functionality and behavior. By standardizing the process, the XSSO is able to accommodate multiple platforms and technologies.

HP-UX

Hewlett-Packard's HP-UX UNIX operating system, like many of the others described here, meets the Department of Defense's C2 requirements and has some additional features for B-level security.

Security features of HP-UX include:

◆ C2 compliance

◆ System auditing (maintains a log of security events)

◆ Access control lists (ACLs) for flexible control over file access

◆ Extended password management facility

◆ Logon restrictions that give administrators control over the times specific users can access the system

◆ Boot authentication, to prevent an unauthorized user from booting up a system

HP-UX provides a superuser-only encrypted password database, system-generated passwords, user-generated password screening, and enforced password aging. The System Administration Roles (SAR) mechanism enables the administrator to delegate security-related tasks to other staff, without having to assign superuser capabilities to those users.

HP-UX's journaled file system guarantees file system integrity through a fast recovery process in the event of system failure. In addition, HP-UX allows for dynamic management of the journaled file system with HP OnlineJFS, which offers features for online disk defragmentation, online disk resizing, and online backup.

Other features relating to security include the capability to maintain consistency between multiple applications, support for dual I/O paths between disks and the system with automatic failover to the second I/O path, and the capability to back up a mirrored logical volume from a second system.

Working with HP-UX is the HP Praesidium/Authorization Server, which offers additional security-related features to the HP-UX environment. Specifically, Praesidium does the following:

◆ Secures Internet, intranet, and enterprise applications with granular rules-based access control

◆ Offers a centralized Internet/intranet application security model that reduces the chance of administrative errors

◆ Offers a browser-based GUI, so customers can use an existing PC to administer the Authorization Server

The HP Praesidium/Authorization Server is a rules-based product that retains some of the same centralized administration and consistency that mainframe users have long been accustomed to. However, it also offers more end-user functionality, and the flexibility that users are accustomed to in a distributed environment. It improves security at the application level by controlling user access privileges and simplifies administration through the convenient graphical user interface, through which the administrator manages rules and privileges for all applications in the enterprise. Furthermore, the custom code that would have to be otherwise created for each individual application is no longer necessary.

Custom code is also often required for specific security tests to verify a user's permission to access an application's information. This also calls for a custom database for holding permission information, access control lists, and various other tools and utilities. The Authorization Server adds the convenience of a centralized rules base that holds privileges information in a common database that is shared across all applications.

The Authorization Server enables authorization decisions to be made based on rules that take into account the privileges of a specific user, as well as the privileges required to run any given application. Each rule is structured as an equation, in which privileges and transaction values are plugged into the equation variables at runtime. All rules are stored in the Authorization Server database. The rules could, for example, allow a user to access an application only during certain hours of the day, within a specific dollar amount, or only for a specified set of account numbers.

Because some privileges will be almost universal, a set of common privileges can be defined as a "profile" and stored in the database. An individual user can then be assigned the privilege of a specific profile, instead of having to assign all of the profile's privileges individually to the user. Through this facility, it is simple for the administrator to modify a group of users' access privileges globally.

The Authorization Server can also control access to Web applications based on URL or CGI scripts. For example, a user can be restricted from a particular Web-based application by limiting that user's access privileges to the CGI script that controls the application.

The Authorization Server includes a browser-based administration terminal. Administration can be carried out either by an individual user, or by a profile of several users.

The Praesidium/Authorization Server runs on an HP 9000 Enterprise Server; HP recommends that it run on its own separate server to protect against tampering.

The Praesidium Enterprise Security Framework (see Figure 6-1) was created to provide a secure basis for electronic commerce, by taking a comprehensive view of enterprise security. The framework is made up of HP and third-party security products that combine to form a complete, end-to-end security solution for the HP-UX environment. These products are organized into three categories, all of which are centrally managed by Enterprise IT Management:

- ◆ **Gateway services.** This category includes products for securing the enterprise's perimeter, and for securing transaction gateway services.

- ◆ **Platform security.** This category includes products to secure the application server, clients, network appliances, and network communications.

- ◆ **Core security services.** This category establishes a central repository, from which authentication, authorization, general policy administration, and monitoring take place.

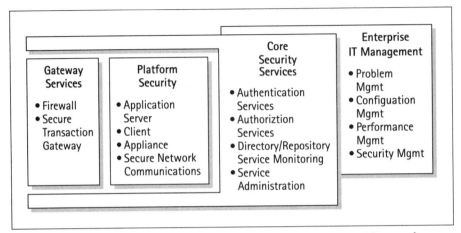

Figure 6-1: The Praesidium framework model (courtesy of Hewlett-Packard Company)

IBM Platforms

IBM's security strategy is organized into two stages. Stage 1 implements an infrastructure on each strategic IBM platform, based on the ISO Security Framework. This infrastructure includes facilities for the following:

◆ Identification and authentication

◆ Access control

◆ Confidentiality

◆ Data integrity

◆ Nonrepudiation

◆ Security management and audit

Stage 2 provides a broader range of security features for the enterprise, based on OSF/DCE (Open Software Foundation/Distributed Computing Environment) technology. These features include the following:

◆ Single sign-on

◆ Security administration

◆ Network security

◆ Distributed data security

IBM's various operating systems, including MVS, VM, OS/400, and AIX provide security for stand-alone environments. In addition, IBM's system security structure permits the attachment of workstations, via LAN/WAN connections, while still accommodating security requirements. This structure accommodates a maximum of flexibility.

The user and resource naming structure for the directory permits the establishment of unique names. It also allows user authentication to be performed once for a user session and allows users to access applications in any system for which they have authorization.

Data integrity and confidentiality services are possible between any two points, and security management and administration will permit control and reporting across multiple systems. IBM's security structure defines the security services required in each system in order to provide for a maximum of interoperability in a mixed environment.

SNA (Systems Network Architecture) security architecture extensions partially address the need to maintain security in a mixed environment; in addition, SAA (Systems Applications Architecture) brings a common API, common user access, and common applications across MVS, VM, OS/400, OS/2 and AIX. In addition, interoperability with non-IBM open platforms, UNIX systems, and other vendors' proprietary operating systems is provided with additional APIs. The subsequent evolution from SAA to an open, distributed model requires greater interoperability, and a system structure that supports distributed processing across multiple strategic platforms. This consistency affords the same level of protection, regardless of where a resource resides. For example, if a user does not have access to a particular resource on an MVS system, moving that resource to OS/2 will not give the user access.

By embracing the ISO security framework, IBM acknowledges the need to conform with open systems security standards. IBM's plan is to implement all of the ISO security protocols as they are adopted.

AIX

AIX 3.2 and AIX 4.0 for the RISC System/6000 provides security mechanisms for user authentication, password complexity, user and port access control, access control lists, auditing, trusted path, system integrity and user-resource limitations. AIX/6000 is a secure operating system that goes beyond traditional UNIX security to include DCE (Distributed Computing Environment) security, ACL enhancements, and other features in furtherance of C2 compliance.

AIX/6000 is available with a hardware key lock. The lock can be configured three different ways:

◆ **Secure.** In this setting, the system cannot boot from a hard disk or from any removable device.

◆ **Normal.** The system can boot from hard disk only.

◆ **Service (Maintenance).** The system attempts to boot from removable devices. If no removable boot device is attached, the diagnostic software from the hard disk is loaded.

Some of AIX/6000's major security features include the following:

◆ **Identification and authorization.** AIX uses standard password authentication; encrypted passwords and user information is kept in an inaccessible directory.

◆ **Access control lists (ACLs).** AIX uses the ACL mechanism along with UNIX mode bits. An AIX ACL permits a user to restrict or permit access for individuals, groups, or combinations thereof. The access permission bits and ACLs can be modified only by the owner of the relevant file or directory.

◆ **Object reuse.** A storage object can be read from or written to by nonprivileged users, and accessed through kernel system calls. Storage objects on AIX include file system objects, heap data, the process's memory address space, shared memory segments, and sockets.

◆ **Audit.** AIX can create an audit trail. Auditable events can be preselected by the administrator, and the audit trail is not accessible by ordinary users.

◆ **System architecture.** All AIX processes have their own address space; a nonprivileged process cannot read or write outside of its own address space.

◆ **System integrity.** Every time the system is cold booted, the RS/6000 performs a power-on self-test (POST) to check proper functioning of hardware and firmware.

In addition, some applications written for the AIX/6000 platform have additional security functions.

OS/400

Security is integrated into the OS/400 hardware and software, and users have selectable levels of installation security available. OS/400 is a C2-compliant operating system. Different levels of security include:

◆ **No protection.** In this level, no security is enforced, and anyone can sign on to the system.

◆ **Sign-on security.** A user ID and password is required. All users are given access to all objects on the system.

◆ **Resource security.** A user ID and password is required. In addition, users must have authority to access an object.

- **Resource security with system integrity.** A user cannot directly access a system object without going through published interfaces. Integrity is enforced at the operating system level and through hardware storage protection.

- **Resource security and enhanced system security.** Additional system interfaces are provided. This level is intended for AS/400 environments with high security requirements, and meets C2 specifications.

Because many security functions are built into the operating system itself, it is not necessary to purchase many of the third-party products that would otherwise be necessary. This does not mean, however, that OS/400 is all you need for security; your own requirements and policy will dictate what third-party products you actually need.

The AS/400 Security Audit subsystem helps customers implement security on an AS/400 system. It performs an audit on the existing security environment and generates a security policy document. The document not only offers the findings of the audit, but also offers specific recommendations. The application's audit examines:

- Exposures due to users with excessive authority

- Use of group profiles and authorization lists

- Security-related control

- Program control

- Physical access

DEC MLS+ and SEVMS

DEC offers a security-enhanced version of UNIX with DEC MLS+ and a security-enhanced version of OpenVMS with its SEVMS offering.

DEC MLS+ is Digital's security-enhanced implementation of DEC OSF/1 version 2.0 software for Alpha systems. A trusted UNIX implementation, DEC MLS+ is designed to meet the B1 level of security, as well as the security requirements for System High and Compartmented Mode Workstations (CMW) as defined by the Defense Intelligence Agency.

The product addresses the need to manage files and directories with different levels of security with its multilevel security (MLS) facility. MLS allows unprivileged users to place files with different required security levels in the same directory.

Additional security features include secure multiuser windows, a secure network interface, and TCP/IP support. DEC MLS+ is a trusted version of the 64-bit advanced kernel architecture, based on Carnegie-Mellon's Mach V2.5 kernel design.

Research

The Defense Advanced Research Projects Agency (DARPA) is leading the way on developing the next generation of secure operating systems with several new projects. The agency's Flux project combines a stripped-down microkernel with tight process control. The kernel itself contains very little—it includes tools for managing address space, mapping, synchronization, threads, and communications. The kernel does not, however, include features for managing virtual memory or peripherals. These features instead are selected through applications. In addition, Flux can run processes in a nested pattern, so parent processes can control the resources used by children.

DARPA's Exokernel project also follows the same philosophy of deploying a minimalist kernel, which does only such tasks as resource allocation, hardware protection, and fault isolation, and focuses on discretionary rather than mandatory access control. This approach departs dramatically from other operating systems in exposing the hardware to application programs.

The Spin project targets higher performance by customizing the kernel to meet the needs of the application. This approach lets users write their own variations of kernel services, and then attach them to the kernel at runtime. However, allowing code to be written to the kernel may cause a security problem. Spin addresses security by requiring kernel extensions to be written in Modula 3, which protects the kernel by restricting how different types of data can be manipulated.

The DARPA Scout project also customizes the operating system but is geared toward communication. Scout's path abstraction mechanism lets everything from the operating system to the application be built around the same set of abstractions. The focus on communications also lends itself to security, because it is possible to define a path's secure attributes.

The DARPA Synthetix project enhances performance by customizing the operating system with compiler technology to meet specific application needs.

SEVMS builds on the security already present in DEC's OpenVMS operating system. SEVMS satisfies the needs of government agencies and other entities with the need to protect classified information.

SEVMS offers mandatory access controls (MAC) and security auditing features for secure stand-alone or clustered OpenVMS systems. The security manager can enforce a system-wide security policy to protect against compromised security. SEVMS meets B1 security standards. Its features include the capability to define and control access between subjects (users) and objects (files, programs, and devices), and the capability to designate sensitivity labels for any user, file, program, or device.

SEVMS enforces security policy through a series of validation and access-checking mechanisms. In SEVMS's mandatory access control system, a nonprivileged owner of information does not have the authority to grant access to other users, unless the access adheres to a system-wide security policy. The security manager alone has the responsibility for classifying data, software, and hardware and for authorizing users.

Security levels and categories are stored in the OpenVMS rights database by the security manager; the manager then assigns security ranges to each user through the Authorize utility. Users are then able to log into any classification within their range of authorization.

In an SEVMS environment, nonprivileged users cannot violate the access control policy. Whenever a subject requests access to an object, the mandatory access control mechanism compares security labels and either grants or denies access.

Summary

Network operating systems come with numerous security features. In this chapter, you learned about the following:

- Network operating systems contain some native security functions; these are often supplemented by third-party add-on programs.

- NetWare uses six security categories to regulate network access: login security, trustees, rights, inheritance, attributes, and effective rights.

- Windows NT security is based on the concept of security access tokens. Every user gets an access token upon login; this token contains information about the user, what the user can access, and a unique security ID.

- Sun Microsystems' Solaris operating system offers four layers of security:

  1. Features that enable the administrator to control login

  2. Tools for setting the overall security state of the system

  3. Support for different authentication and encryption mechanisms

  4. Physical access

- Hewlett-Packard's HP-UX operating system also offers strong security mechanisms, primarily through its Praesidium framework that encompasses HP and third-party products.

- IBM offers an overall security strategy for all of its operating systems, a plan that promotes the establishment of a single security policy for a mixed environment.

Chapter 7

Systems Management Platforms

IN THIS CHAPTER

◆ A look at system management standards

◆ An overview of security options available through the major systems management platforms

NETWORK AND SYSTEMS MANAGEMENT has changed significantly over the last ten years, particularly as the industry moves toward larger, multivendor, client/server environments. As this movement continues, more corporations are deploying mission-critical applications on their client/server networks.

A systems management platform, then, must be capable of accommodating such products from multiple vendors. And ease-of-use features such as a central GUI (graphical user interface) console become even more important, because of the enormous complexity of the enterprise. Part of network and systems management also includes the maintenance of security. If security can be managed from the same console as the rest of the system, the manager's job gets a great deal easier.

Systems management software helps companies control increasingly complex networks. A network management software product typically offers features such as the following:

◆ **Network status monitoring tools.** These utilities monitor the network and generate reports and alarms to indicate the network's status. These are particularly useful in detecting intrusions.

◆ **Error reporting.** These utilities create logs of any generated errors that can be referred back to later.

◆ **Performance analysis.** A performance analysis tool looks at how the system is performing and whether traffic is too high, and may be used to determine whether bottlenecks exist somewhere on the network.

◆ **Network modifications capabilities.** Offices are increasingly mobile; accommodating moves, additions, and changes is a large part of the network administrator's job.

A network management application may be integrated into a broader systems management platform, such as HP OpenView or Sun Microsystems Solstice Domain Manager.

Let's take a look at the standards employed for systems management, and the two biggest systems management platforms on the market, and discuss how you can use them to manage security.

Systems Management Standards

Originally, systems and network management tools were largely proprietary, although the industry has been moving toward standards-based management. Standards establish a common interface for communications between different management applications and system components. By establishing this common interface, the network administrator no longer has to run several separate, unconnected programs; instead, all utilities run through a common interface. One major advantage of this approach is that it lowers the learning curve significantly.

The most prevalent standard is the Desktop Management Interface, which is promoted by the Desktop Management Task Force (DMTF). Another standard is the Systems Network Management Protocol.

Desktop Management Interface

The Desktop Management Interface (DMI) establishes a common, standard interface for different management applications. Several products comply with the DMI specification, including Hewlett-Packard's OpenView, Intel's LANDesk Manager, and Microsoft's Systems Management Server.

The DMI standard was created in 1992 by a group of computer hardware and software manufacturers. It was designed to create a standard for managing desktop computer systems in a way that guarantees openness and flexibility, simplifies inventory and asset management, and improves security management. In terms of security features, DMI makes it easier to prevent unlicensed software from being introduced into the network. It can further be used to restrict the data that each user can access.

The DMI model revolves around a Management Information Format (MIF) database, which is a language that specifies the manageable attributes of each DMI-compliant device on the network. Several MIFs are available for basic components, including the CPU, operating system, disk drives, network interface cards, printers, and other networkable devices.

The DMI's Service Layer runs locally (on the desktop PC), and gathers information from networked devices by accessing the MIF database. Every compliant device communicates with this Service Layer through a Component Interface (CI), and then sends information to the management application (such as OpenView) through a Management Interface (MI). The information stored about each desktop PC is automatically updated to reflect configuration changes.

The MIF database holds information about each product on the system. The information in the MIF is managed at the Service Layer. The information held in the database comes from individual MIF files, which are provided with each product by the manufacturer. (See Figure 7-1.)

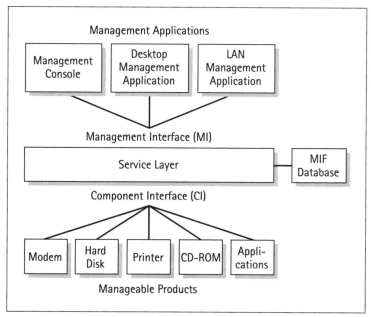

Figure 7-1: The Desktop Management Interface

Figure 7-1 shows a category of management applications that are either remote or local programs used for changing, interrogating, controlling, tracking, or listing all elements of the desktop system. These applications can take the form of a local diagnostics or installation program, or an agent that redirects information from the DMI over the network.

The manageable products shown in the figure include hardware, software, and peripherals that are inside or attached to a desktop computer or network server. Each manageable product contains a MIF file that contains management information about itself. Through this file, each product is capable of providing information to the MIF database.

In the center of Figure 7-1, we see the Service Layer, a desktop-resident program that controls DMI activity. This program runs permanently in the background, and handles Get, Set, List, and other commands from management applications such as OpenView, retrieves information from the MIF database, or passes requests on to manageable products when needed.

The Get command permits the management application to get a current value of individual attributes or groups of attributes. The Set command permits writable attributes to be changed, and the List command permits the management application to read the MIF descriptions of each manageable product, without having to retrieve that product's attribute values.

The Management Interface, shown on top of the Service Layer, shields the management application from the many different mechanisms that may be used to gather management information from products within a desktop system.

The Component Interface, shown below the Service Layer, is in charge of communication between each manageable product and the Service Layer.

DMI is available for DOS, Windows, and OS/2 operating systems, and other versions are under development. Information stored in the MIF can be accessed by any systems management application that supports the DMI standard. The DMI software that runs on the local machines is distributed free of charge, and can be downloaded from several vendors' Web sites (including HP's).

System Network Management Protocol

SNMP stores data in a management information base (MIB), which is similar in nature to the MIF. SNMP is a core service of the TCP/IP protocol suite. It provides a framework for systems to report problems, configuration information, and performance data to a central network management site.

SNMP facilitates the reporting and collection of network errors, and is, as its name implies, fairly simple. SNMP has gained in popularity and, from a manufacturer's perspective, represents a fairly simple network management tool. Implementing SNMP simply involves having each network device report errors to SNMP, and designating one computer to receive the error report collected from SNMP. In a multivendor network of SNMP-compliant stations, one SNMP monitoring station can track network operations of multiple types of computers.

However, SNMP-based management applications may be of less value than those based on DMI, because the SNMP-based ones were designed to work with static network configurations rather than the constantly changing configuration of the desktop PC. The configuration of PCs often changes without the network administrator's knowledge. Although this should be discouraged, it is, unfortunately, inevitable.

SNMP includes a number of security provisions, including the concept of the *SNMP party*. This is a conceptual execution context, in which the operation is restricted to a defined subset of all possible operations of a given SNMP protocol entity. If an SNMP protocol entity processes an SNMP message, it is acting as an SNMP party, and is then restricted to the set of operations defined for that party. An SNMP party consists of:

◆ A unique party identity

◆ An authentication protocol and its associated parameters

◆ A privacy protocol and its associated parameters

◆ A MIB view, where all operations performed by the party are specified

An SNMP protocol entity is a process that performs some type of network management operation, by generating or responding to an SNMP protocol message. Each SNMP protocol entity maintains a local database representing all SNMP parties known to it, and maintains a local database that holds the access control policy that defines access privileges.

HP OpenView

Hewlett-Packard PCs are DMI-compliant. Vectras, for example, come with a full set of management features built into the system BIOS, and only the administrator can change security-related information. DMI features in HP's Vectra include:

♦ **Inventory control.** Individual serial numbers or asset tags can be accessed through DMI.

♦ **Remote system locking.** This feature prevents users from interrupting remote configuration procedures. This is done by enabling the administrator to selectively lock the mouse, keyboard, power-on and reset buttons, or the entire system.

♦ **Remote configuration.** The PC can be rebooted or powered off from a central management console.

♦ **Password control.** C2-level password protection lets the administrator specify that passwords must be set, and also allows the administrator to specify a maximum number of days between password changes, maximum password length, and number of incorrect password attempts allowed before the system access is disabled.

♦ **Advanced security.** Advanced security features prevent unauthorized data transfer through controlling the floppy disk drives. This includes the capability to disable floppy disk drive access, disable writing to floppy disks, and to disable or enable writing to floppy disks from which the system has booted. Similar features are available to control the hard drive. Furthermore, the administrator can control system ports by preventing the transfer of data through serial, USB (Universal System Bus), and parallel ports.

♦ **Health monitoring and reporting.** DMI alerts are generated by monitoring hard disk information using self-monitoring and reporting technology (SMART) and power-on self-test (POST) errors to alert administrators of potential problems.

HP OpenView is an integrated environment consisting of several products. It can manage both NetWare and Windows clients, as well as several different server platforms. A number of third-party products have been written for the OpenView architecture. Currently, over 290 complementary management products are available on multiple operating system platforms, including HP-UX, Solaris, Windows 95, and Windows NT.

HP Security Products

Hewlett-Packard addresses security in its OpenView systems/network management platform through its HP OpenView solutions partner AXENT Technologies. This strategy consists of three products:

◆ OmniGuard/Enterprise Security Manager (ESM)

◆ OmniGuard/Enterprise Access Control (EAC)

◆ OmniGuard/Intruder Alert (IA)

The three HP OpenView security products are multiplatform solutions well-suited to a mixed environment. They come with support for several UNIX operating systems, including HP-UX and Solaris. Let's take a closer look at these three products.

OMNIGUARD/ENTERPRISE SECURITY MANAGER

OmniGuard/Enterprise Security Manager creates, manages, and enforces a security policy in a client/server environment and is used to control the OmniGuard/Enterprise Access Control and OmniGuard/Intruder Alert products. The policies you create with Security Manager can be enforced across all computer platforms, and ESM can accommodate multiple policies that may be in place in different areas of the company.

When a policy violation occurs, the administrator receives a warning of the violation. Some minor problems can be automatically corrected. The tool is intuitive and features pull-down menus and a toolbar, making it relatively easy to manage security policy. Users have a choice between a Windows or Motif interface, and managers without technical background in specific operating systems can still view the security status of all computer systems throughout the enterprise. Furthermore, the tool offers the manager the capability to drill down to receive more specific security details.

ESM is a client/server-based process that includes three primary components: agents, managers, and the graphical user interface. Agents and managers are the heart of the system. Using client/server technology, the manager tells the agents what security checks to perform, then disconnects and waits until the agents complete the check and contact it with the results. The manager then stores the results in its database.

ESM agents can run on several operating systems, and can run all security checks associated with each platform. ESM managers can also run on multiple platforms, and can communicate with any ESM agent, regardless of agent platform. For example, a manager running on a UNIX platform can still communicate with NetWare, UNIX, Windows NT, and other agents.

OMNIGUARD/ENTERPRISE ACCESS CONTROL

UNIX, for all of its advantages, was not designed to be a secure system. OmniGuard/Enterprise Access Control is an add-on designed to augment the native security in UNIX by providing an additional set of access controls. These additional controls can be managed on all systems in the network.

Using the Access Control tool's GUI, the security manager can create a profile for each authorized user. Users can then be organized into logical groups for easier administration. Access controls can be set for account management, password controls, and access restrictions. With account management, the manager can describe general account characteristics; password control permits the establishment of security levels beyond what is available with native UNIX. Furthermore, you can use the access restrictions available to determine the type of access a user or group of users can have, as well as the time of day that they are allowed access.

Access Control comes with a station-locking feature so that the manager can determine when a workstation is idle. If it does not detect any activity on any workstation in the network, this feature clears the workstation's display, terminates the user session, or locks it.

OMNIGUARD/INTRUDER ALERT

OmniGuard/Intruder Alert addresses other security problems as they occur and adds another layer of security to the overall system. This tool automates security monitoring and enables the manager to take action when a violation has been detected. The real-time system monitors audit trail information. If an event occurs that matches pre-established criteria, the system takes one or more of the following actions:

- ◆ Sends an e-mail alarm
- ◆ Broadcasts a message to a device or user
- ◆ Stops the process
- ◆ Causes the violator's program to terminate
- ◆ Disables the user's account
- ◆ Calls a pager
- ◆ Executes a command
- ◆ Appends the event text to a file

Intruder Alert operates by examining either rules or exceptions. It is actually a rules engine, and processes input based on a set of rules that are applied to the particular system it is monitoring.

The software consists of three parts: an interface console, manager, and agent. The interface and manager work as a configuration engine, which permits the manager to configure the set of rules. Agents take the form of daemons or intelligent processes that run locally and execute the rule set.

As with the other tools, Intruder Alert sports an intuitive graphical interface and does not require a high level of sophistication to operate. The system is password-protected, and the user must be defined as an administrator to gain access to the software. Intruder Alert supports multiple platforms that can be grouped in domains according to business function. Figure 7-2 shows Intruder Alert.

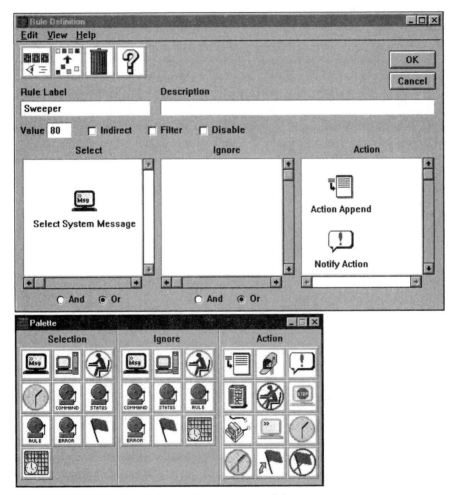

Figure 7-2: With Intruder Alert, intrusion detection policies can be mapped to various domains using a simple drag-and-drop interface.

Although you can use your own internally generated policy to establish Intruder Alert rules, the product comes with prebuilt policies that accommodate a wide variety of attacks and situations. In addition, the product can generate internal reports from the ITAView Monitoring Console, or it can output reports to a database. The product includes a Windows-based relational database called ITAGraph, which has a utility for importing Intruder Alert output, and several prebuilt reports and charts.

Authentication on HP

All too commonly, an organization is unaware that system passwords are constantly sent over the network in unencrypted form. Any attacker with a packet sniffer can capture this information and use it to break into the system. HP accommodates authentication through its Praesidium/Security Service, which allows non-DCE (Distributed Computing Environment) customers to have DCE-like authentication without a DCE/9000 cell.

Praesidium/Security Service applies Kerberos mechanisms to passwords to authenticate users and application servers by exchanging encrypted "tickets." A ticket is an encrypted identification that substitutes for a password. Under the Security Service method, a short-term ticket, instead of a password, is transmitted over the network. Data is encrypted via DES.

Security Service is part of HP's Praesidium security framework. It supports the Praesidium/Authentication Server, which allows the administrator to centralize the authentication function.

HP Praesidium/Security Service provides the following functions:

◆ **Authentication service,** to identify and authenticate users

◆ **Registry service,** to manage the security database

◆ **Login facility,** to process a user's access to security services through a keyed password

◆ **Access Control List (ACL) facility,** for username comparisons and to control who has access to what resources on the network

◆ **Encryption software,** to encrypt transmitted data

Table 7-1 delineates the Praesidium/Security Service framework.

TABLE 7-1 HP's Praesidium/Security Service Framework

Framework	Feature
Gateway Services	Firewall
	Secure Transaction Gateway

continued

TABLE 7-1 HP's Praesidium/Security Service Framework *(continued)*

Framework	Feature
Platform Security	Application Server
	Client
	Appliance
	Secure Network Communications
Core Security Services	Authentication Services
	Authorization Services
	Directory/Repository Service Monitoring
	Service Administration
Enterprise IT Management	Problem Management
	Configuration Management
	Performance Management
	Security Management

Monitoring Security Service is easy through HP DE (Distributed Enterprise)/ Service Monitor, an OpenView tool with a graphical user interface. Security Service also includes the HP Account Manager, which lets the security administrator add and delete users, change passwords and expiration dates, suspend user accounts, and change group memberships.

The DE/Service Monitor provides a service-centric view of a distributed system. It consists of a discovery engine, a database, and an event service. The system administrator can access DE/Service Monitor through either the HP-UX System Administration Manager (SAM) or the OpenView Network Node Manager. The DE/Service Monitor gathers and analyzes data about the status of DCE services across all nodes in the enterprise. It relies on built-in intelligence to spot potential problems, and sends alerts to administrators as needed.

HP TopTOOLS

Hewlett-Packard's TopTOOLS (see Figure 7-3) is a DMI-compliant desktop management application that integrates with OpenView. It offers features for inventory, configuration, fault, and security management. It is available with all HP

Vectra PCs. With HP TopTOOLS, security managers can manage more than 300 DMI attributes.

TopTOOLS integrates the following utilities:

◆ **AssetTOOLS.** This product provides for inventory and asset management. It can execute a full inventory for the system, processor, hard drive, monitor, and network interface card, including information about the manufacturer, model, and serial number.

◆ **ConfigTOOLS.** This utility offers configuration management and troubleshooting in the OpenView environment. It retrieves a wide variety of configuration information, can remotely lock or unlock the PC keyboard, and can enable or disable PC booting from a remote server or floppy drive.

◆ **SafeTOOLS.** This PC health monitoring and fault protection utility is designed to prevent damage and data loss. SafeTOOLS notifies the administrator of any potential problem and suggests a resolution.

◆ **ProtectTOOLS.** This utility prevents unauthorized PC access. Through ProtectTOOLS, the administrator can monitor the configuration of HP hardware, administer passwords, and execute other security-related tasks.

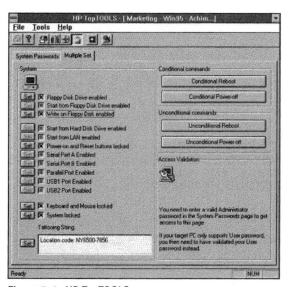

Figure 7–3: HP TopTOOLS

Solstice Domain Manager

Sun Microsystems offers two platforms for systems management: the Solstice Domain Manager for larger enterprise sites and the Site Manager for smaller networks. Sun previously approached systems management through a single product, called SunNet Manager. Dividing the older SunNet Manager into two products provided a consistent pair of management platforms for managing different-sized environments, something that is lacking in other platforms. The same tools, applications, and interface are used in both products, which helps to minimize the learning curve between the two. Furthermore, Solstice Site Manager can send information to Solstice Domain Manager. You can also configure Solstice Domain Manager to receive information from multiple Solstice Site Managers. Both run on the Solaris 2.4 or later operating environment. Domain Manager can be configured either as a stand-alone platform for managing large sites, as a central manager receiving information from multiple Site Managers, or connected in peer fashion to other Domain Managers.

Domain Manager offers facilities to allow it to function in a mixed environment. For example, it can access Novell NetWare Management Agent 2.0, which resides on a NetWare server that is also running TCP/IP. Through this agent, Domain Manager can manage the NetWare server. Furthermore, by importing Novell's ManageWise topology map, Domain Manager can view the NetWare LAN separately from the primary IP network.

Domain Manager can also import the topology map from Novell's ManageWise network management console, enabling Solstice Domain Manager to view the PCs on the NetWare LAN as a separate view from the IP network that it is managing.

While Domain Manager and Site Manager provide for general systems and network management, the separate Solstice Security Manager family addresses security management specifically, and consists of three products:

◆ Solstice Security Manager for Intranets

◆ Solstice Security Manager for Desktops

◆ Solstice Security Manager for Applications

This family provides a comprehensive system for a mixed platform environment, adding mainframe-style security to the client/server environment. Fortunately, it is not as difficult to administer as a mainframe. The security administration has been simplified and is largely transparent to end users.

Solstice Security Manager is built on a scaleable client/server design that facilitates a secure single sign-on from desktops to servers and applications in a large, mixed environment. Each product can scale to tens of thousands of users.

Through Solstice Security Manager, the security manager can enforce a security policy based on dynamic business requirements, depending on how users can access resources, which users can access individual systems and applications, and when they can access them.

Solstice Security Manager for Intranets

Solstice Security Manager for Intranets (SSMI) accommodates the need to administer multiple systems inside the network. This platform simplifies security management by centralizing security-related tasks while still permitting tasks to be delegated to other members of the security team. The capability to judiciously delegate security-related tasks may help keep costs down, while relieving some of the burden on the security manager. Security Manager's Windows NT support makes the product useful for smaller networks as well (under 500 nodes).

SSMI can be used to implement the enterprise-level, single sign-on model discussed in Chapter 6 (see Figure 7-4).

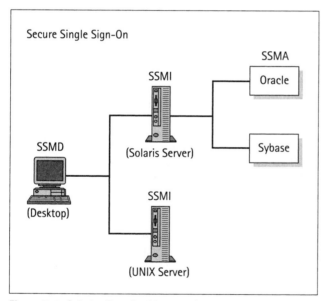

Figure 7-4: Solstice Security Manager for Intranets implements a single sign-on at the enterprise level.

SSMI provides a central security management platform, including single sign-on and auditing for a network of heterogeneous machines and applications. It controls access through access routes, which are specified for each user or user class. The security administrator can use this feature to control access by specifying access method, where users are accessing from or where they are accessing to, and what time or day access is to be granted. Furthermore, SSMI controls authentication by tying it to these access routes, so all users in an access route must use the same authentication method. Methods include password, UNIX password, single sign-on, and secure single sign-on.

Password administration in SSMI is such that the security administrator can establish rules for password length, life span, and format. SSMI also prohibits reuse of passwords.

Features of Security Manager for Intranets include the following:

◆ Central administration of login rights for any UNIX system in the network

◆ Password control

◆ Multiple administrators for security

◆ Logging of user sessions and security-related activities

◆ Security integrity checking and user inactivity monitoring

SSMI offers support for multiple UNIX platforms as well as Windows environments. Some of the key elements of SSMI include the following:

◆ **Access control.** SSMI embraces the concept of access routes, which are specified for each individual user or user class. An access route lets the manager control access to systems by access method, place of origin, and time of access.

◆ **Authentication control.** All users in an access route use the same authentication method. This restriction allows the administrator to define different authentication methods for each access method, depending on policy.

◆ **Password administration.** Easy-to-guess passwords are not allowed. As the administrator, you can set up rules for minimum password length, password life span, and password format. You can ban certain words as passwords. The reuse of passwords is also prohibited.

◆ **Secure single sign-on.** SSMI manages secure single sign-on services between desktops and applications. The authentication process is transparent to the end user and is based on public-key technology.

◆ **User administration.** The administrator can create new users, specify user account and password life spans, and specify automatic time-outs.

◆ **User class and host group.** In environments with possibly thousands of users, access controls can be simplified through the use of user classes. A user class sets out a common set of access rights that applies to all members of the group.

◆ **Blocking users.** Users can be blocked manually or even automatically if certain events trigger it. This feature is used to block intruders from gaining access by impersonating a valid user, without requiring you to destroy the valid user's account information. Events that can trigger a block include too many failed login attempts, invalid password, or an expired password or user account.

◆ **Real-time monitoring.** Probably at any given time in any company at least a handful of people are working on sensitive documents. What happens when those people walk away from their workstations? Whether it's to go outside and smoke, use the bathroom, or get something out of a file cabinet, it's still a security risk. SSMI monitors all workstations, and after a predetermined period of inactivity, logs out the user or locks the display.

◆ **Integrity checking.** This periodic monitoring process checks the system for potential security problems at the operating system level. This feature generates a report file for later analysis.

◆ **Log administration.** Solstice Security Manager logs system activities and user activities for later evaluation.

◆ **Subadministration.** SSMI administration and system administration can be delegated without having to give out the superuser "root" password to a subadministrator.

◆ **Web browser interface.** Administration is done via a distributed Web browser, locally on the SSMI server or securely over the network, via Solstice Security Manager for Desktops with session encryption.

◆ **Replica server.** The master server holds the original copy of the security database. Redundant servers have just read-only copies of the database, which are updated from the master server.

Solstice Security Manager for Desktops

Solstice Security Manager for Desktops (SSMD) is the client software component of the Security Manager family. You use it to manage desktop security. The central focus of SSMD is to provide, from the desktop, secure single sign-on capability to mission-critical applications and servers in a mixed environment. Advanced public-key technology is used for authentication. Sun also plans to make smart card technology available for SSMD. The desktop software offers strong access controls, including boot protection for the host, local file encryption, integrity checks, digital signatures, system monitoring, and automatic screen locking. These features are centrally managed by the Solstice Security Manager for Intranets product.

Some of the advantages of SSMD include the following:

♦ **Single sign-on.** SSMD supports a single sign-on to legacy environments, including NetWare, LAN Manager, and MVS mainframes.

♦ **Secure single sign-on.** SSMD can provide secure single sign-on to UNIX servers managed by SSMI or applications running SSMA.

♦ **Local authentication.** SSMD requires users to log in to the desktop. The user can make three attempts to log in successfully; if login fails after three attempts, the desktop is locked and the administrator will have to unlock it.

♦ **User access control.** The desktop can have different user categories: administration, user, or guest.

♦ **Personal Security Device.** The Personal Security Device (PSD) is an encrypted file on the local disk that contains information about the organization and unit to which the user belongs, private RSA keys, and certificates. Each PSD can contain up to ten keys. One is a personal key and the others are group keys.

♦ **Digital signatures.** With a digital signature, a document can be signed so that a recipient who possesses the sender's public key can have confidence that the document has not been altered and was signed using the private key that corresponds to the signer's public key.

♦ **Boot protection.** This service helps to protect PCs by not allowing access to the hard disk if the system is booted from a diskette.

♦ **File and directory protection.** Specified files or directories can be encrypted automatically to protect data against unauthorized access.

♦ **Real-time monitoring for inactivity.** After a preset period of time, if no keyboard entry or mouse movement has been made, the session can be locked and the password must be re-entered before the workstation can be used again.

Solstice Security Manager for Applications

Solstice Security Manager for Applications (SSMA) gives managers the ability to control access to individual, Solaris-based applications running Sybase or Oracle. This ability is critical to implementing an effective single sign-on mechanism. Sun also plans to expand the technology to Windows NT and HP-UX.

SSMA can reside on a Solaris server running Oracle and Sybase applications. It communicates to desktops running the Solstice Security Manager for Desktops application to facilitate a secure single sign-on and session encryption.

Summary

In this chapter, you learned about the following:

- The major systems/network management platforms contain some native security functions; these are often supplemented by third-party add-on programs.

- A distributed environment is inherently more complex than a centralized one. Because applications, processing, and other tasks are distributed throughout the enterprise, the network manager must address complicated security issues such as access control, applications management, and real-time monitoring.

- The Desktop Management Interface is a common standard for managing different applications. It greatly simplifies network and security management by relieving some of the learning difficulties and making operations more intuitive.

Chapter 8

Network Monitors and Other Security Programs

IN THIS CHAPTER

- ◆ Security programs and enforcing policy

- ◆ "Farmer's Law"

- ◆ Getting in through the Web server

- ◆ A new security standard

- ◆ Giving the Devil his due

SECURITY GURU DAN FARMER, creator of the controversial SATAN program (Security Administrator Tool for Analyzing Networks), tells us that "The security on a computer system degrades in direct proportion to the amount you use the system." This truism is known as "Farmer's Law."

Farmer accurately postulates that most security problems happen because of humans, not because of the computers themselves. The system administrator may make a typo or misconfigure a system, or a user may select a poor password or have sloppy security habits. For example, a user who sticks a note with his password on it squarely on the computer screen's edge is asking for trouble. While education may eliminate many of these instances, in larger environments it is more difficult to keep under control. In other words, the more people on the system, the more instances of security violations will occur.

Because most problems are due to human error or oversight, a rigorously enforced security policy is essential. In fact, most attacks occur when the attacker spots an open hole that could have otherwise been closed by simply enforcing a policy item and deploying a simple feature of the operating system or third-party software. Closing up security holes is usually not technically difficult; indeed, it typically involves deploying features already present in the operating system, or running third-party utilities.

Most commercial business and productivity software is not created to offer strong security. Rather, it is created to offer ease of use, and because of competitive pressures, it is created in the shortest period of time possible. However, specialty vendors can save the day with specialized security products. These third-party products are plentiful and may be just the ticket to securing your network. Some are free, some are cheap, and some are outrageously expensive but worth every penny.

Welcome Screens

It is common practice for a welcome screen to appear after a network connection has been made. The presence of a welcome screen causes some legal confusion, because it may be argued that the system is inviting the person who has made the connection (who may be an unfriendly attacker) to log in. The welcome screen also identifies the company name and often includes other information that may be valuable to an attacker.

Instead of merely welcoming the user and requesting a password, a welcome screen may also take an extra precaution in light of this gray area. Before logging in, the user should be asked to confirm, with a simple yes or no response, whether they are authorized to use the computer, and if they agree to access only data to which they are entitled.

While this precaution will not deter an unscrupulous attacker, it may eliminate this touchy legal question should it arise, and may further provide an audit track that can be used later should an employee misuse the system.

Monitoring the Web Server

The server itself must be continuously monitored and protected. Firewalls are wonderful tools, but they are not meant to be islands of security. The firewall is only one piece of a very large puzzle. Attackers may still be able to get through the firewall; or, if an attack has an internal origin, the firewall will not stop the attack. No firewall, software, or device can completely prevent attack, but you can take steps to find out immediately when an attack occurs.

A standard way that attackers get to sensitive machines is to first gain access to a machine (such as a Web server) that is easier to hack into. The hackers then use that as a starting point to jump to other points on the network using Telnet, rlogin, RSH, FTP, or RCP. Software tools such as WebStalker can detect when this type of jump is being attempted. WebStalker Pro is included in the CD-ROM that comes with this book. It goes beyond the functionality of the firewall and can detect the following activities:

◆ Unauthorized users logging into the Web site

◆ User attempts to illegally take over Administrator privileges and, therefore, take over the Web site

◆ A hacker using your Web site to jump to other machines that may hold sensitive data

◆ Vandalism of the Web site

◆ An illegal shutdown of a Web server

WebStalker Pro uses an intuitive interview process to help you create a security policy to protect the Web server.

Assume, for example, that someone has vandalized your Web site. You then decide to implement WebStalker Pro to prevent further occurrences of vandalism. The six steps involved are all fairly straightforward:

1. Begin the WebStalker Pro interview by clicking Start Interview to Customize the Security Policy.

2. Select the type of activity you want to monitor. Several options are available, including illegal logins, illegal privilege usage, daytime and nighttime hours, illegal file access, and illegal Web server shutdown. Selecting Illegal File Access specifically addresses the vandalism issue, and brings you to another menu.

3. You are shown a set of permissions for daytime and nighttime usage. You can set permissions to allow all users access, selected users access, or no users access. The Selected User option enables you to specify who has access and keep out the rest.

4. You are then taken to a file menu, where you select the files for which access should be restricted.

5. Then, you decide how you want WebStalker Pro to respond when it detects an illegal file access. You can select more than one option from the following:

   ■ Kill the offending process

   ■ Kill the offending login

   ■ Disable logins by the offending user

   ■ Shun logins by the offending user

   ■ Generate an SNMP trap

   ■ Page the administrator

   ■ Pass a message to syslog

   ■ Send mail to the administrator

   ■ Record the incident in the log file

6. In this step, you specify an e-mail address to which the program sends notifications if an illegal file access occurs. You can specify different addresses for daytime and nighttime.

Open Platform for Secure Enterprise Connectivity

Check Point Software's Open Platform for Secure Enterprise Connectivity (OPSEC) presents a platform for integrating and managing enterprise security through an open and extensible management framework. OPSEC includes a series of published APIs, supports industry-standard protocols, and offers a high-level scripting language. OPSEC enables you to define enterprise security by a single, enterprise-wide policy, and enables you to integrate several different security applications into Check Point's FireWall-1 system.

An alliance between Check Point and Haystack Labs (now Trusted Information Systems) serves as an example of how a firewall can work with additional monitoring software. Haystack's WebStalker Pro monitoring software can now be integrated with Check Point's FireWall-1 system through the open OPSEC standard. This integration immediately communicates information about attacks to the firewall, which in turn blocks the attacker's access to key servers.

OPSEC has been made into an industry-wide standard through the OPSEC Alliance, an open industry group founded by Check Point Software Technologies. The goal of the OPSEC Alliance is to guarantee interoperability at the policy level between multiple vendors' security products, by providing an open and extensible framework.

A number of standard protocols already ensure multivendor interoperability between security products. OPSEC supports several of these standards, including:

◆ **Remote Authentication Dial-In User Service (RADIUS).** RADIUS is a proposed IETF (Internet Engineering Task Force) standard used for the authentication of dial-up users. Through RADIUS, different vendor security products can be used to authenticate a connection, so long as the equipment at either end of the connection is RADIUS-compliant.

◆ **Manual IPSec, SIP, and ISAKMP (Internet Secure Association Key Management Protocol) Encryption Protocols.** Encryption algorithms such as DES guarantee the privacy of information being transmitted electronically. However, in addition to the encryption algorithm, a common protocol must be specified to define the packet formats and a common key management scheme. Standardization of this common protocol is being developed by the IETF IPSec (IP security) working group. The first such specification, Manual IPSec, has already been ratified. Manual IPSec requires manual configuration and exchange of keys.

◆ **ISAKMP Oakley Standard.** As a follow-on to Manual IPSec, the ISAKMP Oakley Standard has been proposed. ISAKMP Oakley handles key exchanges transparently for end users. **SKIP (Simple Key Management for IP)** is another IPSec standard protocol that is commonly used on Sun Microsystems platforms such as Solaris, which also features an automated key exchange mechanism.

◆ **X.509 Certificates.** X.509 forms the basis of Public Key Infrastructures (PKI), which use certificates and Certificate Authorities to guarantee that users are who they claim to be, or that they have the authority to undertake a specific transaction, such as a credit card payment. X.509 certificates are used by ISAKMP as a way to obtain the public keys used to establish an encrypted connection, and to verify the authenticity of the parties involved in the transaction.

◆ **SNMP (Simple Network Management Protocol).** This is the protocol used by network devices to exchange management information with a central management console. Most network management systems, such as HP OpenView or Sun Microsystems' Solstice, can exchange messages with an SNMP-based system.

◆ **Lightweight Directory Access Protocol (LDAP).** LDAP is a standard for exchanging information between directory services. OPSEC-compliant applications use LDAP to integrate naming services. LDAP can be used to retrieve user information such as X.509 certificates stored on a central directory. LDAP can further be used to set up a centralized account management system, and it can unify the storage and retrieval of other user-related information across an enterprise.

OPSEC-specific APIs, defined by Check Point, include:

◆ **Content Vectoring Protocol (CVP).** CVP is used to implement content validation and checking of messages or attachments.

◆ **URL Filtering Protocol (UFP).** UFP is used to enforce access control to external Web sites.

◆ **Suspicious Activity Monitoring Protocol (SAMP).** SAMP is used to integrate applications that detect suspicious activity with Check Point's FireWall-1.

◆ **Log Export API (LEA).** LEA is used by external applications to retrieve log information for processing.

Application Management

A particularly effective approach to security management is to use a *security framework* as opposed to merely collecting separate, unintegrated security applications. A framework, such as BMC Software's PATROL or Enhance Systems' OmegaVision, integrates a number of application management and security-related products into a common management framework. These offerings typically take a "best-of-breed" approach, and offer a single console view of the entire network, increased automation, and the capability to correlate management processes across systems.

Application management is the process of managing services provided by an application. It involves the central management of those applications' critical elements. It extends the processes of client/server systems management disciplines to the application level, and optimizes the service provided to end users by integrating and centralizing management of the system's critical elements – including databases, middleware, and other processes. Part of this central management, of course, is security.

Applications management minimizes costs and improves service levels in several ways, including maximizing application uptime, automating application management tasks, and speeding the deployment of new applications.

Incorporating security management into the application management function helps improve service levels by reducing data corruption and data theft and by maximizing computer uptime.

The application management function should ideally support a mixed computing environment and should be policy-based. As discussed in Part I, the first and most important element of implementing a secure network is creating a policy. Only after creating the policy can software be implemented. You should be able to customize this software to meet your company's specific security policy. Furthermore, the software should be capable of monitoring the system to spot instances in which the security policy has been breached, provide for authentication, and provide for access controls.

Both Enhance Systems' OmegaVision and BMC's PATROL use a third-party, "best-of-breed" approach to combine integrated products into a common application management platform. These third-party offerings include a number of security-related products that address security needs such as the following:

◆ Event monitoring

◆ Backup and recovery

◆ Customizing and controlling the attributes of specific applications

BMC's PATROL Management suite integrates AXENT Technologies' AXENT OmniGuard security management solutions to add security management to the application management infrastructure.

Unify offers a similar plan with its VISION application management strategy. AppMan, part of the VISION development environment, addresses all major areas of application management. VISION includes an event facility for automatic monitoring and alerting for predefined events. It also includes an SNMP agent, so a VISION event can generate an SNMP trap that can be received by the major network management platforms (NetView, OpenView, SunNet Manager). As with the other products mentioned, Unify plans to integrate popular security management systems into AppMan.

The need for application management is even more evident as the computer industry evolves away from centralized computing to embrace the client/server paradigm. As mission-critical applications become part of a distributed environment, it is important that some of the same rigorous management that has always been applied to a centralized environment also be applied to distributed applications.

Application management encompasses the configuration of each application. Configuration is an essential consideration in a secure environment; without centralized control over configuration, a worker may unintentionally misconfigure the system and may even bring down the entire network. Therefore, application management must be able to track all configurations throughout the distributed enterprise. One standard used for this purpose is the Desktop Management Task Force's Management Information Format (MIF), which is adhered to by many application management products.

A major purpose of application management is to ensure that security policies are not unintentionally violated by applications. This responsibility falls to the application developer, who must ensure that applications do not transmit unencrypted passwords or violate any other security policy.

Lastly, asset and license management is also a critical part of application management; this process should also be automated and flexible. Automated license management not only saves time, but it can also save money by keeping track of how many licenses are actually needed (so you don't overbuy). And it helps prevent piracy or the presence of unauthorized software.

Proxy Servers

A firewall may serve as a first line of defense, but by no means can it offer a complete security solution. In fact, Dan Farmer, the creator of SATAN, goes so far as to say "a firewall isn't that important," when compared to the importance of a strong security policy. One major disadvantage of a firewall is that it keeps internal users from taking advantage of technologies such as streaming audio.

A *proxy server* may be a good alternative to relying solely on a firewall for protection. This software-based utility works with the firewall and functions as a piece of middleware that sits between the internal network and the Internet. Whenever an internal user wants to issue a command or make a request, the request is made to the proxy server, which runs on a firewall machine. The proxy server then forwards the request to the remote server outside the firewall, takes the information, and transfers it on to the requester. Consequently, the internal users never have direct contact with remote Internet hosts but can still take advantage of all of their services, such as streaming audio.

A proxy differs from a standard packet filter solution. A packet filter determines whether a packet can be forwarded based on its IP address or TCP port number. The proxy goes a step further than the packet filter by making a connection with the secure internal network and the insecure Internet simultaneously. Although performance will be somewhat slower than a standard packet filter solution, it is much more secure.

Besides transferring requests and information, some proxy servers can also store data in a local cache to improve performance. Caching enables a frequently requested Web page to be stored locally, so it does not have to be retrieved every time. The cache should be kept on the proxy server rather than on each individual client to save overall disk space and provide for more efficient distribution of frequently requested documents.

Proxy logging can also provide a good audit trail for attack analysis. A great deal of transaction data can be logged, such as client IP address, date and time, URL, byte count, and fields in any HTTP transaction.

Several commercial proxy servers are available, including the Microsoft Proxy Server discussed in Chapter 16, or Netscape Communications' Proxy Server offering.

Risk Analysis Tools

Risk analysis, as discussed in Part I, represents an early part of security implementation. The results of the analysis will mold the security policy. In turn, the policy will mold what specific products and procedures are implemented.

Software tools are available to help with risk analysis. An appropriate risk analysis tool will get you through the risk analysis process by automating many of the tasks involved. Risk analysis tools focus mainly on three tasks: collecting data, analyzing data, and generating output.

The National Institute of Standards and Technology (NIST) makes the following recommendations concerning risk analysis:

♦ The software should contain modules for data collection, analysis, and output.

♦ It should be compatible with all software and hardware currently in use.

♦ The type of information required from the software's reporting facility should be clearly defined.

♦ The tool should maintain a history of all information collected for subsequent review.

In general, the risk analysis software should help you address the following questions:

- ◆ What can go wrong?

- ◆ What is the likelihood of each incident occurring?

- ◆ What is the impact of each incident?

- ◆ How can each incident be prevented or minimized?

- ◆ What is an acceptable level of risk?

Risk management involves the selection of various safeguards that address specific threats, and is basically an organized process for finding your system's vulnerabilities. The risk management/analysis process involves defining the sources of potential threats, and which assets are vulnerable to loss or other damage. The risk management software should help in this process. While safeguards may never completely eliminate every possible threat, they can reduce the likelihood of threats, minimize their impact, and reduce losses to an acceptable level. The risk analysis software helps the security manager determine where the greatest risks are most likely to occur and decide where to apply safeguards for the best results.

The risk analysis process identifies all critical assets that need protection and also considers each asset's environment.

An automated risk analysis tool can usually evaluate weaknesses much more quickly than if the process were done manually. Not only will a quick analysis save time and money, but it also minimizes the possibility that the results are outdated by the time the study is completed.

These tools use a variety of techniques to analyze risk; some use estimation schemes, and some use fuzzy reasoning, event trees, Monte Carlo simulations, or other mechanisms.

One potential risk of the risk analysis software itself is the database it generates. This database contains a great deal of information about the company's vulnerabilities and other sensitive data. If this data should happen to fall into the wrong hands, it can cause as much trouble as it could potentially save you. Some risk analysis tools have built-in security controls to prevent an attacker from accessing this data. In addition, the risk analysis database file should be access-controlled.

The risk analysis process differs from the security audit discussed in Chapter 9. Whereas a security audit reviews an existing system and spots security problems, a risk assessment is more of a planning tool designed to create or improve a system. It identifies current threats and potential threats, what assets face possible danger, and where controls are required. A recommended procedure for risk analysis follows:

1. Organize a task force to conduct the analysis. The task force gains the support of management in carrying out the analysis and all that it entails.

2. Identify all assets subject to loss and rank their importance.

3. Identify all potential threats to the identified assets.

4. Identify all controls that are already in place, and areas where no controls exist.

5. Identify vulnerabilities. A vulnerability exists whenever a potential threat exists, an asset is subject to loss or damage, or mitigating controls are lacking.

6. Evaluate vulnerabilities in terms of potential loss.

7. Identify what actions or controls may reduce risks and losses.

8. Recommend a plan to reduce risk to an acceptable level.

9. Execute the plan and establish ongoing maintenance.

So where are the weak areas you are supposed to pinpoint? They could be in several places, but the first place to look is beyond the computer itself. One of the biggest vulnerable areas is in the manual handling of data before it is entered into the computer, or after it has been retrieved in hard copy form. Certain types of data may be highly sensitive, and may be afforded a great deal of control once it is in the system, but while that data is still sitting on the data entry clerk's desk, it is just another piece of paper that anyone can see. Policy should dictate a secure procedure for entering sensitive data into the system. For example, policy should state that clerks entering sensitive data should be in a controlled location; failing that, caution should be taken so that the sensitive data is never left unattended.

SATAN

The Security Administrator Tool for Analyzing Networks (SATAN) program, created by computer security expert Dan Farmer in 1995, has been both controversial and useful at the same time. The SATAN program gives computer network administrators a tool for finding security vulnerabilities in their UNIX networks and filling in the holes before they're used by attackers. It can recognize several common security problems. With each problem it detects, it offers a brief tutorial to explain the nature of the problem and what you can do to correct it. The tool does not actually break into the network, but merely gathers information that is available to anyone with access. The notorious tool has shown that an incredibly large percentage of the World Wide Web is vulnerable to attack.

SATAN is a double-edged sword, though; hackers can use it to infiltrate computer networks. SATAN is easy to use, highly automated, and attractively graphical, which makes the network administrator's job easier — unfortunately, however, it also makes the hacker's job easier.

Some of the more common problems found by SATAN include the following:

◆ NFS (Network File System) file systems exported to arbitrary hosts

◆ NFS exported to unprivileged programs

◆ NFS exported via the portmapper

◆ NIS password file access from arbitrary hosts

◆ Old (that is, before 8.6.10) Sendmail versions

◆ REXD access from arbitrary hosts

◆ X server access control-disabled

◆ Arbitrary files accessible via FTP

◆ Remote shell access from arbitrary hosts

◆ Writable anonymous FTP home directory

SATAN sports a clean, intuitive interface that is built with HTML pages and makes strong use of HTML forms for entering information. When the program detects a vulnerability, it describes it and may explain how an intruder would use it to execute an attack. SATAN is built on an inference engine, which contains five rule bases that permit the program to deduce problems based on a set of known facts. For example, SATAN can easily detect which version of Sendmail is being used. If the system is running a version earlier than 8.6.10, it is easy to deduce that a vulnerability exists. New rules can easily be added to these bases.

Farmer did an informal study in 1996 that revealed some startling results. His paper, "Security Survey of Key Internet Hosts & Various Semi-Relevant Reflections," (http://www.trouble.org/survey) discusses his informal security survey of 2,200 computing systems on the Internet. For his study, Farmer selected high-profile and commercial Web sites such as banks, government agencies, and newspapers. Permission was not sought ahead of time, although Farmer's study was nonintrusive. According to the study, nearly two-thirds of the sites had a serious security problem.

This is especially frightening when considering the current push toward Internet-based electronic commerce. Banks are starting to offer Internet-related services; one must wonder whether they are indeed safe and secure. Because of this concern, Farmer chose to focus on banks, government agencies, and other sites engaged in Internet commerce. Farmer deduces that more than 60 percent of these sites could be broken into and network functions impacted by an outside attacker.

Despite the fact that Farmer made no attempts at hiding his presence, only three sites out of more two thousand contacted him after his study. It is interesting to note that although Farmer is well-known as a security expert, the methods he used were minimal and could be used by anybody with marginal experience. This fact makes his survey all the more frightening. Farmer used the SATAN program, which is widely available, at a minimal scan level.

Farmer says that even more of the hosts could be compromised through more advanced techniques, such as spoofing, or name service attacks. Although Farmer drew the line at illegal procedures, an attacker intent on destroying a network would not necessarily have the same consideration. Thus, an even greater majority of sites than the 60 percent Farmer cites would be vulnerable to attack by an unscrupulous attacker.

In his paper, Farmer says to keep in mind that no hosts were actually broken into during the course of his study. "However," he warns, "there are many ways to detect potential problems without actually breaking into a system. Some of these problems are due to ignorance or host or network misconfigurations, but many of them are taken from CERT advisories." Specifically, the problems Farmer was able to examine included FTP, NFS, Sendmail, and WWW server-specific vulnerabilities.

Farmer marvels at the simplicity with which he, or even less sophisticated tinkerers, can gather information from a remote host simply by connecting to it. Much of this is pure deductive logic. Farmer gives an obvious example:

> You can often tell what sort of system it is and what vulnerabilities exist – for instance, if you determine that a system is running the Apache Web server, you can deduce that it is a UNIX system, because the Apache server only runs (currently) on UNIX hosts. Furthermore, if a CERT advisory warns you about security problems about a version of Sendmail and tells you to run a new version of it, you can tell if a system is vulnerable or not by connecting to the SMTP and looking at the version number listed. Most network services are very friendly and will give you all sorts of information if you ask nicely. This is one of the main methods that SATAN uses to determine weaknesses in remote systems.

Farmer points out that most attackers are not computer geniuses or even all that sophisticated. Most of the problems that occur are simply the result of carelessness or inattention on the part of the administrator.

Farmer's report points out several common reasons why systems become insecure. The solutions to these problems may be simple, but they are not always obvious to the administrator and are often overlooked:

♦ **Running too many services on one server.** Configuration problems and confusion relating to the Web, name service protocols, and other network services can contribute to security problems.

♦ **Commercialization.** Stiff competition often results in poorly designed and tested software. Because security is not high on the list of customer desires, it is often neglected in the development stage.

◆ **Lack of a total solution.** Site security cannot be achieved simply by installing a firewall and letting it run. Farmer's Law states that "the security on a computer system degrades in direct proportion to the amount you use the system," despite the presence of a firewall and other tools. The firewall is a useful tool, although it is only one small part of a total solution. Tight security actually involves two areas: secure communication and secure endpoints. Secure communication involves cryptography, authentication, and encryption. Unfortunately, current government laws prohibit the use of any reasonably useful encryption technology. The endpoints, both clients and servers, should also be reasonably secure.

Farmer offers three solutions that are essential to good security:

◆ Continuous monitoring.

◆ Employing a third party to periodically run security programs, patch security vulnerabilities, and provide information about the latest bugs and security programs relevant to your system.

◆ Receiving a "stamp of approval" or certification of security. This is currently not possible, as no organizations exist to monitor sites and issue security assurances.

CIAC (Computer Incident Advisory Capability) recommends the following steps for preparing your network for SATAN:

◆ Examine your system for the vulnerabilities that SATAN is capable of spotting and implement security fixes.

◆ Read CIAC's advisories on those specific vulnerabilities.

◆ Contact your software vendors for information on the availability of any security patches that have been created, and make sure that all such patches have been installed.

◆ Use a security tool to help assess and improve your site's security. You may choose to run SATAN itself on your site to determine what vulnerabilities it may spot. However, make sure to read the documentation and use SATAN with caution. It is possible to accidentally probe a system that you did not intend to probe; that system may see that probe as an unfriendly attack. Select the probe level appropriately and with caution.

◆ If you run SATAN, make sure that nobody else has read access to the SATAN directory.

CIAC, an organization operated by the U.S. Department of Energy, provides advisories on computer security issues, discussion forums, and a virus database. Although it was organized primarily to provide incident handling services to the Department of Energy and its contractors, its useful advisories are freely available at `http://ciac.llnl.gov/`.

Standardizing Security

In his paper, "Security Survey of Key Internet Hosts & Various Semi-Relevant Reflections" (`http://www.trouble.org/survey`), Dan Farmer brings up the idea of a "stamp of approval" or certification of security for attesting to the thoroughness and effectiveness of any security implementation. To receive this certification, a firm's security policy would have to meet a set of security standards and have certain security practices in place.

Because every company has a different policy based on its own individual needs, such a certificate would not mandate specific security tools or procedures. Instead, the tools and procedures used would depend on the policy itself.

This type of "standard" is not uncommon. Accounting has a set of Generally Accepted Accounting Practices, and surfers (ocean surfers, not Web surfers) have a set of rules they live by. But alas, the computer industry has no set of Generally Accepted Computer Security Practices, no official set of guidelines, no central authority from which guidance can be derived.

The United Kingdom has taken the first step toward implementing this type of certification. Great Britain's Department of Trade and Industry introduced a new British Standard in January 1997 (BS 7799), known as the "Code of Practice for Information Security Management." The standard started being enforced by the end of 1997.

BS 7799 introduces a common framework for companies to develop, implement, and measure their security management. BS 7799 includes a recommendation for the development of a business continuity plan, which would promote disaster recovery after an emergency. The code is based on the security practices already in place by some of the country's leading international firms.

Consultants are already in place to audit British companies for BS 7799 compliance. The code may break out of the U.K. eventually, as it is currently under review by ISO for acceptance as an international standard. BS 7799 has received almost universal acceptance in larger companies with more than 10,000 employees.

The National Computing Centre's Information Security Breaches Survey 1996 showed that overall, 47 percent of about 9,500 respondents were aware of BS 7799. One of five had reviewed their own standards against BS 7799, and 50 percent said that they plan to do so.

Interestingly, nearly 80 percent of the respondents reported at least one security breach, and the number of respondents reporting computer-related theft has risen 60 percent since the previous survey, which took place in 1994. The survey also showed an increase in incidents that resulted from user error, up from 23 percent in 1994 to 34 percent in 1996. The latter statistic underscores the need for centralized security management and strict controls over user configuration. The Centre shows the average cost of an incident to be nearly £16,000, with the most expensive incident being a theft worth £750,000.

Although implementation of a standard may not eliminate attacks and security breaches completely, adhering to standards will minimize the impact of a breach and reduce the number of attacks that are possible due to poor security.

We often learn our lessons too late, after an attack has already occurred. The Centre's survey confirms this fact by reporting that in 56 percent of reported incidents, corporate security standards were amended or new measures were implemented after the incident.

The United States National Institute for Standards and Technology (NIST) has no corollary to BS 7799, but does offer some general advice for security. NIST's Minimal Security Functional Requirements for Multi-User Operational Systems highlights eight major security functions that are important to any secure system:

- Identification and authentication
- Access control
- Accountability
- Audit trails
- Object reuse
- Accuracy
- Reliability
- Data exchange

(continued)

Standardizing Security *(continued)*

NIST's research and development focuses mainly on the development of a common, interoperable cryptographic security technology, Public Key Infrastructure, and APIs for cryptographic modules. NIST's development efforts in this area include standards, guidance on the use of cryptography, and conformance testing. Specifically, these recommendations include the following FIPS (Federal Information Processing Specification):

- ◆ **FIPS 140-1.** Security Requirements for Cryptographic Modules

- ◆ **FIPS 46-2 and 81.** Data Encryption Standard (DES) and DES Modes of Operation

- ◆ **FIPS 186 and 180-1.** Digital Signature Standard (DSS) and Secure Hash Standard (SHS)

- ◆ **FIPS 113.** Computer Data Authentication, which specifies the generation of a Message Authentication Code (MAC) from ANSI X9.9

- ◆ **FIPS 171.** Key Management Using ANSI X9.17

Validation testing for the first three standards falls under the Cryptographic Module Validation Program, which is overseen by NIST and the Communications Security Establishment of the Government of Canada.

Further NIST research involves examining secure, interoperable systems, and advanced measures such as intrusion detection, firewalls and scanning tools, vulnerability analysis, access control and incident response, security metrics, and Internet security.

While SATAN can be used against you, you can use it to your benefit and as a means of evaluating your own network. SATAN is easy to use, and once you execute it, the program walks you through all of the procedures required to analyze your system.

Once executed, SATAN asks you for the name of the system you want to evaluate, and what level scan you wish to perform. SATAN can be configured at one of three scan levels:

- ◆ **Light.** A light scan is the least intrusive. In a light scan, the program gathers information from the Domain Name Service, and establishes which Remote Procedure Calls the host offers and what file systems it shares over the network.

- ◆ **Normal.** A normal scan probes for the existence of common network services, such as finger, remote login, FTP, or Gopher. Once SATAN obtains this information, it determines the operating system type and release version.

- ◆ **Heavy.** A heavy scan is the most intrusive, and discovers everything a normal scan does, but in more detail. A heavy scan also checks for specific vulnerabilities.

SATAN Remedies

Clearly, SATAN is a wonderful tool for discovering where your network's weak spots are – so long as other less benevolent individuals don't use it for the same purpose. You can, however, find out if someone is attempting to use SATAN on your network. The best way to protect your network against a SATAN-based snoop is to run SATAN yourself and fix all the vulnerabilities it reports. However, other products can help you detect a SATAN attack in progress.

USING GABRIEL

A free SATAN detector, called Gabriel, is available on the Internet (http://www. lat.com/gabe.htm). This tool issues a warning to the network or security administrator if anyone attempts to use SATAN or another similar tool on your network.

Gabriel was created by UNIX security software vendor Los Altos Technologies. It detects any unauthorized network probing by looking for suspicious hosts. Gabriel examines all TCP (Transmission Control Protocol), UDP (User Datagram Protocol), and ICMP (Internet Control Message Protocol) packets and records them in a database. Gabriel then scans the database periodically to determine if any hosts are requesting connection to a large number of services.

Gabriel is available only for Sun platforms. It comes prebuilt and is written entirely in C.

USING COURTNEY

Another similar program is Courtney, which was developed by CIAC. Courtney monitors the network and identifies the source machines of SATAN probes or attacks.

Courtney works with tcpdump to count the number of new services a machine executes within a certain period of time. If a given machine connects with several services within that period of time, it is reasonable to deduce that a probe is underway.

You can find Courtney at http://ciac.llnl.gov/ciac/ToolsUnixNetMon.html#Courtney.

Summary

In this chapter, we talked about the following:

◆ A firewall is only one small part of an effective security system. The firewall and other security software packages are merely tools that can be used to execute a strong security policy.

◆ A proxy server adds software to the firewall. It takes requests from users inside the firewall, and reissues the requests to the remote host. Information is then taken from the remote host by the proxy, and redirected to the internal user.

◆ Application management is the process of managing the services provided by an application. It encompasses central management of security from an application perspective, and includes event monitoring, backup and recovery, license and asset management, and configuration management.

◆ SATAN is a user-friendly tool that you can use to figure out how to break into a system, or to determine how somebody else might break into your system. In the latter case, SATAN points out your network's vulnerabilities and provides advice on correcting problems.

◆ The British Standard (BS) 7799, the Code of Practice for Information Security Management, may have the potential to be an international standard. BS 7799 lays out a set of generally accepted security practices that help minimize the impact of security breaches.

Chapter 9

Security Audits

I'VE OFTEN MADE THE point that policy is the most important part of security; indeed, it is even more important than the software and hardware tools that are used to carry out the policy. Policy forms the framework, the foundation of the actual security implementation. Without it, the best security software in the world is ineffective.

Secondary to policy, but still of great importance, is auditing. Auditing gives you a guarantee that things are working according to plan. The purpose is to make sure that the security policy, which you have already put in place at this point, is being carried out. Policy without implementation is useless; and to take security issues a step further, implementation without auditing is also of little use – because of the obvious importance of knowing whether that implementation is actually doing what it was meant to do.

In a big, multivendor network, it is important to have such a guarantee. In a small network of just a few computers, it may be possible to see whether everything is working and whether it complies with policy through an informal and cursory review; however, with a network of a significant size, a formalized audit and formal auditing tools are an absolute necessity.

The Usefulness of an Audit

Audits have a number of direct and indirect benefits in addition to enhancing the network's general security and integrity. Audits can be useful in subsequent troubleshooting because the help desk can have a ready resource of configuration information on every machine. It can also help protect against viruses by making sure that executables do not change between audits. It ensures that no pirated copies of software exist in your network and can even save money by tracking how many copies of a particular program have been legitimately purchased. Most software companies offer volume discounts – if every department in your company buys ten copies of a program independently of each other, your company may qualify for a volume discount and not know it.

Having a thorough knowledge of what software is installed on the company's computers is extremely important for a number of reasons. A company will want to know whether it may be subject to prosecution because unlicensed software is being used; it may also wish to have knowledge of any unauthorized software, such as games, custom-made programs, and so on.

You have two reasons to control unauthorized software on the network. The first and most obvious is simply a productivity factor – if too many people are loading the latest version of DOOM on their PCs, you may not be getting your money's worth out of them. Of course, how much freedom your employees have in terms of games and Internet access is in large part a Human Resources issue that goes beyond the scope of this book.

The second reason, however, pertains more closely to security. If unauthorized programs exist on the network, that means someone other than the network administrator probably installed it. Very likely, someone not even in IS installed it. When that happens, you've lost control over your network configuration. It's simply too easy for someone to cause serious network problems without meaning to when trying to install a program.

A software audit results in a complete list of all software contained on all of the company's computers. The software audit is *not* done by disseminating a questionnaire to every user and asking them to fill it out, and it is *not* done by reviewing accounting records to see what has been purchased. It is done by actually looking at all the files on every computer and seeing what executable programs reside there. Several programs are available to automatically carry out this task by scanning every computer's hard disk and reporting what software is inside.

You may be able to audit your system using software already built in to the operating system, or you can add a network auditor to perform the audit.

Network Auditing Tools

Most network operating systems have at least some minimal type of automatic audit facility. Such features typically log all unsuccessful login attempts and system usage in a separate file that can be examined later by the security manager. Make sure that the audit feature of your network operating system is enabled, and that the log files are protected against tampering. An attacker may attempt to delete or tamper with the audit log in order to hide his or her presence.

A network auditor (or LAN auditor) is comprised of a client module and a server module. The client module monitors workstation activity and sends data to the server module, which in turn generates reports for subsequent analysis and review. The client module may determine available memory, watch to see who is accessing specific sensitive files, or identify unauthorized programs on the network.

Sometimes they can also be used to centrally manage configuration, an especially useful but often overlooked aspect of security management. Leaving workstation configuration up to each individual end user may be convenient for the administrator (at least until the system crashes), but it can easily spell disaster.

The LAN auditor should be able to record information about the software on each machine, as well as details about the hardware and configuration. The program typically contains a database of known applications, which can be updated periodically. In addition, this database should be configurable by the administrator so that custom software packages can be added to the database.

The Auditing Process

You should document your auditing process in your security policy. When writing your policy you should consider numerous factors: the users on your system, performing security drills periodically, testing parts of your auditing process, the steps to take in your audit, and how you can use the information you gather in your audit.

Human Relations Factors

Attempts to control what an individual can or cannot do with the computer that sits at his or her desk is often met with resistance and resentment. Workers who spend all day at the computer tend to regard the computer as "theirs," even though it actually belongs to the company. They tend to feel that they should be allowed to do with it what they will, load whatever programs they want to use, and prevent other people (such as network security administrators) from looking under the hood.

Resistance also comes from management, who may see audits and other procedures that do not directly contribute to the bottom line as deserving of less funding than other projects. Nonetheless, auditing of various types – financial audits, tax audits, and many other types of audits – are a normal part of business life. A security audit is no different.

Knowing this, you must therefore approach the audit carefully and with a lot of tact. Present the idea to management as an essential part of business, that although it does not *directly* contribute to the bottom line, it contributes *indirectly*, and is necessary even if it didn't. As mentioned previously, it could contribute indirectly by finding opportunities for volume discounts, and by avoiding costly fines and lawsuits by eliminating pirated software or illegitimate copies of programs.

On the positive side, auditing provides a measure of accountability. Introducing accountability into the computer environment gives management a look into the activities of users, and what information they may possess or have access to. Auditing and accountability enables the company to undertake a paradigm shift, where it moves away from the older model of keeping people out to a newer model of allowing people in but monitoring their activities as they go.

Security Drills

As part of the audit process, a scheduled security drill may be conducted periodically to determine whether the procedures laid out in the security policy document are effectively implemented, and adequate to meet an anticipated threat. A drill is a very good way to test your policies and procedures.

The drill can focus on the most likely threat, or drills may alternate between possible scenarios; for example, every other drill could focus on the possibility of natural disaster, and every other one could focus on an intrusion by an outsider. When planning a drill to test your procedures and policies regarding a natural disaster, focus on those systems that will be called into action following the disaster — such as backup and recovery mechanisms. For a drill that tests your abilities to react to an intruder, arrange for an actual penetration of the system by a trusted individual. Many consultants are available who can attempt to "break into" your system for a fee.

Testing

An all-out "drill" can be disruptive to your day-to-day operation, and as such, should be an infrequent event. However, the testing of individual procedures can be done more frequently. Backup procedures, for example, should be checked regularly to make sure that data can be recovered from the tapes or other backup media. Log files should also be checked periodically to make sure that the information meant for them is actually being logged onto them.

When creating the tests that audit security policy, it is important to identify what specifically is being tested, how the test will be conducted, and what results are expected. A provision for testing and auditing should be laid out in the security policy document itself.

All aspects of the security policy, whether procedural or automated, should be tested. All tests should be comprehensive, encompassing all possibilities. For example, if testing a user logon process, both valid and invalid usernames and passwords should be used as part of the test to demonstrate proper and improper usage of the logon program.

Audit Steps

Once the procedures have been written and implemented, the auditor or auditing team takes on the task of assessing the effectiveness of these procedures. This process involves five key steps:

1. The first step of the audit is to review the system being audited; that is, review the policy behind it, its implementation, and technical details.

2. Second, the auditor examines the overall environment in which the security system is operating, and identifies techniques used to control this environment.

3. A line-by-line analysis is then undertaken to determine the effectiveness of each component of the security system.

4. A composite evaluation is then created, in which the total security system is assessed. In this step, the auditor determines in general whether the security system meets the objectives laid out by the policy document. To complete this phase of the audit, the auditor may wish to compare the results of the audit with the goals of the design team to see whether the system is accomplishing what it was meant to do. The design and audit processes are very close. Although the designer and auditor have separate functions, both work from the same base set of requirements, and the design and audit teams should communicate and cooperate – this is to make sure that the same factors that underlie the design process are taken into account for the audit.

5. In the last step, the auditor or auditing team prepares a report to document and illustrate the findings. This report should include recommendations for enhancing specific areas of security if a weakness is spotted, as well as recommendations concerning the overall security environment.

Asset Management

Part of the security audit process is asset management. By auditing and tracking what software and hardware exists where, the manager is able to keep track of configuration information, and prevent the introduction of unauthorized equipment and software.

Besides ensuring that your company is complying with software license agreements, asset management software helps control how much money your company spends on software. Asset management attempts to address these questions:

♦ Is the company buying more software than necessary?

♦ What are the terms of the software licenses? Do you need to purchase one copy for each user? Or do you have a "floating license" that allows any user to take advantage of a "pool" of licenses that are readily available?

♦ Which individuals in your company need to use which software products?

♦ Has the company been buying software for employees who do not use it?

Asset management is, therefore, not only a tool to address security issues (such as piracy and unauthorized system configuration), but cost-saving issues as well. This plays well for upper management, who often see security as a necessary evil that does not contribute to the bottom line.

Although asset management can be done manually, in a large network it is tedious and time-consuming. Vendors including Tally Systems Corp., Global Data

Security, and others offer automated software tools to take control of this area of the audit process.

The software industry loses millions each year to piracy. According to the Software Publishers Association, worldwide losses to piracy were over $8 billion in 1994. Piracy is more widespread than many managers realize. End users, file clerks, secretaries, and others who would never think of pocketing a wristwatch from the department store often think nothing of making an illegal copy of a computer program. Workers often make copies of a program from the workplace to take home, or bring in unlicensed software from home and circulate it at the workplace. The introduction of unauthorized programs, besides causing potential configuration problems, may put your company in legal jeopardy. The Copyright Act makes it illegal in the United States to reproduce copies of protected work, including software, and imposes penalties for doing so.

The Software Publishers Association and Business Software Alliance both have piracy hotlines that encourage individuals to report piracy. Both organizations receive plenty of calls, and have brought actions against many organizations in the United States and Canada. In most cases, companies are given an opportunity to submit an audit report that is compared to purchase records. Unauthorized copies are then destroyed, and legal copies are purchased.

Three types of licenses exist for software: licenses that specify one license for each PC, concurrent licensing, and site licensing. The first type is the simplest, and requires one copy of the application to be purchased for each PC on which it will run. Concurrent licensing is becoming more prevalent however. This type of licensing reduces costs by installing the software on a network drive, and enabling users with access to the network drive to share the application. For larger sites, a site license may be purchased. These typically offer volume discounts for heavy usage.

While it is important to understand what type of license you have, it is also important to maintain control over how many licenses are being purchased and how many are actually being used. In some cases, an audit may reveal, for example, licenses purchased for every person in a department, when only half the people in the department actually need the application.

Part of asset management is education. The individual in charge of asset management must educate every individual in the company about piracy and asset management, and must also make sure that everyone knows the consequences of piracy. This information should be laid out clearly in the policy manual.

As part of the asset management process, you should first set a standard for basic applications. Instead of each department using a different word processor and spreadsheet, define a single standard for these basic applications. This makes license compliance easier to monitor, and can lead to volume discounts.

After educating employees and defining a standard, a methodology should be designed for ensuring license compliance and determining appropriate purchase amounts. This methodology should specify a way to count all installed licenses, determine what software is being used, and discover whether each user actually needs the software allocated to him or her.

Desktop asset management applications are widely available to carry out these needs. The following are the three types of asset management applications:

◆ **Inventory.** These applications discover all software that exists within the enterprise.

◆ **Metering.** These applications define who is using software, and who needs to access it.

◆ **Distribution.** These applications automatically install and upgrade software.

Some offerings, such as Tally Systems' Cenergy, combine all of the preceding functions.

Another important factor in asset management software is multiplatform support. Rather than employing multiple, operating system-specific asset management tools, it is more efficient to purchase one that is capable of supporting multiple environments, and compiling asset information from these environments into a single database.

These tools can either enforce asset policies passively or actively. A *passive* tool monitors and illustrates software usage patterns. An *active* monitoring tool, on the other hand, allocates licenses, imposes restrictions, and prevents users from accessing an unavailable application. For example, if you have a floating license for 50 users of Microsoft Word, the first 50 authorized people to request it will gain access to it. The 51st user, however, will be notified that no licenses are currently available, and will instead be placed in a queue to await access. If queuing happens often, it's time to buy more licenses. If it never happens, maybe you have too many.

Summary

This chapter covered the following topics:

◆ Network auditing helps guard against accidental system problems that may be caused by unknowledgeable end users misconfiguring a system.

◆ The network audit can positively impact the company's bottom line. For example, the audit keeps track of exactly how many copies of a program exist throughout the enterprise. Your company may use this information to negotiate volume discounts with your software providers.

◆ Testing and security drills are often a big part of the audit process. Although these drills may be disruptive, they are excellent tools for making sure your policies and procedures are working according to plan.

Part III

Hardware and Network Design

Chapter 10

Remote Access

IN THIS CHAPTER

- ◆ Security considerations with remote access
- ◆ Remote control
- ◆ Remote access software

IN THE PAST, MOST or all of a company's employees worked in a central physical location. This made it easy to keep track of data, sensitive information, and physical equipment. Salespeople were an exception, but most of their information still stayed in the office. While away on a sales call, a sales representative needing information would telephone the secretary, who would physically retrieve a paper file from a filing cabinet and read information to the salesperson over the phone.

Laptop computers, networks, remote access software, and the Internet have changed all that. Workers can go anywhere, physically or virtually, and take the entire corporate network with them. Depending on his or her access privileges, a worker vacationing in Maui can have access to practically all the same data he or she could access while in the office. The growing sophistication of remote control and remote access solutions brings the power of the corporate network directly over the phone lines to the Maui beach, where the remote worker can control everything but the break-room coffee pot. (And Microsoft's working on that one.)

Remote Access Security Considerations

A connection from a remote user could originate from anywhere on the Internet, from a dial-up line, or from a worker who is traveling or telecommuting. Although remote access has numerous advantages, it also poses a possible security threat. As such, all types of remote connection should be subject to the firewall's authentication service to gain access to the network's services. The security policy needs to address remote users. Specifically, it should state that remote users should never attempt to access the system by calling in to an unauthorized modem on the company premises that may be behind the firewall.

In addition, you should implement a separate dial-in policy. Dial-in capability enables authorized users to still have remote access to the system, even if they are in a location where Internet access is unavailable. This capability, however, may also present another vulnerability, in that it establishes a direct path to the network that could potentially be hijacked. Consequently, be sure to consider dial-in and dial-out features when selecting and configuring the firewall and take strong security measures so that these features do not become a new avenue of attack. In addition to prohibiting the use of unauthorized modems behind the firewall, the security policy should reflect the use of the firewall's authentication facilities and how they are used in respect to dial-in and dial-out capability.

Also pertinent to the remote access policy is the use of SLIP (Serial Line Interface Protocol) and PPP (Point-to-Point Protocol) connections. SLIP establishes a point-to-point link for connecting two TCP/IP devices over a standard serial line (such as a common telephone link). SLIP is commonly used to connect modems to the Internet. For the most part, SLIP has been superseded by PPP, which is a standardized method of accomplishing the same thing. It is possible to use a SLIP/PPP connection to establish a connection to a site protected by the firewall. This "back door" around the firewall may also present some serious security problems. The security manager may want to establish a policy prohibiting setting up an unauthorized Internet connection for this purpose.

Remote Control

Remote control systems enable a remote user to take control over another computer. With a remote control connection, a remote user can manipulate a computer at another location as if he or she were sitting right in front of it. This can be useful when workers at home or on the road need to access their desktop office computer from their present location. Although remote control brings great power and productivity, it also brings great risk.

Your security policy must be clear on the issue of remote control. It may be necessary to encrypt the remote control link that exists between the remote user and the computer being controlled, depending on the data being transmitted. The policy should also state that the discs used on the traveling laptops should be encrypted if they contain sensitive information, such as sales data, customer lists, or rate sheets. Because the risk of a laptop being stolen is great, it is absolutely essential that the data contained on it does not fall into the wrong hands.

Remote control software should have a good selection of security features. For example, Avalan Technology's Remotely Possible remote control software (see Figure 10-1) includes the following security features:

◆ Login name and connection

◆ Password

- ◆ Access privileges

- ◆ Callback and roving callback

- ◆ Host confirmation

- ◆ Blank host screen

- ◆ Disable host keyboard and mouse

- ◆ Data encryption

- ◆ Start before logon

- ◆ Reboot on disconnect

The callback feature is of particular importance. With callback, a remote user dials in to the network, enters a user ID, and hangs up. The system then calls the user back at a predetermined number and establishes a session. Callback is meant to address the possibility of an attacker stealing a user ID, and using it to call into the system from another location.

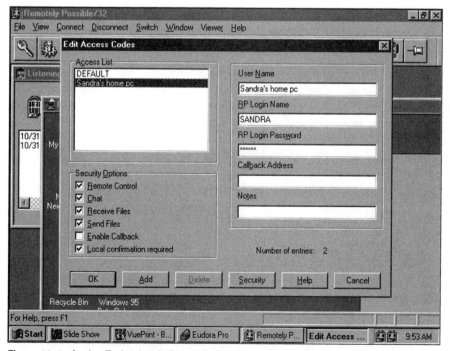

Figure 10-1: Avalan Technology's Remotely Possible software offers a variety of security features for remote control.

Remote Access Software

Plenty of tools are on the market for establishing remote access to the corporate network. Remote access differs from remote control in that it transforms the remote station into a de facto node on the network, with all the privileges that come with it. In effect, no difference exists between the remote machine and any desktop machine in the office.

But are these tools secure? Some are. Lantronix's Remote Access Server 32, for example, is more than a remote access device – it's a router with packet filtering capability. Packet filtering lets the administrator control what goes over a given link by automatically filtering out or disallowing packets that fall into certain restrictions – for example, packets from a certain domain or address. Security on the Lantronix device includes the following:

♦ Password Authentication Protocol (PAP)

♦ Challenge Handshake Authentication Protocol (CHAP)

♦ Remote Authentication Dial-In User Service (RADIUS)

♦ Kerberos

♦ SecurID security

♦ Callback security

Your routers should support the three industry-standard handshaking protocols listed previously – PAP, CHAP, and RADIUS. RADIUS provides a centralized server for a single point of authentication on the network. CHAP and PAP are methods of authenticating a PPP connection.

Remote access products such as Microcom's LANexpress 4.0 also build in security to provide remote users with secure access to the LAN. Security is essential when remote access is being used, because that remote access represents a potential entryway and brings numerous obstacles to security. Any time access to the network is allowed from outside, potential danger looms. The link could be hijacked, the user ID could be stolen and, if not configured properly, it could be used to bypass the firewall.

End-to-end solutions such as LANexpress provide the greatest security. This particular solution includes the remote client software, a dedicated remote LAN access server, and remote management software. The management software is an especially crucial piece of the puzzle. Through this element, you can run the entire remote LAN access solution. LANexpress' expressWATCH management software relies on standard SNMP (Standard Network Management Protocol) for management, which again brings an extra measure of openness in multivendor systems. SNMP enables any number of standard-compliant network management platforms to control an SNMP-compliant device or application.

An audit trail is an important part of a remote access solution. The audit trail should show all dial-in and dial-out activity, including start time and end time, the user ID for each call, security level, phone number, number of bytes received or transmitted, modem port number (a modem configuration setting) from which the call was received or dialed, and the termination code. The remote access solution should also include some sort of event monitoring and alarm notification. With expressWATCH, you can enable or disable privileges for dial-in or dial-out security from any workstation on the network or from a workstation dialed into the network over LANexpress.

Ideally, remote access security will work with the network operating system's own native authentication services. In Novell and Microsoft environments, for example, all users have an existing username and password. Authentication in LANexpress adds an extra layer of security by first requiring authentication to make the remote connection and then requiring users to go through the authentication procedures of the operating system as well.

An efficient remote access system offers several security options, so the administrator can select the most appropriate setting for each circumstance. LANexpress offers several options:

- **None.** This setting prevents a user from establishing any dial-in connections to the LANexpress server.

- **LANexpress passthru.** Users must provide the server with a username and password before accessing the network.

- **Fixed dialback security.** Remote users first must enter a username and password. The LANexpress server then disconnects the call and calls the user back at a predefined telephone number.

- **Roving dialback.** This option is similar to the preceding option, but is more suited to users who may not be at a fixed remote location. Remote users first must enter a username and password. The LANexpress server then asks the user to enter a callback number, disconnects the call, and then calls the user back at the number that was entered.

- **Roving passthru.** This option enables the user to enter a "P" at the dialback prompt instead of entering the dialback telephone number. This action immediately connects the user to the network. This option may be useful if the remote user is in a location that cannot accept a direct callback. However, use of this option should be extremely limited, because of the obvious security risk involved.

Dial-out security is handled through an internal database stored on the LANexpress server, which contains a username and password for all privileged users. Users attempting to gain access will be suspended after three incorrect attempts.

Summary

This chapter covered the following topics:

- ◆ Remote access, remote control, and the Internet have enabled our corporate networks to go far beyond their traditional boundaries. Yet these new conveniences bring new security risks that must be addressed.

- ◆ Remote access software enables a remote computer to take over another computer in a different location, usually through a modem-to-modem link. Remote access software, on the other hand, enables a remote computer to participate as an equal node on the network.

Chapter 11

Virtual Networking

IN THIS CHAPTER

- ◆ Creating a Virtual LAN
- ◆ Virtual Private Networking

LARGER NETWORKS ARE TRADITIONALLY segmented into more-or-less permanent sections, or subnets. A lot of moves, adds, and changes take place within these divisions and every time one occurs, an administrator must reconfigure the affected subnets, and make changes at the physical level. Virtual networking enables you to do this at the software level. Virtual networking makes network management simpler, and also introduces an additional layer of security.

Virtual LANs

A Virtual LAN (VLAN) is essentially a broadcast domain. As with a router's broadcast domain, the devices in the VLAN receive all broadcasts and frames with unknown destination addresses, so long as the frames originate inside the same VLAN.

The VLAN is actually very similar to the old hub and router configuration, except that in a hub and router network, frames are broadcast within a hub and routed between hubs. In a VLAN, frames are broadcast within the VLAN and routed between VLANs. The broadcast domain in the VLAN does not have to be a single port on a router, as is required in the older hub-and-router network. The broadcast domain instead can be made up of devices connected to a single port on a switch, users on multiple ports on a single switch, or users attached to multiple ports on different switches.

VLAN Advantages

A VLAN offers several advantages over a traditional hub and router broadcast domain. These advantages make the VLAN more powerful and secure, as well as easier to manage.

The VLAN model allows for a more policy-based management structure. A VLAN is a logically-defined group of endstations that communicate as though they were on the same physical network. Endstations in a VLAN can, however, be located on different segments, which enables the manager to group workers together according to function rather than physical location. It also enables the manager to assign priorities to different types of traffic. The result is that the network can be managed from a business perspective rather than a purely technical perspective.

Simpler management always translates, at least indirectly, to stronger security — simply because simplicity provides fewer opportunities to make mistakes. It also enables much easier adds, moves, and changes.

A traditional router-based network uses a Layer 3 (of the OSI model) address to move data between LANs. Every computer on a TCP/IP network requires one of these addresses, called an IP address. These addresses identify the domain where the frame's destination device is located. Each network address corresponds to a workstation and the segment to which the workstation belongs.

The network administrator must assign addresses and enter them manually into each workstation. Up-to-date IP addresses must be carefully maintained. Typically, this information is maintained in a text-based configuration file, with updates made manually. Of course, any time configuration data is changed manually, the potential exists for human error. But the modern corporation is a very mobile creature; we get promotions, demotions, change offices for a better view, or move across the hall to join a different department. When changes happen, or as more devices are added to the network, managing these addresses becomes more difficult, costly, and error-prone. The network manager must then manually change the network address and other gateway details. If this happens often, it becomes an administrative burden.

A DHCP (Dynamic Host Configuration Protocol) server can relieve this burden by automatically assigning TCP/IP addresses to nodes across a network, and facilitating the central administration of those addresses. The problem with this is that it becomes impossible to implement a deterministic security policy. Because DHCP assigns an address based on the subnetwork number to which the router port belongs, if a workstation moves to a new subnetwork, the Layer 3 policy may then become invalid. New firewall rules may then have to be set. Organizations using DHCP still must manually synchronize the configurations of the Domain Name Service (DNS) and DHCP servers.

The problem is further complicated by the increasingly widespread use of TCP/IP, and the proliferation of network devices. Some of these administrative problems can be addressed with a DHCP software product such as MetaInfo's Meta IP/Manager. This product offers an industry-standard server implementation of DNS and DHCP, as well as a central management server and database. Meta unifies the process of managing IP addresses, and eliminates the need for manual configuration and synchronization.

A switching-based network like a VLAN, on the other hand, uses Layer 2 technology (the data link layer of the OSI model) based on the workstation's medium access control (MAC) address. MAC corresponds to Layer 1 (physical layer) of the

OSI reference model. VLANs track workstations by their MAC addresses, and thereby guarantee that it remains in the same VLAN regardless of location. With the VLAN model, it is no longer necessary to modify the Layer 3 (network layer) security policy for every move.

The VLAN model offers an inherently better security environment. A hub-based network, for example, is susceptible to attack by anyone with a protocol analyzer. An attacker could simply plug the analyzer into any connection on the hub and intercept all data being transmitted on that segment. When each network device is connected to its own port on a network with a switched VLAN, that sort of attack is no longer possible. Although an attacker could still use the protocol analyzer to try to gain information, the attacker would only get information from the single device attached to the port, instead of from all devices on a segment.

VLAN Types

Several different types of VLANs exist. Xylan's VLAN implementation, called AutoTracker, works with Xylan switching products. AutoTracker can support several different LAN types, including the following:

- ◆ **Port-based virtual LANs.** This type of VLAN is the simplest implementation, but offers the most control and security. A device is assigned to a VLAN based on the ports to which it is physically attached. Port assignments are static and can only be changed by the administrator.

- ◆ **MAC address VLAN.** Configuration of the MAC address VLAN is more complex. This type of VLAN consists of a grouping of MAC addresses, which AutoTracker transforms into a broadcast domain. Because identification is based on MAC addresses, this type of VLAN is also one of the more secure options. Before a machine can gain access to the VLAN, it must have a recognizable VLAN address.

- ◆ **Layer 3.** In a Layer 3 VLAN, the manager assigns traffic with different protocol requirements to separate VLANs.

- ◆ **Protocol policy VLAN.** This type of VLAN is based on protocol criteria within a frame. In this type of VLAN, the manager could, for example, designate a field within a frame to determine VLAN membership.

- ◆ **Multicast VLAN.** A multicast VLAN sends traffic point-to-multipoint or multipoint-to-multipoint. It is useful for applications such as newsfeeds or video-conferencing.

- ◆ **Policy-based VLAN.** This type of VLAN lets managers combine VLAN policies to create flexible VLANs. Devices can be assigned to VLANs based on the policies. Each switch in the network understands all of the various VLAN policies.

♦ **Authenticated user VLAN.** This is a highly secure type of VLAN that requires users to be authenticated by a server before gaining access to network resources.

Virtual Private Networks

Networks in general have undergone a dramatic transformation over the past few years. They have evolved from a simple means of sharing resources to a more strategic investment. Often, this emerging strategy involves bringing in trading partners, remote workers, and others into the network. One of the most effective ways to do so is by establishing a Virtual Private Network (VPN) over the Internet. This approach can save a great deal of money, because dedicated leased lines become unnecessary, and also offer greater flexibility.

A VPN establishes a secure link between multiple locations over a public network. Traditionally, a VPN involved dedicated, leased lines and a proprietary security system and was quite costly. Until recently, this was the only way to connect multiple remote LANs — with private leased lines that ran between sites. In addition, while the older model did secure the communications channel, it did nothing to secure the corporate networks that were participating in the VPN. This approach worked well and was generally secure, but it was also costly and difficult to administer.

The Internet presents a different approach to connecting sites that is significantly less expensive, requires less hardware, and less administration. Recently, companies have started to implement VPNs over the Internet. More corporate networks are moving toward an intranet model based on TCP/IP, and more remote employees are needing to access the corporate network. In addition, more companies are bringing in trading partners to their network, creating an *extranet*. Because of these trends, interoperability has become a major issue, and proprietary VPN systems have become too limiting.

The new model for a VPN carves a "private" network out of the public Internet, enabling nodes or subnets in one location to connect to nodes or subnets in another location, creating a de facto private WAN for the enterprise. This differs from the VLAN, which segments a large network into subnets, and manages the connections via software.

The two types of VPNs are *directed* and *tunneled*. The directed VPN uses IP and addressing and establishes directional control of data over the VPN. It encrypts data, and includes authentication that is based on the user, not on the IP address. The tunneled model, on the other hand, uses IP frames as a tunnel for sending packets. In this model, the source and destination cannot be identified, and the connection is bidirectional. In the directed model, if the network is attacked, the intruder can only access the destination network, but in the bidirectional model, an attack opens up both source and destination networks.

The VPN is also effective as a tool for supporting remote workers. Remote access has been around for years, although it has been largely based on dial-up connections. VPN provides remote access to the corporate network over the Internet. The older dial-up model of remote connection also posed some security problems. Because this model uses multiple connections, one for each individual needing access, multiple points of entry exist. Each connection must have authentication, and many remote-access solutions offer only limited security features and no encryption. Internet-based VPNs, on the other hand, handle remote access through a single Internet connection. Instead of multiple points of entry, just one exists.

You actually have three ways to connect remote sites:

◆ The dial-up model

◆ Leased-line VPN

◆ Internet-based VPN

The leased-line model is the most costly, and also comes with high recurring costs for the line itself and related services. This model can be secure, although the security measures again tend to be costly and largely proprietary. This requires authentication and encryption hardware and software to be installed at each end of the connection. Although doing so secures the channel, it does not secure the network itself at either site.

The Internet model for VPNs links multiple sites through a single Internet connection at each site. This is less costly than the leased-line model and also has low recurring costs. Also, because it is such a simple solution, it is highly scaleable.

Security is of particular concern, because the Internet was not, after all, designed to send mission-critical data. To meet these security needs, a VPN must address privacy, integrity, and authenticity. Privacy can be ensured through encryption, which makes sure that an intercepted message cannot be read. Methods of guaranteeing integrity see to it that data cannot be tampered with. Authenticity, of course, ensures that the sender's identity is verified.

VPN Security

Leased lines have long been used to establish secure, private connections between sites. Connecting sites with a leased line was inherently secure, because the line was only available to the two sites. Connecting sites across the Internet, on the other hand, sends data over the public network and makes it vulnerable to hacking. A VPN can offer the same level of privacy and security, and at a substantially reduced price, by using firewalls and encryption to make sure data is transmitted between sites safely. Additional management issues must be addressed, however. VPNs require the administrator to consider several issues, such as encryption, performance, price, and interoperability. Most network managers are willing to go the extra mile to reap the savings.

A VPN is made up of multiple sites that can communicate securely while still being capable of communicating with other sites on an unsecured basis. The VPN uses an encrypting device, sitting at the edge of the private network, that uses encryption and authentication to secure the link. With encryption, only the other corporate sites with corresponding encryption keys can decrypt the data.

Most VPNs run over a native IP backbone. Generally, you have three ways to implement a VPN: with a firewall that runs encryption, with a router that runs encryption, or with a stand-alone encryption unit. Because of the lack of compatibility, networks with routers or firewalls from different vendors have to run a stand-alone unit.

In addition, encryption can be hardware- or software-based. While dedicated chips frequently offer better performance, software running on a dedicated machine can also be effective. The hardware-based encryptor may be less vulnerable to attack, however. If the encryption key is kept on a chip inside a physical device, it is less likely that the key will be stolen. A software encryptor, on the other hand, may run on top of an insecure operating system and is thus vulnerable to attack. As long as the medium access control (MAC) address is visible, which it is in a typical operating system, the encryption key can be attacked. Use of a trusted operating system (a highly specialized type of operating system with additional security features) shields the MAC address and makes it less vulnerable to attack.

Four encryption algorithms can be applied in the VPN implementation:

◆ Data Encryption Standard (DES)

◆ Triple-DES

◆ International Data Encryption Algorithm (IDEA)

◆ RC4

Triple-DES and IDEA are the strongest, using key lengths of 112 and 128 bits. However, federal regulations greatly restrict encryption products greater than 56 bits (see Chapter 5 for more information about encryption regulations). In fact, even 56-bit encryption is limited; most companies are still limited to 40-bit encryption. Forty-bit encryption is only marginally useful and can be cracked easily. Fifty-six-bit products are available, although using them requires allowing a third party to hold the key in escrow. This key recovery gives the government a "back door" to your data. This places a big limitation on domestically-made VPN encryptors.

Besides encryption, most VPN devices also shield the source and destination IP addresses. This technique, which is referred to as *tunneling*, encapsulates the header and payload of each packet inside of a new header. The VPN encryptor then scrambles the data payload and the IP packet's header (which contains source and destination information) before the encapsulation, making the contents unreadable.

Exchanging the encryption key, however, can present a security vulnerability. A manual system of key exchange is prone to attack. Under this method, a session key is randomly generated and then transmitted to the second site via telephone or registered mail. This is inherently a weak approach, because a hacker can intercept the key during transmission. A more effective method may be to use a dynamic system, in which the key is encrypted and distributed over the network on demand. The authentication in a VPN is done both at the packet level and at the encryptor level whenever a new device is added.

At the packet level, an encryption device applies a digital stamp to the encrypted data. This stamp can then be used by the recipient to verify the source. At the encryptor level, a new device is manually authenticated, or authenticated with a digital certificate. The manual approach hard-wires the private and public key pairs to the device before shipping. The digital certificate approach, on the other hand, does not include hard-wired keys, but instead randomly generates a key pair, signs a certificate with a private key, and then sends it to a certificate authority, such as VeriSign, for approval.

Most VPN encryption solutions also include remote access software, which loads onto a laptop so users can communicate securely with the central encryption device over a modem.

Although encryption may degrade performance somewhat, the degradation is usually minimal and well worth it. Tunneling may avoid the degradation completely. Tunneling is part of the evolving IPSec standard, and some vendors also offer proprietary tunneling mechanisms. IPSec is supported by many VPN products. This standard defines how VPN encryptors perform authentication and negotiate the algorithm and encryption key. However, at the present time, IPSec is still being defined and amended and does not yet present a solid, interoperable mechanism – although it is certainly a step in that direction. For more information on IPSec, see Chapter 21 on TCP/IP.

VPN Software

Creating a VPN over the public Internet need not be a security risk. In fact, it can be a way to use the Internet in a secure manner. Products such as Aventail's MobileVPN and Aventail PartnerVPN use a *directed* VPN model as opposed to the traditional, open-ended tunnel model to achieve a greater level of security. The directed model provides directional control of information across the VPN, encrypts data, and offers user-based authentication. A directed VPN, through its directional control, eliminates the possibility of a user inheriting another office's or company's security flaws.

The Aventail solution addresses the security risks that many other VPNs still face. It is based on circuit-level proxies that operate at the session layer of the OSI model (see Figure 11-1). As such, the Aventail proxy will proxy all network traffic, not just packets or applications.

Aventail's solution applies authentication to the user instead of an IP address – eliminating the possibility of a man-in-the-middle attack. In this type of attack, intruders place themselves between two parties, and masquerade as one of the parties. The best way to thwart this type of attack is the use of digital certificates or digital signatures.

Aventail VPN is a client-server solution that is based on strong encryption and a directed architecture, which provides a greater measure of security than the standard tunneled VPNs. The directed model assumes that corporations want to control exactly what information is passed across established data channels. Tunneled VPNs create portals into corporate networks based on the assumption that the companies share a two-way, trusted relationship. The bidirectional nature of tunneled VPNs makes each participant susceptible to the other's security flaws. This is because the tunnels are created with IP frames that are disassociated from the user or destination. If someone were to attack either end of a tunnel VPN, both ends would be subject to damage. If the security of a directed VPN were breached, however, the intruder would have access only to the attacked network. Directed VPNs encrypt all data, authenticate each user (not machine), and provide granular access controls to safeguard each end of the link.

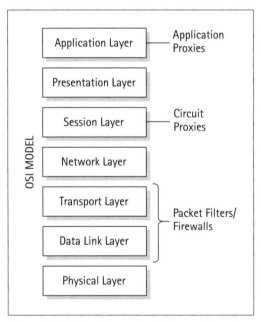

Figure 11-1: Network security devices and how they correspond to the OSI model

Aventail's MobileVPN functions as a circuit-level gateway, acting as a proxy at the session layer to handle remote connections. Because these connections go through a proxy, no direct connection to the corporate network actually exists. Figure 11-2 shows Aventail's VPN model.

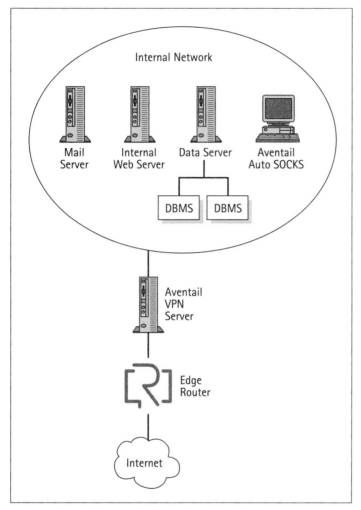

Figure 11-2: Aventail's Virtual Private Network solution

According to VPNet Technologies, vendor of the VPN Service Unit 1000 stand-alone unit, the biggest security threats occur from within the WAN, where an intruder can intercept data without detection. Common attacks include the following:

♦ **Data sniffing.** This involves capturing data packets while in transit. The packet is captured, read, and then sent on to its destination, so neither sender nor recipient are aware of the interception.

◆ **Data tampering.** This involves intercepting a packet and modifying its contents before the packet is sent on to its destination. One type of tampering is packet spoofing, where a hacker attempts to portray himself as a legitimate user by altering the packet.

◆ **Denial-of-service attack.** This type of attack has received a great deal of press recently and has the potential to bring down a major network. The denial of service attack bogs down the network by sending too many consecutive requests for connection.

All three of these problems are WAN-oriented; however, most security products are LAN-based. A firewall, for example, may be useful for protecting the LAN, but cannot protect data while it is moving across the WAN.

Performance is another major issue. While a leased line guarantees performance levels, using the public network involves sharing available bandwidth between several users.

Technologies are available to address the triple issues of security, performance, and scalability, such as VPNet Technologies' VPLink solution. VPLink is based on three technical disciplines:

◆ Security technology

  ■ Encryption

  ■ Authentication

  ■ Key management

◆ Networking technology

  ■ IP, frame relay, ATM

  ■ Data compression

◆ Integration technology

  ■ Chip level (ASIC integration)

  ■ System level (APIs)

VPLink incorporates industry-standard encryption, authentication, key management, and data compression, offering close integration at both the chip and system level. The company's real-time hardware, software, firmware, and ASICs (Application-Specific Integrated Circuits) are all unified by the VPLink architecture and the Secure Networking API (SNAPI). Through SNAPI (see Figure 11-3), VPLink can establish a consistent interface to all VPLink services.

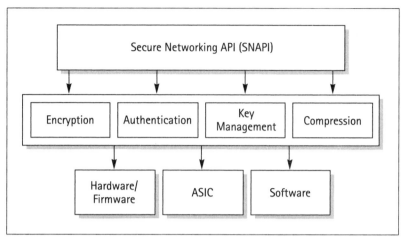

Figure 11-3: VPNet Technologies' Secure Networking API (SNAPI)

SNAPI is an asynchronous service interface that gives developers access to standard security, cryptographic, and compression technologies. Through SNAPI, a common set of security services can be implemented in various hardware devices, software, firmware, or ASICs. VPNet and other developers can use this set of APIs to develop low-end, software-based VPN solutions, firmware products, and high-performance secure routers.

VPLink provides for both core security services and core network services. Security services include encryption and other technologies, including secure hashing functions and key management systems.

Secure hashing guarantees the integrity of data as it travels over the VPN, as well as validating the data's origin. Hashing creates a fingerprint (hash) of a piece of data, sometimes known as a digital signature, and makes it tamperproof. If an intruder alters a message, the hash no longer matches and the intrusion will be detected.

Key management is also essential. A VPN solution should support several key management protocols. VPLink implements the SKIP (Simple Key Management for IP) protocol, which boasts low overhead and good scalability.

Most authentication protocols deal with session-oriented key management schemes. However, most network layer protocols, such as IPv4 and IPv6, are sessionless, datagram-based protocols. SKIP is well-suited for use with sessionless datagram protocols, and SKIP has been especially designed to work with the IP Security Protocols (IPSec).

SKIP is a set of IP-layer encryption protocols, which provides a system for encrypting any protocol within the TCP/IP suite. Once installed, any two systems implementing SKIP can transparently encrypt and authenticate any traffic that moves between them.

SKIP provides four separate network security services:

◆ **Access control,** for protecting data from unauthorized use

◆ **Encryption and decryption,** to ensure confidentiality

◆ **Authentication,** to ensure the integrity of data

◆ **Key and certificate management,** for efficient administration of security policy

Encryption, authentication, and key management may be essential to a VPN, but they also add overhead. VPNet addresses the overhead problem through real-time data compression – that is, data is compressed prior to encryption to mitigate the effects of packet expansion. Furthermore, a piece of data that has been both compressed and encrypted is seen as more secure than data that has only been encrypted.

Digital Secured Networks Technology's NetFortress simplifies the process of creating a VPN. The NetFortress device appears as a simple "black box" that, remarkably, requires no configuration. It works by encrypting everything at the network layer with a unique key, so anyone on the outside attempting to infiltrate will be able to read only the source and destination IP address. The data within the packet is rendered unreadable.

The DSN black box sits at the perimeter of each LAN, between it and the Internet (see Figure 11-4).

NetFortress is in a sealed box that cannot be logged into, and therefore, cannot be compromised in the same way as a firewall can. It works at the IP layer, which is a lower layer than where the firewall works, and below the level of most hacker attacks. Its security protocols are implemented without human intervention, and require no special configuration. Setup is incredibly simple. Setup consists of plugging the device into a host computer or client LAN on one side, and the open network on the other side. It has two Ethernet interfaces, which can accept either thin coax or 10BaseT connectors. Configuration is automatic. When the client transmits the first message through the host box, NetFortress burns the client's IP and MAC addresses into memory; this action permanently ties the box to its host computer. Further, the host box shields its host's MAC address, by answering Address Resolution Protocol (ARP) requests with its own MAC address. An outsider, therefore, does not have access to the host's MAC address, only that of the NetFortress box.

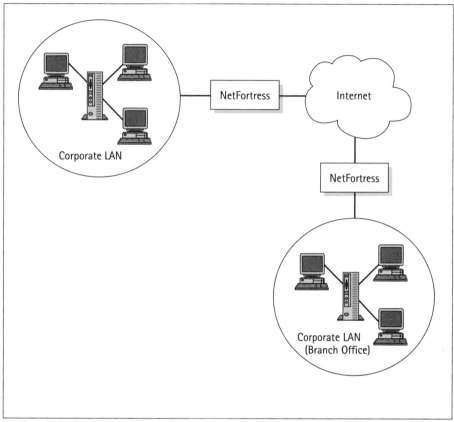

Figure 11-4: Digital Secured Network Technology's NetFortress establishes a VPN by sitting on either side of the Internet, and encrypting everything at the network layer with a unique key.

Summary

In this chapter you learned about the following:

- ◆ A Virtual LAN (VLAN) is a new type of broadcast domain that enables subnets to be configured based on logical association, rather than physical location of the participants. The VLAN model also offers tighter security.

- ◆ A Virtual Private Network (VPN) uses tunneling and encryption to create a private, secure network over the public Internet.

Chapter 12

Firewalls

IN THIS CHAPTER

- ◆ Examining the different types of firewalls
- ◆ Understanding the difference between a firewall and a packet-filtering router
- ◆ Creating a firewall policy
- ◆ Implementing a firewall

THE RAPID EXPANSION OF the Internet has provided tremendous opportunities to access an unparalleled amount of information. A company connects to the Internet to gain access to this information and to share information with the public. However, once a company connects its corporate network to the Internet, that company's private information becomes vulnerable to hackers. Network break-ins can and do occur – more often than most network managers realize. When networks are connected together as part of an internetwork, and that internetwork is, in turn, connected to the public Internet, the risks are especially great.

Ways exist, however, to share public information and still protect private information. One such method is to install a *firewall* between the private corporate network and the public Internet. A firewall is typically a system used to enforce an access control policy between two networks. The firewall sits between two networks, such as a corporate network and the Internet, examines all traffic that goes through the two networks, and only allows authorized traffic (as defined by the security policy) to pass through. The firewall enforces an authentication system that allows only authorized individuals to gain access to the private network.

We usually think of a firewall as protecting a corporate network from the Internet, but it can also be used to enforce security in any type of internetwork or corporate WAN. Many valid reasons exist to apply a firewall to a WAN, even if it is not connected to the public Internet. For example, a large organization's product development department may want to protect its own network from people on other networks within the company. That's because corporate spies abound – in fact, a great deal of network intrusion actually comes from within the company. Thus, an effective way to reduce the risk of attack from an internal source is to segregate a company's networks with a firewall.

When a firewall is deployed in an internal WAN, it is often referred to as a *gateway*. The gateway blocks the transmission of certain types of traffic.

Unfortunately, it's never as simple as just putting up a firewall. Security expert and SATAN designer Dan Farmer claims that "A firewall isn't that important, really. A security policy is by far the most important piece of the puzzle; more than everything else put together. Actual adherence to policy is number two." Merely implementing a firewall does not by itself solve all of the network's security problems. Often, a manager will put in a firewall and then neglect everything else. Then, if the firewall is attacked, a neglected network can be an attacker's playground where widespread damage could occur.

So, a firewall is one piece of the security puzzle. It should be as impenetrable as possible, keeping in mind, however, that a firewall (or indeed, any security device) has the potential to be breached, no matter how secure and robust.

Types of Firewalls

It's difficult to pin down a precise definition of a firewall because several different types of implementations are available. In this chapter, we focus on the following:

- Packet filtering firewall
- Dual-homed gateway firewall
- Screened host firewall
- Screened subnet firewall

Packet Filtering Firewall

The packet filtering firewall (see Figure 12-1) is the most common firewall type and the best suited for simpler networks. This approach simply involves installing a packet filtering router at the Internet gateway and then configuring the filtering rules to block protocols or addresses.

The packet filter looks at every packet before it is sent, and then decides whether to allow it to be transmitted, or to discard it. It accomplishes this by examining the packet and comparing it against a set of rules that indicate which types of packets are permitted and which are not. IP packet filtering is executed at the lower levels of the IP protocol stack. IP runs on each host, and is responsible for routing packets to their appropriate destinations.

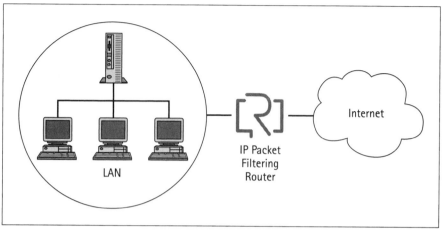

Figure 12-1: Packet filtering firewall

The packet filtering router can filter IP packets based on these fields:

◆ Source IP address

◆ Destination IP address

◆ TCP/UDP source port

◆ TCP/UDP destination port

A packet filtering device examines the packet header, which describes the connection, and the protocol being used. The packet filter enables you to filter packets based on the following:

◆ Source and destination IP address.

◆ Source and destination ports. These ports identify the application for TCP/UDP, such as FTP, Telnet, SNMP, or RealAudio.

◆ TCP. This is the connection-oriented protocol used for most services, such as FTP and Telnet.

◆ UDP (User Datagram Protocol). This is the connectionless protocol used by SNMP and RealAudio.

◆ ICMP (Internet Control Message Protocol). This is the low-level management protocol for the Internet.

◆ Whether a packet is the first packet of a new TCP/IP connection, or a subsequent packet.

◆ Whether the packet is destined for, or originated from, a local application.

◆ Whether the packet is inbound or outbound.

By itself, the packet filtering firewall is a limited option because it offers no logging capability and can become overly complex to manage if you need to apply numerous filtering rules. Some router vendors may call a packet-filtering router a "firewall," and may tell you that this is all you need to protect your internal network. Nothing could be further from the truth. Packet filtering may be adequate for protecting an isolated system, but it is not enough to protect your internal network from outside attack. It is, nonetheless, an important part of an overall strategy.

TCP and UDP port filtering is exceptionally useful. For example, the Telnet daemon lives at a specific port (usually port 23). Configuring the firewall to block TCP and UDP connections to and from given ports enables you to have a policy that states that different types of connections can be made only with specific hosts. However, not all packet filtering routers are capable of filtering TCP and UDP.

Besides Telnet (port 23) and FTP (ports 20 and 21), the policy should reflect restrictions on other protocols that are inherently vulnerable, including SMTP (port 25), DNS (port 53) and RIP (port 520). The latter protocol (Routing Information Protocol) can be spoofed to redirect a packet. Other protocols that could hold the potential for misuse, and should therefore be regulated, include UUCP (port 540), and NNTP (port 119).

PACKET FILTERING

General-purpose routers offer some firewall-like protection, but they can examine only one packet at a time and thus do not offer a very fine level of control. A router can be imbued with some firewall features. Special-purpose firewalls are designed for security from the beginning, although they still require a good deal of configuration, know-how, and policy-making along with them. Packet-filtering routers are the most basic type of firewall. They provide only limited functionality. Packet filtering routers are often difficult to configure and maintain because the rules are complicated and you usually have no way to verify the correctness of the rules outside of examining them manually.

All firewalls execute IP packet filtering, usually through a packet-filtering router. These devices filter out packets as they pass based on a set of rules imposed by the security manager. Filtering can block connections to or from specified hosts or networks or to specified ports. The capability to filter specific ports is especially useful. As mentioned, the Telnet daemon usually exists at port 23. You can use this type of knowledge to implement a policy that limits what type of connections can be made to each host.

Some packet filtering routers do not have any logging facilities, so if a hazardous packet does get through, the packet may not be detected until later.

Packet filtering rules can get complicated because you'll often need to make exceptions, such as allowing Telnet services through port 23 as just described. Once you start making exceptions, you may need to establish a separate rule for each system.

Packet filtering routers represent the first generation of firewalls. For the most part, packet filtering is transparent to end users. However, these devices can sometimes be bypassed with sniffers, spoofers, and other hacker equipment.

Packet filtering routers function only at the lowest layers of the OSI model, or the physical connections. Other firewall technologies may examine higher layers; the best firewall implementations will examine all layers of the OSI model.

PROXY SERVICE

Some of the weaknesses of packet filtering routers can be mitigated by adding software applications that forward and filter connections for Telnet and FTP services. This is known as a *proxy service*, and the host that runs the proxy service is an application gateway.

This configuration is set up so the packet filtering router blocks all incoming Telnet and FTP connections, allowing them to go to only a single host. This host is the Telnet/FTP application gateway. The combination of a packet filtering router and an application gateway offers a higher level of security. The steps involved in using this configuration are as follows:

1. The user Telnets to the application gateway and inputs the name of an internal host.

2. The application gateway examines the user's source IP address and determines whether to allow or deny the connection.

3. The user enters a password.

4. The proxy service establishes a Telnet connection between the internal host and the application gateway.

5. The proxy service transfers data between the two connections.

6. The application gateway logs the connection.

One advantage of the proxy is that the names of internal systems do not have to be made public, because the application gateway, or proxy, is the only host whose address must be made known to outside systems. Under this type of configuration, a user cannot access a service for which no proxy exists. The proxy service can also filter protocols, which offers an additional layer of security.

While it is important to address firewall issues in your security policy, you should also build in some flexibility because of the Internet's changing nature. You may need to allow access to a certain protocol that emerges later to accommodate new tools or requirements. For example, the RealAudio player from Progressive Networks provides users with the opportunity to listen to streaming audio feeds. A firewall that blocks UDP (User Datagram Protocol) will not permit RealAudio to pass through.

Installing an applications proxy firewall is often difficult because it closes all paths between the network and the Internet. You can then configure the firewall to allow Internet access only to users who require it. To implement this type of firewall, you need to do a great deal of advance planning. The IP addressing scheme is important when implementing this sort of firewall because all of the traffic leaving the network appears to originate from a single IP address. That single address is the address of the firewall's interface. This scheme is important in preventing hackers from gaining information about the IP addresses of your internal devices.

Although this IP address must be "official," it is possible to use "illegal" IP addresses (not assigned by InterNIC) internally. This maneuver adds another layer of security because it prevents an attacker from routing packets to the internal network. However, changing the internal IP addressing scheme can be complicated, because other applications and gateways may refer to those IP addresses, so you would have to change all of those references as well. An address management scheme, such as Dynamic Host Configuration Protocol (DHCP), can be helpful in managing the assignment of IP addresses within your network.

Dual-Homed Gateway Firewall

A dual-homed gateway firewall (see Figure 12-2) may be a better solution for more complex networks. The dual-homed configuration places two network interfaces on a host and disables the host's IP forwarding capability. In other words, the dual-homed gateway has connections to two networks. One connection is to the internal, secure network, and the other is to a perimeter network that has access to the Internet via a router. This option completely blocks IP traffic between the Internet and the internal network.

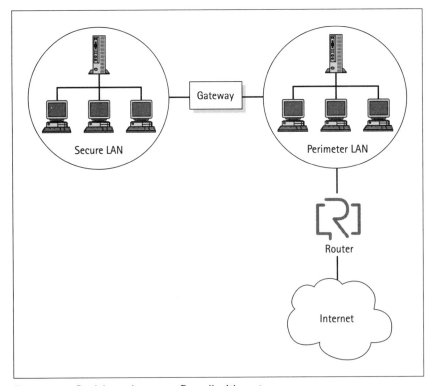

Figure 12-2: Dual-homed gateway firewall with router

Typically, the dual-homed option is used to deny access to all services that are not expressly permitted. For example, this type of firewall can be used to segregate traffic, allowing an information server to be accessed from the outside while denying access to all other servers.

The gateway can, therefore, send and receive data from local applications, but packets cannot be forwarded through it via IP. Internal users make use of proxy servers on the gateway to access servers on the Internet. A mail proxy transfers mail between an internal mail server and mail servers on the Internet.

Because two domain name servers exist, the names of the internal hosts are not visible to anyone on the Internet; however, internal users still have access to all systems, including the public server on the perimeter network.

In this type of configuration, spoofing is prevented by not allowing packets with internal IP addresses to be received on the LAN adapter connected to the perimeter network. In fact, the IP addresses used in the internal network are never even seen by anyone on the Internet, and do not even need to be valid IP addresses.

Screened Host Firewall

The screened host firewall (see Figure 12-3) offers a little more flexibility than the dual-homed option. It combines a packet-filtering router with an application gateway on the protected side of the router. Unlike the dual-homed gateway option, it requires only one network interface. The application gateway sends Telnet and other services to individual systems if a proxy exists for them there; the router also filters out any dangerous protocols and prevents them from reaching the gateway or individual systems.

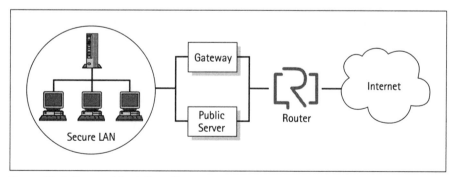

Figure 12-3: Screened host firewall

In the screened host firewall, the separation of the internal network from the perimeter network is logical, rather than physical. That is, the packet filtering rules are used to only allow traffic between the Internet and the gateway and public servers.

Because it is a logical, and not a physical separation, this configuration is less tolerant of errors, and if the public server does happen to get attacked from the outside, it can be used as an entryway into the internal network.

Although the screened host option is more flexible, it may be less secure, because the router can pass specific, less vulnerable services (such as NNTP) around the application gateway and directly to individual systems. This option can also be more difficult to maintain because you have to configure both a router and an application gateway.

Screened Subnet Firewall

The screened subnet firewall option is similar to the dual-homed and screened host firewall options. With this setup, each component of the firewall is located on a different system. Although this setup is more complex, it offers more flexibility and greater throughput.

In this configuration (see Figure 12-4), two routers create an inner, screened subnet that contains the application gateway, information servers, modem pools, or other systems to which access should be restricted.

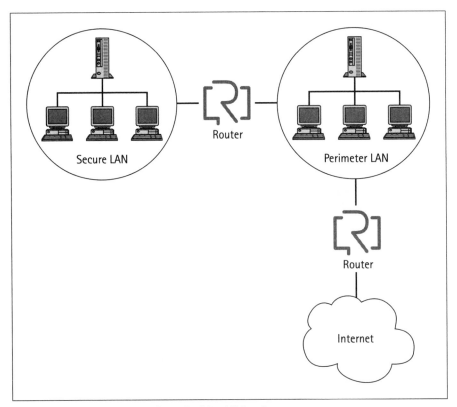

Figure 12-4: Screened subnet firewall with additional systems

Under this type of firewall configuration, no system can be directly accessed from the Internet; the routers direct the traffic to specific systems. The outer router restricts Internet access to specific systems and blocks all other traffic to the Internet that may be originating from systems that do not require Internet access. The inner router sends traffic between systems on the screened subnet.

Firewall Pros and Cons

A firewall is not an "install it and forget it" type of device. Configuration can be complex and tedious and require a great deal of planning. You should also consider the limitations of firewalls. Before actually creating your firewall policy, you should document several factors; for example, what Internet services will be used and from where, will encryption be required, and what costs will be imposed in terms of network usability.

You must consider every possible entryway when configuring the device, so you leave no vulnerabilities. You also have to weigh the amount of security you implement with the firewall against end user ease of use. If the firewall makes the network too difficult to use, end users will rebel, seek workarounds, and not use the security measures provided.

Something else to keep in mind: a firewall is *not* just a router. A firewall represents, or should represent, an entire approach to security. It is a tool for implementing a larger security policy that defines access and services. For the most part, the firewall's purpose is to regulate access to and from a protected network. The firewall implements the network access policy by routing all connections through it, so that it can examine each piece of traffic and determine whether the transmission should be allowed to pass into the internal network.

Pro

All firewalls are not alike and may not even consist of the same hardware. Although a firewall is commonly implemented as a router, it can also be a PC, host, or a set of PCs or hosts. As such, it is not the hardware itself, but its function that defines the firewall. While the physical device itself does not comprise the entirety of a good security system, it does offer some protection. It can, for example, offer the following services:

- ◆ **Protection for vulnerable services.** The firewall can minimize the risks to hosts by filtering out any inherently insecure services. By allowing only certain protocols to pass through the firewall and into the network, you expose the environment to fewer risks.

- ◆ **Protection against routing-based attacks.** Examples of this include attempts to redirect routing paths.

- ◆ **Controlled access to systems.** The firewall can allow outside users to access specific hosts, while denying access to other hosts containing more sensitive data.

- ◆ **Centralization of security software.** Centralization on the firewall system instead of distributing it on multiple hosts leads to simpler management.

- ◆ **Privacy.** The firewall can block services such as finger and Domain Name Service (DNS), which may provide attackers with information about users' identities.

- ◆ **Statistic collection.** The firewall can log information about access and provide the manager with information about network usage. The manager can use this information to watch for stealthy attackers.

- ◆ **Policy enforcement.** The firewall provides a means of enforcing the network access policy.

And Con

The firewall does have some drawbacks and limitations. For example, although a firewall can block services that may be harmful, it may block services that would be helpful as well. Suppose that some users want to access Telnet for a legitimate business purpose, but the security policy does not allow for it, and the firewall blocks this type of access. The security policy must carefully balance the types of accesses desired and needed by different end users against the potential risk.

A "back door" attack may also be possible, even with a firewall in place. Modem access, for example, may enable an attacker to bypass the firewall completely. An intruder with inside knowledge could, for example, dial up a modem directly, if the modem sits within the network and therefore behind the firewall. Once connected, the attacker could potentially gain access to the rest of the network. Regrettably, it is not possible for the firewall to protect against this sort of unauthorized access. The firewall does not protect against attacks from the inside – which is a very large risk indeed in most companies of any size.

Another limitation of firewalls is that they cannot protect against viruses. No firewall can prevent legitimate users from unknowingly downloading a virus-infected program or file. Because files are usually compressed or encoded for down-loading, it is impossible for the firewall to accurately scan them for virus signatures. Consequently, you'll need to supplement the firewall with a separate antivirus strategy.

Still another limitation of the firewall is that it could cause performance problems. Because all traffic must pass through the firewall, the firewall represents a potential bottleneck. However, this is seldom the case except for extremely high-traffic networks, because most firewalls are capable of passing data through at T1 rates (1.5Mbps).

A firewall tends to concentrate security in a single spot. This can be either a good or bad thing, depending how you look at it. With this type of concentration, you have the potential of compromising the entire network through a single point. In other words, if the firewall fails, the entire network could be attacked. However, distributing security over multiple hosts also holds some disadvantages. Although a distributed solution may disseminate security and minimize risk, it also is more difficult to manage. As a result, you have more places to make mistakes.

Despite the limitations of the firewall, it still comprises an important part of the overall security strategy and should be included as part of the security policy.

Firewall Policy

Although you have many ways to configure firewalls and firewall components, the technical details must take a back seat to the firewall's function as a tool to enforce security policy. That policy is divided into two areas: a network service access policy and a firewall design policy. The network service access policy defines what is allowed and what is denied regarding the network; the firewall design policy describes the technical details of how the firewall limits that access.

The network service access policy should not only restrict the use of internetwork services but other types of network access as well, including dial-in or SLIP connections. The service access policy may include a provision that disallows access to a site from the Internet, but allows access in the other direction—that is, from the site to the Internet. Or your policy may allow some access from the Internet, but only to specified servers or directories. In the latter case, you should require authentication before permitting access.

The firewall design policy, on the other hand, is more technically oriented and related to the implementation and configuration of the firewall components. This policy is based on the capabilities of the physical equipment and follows one of two general policies: permit all services that are not expressly denied or deny all services that are not expressly permitted.

Allowing all services that are not expressly denied is the less effective policy of the two because it allows more avenues for an intruder to gain access and requires the manager to consider all possibilities. It could also potentially enable users to access new services that are not expressly denied or addressed by policy, or could even enable access to a denied service if it is accessed at a nonstandard TCP/UDP port. The second option is more effective, although more difficult and often overly restrictive. However, in most circumstances, the "deny everything not expressly allowed" methodology should be employed, despite its inherent complexity.

You can use advanced authentication techniques along with the firewall to mitigate the all-or-nothing scenario. This way, the users who need access to such services as Telnet or FTP can have it. Advanced authentication techniques such as smart cards or authentication tokens represent a strong way to provide limited access to these services. The best advanced authentication option is a one-time password system that generates a unique response for every login. Because the password is for one-time use only, an attacker who "overhears" the password will be unable to reuse it. Although this solution can be deployed on each host, implementing it is much easier on the firewall itself. These one-time passwords can be implemented through separate hand-held devices or programs (such as S/Key) designed to generate one-time passwords.

Swiss banks that accept electronic payment orders use a method similar to one-time passwords to authenticate whoever is executing an order on a numbered account. If the account holder authorizes the bank to accept electronic funds transfers, the bank securely delivers a list of individual session passwords of from four to six digits in length. It is the account holder's responsibility to keep this list physically secure. When the account holder gives an order, the account holder must give the bank a user ID and password, and the next key from the list. The account holder then crosses off the key after one use, and then goes down the list for subsequent transactions. In this way, if the session between the account holder and the bank is intercepted, the outsider will still not be able to execute transactions, because the one-time password cannot be used again.

The S/Key one-time password system, originated by Bellcore, provides authentication over networks that are subject to attack. With S/Key, the secret password never has to cross the network during login, or when executing other commands requiring authentication (such as the *passwd* or *su* commands in UNIX).

S/Key is actually a very simple mechanism that protects a user's passwords against a passive attack. It does not, however, protect against active attacks. Nevertheless, it is easily added to any UNIX system without any additional hardware, and without requiring the system to store any sensitive information. It can be used with PCs or nonprogrammable terminals.

Next-Generation Firewalls

The first generation of firewalls were the packet filtering routers. They and other older generation firewalls have moved consistently in the direction of examining more of each packet, thereby giving attackers fewer opportunities to attack. This has given rise to a new generation of firewalls – a second and a third generation.

Second Generation

The second generation of firewalls – application and circuit gateways (also called *proxies*) – represents a more specialized type of service. These types of firewalls connect the local network to an external network (such as the Internet) through a secure workstation running specialized applications. Users can communicate with secure systems through a proxy, which shields data and other servers from attackers.

Circuit gateways focus on the transport layer of the OSI reference model and rely on the network TCP/IP connection to work as the proxy. The circuit proxy (or gateway) sits between the network router and the Internet. The only address that is transmitted to the outside world is that of the proxy, so addresses of network devices are hidden from view and safe from attack.

An *application gateway* works a little differently. While it provides a higher level of security, it is, nonetheless, visible to the user attempting to send traffic through the gateway. An application gateway has one program for every given service, such as Telnet or FTP. The program performs authentication on the user, and then restricts that user's privileges based on factors such as time of day or location of origin. The application gateway works as a sort of one-on-one proxy for one specific application. Consequently, a proxy agent must exist for each IP service.

The application gateway option is naturally more flexible, although it does need more maintenance. In addition, some performance delays may be evident because data must be processed by both the gateway and proxy agent.

Third Generation

Stateful Multi-Layer Inspection (SMLI) represents a third generation of firewall technology. This new class of firewall can be applied internally and externally, over different protocol boundaries, and with numerous advanced functions. SMLI is similar to the application gateway model in that it examines all seven layers in the OSI model. But instead of relying on a proxy, SMLI relies on a traffic screening algorithm optimized for high throughput. Each packet is examined and compared against known states of friendly packets. SMLI examines the entire packet (both address and application data). Because it does not use a proxy, it overcomes the performance problems of the application gateway model.

The SMLI solution enables all applications to run natively over the firewall, because no proxies or modifications need to be made. The user also does not face additional passwords or validation procedures, so the solution is transparent to the end user.

The ON Guard (ON Technology) implementation of SMLI delivers a more complete examination of all seven layers. It provides for application-level security without the limitations imposed by proxies; furthermore, end users are not limited to using only specific applications.

In the past, firewalls were largely UNIX-only beasts that were difficult to configure and operate. However, recently more offerings have been made on Windows NT and other platforms, giving users the capability to run their firewalls on more familiar and comfortable Intel-based PCs.

Offerings such as ON Technology's ON Guard overcome the complexities of UNIX. ON Technology uses its own secure, special-purpose operating system, Secure32OS, designed specifically for firewalls. Although UNIX may offer some advantages, a UNIX-based firewall may also have several drawbacks. Besides its complexity, and the probability that outside consultants will be required, source code is widely available and highly documented. Attackers live to hack UNIX. Proprietary firewall operating systems such as Secure32OS, on the other hand, are more difficult to hack because the information about these systems is unavailable to attackers.

OPSEC (Open Platform for Secure Enterprise Computing)

The Open Platform for Secure Enterprise Connectivity (OPSEC), designed by Check Point, promotes a single platform for enterprise-wide security. This single platform integrates all aspects of network security through a single, extensible framework. OPSEC has published APIs, so third-party applications can plug into the OPSEC framework. The integrated applications can then be managed from a single, central location and from a single policy editor.

Check Point Software Technologies uses OPSEC to unify its FireWall-1 enterprise security suite.

In April 1997, Check Point announced the OPSEC Alliance, an industry-wide organization dedicated to providing enterprise-wide security solutions. OPSEC and the OPSEC Alliance hope to facilitate interoperability at the policy level and between security products. More than 75 companies have joined Check Point in the OPSEC Alliance. Members of the alliance cover a wide range of security technologies, including encryption, authentication, content security, network infrastructure, and application software.

Check Point has published the following APIs for third-party integration:

♦ **Content Vectoring Protocol (CVP).** This allows for the integration of virus scanning software and other content inspection programs.

♦ **Suspicious Activity Monitoring Protocol (SAMP).** This API allows for the integration of suspicious-activity monitoring programs and permits the modification of access privileges upon detection of suspicious activity.

♦ **URL Filtering Protocol (UFP).** This API allows for the integration of URL list services for limiting access to specific Web pages from behind the firewall.

In addition, OPSEC supports the following open standards:

♦ **RADIUS.** Permits interoperability with new, third-party RADIUS authentication servers.

♦ **SNMP.** Allows for interoperability with most mainstream network management software, including HP OpenView, SunNet Manager, and IBM NetView.

♦ **LDAP (Lightweight Directory Application Protocol).** Enables OPSEC to extract user information from other LDAP-based directories.

♦ **ODBC (Open Database Connectivity).** Enables third parties to download Check Point log information to any ODBC-compliant database.

♦ **Fortezza.** A government standard for hardware-based token authentication.

◆ **IPSec ISAKMP (Internet Secure Association Key Management Protocol).** A mandatory key management scheme defined for the IETF (Internet Engineering Task Force) IPSec standard. This allows for Virtual Private Networking.

◆ **SKIP (Simple Key Management for Internet Protocols).** An optional key management scheme defined for the IETF IPSec standard.

Check Point FireWall-1 is based on a stateful inspection technology. *Stateful inspection* incorporates both communication-derived and application-derived state and context information, which is stored and updated dynamically. Through this approach, the firewall has full application-layer awareness but does not require a separate proxy for every service that must be secured. In addition, through its OPSEC framework, FireWall-1 offers strong cross-platform support for Windows 95, Windows NT, UNIX, and internetworking equipment from Check Point's OPSEC partners.

Stateful inspection may well represent the next generation of firewall technology – the next evolutionary step after application-layer proxies. Stateful inspection understands the state of any communication through the firewall, including packet, connection, and application information. Packet filters, for example, cannot track the application or connection state. An application proxy can track only the application state, but not the packet or connection state.

Stateful inspection, as implemented through Check Point's FireWall-1, examines communications at Layers 3 through 7 of the OSI reference model. (Application gateways only examine Layers 5 through 7.)

Allowing Remote Access to Users

Larger networks with a distributed workforce often allow remote workers to dial in to the network via modem. However, this capability represents a potential for attack by providing a back door around the firewall. This back door could swing open, for example, if the modem exists on the internal side of the firewall (for example, inside of a network-attached PC). An attacker with inside knowledge of the modem's existence could, therefore, directly access the modem, and bypass the firewall.

Instead of having modems distributed throughout the network, the more secure option is to use a single modem pool and to apply security to that pool.

Dial-in via modem works like this: users dial in and connect to a terminal server, which connects the modem to the network. After connecting to the terminal server, the remote user can Telnet to other host systems within the internal network. If a user can connect to any host system after connecting, the system has a very large potential problem. However, you can usually configure a terminal server to restrict connections to given systems (for example, Telnet access can be denied to certain hosts) or to require some sort of authentication on the part of the remote user.

You can secure the modem pool by locating it outside the firewall. Doing so forces all modem connections to pass through the firewall. However, this also connects the modem pool directly to the Internet and opens another vulnerability to attackers who may attempt to access the modem pool directly from the Internet. You can mitigate this vulnerability by configuring the terminal server to reject any dial-in connections to any system outside of the application gateway(s).

Alternatively, you can use the modem pool with a screened subnet firewall and locate it on the inner subnet, thereby affording greater control and security. With this option, a router is connected directly to the Internet and prevents any routing between the Internet and the modem pool.

Demilitarized Zone (DMZ)

A DMZ is a way of configuring the firewall to ensure the greatest level of security. The DMZ (see Figure 12-5) adds an extra layer of protection by establishing a server network that exists between the protected network and the external network (the Internet). The DMZ is attached directly to the secure point of access and is usually implemented as a third interface on the device that runs the security application. A firewalled network with no DMZ positions all resources behind the firewall. The term is named after the zone that separates North and South Korea, a sort of political "no-man's land." A network DMZ does offer protection, but, if the firewall is compromised, the entire network is vulnerable.

In Figure 12-5, if network resources (HTTP, FTP, and so on) were located behind the firewall instead of in the DMZ, an attack that reached those servers would have broken through the secure access point and would face no further security measures. However, when those resources are located in the DMZ, traffic to and from these resources has to pass through an access point that is secured by the same security policy.

Hosts on the perimeter network (DMZ) are accessible from the outside (the Internet), while hosts on the internal network are not accessible from the outside. Therefore, the DMZ serves to isolate the internal network from the Internet. Of course, any host that is visible to the Internet has the potential to be attacked. And once a host is attacked, an intruder could potentially use that host as a jumping-off point to gain access to the rest of the network. However, if an attacker gains control of a machine in the DMZ, the internal network is still secure.

Notice that two routers exist in the preceding configuration, one interior and one exterior. The interior router handles most of the packet filtering, and defines what outbound services are permitted. The exterior router limits access such that the only services that are allowed are those services provided by the perimeter network. For example, if the perimeter network contains HTTP and FTP servers, the router is configured to allow only HTTP and FTP services and to deny everything else.

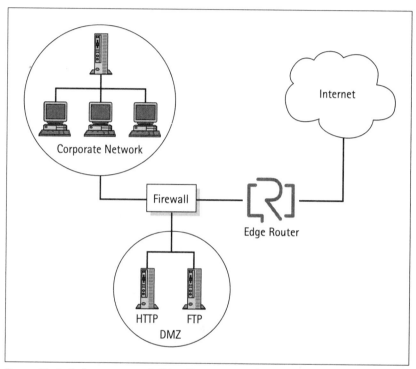

Figure 12-5: Perimeter network ("demilitarized zone")

Implementing Firewall Services

You have many factors to consider when implementing a firewall, including the following:

- ◆ Access control
- ◆ Authentication
- ◆ Encryption
- ◆ Router security management
- ◆ Network address translation
- ◆ Content security

- ◆ Connection control

- ◆ Auditing, logging, and alerting

If you will be deploying an information server to provide public access to information, this deployment may also become part of the firewall specification. You do not have to compromise the network's security to provide public access to data, and the policy should reflect this philosophy. One option open to you is to set up a separate Web server that is not part of the internal network and place all the public information and files on that server only. That Web server would have only an external connection to the Internet and no connections at all to the internal network. As a result, you eliminate the possibility that the internal network would be compromised, even if the Web server is attacked.

Access Control

Access to the Internet brings corporations the advantage of widespread access and an easy way to share information. However, it also brings the risk of attack and unauthorized access. Access control is a critical part of security policy that must be implemented by the firewall.

Access control policy specifies what and who can enter or exit the corporate network. To maintain access control, the security manager must have a clear picture of all services and applications that are available. Earlier packet filtering routers could not do this task because they were not aware of applications. Second generation firewalls, or application proxies, *are* application-aware, but consume a great deal of overhead. Later technologies that use stateful inspection and other advanced techniques build on this application-layer awareness, while providing faster support for new services.

Access control not only addresses what can pass into the network, but should also enable the security manager to specify rules as to what time each user can access which service.

Access control protects against measures such as IP spoofing, denial-of-service attacks, or the "ping of death":

- ◆ **IP spoofing.** In this type of attack, an intruder gains access to the network by changing a packet's IP address to make it look as though it originated in a part of the network with more access privileges. For example, an attacker may undertake an IP spoof to make a packet originating on the Internet appear as though it were local.

- ◆ **Denial-of-service attack.** Under this type of attack, a hacker initiates a TCP connection with a client and issues a request to a server with the SYN flag set in the TCP header. Under normal circumstances, the server then sends a SYN/ACK (acknowledgment) back to the client, and the client sends an ACK back to the server, and data transmission occurs. However, the denial-of-service attacker spoofs the client IP address to be that of an unreachable host, so the preceding acknowledgment process can never be completed.

♦ **Ping of death.** A large PING packet (greater than 65508 bytes) cannot be handled adequately by almost any operating system kernel. Therefore, when such a packet is sent, the systems are likely to crash and reboot. A firewall that can prevent packets larger than 64KB from passing through will effectively prevent this type of attack.

Another element of access control is to "stealth" the firewall, or hide its access point from unauthorized users. This makes the firewall inaccessible to any user or any application outside of management and configuration purposes. Network Address Translation is used to conceal internal network addresses from the Internet.

Authentication

Enterprise resources must be protected through authentication. Some firewalls centralize these authentication services as well as provide tracking and logging services for subsequent review.

You have three types of authentication to consider in your security policy:

♦ **User authentication.** This authentication provides access on a per-user basis to various services such as FTP, Telnet, or HTTP. Authentication may be based on a password scheme, digital signature, or other secure mechanism. This access is granted regardless of the user's IP address. Placing authentication on the firewall prevents authentication from taking place directly on the requested server, thus centralizing the process at the firewall. The firewall intercepts the access attempt, directs the connection request to a security server, and then authenticates the user. After authentication, the firewall opens a second connection to the requested host.

♦ **Client authentication.** This type of authentication, on the other hand, grants access based on the specific IP address. Authentication of this sort is not based on specific services.

♦ **Transparent session authentication.** This authentication is used to authenticate any service on a per-session basis. As implemented by Check Point's FireWall-1 gateway, transparent session authentication works as follows: The user initiates a connection to the server. The gateway, which sits between the user and the destination, intercepts the connection and initiates a connection with a session authentication agent. The agent carries out the authentication, and then the firewall allows the initial connection to continue.

Content Security

Downloadables such as Java applets present a new type of risk to the Internet — a type of risk that cannot be detected by a traditional firewall solution. Content security protects the network against malicious content, such as computer viruses or Java/ActiveX applets written to do harm to the network or compromise its security. Virus scanning, in many enterprises, is left up to individual end users. This approach is only minimally successful — ideally, virus scanning should be a centralized and regulated process.

Implementing virus scanning at the firewall provides the greatest level of protection. Again, Check Point facilitates this integration by enabling its OPSEC partners to provide the antivirus software to work with its FireWall-1 offering.

A supplementary solution often must be considered to handle the risk of allowing access to Java applets. Java applets bring us a lot more than dancing logos; they can be used as part of a critical operation. But most security managers are afraid to have users download Java applets from the Internet and usually block access to them completely. The mere idea of allowing end users to download active programs from the Internet indiscriminately goes against everything a security manager believes in. Although a full block may be the best solution for environments containing highly sensitive data, on some occasions Java applets may be necessary. While Java does offer many security-related features, it is still theoretically possible for a rogue applet to get through and cause at least limited damage.

Several high-profile firewall vendors, including Check Point Software Technologies Ltd., Digital Equipment Corp., Milkyway Networks Corp., Network-1 Software & Technologies, Inc., and Trusted Information Systems, Inc., have signed up with Finjan, Inc. to strengthen their firewalls against Sun Microsystems Inc. Java applet attacks.

Finjan's SurfinGate Java (see Figure 12-6) is one of the earliest software tools capable of scanning and examining Java applets entering the corporate network. A gateway-level firewall, SurfinGate takes a new approach to handling potentially hostile Java applets. Instead of simply denying access, the product examines all downloadables seeking passage through the gateway. SurfinGate creates a digital signature on the fly, scans the applet's byte code to develop a security profile, and compares the results to an existing security policy to determine whether it should be allowed to pass through.

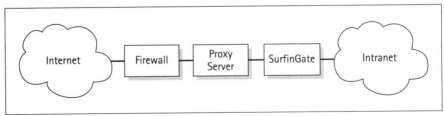

Figure 12-6: Finjan's SurfinGate adds an extra layer of protection inside the firewall to protect against hostile Java applets.

Another function of the firewall can be URL screening; this can restrict access to specific Web pages that may be harmful, wasteful of employee time, or too large for the network to handle. You can also address Java and ActiveX attacks at the firewall, either via an attached program, such as SurfinGate, or by the firewall itself. When implemented at the firewall itself, protection against Java and ActiveX usually consists merely of stripping Java and ActiveX code according to specific conditions. Some firewalls can, for example, strip Java applet tags from HTML pages, strip Java applets from replies, and block suspicious connections.

The firewall should also offer fine granularity over SMTP support. SMTP supports e-mail and file attachment, and support of this protocol is essential to continued communication. However, the firewall should include controls over SMTP connections, in order to shield an outgoing e-mail message's *From* address behind a standard, generic address. This function conceals the internal network structure and internal users from the public Internet.

Some firewalls support a proprietary, hardened operating system. This is because users with access to an underlying operating system could potentially jeopardize the integrity of the firewall and expose network resources to attack. The hardened operating system protects the firewall by restricting access to critical processes, configuration files, data files, and utilities.

Firewall Logs

All firewalls generate a log file of information that you can use for analyzing firewall security and management. This log enables the manager to see where users are going on the Web, how much bandwidth is being used, and other details.

This log is important for tracking misuse of the company's access policies. A single improper, unauthorized use of the Web for recreational or personal purposes could have a dramatic effect on the network. For example, a rogue employee who spends his or her lunch hour downloading pictures from the Web could not only harm productivity, but could even produce a negative impact on the entire network's performance. Even a small amount of misuse can add up quickly. An organization with 200 employees, with average salaries of $25,000 annually, could lose $300,000 a year to nonproductive time if every employee spent only 30 minutes a day misusing the Internet.

Although some companies can simply prohibit employees from having Internet access, this is not a possibility for many firms, because it would harm the company's competitiveness. In these cases, the firewall log is a must-have. The problem with these logs, however, is that they are often confusing to read and quite abstract.

TELEMATE Software's TELEMATE.*Net* is one of a new breed of firewall software tools that reads complicated firewall log files and generates an intuitive and informative management report. These translated versions of the log files help you control costs and detect misuse among users more easily than was possible with the original log file.

TELEMATE.*Net* is the first product to address the burgeoning Internet management issue at a strategic level. Version 1.1 of TELEMATE.*Net* is also unique in that it reads Internet data directly from firewall log files rather than taking data from other devices added to the network that could limit or interfere with the transfer of information. These capabilities make tools such as TELEMATE.*Net* particularly valuable as a means of monitoring compliance with the company's acceptable-use policy for the Internet.

Summary

In this chapter, you learned about the following:

◆ Firewalls are only one small part of an overall security structure, and only one of several tools that you can use to implement the security policy.

◆ Firewalls also have some disadvantages and drawbacks. While they can block access to particularly vulnerable services such as Telnet and FTP, some network users may have a legitimate need to access these services and may be prevented from doing so by the firewall.

◆ Telnet, FTP, and other services can be provided in a firewalled network through use of an application gateway. The firewall sends all requests for particular services to a single server, which usually enforces security through authentication and passwords.

◆ General-purpose routers do offer some basic firewall services. However, packet filtering routers function only at the lowest layers of the OSI model, or the physical connections. Other firewall technologies may examine higher layers; the best firewall implementations examine all layers of the OSI model.

Chapter 13

Security Devices

THE NEED FOR STRONG network security has created a market for a wide variety of security gizmos, doodads, and whatzits. Besides the traditional collection of antivirus software, firewalls, and network monitors, the never-ending quest for keeping secrets has led to the creation of devices such as Miros' TrueFace CyberWatch, which uses face recognition technology to control access, and numerous other solutions. Devices that record a user's fingerprint, voiceprint, or face pattern have just started to mature. Although these methods may seem intrusive, for the legitimate end user they are much easier to use than tokens or passwords.

Face Recognition Devices

Passwords can be broken or stolen, encryption can be cracked. But nobody can steal your face. Face recognition devices use video technology to create an image database of authorized users.

These neural network-based systems are not easily fooled. They typically use two views of each live face presentation. The use of two views provides a stereo view of the face, which makes it impossible for someone to simply use a photograph of an authorized user to attempt to gain unauthorized entry.

The Miros TrueFace CyberWatch software works with a small video camera and takes a picture of each user. The pictures are stored in an image database. CyberWatch then takes a picture of a user when he or she requests access. The picture of the user requesting access is compared against the pictures in the image database. If a user is not verified, a picture of the intruder will be stored for subsequent audit.

TrueFace relies on neural network technology, which learns how to compare faces from its own experience. This is similar to how the human brain functions by learning as it goes along. Miros' proprietary neural network design uses features from each part of the face to determine the similarity between two facial images – not just the distances and angles between the eyes, nose, and mouth. So, you don't need to worry if you sprout a lip broom – the software is able to compensate for variations such as suntan and beard growth.

Although the concept of video camera security may be attractive, especially in sensitive locations, widespread user acceptance of such a plan may be difficult because users may perceive the technology as intrusive.

In a move that pushes the envelope of face recognition technology, Miros recently announced an alliance with Mr. Payroll Corporation, a convenience store check cashing service, to present the world the first fully automated check cashing system using biometrics. Miros will integrate TrueFace with the Mr. Payroll check cashing system to provide a solution for ensuring that the users of the automated system are who they claim to be. Because the TrueFace system both identifies and verifies faces, customers of the Mr. Payroll system will no longer have to wait for manual identification checks. Instead, they will be automatically identified when they use a Mr. Payroll machine.

Theft Recovery Software and Services

Because of their small size and mobility, laptops are particularly vulnerable to theft. Although you can insure the machine itself against loss, you cannot do the same with the data it contains. In addition to providing sensitive data, a stolen laptop may give a thief access to passwords or phone numbers that could be used to further compromise the private computer network. Therefore, the security policy for your laptops should include the following three precautions:

- ◆ Encrypt sensitive data
- ◆ Back up all data on the laptop regularly
- ◆ Use a theft control system

In addition to these precautions, you can use *computer tracing software.* Although it does not prevent the theft itself, this type of software facilitates recovery through an unusual "stealth" technology. Absolute Software's CompuTrace software, for example, runs undetected, and silently and automatically calls the CompuTrace Monitoring Center on a weekly basis. Absolute's monitoring service collects all the details of each call made by each laptop and places it into a reporting system. You can access these reports through Absolute's secure Web site via e-mail or fax.

If a laptop is stolen, the owner reports the theft to CompuTrace, which then goes into "Alert" mode. When the stolen laptop is connected to a phone line, it will dial out, unbeknownst to the thief, and tell the CompuTrace Monitoring center where it is calling from. Absolute will then immediately report the computer's location to the owner and notify the police. The police can then obtain the street address of the location from where the PC called and attempt to retrieve it.

Versions of the product are available for both LANs and stand-alone workstations.

Web Site Blocking Tools

Depending on the nature of your business and your views on productivity, you may want to limit your workers' Web activity. Although many workers may see this as an invasion of privacy and resent the control, it may be necessary for some people who spend too much time in chat rooms, newsgroups, or even at pornographic sites during company time. Too much Web cruising unrelated to business can be counterproductive, so you need to be able to monitor who's doing what on the Web.

Keep in mind that, more than likely, not everyone in the company needs to have Internet access. Part of a good security policy includes establishing who needs Internet access and who doesn't, and then allocating it accordingly. This sort of policy not only helps minimize Web cruising not related to business, but it also limits the number of users who could potentially cause harm to the network.

In the end, it comes down to this question: do you want to limit your employees' Web access? It's your call, but if you want to, there are plenty of tools with which to do it.

Tools such as LittleBrother Pro, from Kansmen Corporation function as a sort of network monitor. Unlike standard network monitors, which generate statistics on which external users are using a site, how often they visit and how long they stay (information that is often used by the marketing department), LittleBrother monitors the activities of internal users. LittleBrother is a little different than other blocking tools on the market in that it goes beyond merely blocking sites – it also generates a report with detailed statistics. The manager can use this report to decide who is abusing Web privileges and who is using them appropriately.

LittleBrother generates several easy-to-read management reports (see Figure 13-1). The Daily Overview report lists each day's usage overview in a row. Each day's usage is rated into the following divisions: productive, unproductive, neutral, and not rated. This report gives you an overview of how productive (or unproductive) your Internet access is each day. The report can show either the top user or top site in each rating division.

Besides monitoring Web and LAN resources, LittleBrother can also watch over FTP and newsgroup traffic and generate reports by user, site, protocol, and bandwidth consumed. In addition to summaries and reports, the product can also designate specific sites as off-limits to enforce rules.

Date	Productive	Unproductive	Neutral	Not Rated
	Daily overview for sites			_ □ ×
	From 03/25/97 14:00:00 to 04/01/97 16:43:00			
04/01/97	23% [microsoft.public.active...	16% [www.playboy.com]	6% [home26.netscape.c...	55% [milpitas01.pop.i...
03/31/97	10% [comp.security.firewalls]	42% [rec.autos.sport.f1]	3% [mail.hooked.net]	45% [milpitas01.pop.i...
03/30/97	0%	0%	0%	0%
03/29/97	0%	0%	0%	0%
03/28/97	6% [ftp.kansmen.com]	7% [guide-p.infoseek.c...	11% [testdriveftp.netsca...	75% [207.200.74.40]
03/27/97	10% [ftp.kansmen.com]	12% [members.aol.com]	13% [home28.netscape....	64% [milpitas01.pop.i...
03/26/97	20% [microsoft.public.proxy]	25% [www.playboy.com]	18% [milpitas01.pop.inte...	36% [milpitas01.pop.i...
03/25/97	27% [microsoft.public.vc.lan...	10% [www.cnn.com]	28% [milpitas01.pop.inte...	35% [206.84.226.17]

Figure 13-1: A LittleBrother management report

Physical Security Devices

I've talked a lot about how to prevent people from breaking into the network and how to minimize the damage they can cause if they get past security. But how do you keep people, either from the inside or from the outside, from walking out with computer equipment? Most workers will assume that someone wearing overalls and carrying a clipboard is in a position of authority, and if they are carrying out an armload of routers, it's probably because they're going out for repair.

Simple policy points may address some of these concerns. For example, all service people should be required to sign in and out of the building. The receptionist should be given advance notice of any service people who are expected, perhaps with a schedule update daily.

You might also decide on a network configuration that employs a *server farm*, where all servers are kept in a single location. This is convenient and enables simplified management, not to mention added security if the server farm is located in a secure, locked room with limited access. Only those individuals who require access should possess a key. Unauthorized personnel, clerical staff, and others who do not need to be in the room can be successfully kept at bay. Allowing clerical staff unlimited access to the computer room for the purpose of delivering internal memos, mail, and other routine material defeats the purpose of securing the room. You can avoid this intrusion by locating a simple stack of in-boxes directly outside the door, one in-box for each individual who works inside.

In some cases, however – particularly with expensive PCs that contain exceptionally sensitive data and when a secure room is not an option – additional physical security may be appropriate. You might consider a physical device to lock down equipment.

Companies such as PC Guardian offer a wide variety of physical antitheft devices and cabling systems designed to prevent the pilfering of the CPU, internal components, monitors, keyboards, mice, peripherals, and other equipment in your office. These types of devices typically consist of a steel security cable, which is anchored to a stationary object and then attached to the equipment using either a screw-mount or adhesive fittings.

Limited Access to the Power Switch

In a highly secure environment (such as a military installation), sensitive computers are either locked away, or access to them is limited by exposing only the computer's keyboard, monitor, mouse, and printer to users. The power switch, CPU and removable media drives can all be locked away so that only authorized personnel can access them. In this type of highly secure system, unauthorized users should also be kept away from the power and reset switches, if the security policy states that the right to shut down the computer is limited.

On some hardware platforms, the system is protected through a power-on password, which prevents an unauthorized user from starting an alternate operating system (which would compromise security).

Disk Drive Locks

A physical drive lock, a simple device not likely to cost much more than $20, could prevent sensitive documents from falling into the wrong hands. The lock prevents all unauthorized personnel from accessing the disk drive, thereby preventing the introduction of unauthorized software or the unauthorized copying of information. Figure 13-2 shows an example of a disk drive lock from PC Guardian.

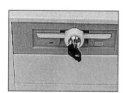

Figure 13-2: A physical disk drive lock provides added security.

Notebook Physical Security

Notebook computers are unusually vulnerable to theft because they are small and mobile. Caution must be used especially when traveling; airport thieves target business people traveling with notebook computers. A passing thief can easily hide a notebook under a jacket or in a briefcase. Short of handcuffing the notebook to your wrist, you can still protect yourself against theft, whether you are traveling or at the office.

One option to consider is a security cable, which attaches at one end to the notebook and at the other end to a stationary device. Such cables are widely available. A notebook security cable from PC Guardian is shown in Figure 13-3.

Figure 13-3: A security cable guarantees that a thief does not walk away with a notebook computer under his or her coat.

Smart Cards

Smart cards are little credit-card sized devices capable of holding a great deal of information about an employee or a user. They can be used in conjunction with remote access as a means of restricting access to secure areas of a building or, more commonly, for secure electronic commerce.

Smart cards are ideal for safeguarding the integrity of shared information because they contain an embedded memory chip or microprocessor. This is more secure than a magnetic stripe card, typically used in credit cards, where information contained in the magnetic stripe can be accessed, copied, or altered directly. Information on a smart card, on the other hand, cannot be accessed directly. The embedded microprocessor encrypts the cardholder's information before sending it to the card reader. The card reader then decrypts the information.

Until recently, smart card technology was limited to major corporate users, and was expensive to implement due to a lack of standardization. For the most part, the smart card industry consists of a few large organizations that provide turn-key solutions to large companies such as banks or telecom companies. However, fewer solutions exist for smaller companies needing a more flexible and customizable solution.

Some incompatibility issues must still be resolved before smart cards can be widely deployed as a security solution in a mixed environment. Much of the incompatibility revolves around the support equipment for the cards. Hardware and software is usually designed to work with only one specific type of smart card. Some examples of smart card applications currently in use include:

◆ **Authentication.** A smart card can hold password and authentication information, to protect the integrity of exchanged information such as financial transactions and sensitive data. In this case, only the holder of the smart card is authorized to conduct certain transactions.

◆ **Computer security.** Smart cards can prevent misuse of computers and improper access of sensitive data by controlling access to PCs, networks, directories, and files. Again, the smart card contains access information, which either allows or denies access to specific documents or devices.

◆ **Electronic commerce.** Smart cards are a perfect secure solution for electronic shopping. In this application, the smart card contains credit card information, shipping addresses, and other data.

Depending on the smart card application, different types of smart cards exist. Applications requiring strong security should rely on microprocessor-based smart cards, because these offer the greatest security, the most memory, and the fastest operation. Memory-based smart cards, on the other hand, are best used for lower-security applications such as department store club cards or for storing records.

Aladdin Smart Card Environment (ASE)

The Aladdin Smart Card Environment (ASE), a proprietary standard offered by Aladdin Knowledge Systems, provides an integrated, modular, PC-based development environment for creating smart-card based applications. These include:

♦ ASEDrive, a PC-based read/write smart card drive

♦ ASESoft, a library of software interfaces and cryptographic tools

♦ ASECards, a set of smart cards for various uses

ASE was designed to help smaller organizations take advantage of smart card technology and to promote security and compatibility. It is essentially an integrated, modular environment for creating PC-based smart card applications. The ASEDrive smart card drive unit supports both microprocessor-based and memory-based smart cards that meet both ISO 7816 and I2C standards, so it supports all industry-standard smart cards. In addition, the API included in ASESoft offers a secure working environment, which includes a proprietary encryption algorithm and antidebugging mechanisms to safeguard data integrity.

Different levels of security can be implemented in the smart card software. For example, Data Encryption Standard (DES) can be used to encrypt financial data, and the DES secret key can be stored on a smart card. RSA, another common encryption algorithm, can also be used to store digital signatures on a smart card for message verification or authentication. Some microprocessor-based smart cards are available with a built-in DES or RSA algorithm from vendors including AT&T, Verifone, and Gemplus.

Hardware Locks

The term *dongle* is usually preceded by a swear word. A dongle is a small hardware device that ships with some software programs. The device must be plugged into the computer's parallel port before the software can be used. The dongle is hard-coded with a unique serial number that corresponds to the software program. When the program runs, it checks for the presence of the device. If the device is not plugged in, the program will not run (or will run only in a limited fashion). The dongle can be used to set an expiration date on the software, restrict features that can be used, or limit the number of times the software can be executed. They are annoying because they require end users to take additional steps to access their programs. But they are also the most effective way to prevent software piracy. This is important when you consider the statistics: according to the Business Software Alliance, losses from piracy total $13 billion annually.

Corporate and commercial developers sometimes use these little hardware devices to protect software. Aladdin's HASP (Hardware Against Software Piracy) serves as an example of how to prevent piracy and secure software products against unauthorized use.

The hardware key contains an ASIC (Application-Specific Integrated Circuit) chip. In the Aladdin system pictured in Figure 13-4, the protected software sends queries at runtime to the HASP key connected to the computer. The key then evaluates each software query and issues a response. If the response returned by the key is correct, the software can be activated. If the response is incorrect, the developer can configure it to prevent the software from activating, or switch to a demo mode.

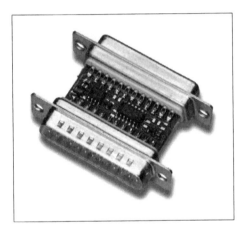

Figure 13-4: Aladdin Knowledge Systems' HASP software protection system

Dongles are used primarily in stand-alone applications, but can also be applied to networked environments. Sentinel Software Protection's NetSentinel, for example, is a network version of that company's Sentinel line. NetSentinel gives developers a tool to ensure that only authorized LAN sites are running their applications, and that site license limits for concurrent usage are being observed. The device itself can be installed either on a designated workstation or on the file server. The device then tracks requests for application use.

Summary

In this chapter, we talked about the following:

♦ The need for strong, yet easy-to-use security has created a market for security devices that grant access based on a user's fingerprint, voiceprint, or face pattern. Although these security devices may seem overly intrusive, in reality, they are much easier to work with, and do not require end users to remember passwords or use tokens.

◆ Face recognition systems work by installing a small video camera on the PC, which allows the PC to actually recognize each user by comparing a video image against a database of pictures. If an attacker attempts to gain access, the video camera records a picture of the attacker for later identification.

◆ Specialized theft recovery software can be installed to track laptops in case they are stolen. This software, which is invisible to the thief, automatically calls a central number as soon as the laptop is connected to a phone line, and provides authorities with the phone number from which it is calling.

◆ A great many pieces of hardware are lost to theft, either from employees who walk out the door with them, or thieves who walk into an office dressed as service people carrying a clipboard. Inexpensive physical security devices can be used to lock PCs, printers, scanners, and other peripherals to a stationary surface.

◆ Smart cards represent one of the newer types of security devices. Microprocessor-based smart cards in particular can be used to enhance security by storing encryption keys and controlling access to systems.

Chapter 14

Redundancy

IN THIS CHAPTER

- ◆ Redundancy as protection against accidents and disasters
- ◆ Redundant cabling and fiber
- ◆ Redundant servers
- ◆ RAID systems and redundant storage
- ◆ Redundancy in different network types

EARLIER IN THIS BOOK, we discussed the two main focuses of a security policy: protecting against harmful intruders, and protecting against the failure and data loss that can result from accidents or disasters. We've covered a lot of ground on the former, but it's just as important to address the latter part of the security policy. You can protect against loss from accidents or natural disasters by reinforcing the network with *redundant configurations*, or *redundancy*.

Having redundancy on your network means adding extra, duplicate elements to compensate for any malfunctions that could occur in the main equipment. Almost any element in a network can be duplicated, depending on the level of security desired. The most common type of redundancy is the data backup, although the concept is often applied to cabling, server hardware, and network devices such as routers and hubs.

Hardware redundancy is also applied to hard disks, servers, and cables. Hard disks can be duplicated through disk mirroring or disk duplexing, or through a RAID (redundant array of inexpensive disks) configuration. Hardware redundancy is necessary because despite the manufacturers' best efforts, hardware components are not perfect and can fail. The failure may not even be the fault of the manufacturer, but may be the result of a power surge, user error, misconfiguration, or sabotage. A spare or redundant component can be provided to replace an equivalent component that may fail. The typical redundant operation installs two equivalent components, both ready to operate. Only one is active, the other stands ready to take over if needed. The active component carries out self-tests, and when a failure occurs, the role of active component is typically switched over to the backup component automatically.

Data redundancy generates extra copies of data, such as database records or important documents, and stores them in a separate location. Part of data redundancy is software redundancy, which generates extra copies of critical code to compensate in case the original code gets corrupted.

In the following sections, we look at redundancy in hardware and software, and how different networking strategies approach the issue of redundancy.

Reliability, Availability, and Serviceability

The three areas of reliability, availability, and serviceability (also called RAS) describe metrics used to measure a system's capability to operate continuously and to reduce service times. *Reliability* is the technology used to minimize system failures and ensure data integrity. *Availability* concerns the accessibility of the system's data and applications. And *serviceability* addresses the need for a short service cycle (downtime) in the event of a failure.

Reliability is built into the technology and is a function of manufacturing and component selection. In general, reliability minimizes the possibility of failure. An important measure of reliability is Mean Time Between Failure (MTBF).

Availability is a measure that shows the time any given resource is accessible and usable. Availability is built on top of reliability, and it is usually measured as a percentage of total uptime.

Serviceability is a measure of the time required to isolate and repair a problem, or to restore a system following a failure.

Meeting these requirements is largely a matter of configuration. For example, you can configure a base system for a higher RAS level by adding a redundant control board, mirroring disks, and other measures. Generally, increasing system redundancy adds significantly to the RAS level. You need to add in software along with the additional redundant systems to detect failures and switch over to the secondary components. All of this adds to the cost, but in an environment running highly sensitive or mission-critical data, these types of extraordinary and costly steps sometimes must be taken.

Sun Microsystems' SunTrust defines a set of features on the Ultra Enterprise 10000 server that delivers RAS capabilities. SunTrust incorporates three main architectural elements that promote RAS:

◆ Gigaplane-XB crossbar interconnect

◆ Dynamic reconfiguration

◆ Integrated System Service Processor

Gigaplane-XB Crossbar Interconnect

The Gigaplane-XB crossbar provides communications between processors, memory, and I/O. It implements a high-speed, point-to-point connection between system boards and implements Sun's Ultra Port Architecture (UPA) using a crossbar rather than a bus. This type of interconnect affords a higher level of system availability. This model is superior to a bus architecture, because it can provide up to 12.8Gbps of bandwidth at a low constant latency, thereby enabling fast, uniform memory access.

The Gigaplane-XB uses separate paths for addresses and data, and the Global Data Router and Global Address Bus provide for redundancy and smooth recovery in case of failure. The Global Data Router routes 16 bytes in parallel through two 8-byte routers with independent power and clocks signals. This way, if one router fails, work can continue on the other router after the system recovers. The Global Address Bus uses four independent buses but can operate on fewer if a failure occurs.

Up to 16 system boards (64 processors) can be mounted on the Gigaplane-XB, which controls fast communications between these boards and external connections. The Gigaplane connects system boards through one global data router and four global address buses. Using separate buses enables data and address topologies to be independently optimized, depending on purpose. A global data router provides for a direct, fast path between any two processors in the system. Similarly, using four global address buses permits four simultaneous address transfers to take place throughout the system.

Dynamic Reconfiguration

Dynamic reconfiguration enables a physical or logical restructuring of the Ultra Enterprise 10000 server while the system is active.

Integrated System Service Processor

The Integrated System Service Processor (SSP) is the central console that monitors the system and enables the operator to carry out management and maintenance tasks. The SSP is a specialized workstation that communicates with the 10000. SSP monitors system status and provides an interface for managing system partitioning and dynamic reconfiguration. It also protects the system from environmental conditions that could cause damage, provides for recovery from fatal errors, and automatically reconfigures the system after testing for component faults.

Sun Microsystems' Ultra Enterprise 10000 serves as an example of a system with a high degree of redundancy. This server achieves high availability and data integrity through component redundancy and other areas such as error detection and correction and online transparent servicing. The Enterprise 10000 can be configured in such a way that no single point of failure exists in the hardware configuration.

The Ultra Enterprise 10000 incorporates several redundant components, including memory, processors, I/O ports, system boards, centerplane control boards, power supplies, and cooling fans. Consequently, in the event that a component fails, the system still enjoys uninterrupted availability. When a component fails, the system automatically isolates it, takes the component offline, and logs the error for servicing.

Some failures occur as a result of power loss or power fluctuations. The Sun system minimizes this risk through its redundant power supply architecture. This architecture includes redundant AC wiring, redundant DC power supplies, system-board power supplies, and hot swapping capability.

The Enterprise 10000 offers multiple, modular power supplies. The base model has five power supplies, but can operate on four. Consequently, if one supply fails, the other four can meet power requirements without affecting performance. Furthermore, each side of the centerplane has its own power distribution bus, and each system board maintains its own power supply locally with on-board regulators.

All components of the server can be configured for redundancy, and each link can be made redundant. Administrators have the option of redundant control boards, centerplane support boards, system boards, disk storage, bulk power subsystems, bulk power supplies, peripheral controllers and channels, and the System Service Processor. Having a fully redundant system such as the Sun 10000 always allows for recovery from a system crash using standby components.

Redundant power and cooling is an important but often overlooked part of a mission-critical server. This feature helps the server survive a failure of the power supply or fan without interrupting the system's operation. The 10000 includes this facility and also adds an optional, duplicate power cord that can be connected to separate in-house circuits.

Redundant Cabling

You can achieve high availability in your network using *link redundancy* (redundant cabling). This type of redundancy provides a parallel path that runs next to the main data path and a rerouting methodology that can establish an alternate path in case the main path fails. A redundant, parallel path can be either an exact and parallel duplicate of the main path or a less expensive alternative that may carry data more slowly. The latter option is less expensive, but still keeps the network going if the main path goes down. For example, a mission-critical ATM (Asynchronous Transfer Mode) backbone network may have a less expensive, 100Mbps (Fast Ethernet) backbone established as a backup.

One alternative to redundant links is a *meshed network*. A meshed network is a network made up of multiple, high-speed paths between several endpoints (see Figure 14-1). A meshed network enables transparent rerouting around a broken link, in effect creating a self-healing network.

These multiple paths are used for regular data transfer during normal network operation. If one path fails, the network reroutes traffic over an alternate path. For example, in the configuration shown in Figure 14-1, if the B–D data path fails, traffic can be rerouted through any of the remaining endpoints to reach its destination.

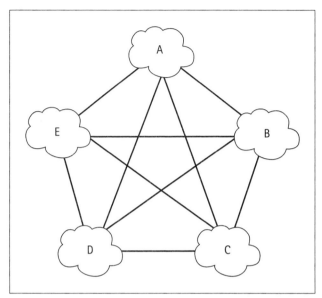

Figure 14-1: A meshed network offers a high degree of fault tolerance.

Corporate users who rely on dedicated lines to link LANs into a WAN may want to implement redundancy in this area as well. Companies such as Dataprobe (http://www.dataprobe.com) offer automatic end-to-end restoration switching systems to achieve this redundancy.

You can achieve a redundant line backup for digital circuits through a dedicated backup link (see Figure 14-2). The backup link can be an equivalent digital or analog leased line. To get the highest reliability, you should use an alternate carrier for the backup, so if the primary carrier goes down, the backup will still work.

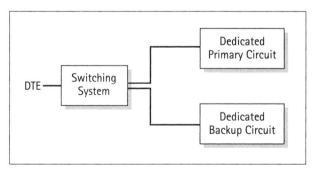

Figure 14-2: Redundant line backups offer an alternate path that can take over in case of failure.

Redundant line configurations detect circuit failures in the primary circuit by monitoring control leads in the DSU (Data Service Unit) interface. If the configuration detects a failure, it automatically establishes a secure backup path by switching terminal equipment at both ends of a data circuit to the spare redundant line. Typically, if the circuit is operating in backup mode, the primary path should be tested continuously. When the primary path has been restored, the backup circuit should be automatically dropped, and terminal equipment switched back to the primary data path.

Both primary and backup circuits should be monitored continuously and tested by the switching equipment. If a failure is detected, even though the switch-over is automatic, the switching device should still be capable of generating an audio or visual alarm or triggering a pager to alert the appropriate staff. It is also desirable to have manual controls, to allow an operator to initiate the backup path or return to the primary path as needed.

Redundant Servers

You can secure critical data on a server by mirroring that data to a standby machine, or a *redundant server*. Sounds expensive, right? Not necessarily – you can mirror data from several machines onto one particular server. Vinca Corporation's StandbyServer Many-to-One for NetWare is an example of how you can provide this type of security to several servers by mirroring them to a single, standby machine (see Figure 14-3).

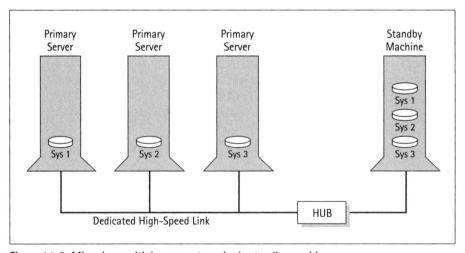

Figure 14-3: Mirroring multiple servers to a single standby machine

In the configuration shown in Figure 14-3, the standby machine functions as a real-time failover machine for several primary servers. The standby machine detects all hardware and software failures in the primary machines and automatically takes over for any failed server.

The most basic approach to redundancy is to keep a spare machine available and to transfer the disk devices manually. Although this works quite well, it takes time and requires skilled technicians, and is therefore less desirable than an automated method.

Redundant Storage

In a secure enterprise, data must be duplicated for many reasons. The foremost reason is to provide a backup in case the original copy is destroyed or becomes inaccessible due to software or hardware failure. Another reason is to provide a backup for disaster recovery – a critical function that helps get the enterprise back up and running after a disaster in the shortest amount of time possible. Duplicated data is also used in data mining and data warehousing applications, to address the year-2000 problem, and for application testing and change control.

Any type of data backup is really a type of redundancy. Although backing up data to the same server may offer some protection, if the server goes down, both the original and backup data are inaccessible. Therefore, it is better to use two smaller servers rather than performing a backup to the same server.

Other methods for protecting your data include disk duplexing, disk mirroring, and disk striping. You can also use *disk arrays* to achieve data redundancy. These arrays, known as redundant arrays of inexpensive disks (RAID), place multiple hard disks in a single case and mirror data between the disks. If one disk fails, the others immediately go into action.

Disk Duplexing

Disk duplexing is a method of protecting data that involves using two or more hard disks. With disk duplexing, a separate channel exists between the PC and each hard disk. Data is automatically written to both disks and sent through the separate channels simultaneously (see Figure 14-4). If one disk fails, data continues to be written to and accessed from the remaining disk.

Disk Mirroring

Disk mirroring also uses two hard disks to duplicate data, but only a single channel (see Figure 14-5). Whereas duplexing writes data to both disks simultaneously, because mirroring uses a single channel, the two writes must be made one after the other. The disadvantage of mirroring as compared to duplexing is that if the channel fails, neither disk is accessible.

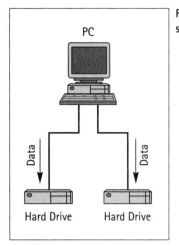

Figure 14-4: Disk duplexing protects data by establishing separate channels.

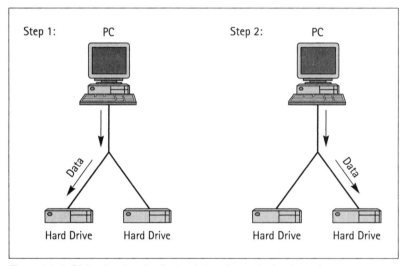

Figure 14-5: Disk mirroring duplicates data using a single channel.

IDE (integrated drive electronics) drives cannot be used in a mirroring configuration, because one IDE drive is automatically designated master and the other slave. Because of the automatic master–slave relationship, disk mirroring is impossible – if the master drive crashes, you cannot use the slave drive.

Disk Striping

Disk striping combines partitions on separate hard disks into a single volume. With this setup, data can be read from and written to multiple partitions simultaneously. Disk striping with parity (error correction) adds another measure of security by distributing parity information across all partitions. This way, if one partition fails, the parity information contained on the other partitions can be accessed to rebuild the missing data.

RAID

A RAID (redundant array of inexpensive disks) system has nothing to do with cockroach spray or with cops shutting down a speakeasy. In fact, RAID is a system that uses multiple disk drives, where data is written across all disks in a predefined order. RAID systems typically use four or five drives, although more can be used. To the end user, the array is seen as a single drive, and all the drives in the array can be accessed in parallel. The RAID system can be an integral part of the enterprise's overall security environment.

The purpose of RAID is to mitigate the effects of a failed disk drive. And no matter how good your equipment is, eventually your company will suffer from a failed disk drive. Instead of losing all of your data, however, you can protect your information through a redundant system such as RAID. A RAID system provides for immediate online availability of data if one disk drive fails.

RAID has six levels, each one dealing with data in a different way:

- ◆ **Level 0** data striping writes data a block at a time across each drive, with one block allocated to each drive. Level 0 disk spanning involves writing data blocks to the next available disk. When a disk is occupied or full, it is skipped over. Level 0 has no fault tolerance.

- ◆ **Level 1** RAID accommodates both disk mirroring and duplexing. Disk mirroring involves using a single channel to write the same data to two different hard disks.

- ◆ **Level 2** RAID accommodates both data striping and bit interleaving. Level 2 RAID is slow and one of the less reliable options. In this level, each bit is written to a separate drive, and checksum data is written to separate checksum drives.

- ◆ **Level 3** RAID adds parity checking to Level 2. Under Level 3, a single parity bit is written to a parity drive instead of checksums being written to checksum drives.

- ◆ **Level 4** is similar to Level 3, except that an entire block is written to each hard disk at one time, instead of a bit at a time.

- ◆ **Level 5** is similar to Level 4, except that the parity or checksum data is distributed across regular disks instead of special-purpose disks. Under Level 5, overlapping writes are allowed, and disks are accessed only if necessary. Level 5 is considered the most reliable.

Let's take a look at RAID implementations at a couple of companies.

HEWLETT-PACKARD AUTORAID

Most RAID systems extract a price in terms of performance and administrative overhead in exchange for the protection they offer. A subsystem without fault tolerance may not offer as much protection for critical data, but performance is usually much better.

HP overcomes some of the limitations of traditional RAID technology. HP's AutoRAID technology represents the next generation in redundant storage technology. The system is based on a set of algorithms within the subsystem controller that manages data block addresses. When data is stored to a drive, the computer system stores it in blocks, of which each one has a unique address that is used for later retrieval. Most RAID systems use a static algorithm to translate the host block address to a location on the physical disk. HP's approach uses a dynamic algorithm to intelligently map any host block address to any disk drive address and to change the mapping while the system is operational. Consequently, the controller can move data to any location on the drive without affecting the data or how the host addresses that data.

The five RAID levels and their impact on subsystem performance are less relevant in the HP system, because the AutoRAID technology continuously optimizes for both cost and performance as if the manager were tuning it manually.

With a traditional RAID system, performance varies depending on the RAID level. AutoRAID understands the differences between the different levels and the trade-offs involved and dynamically adapts to meet the demands of the host.

AutoRAID's block address translation facility enables the subsystem controller to convert data stored in one RAID level to another RAID level without causing problems on the host. This dynamic data migration technique can keep active data in RAID 1/0, which offers the best performance, and less active data in RAID 5, which is less costly.

In addition, AutoRAID introduces the concept of log-structured RAID 5 algorithms to minicomputers and PCs. Log-structured RAID 5, previously limited to higher-end mainframes, boosts performance over traditional RAID 5. Traditional RAID 5 uses block striping and writes sequentially addressed host blocks to different disks within the array. An XOR (exclusive OR) of all data within a stripe is sent to another disk to allow for redundant information. Traditional RAID 5 is, however, inefficient in this regard. It requires a read–modify–write, or four separate disk IOs, for one random write. Log-structured RAID 5 is also block striped, but each block does not have to be from a sequential address. As a result, data can be gathered from multiple random addresses and written in one complete stripe. The result is performance that is more like RAID 3, with RAID 5 fault tolerance.

Configuration of the disk array is accomplished quickly by AutoRAID. The system dynamically selects the appropriate RAID level, so reconfiguring the array to change RAID levels is not necessary.

AutoRAID's mapping technology views each disk as a block of storage instead of as an entire disk. As new disks are added, the disk's blocks are added to the pool of available storage. The storage controller relies on the map to use each block independently to achieve the best performance. Another innovative feature is that adding a new disk boosts performance of the subsystem. When a new disk is installed into the array, AutoRAID redistributes data evenly across all disks in the subsystem. This balancing allows for greater concurrent operations, which leads to better performance.

IBM RAMAC SNAPSHOT

IBM's SnapShot solution takes a different approach to data duplication. The product provides a virtual second view of data in near real time, while minimizing storage expense. But like most security and safety areas, management often considers data duplication to be either a necessary evil or even unnecessary because it does nothing to immediately impact the bottom line (outside of costing money). Furthermore, data duplication often involves downtime or a high amount of CPU power that may drain the network. Consequently, data backup and duplication causes an inconvenience for everyone.

Virtual storage, as implemented by IBM RAMAC SnapShot, avoids the overhead typically associated with data duplication. Using the virtual disk architecture of IBM RAMAC Virtual Array Model 2, IBM RAMAC Virtual Array, or StorageTek Iceberg disk arrays, SnapShot creates multiple views of data within the system, rather than actually copying the data. Applications see these multiple views as multiple copies, thereby minimizing additional storage requirements.

The RAMAC Virtual Array storage system uses an advanced storage architecture, where logical volumes are not mapped directly to physical volumes within the subsystem. It optimizes storage capacity by storing only data that is actually written; it does not keep open capacity for unallocated space, or for allocated but unused space. RAMAC Virtual Array provides for dynamic configuration, so users can add or change logical volumes as needed.

The virtual storage architecture creates virtual volumes, which are represented as a set of pointers stored in a series of tables. SnapShot creates a new view by copying only the pointers; the actual data is not copied. This option also enables nearly instantaneous recovery and less downtime due to application failure.

Virtual array storage was first introduced by StorageTek in 1994. The company's DASD (direct access storage device) product, known as Iceberg, differed from other disk hardware in that it was the only one to use this virtual disk concept. StorageTek has since entered into an alliance with IBM to make Iceberg available as the RAMAC Virtual Array.

Virtual storage is actually not a new concept and is used in several operating systems – most notably in IBM's MVS (Multiple Virtual Storage). RAMAC Virtual Array enables the computer to use more of the available physical disk space while still maintaining the same view of the DASD volume. The system merely changes how the subsystem physically stores data on the disk.

In the RAMAC configuration, no one-to-one mapping exists between the MVS view and the actual volume that contains the data. This system uses a log-structured file approach for storing data. This method maps the MVS view of the disk to the physical location of the data on the array. When data is updated, updates are not written back to the same location on the array, but are written to a new, unused area in a compressed format.

RAMAC Virtual Array's fault-tolerant design retains access to data in the event of a drive failure. It provides for near-instant copying of data through the SnapShot facility. Traditionally, copying data can take hours; SnapShot can accomplish copying functions within seconds. And because SnapShot functions within the Virtual Array device, it eliminates CPU time and channel use that would otherwise slow down the copying function in another system.

Redundancy in High-Speed Networking

Some networks have redundancy built in. Let's look at the high-speed networking redundancy in Fast Ethernet, FDDI, and SONET.

Fast Ethernet

You can enhance critical Fast Ethernet devices with redundant cabling links. Digi International, Inc., offers the 240TX Redundant Port Selector, a fault-tolerant 100BaseTX transceiver, for this purpose. The device provides redundant cabling links for critical Fast Ethernet devices, such as file servers or network switches. It is particularly useful for Fast Ethernet environments where fault tolerance is a requirement.

The 240TX offers a redundant UTP (unshielded twisted pair) path from one server port to two switch ports. If a failure occurs on one switch port, the Digi device automatically switches to the second port without the delay usually associated with redundant connections. Minimal delay is especially important to Fast Ethernet networks that require minimal downtime.

FDDI

FDDI (Fiber Distributed Data Interface) technology offers an optional bypass switch at each node for overcoming failures. When a node fails, it is bypassed optically, effectively taking it out of the loop but preserving the integrity of the network itself.

As many as three sequential nodes can be bypassed. If the cable breaks, the dual ring topology uses redundant cable to accommodate normal 100Mbps traffic without any performance degradation. If both the primary and secondary cables fail, the stations next to the failures will automatically loop the data around the rings, creating a new C-shaped ring from the remaining portions of the two original rings that are still operational.

FDDI uses a dual counter-rotating fiber ring topology to provide fault tolerance. Therefore, if the active ring breaks or suffers from a failure of some sort, stations adjacent to the fault will automatically loop onto the secondary ring, and the network will continue operating.

A typical FDDI concentrator has two buses that accommodate two FDDI backbone rings.

SONET

SONET (Synchronous Optical NETwork) technology relies on fiber-optic rings to carry data over great distances with guarantees of high availability (fault tolerance).

Originally created as a cost-effective platform for multivendor interworking, SONET offers the advantages of high performance, compatibility, and back-to-back multiplexing. Furthermore, it can carry a wide variety of traffic, including Asynchronous Transfer Mode (ATM). SONET is inherently redundant and fault tolerant by design.

Although this technology is limited to telecom organizations and very large enterprises, it does offer numerous security advantages. Many of the Bell companies are deploying SONET on their carrier backbones and are starting to offer public ATM services based on ATM transport—thereby giving the little guy a chance to take advantage of SONET.

One security advantage is that SONET is difficult to tap into, so an attacker who can't use a protocol analyzer to read Ethernet packets off a copper wire will be unable to do the same snooping on a SONET network. In addition, you can configure SONET services with redundant rings.

SONET's built-in redundancy enables automatic rerouting of traffic, within milliseconds, when you have a damaged cable or other type of outage. Every SONET frame (packet) includes instructions about where it should go if it cannot reach its original destination. These rerouted frames are detected by the multiplexers of the SONET network; these multiplexers then tell the switch to send the rest of the traffic headed for the outage to the alternate path.

SONET is a transmission technology—unlike ATM, which is a switching technology. Switching addresses how data is routed over the network; transmission addresses how data is encoded and transported over the network.

Although a point-to-point, dedicated SONET line is faster, the dual-fiber SONET ring offers greater security and protection through its redundant configuration. The dual-fiber ring guarantees the previously mentioned automatic rerouting feature in case of an outage. In this configuration, each SONET ring has two circuits. If one circuit is cut or damaged, the traffic reverses and flows in the opposite direction on the same ring to avoid the damaged area. If the ring is broken in two places, traffic is rerouted onto the second circuit.

SONET's "self-healing" ring is based on a technique called Bidirectional Line-Switched Ring (BLSR). BLSR achieves a high level of survivability. The BLSR can be made up of either two or four fibers.

Summary

In this chapter, you learned about the following:

◆ A redundant configuration helps to reinforce the network, and provide protection against data loss due to disaster or outage.

◆ Redundancy can be applied almost anywhere to add additional security and protection: to the server and its components, to storage, or to the network infrastructure itself.

◆ A RAID system provides for data duplication by copying data across several disks.

◆ Several high-speed technologies, most notably SONET, have some type of built-in redundancy.

Part IV

The Internet

Chapter 15

Preventing Telephone Fraud

IN THIS CHAPTER

- ◆ Cellular telephone fraud and "cloning"
- ◆ Detecting telephone fraud
- ◆ The future of cellular
- ◆ Internet telephony and encryption

CELLULAR TELEPHONY GIVES US the capability to use our cars as an extension of our offices. Now we can start work even before we get to work, transforming that leisurely drive down the coastal highway into a meeting with the marketing department.

However, cellular telephony brings risks as well as conveniences. For instance, others can listen in on cellular calls. Bits and pieces of conversations can often be overheard accidentally, and some people with no social life even get a thrill by using a radio scanner to regularly listen in on other conversations.

The radio scanner maneuver became more difficult with the FCC ruling, which went into effect after April 1994, that forbids the manufacturing or importing of scanners that can tune into a cellular telephone frequency. For the most part, scanner owners are harmless snoops, but thieves and corporate spies may be using the same techniques. Be careful what you discuss on the cellular telephone, and avoid discussing sensitive and private issues.

Because of the inherent risk of having a cellular conversation overheard, never give out sensitive information such as a credit card number over a cellular phone. If an unsavory type overhears this information, you may become a victim of credit card fraud.

How do you keep your cellular conversations from being overheard? Unfortunately, it's neither easy nor cheap to prevent cellular snooping. The best way is simply to use only standard, wired telephones when discussing sensitive topics.

Cellular Awareness

Telephone fraud has turned into a big business. During the 1996 summer Olympic games, Hewlett-Packard worked with BellSouth on a pilot project using HP's acceSS7 fraud management system, which can identify illegal calls within seconds. BellSouth used the system to stop and detect phone fraud at the Olympics in Atlanta. The system was able to flag any activity that was out of the ordinary, and gave HP the ability to field-test their system under extreme conditions.

During the pilot, BellSouth was able to pinpoint suspicious activity at several pay phones in the area. The phones had been tampered with to enable users to make direct-dial international calls without paying. HP's system alert enabled BellSouth to shut down those phones immediately.

HP's acceSS7 fraud-management toolkit monitors Signaling System Number 7 (SS7) network links in real time and looks for a variety of user-defined fraud scenarios. SS7 is a digital switching network used by many local-exchange carriers and regional Bell operating companies.

The toolkit generates network alerts by building and maintaining a prioritized list of fraud cases so that network operators can focus their investigations on tracking down phone-fraud criminals and disconnecting fraudulent operations. It uses Call Detail Records (CDRs), which are created in seconds by the HP acceSS7 platform. The CDRs are passed to a detection and analysis engine where they are compared against selected fraud scenarios, which can be expanded as criminals develop new ways to defraud service providers.

According to HP, telecommunications fraud is a $3.7 billion problem for carriers, manufacturers, and consumers. Fraud can take many forms, including calling card or credit card theft, switchboard hacking, or taking telephone service under a false name. HP's product monitors the system in real time and looks for specific suspicious actions, such as call length, calls to high-fraud destinations, and suspicious use of call-forwarding.

If you're going to use a cellular phone, you should be aware of potential fraud and be prepared to take precautions against fraud.

Cellular Cloning

Cloning, or the duplication of the cellular phone's electronic serial number (ESN), is a very common type of cellular fraud. The ESN, a unique number programmed into the cell phone by the manufacturer, is used to identify the subscriber. An ESN reader can sometimes be used to capture this number—the thief then reprograms the number into another cellular telephone's computer chip. Digital cellular telephones are less likely to be cloned, because it is more difficult to pick up the digital frequencies.

Unfortunately, most cellular telephone users learn of fraud only after they receive their bill and see a list of calls they never made. Most cellular providers have a policy of not charging the customer for cloned calls. This is generally accepted practice throughout the industry, but make sure that your cellular provider adheres to this policy. Fortunately, you can take specific steps to prevent this type of fraud:

♦ Use the telephone's lock feature when it is not in use.

♦ Keep any documentation referencing the phone's ESN in a secure location.

♦ Check your cellular phone bills thoroughly.

♦ Understand your provider's policies about charging for fraudulent calls and find out what specific antifraud features they offer.

Call Accounting

Telephone fraud can be hard to detect if a company typically has several lines and a large bill to begin with. One company out of four has been the victim of telephone fraud or hacking. Costs can quickly mount to the tens of thousands of dollars, and can have a significant impact on a company's bottom line if it goes unchecked. The accounts payable department may not want, or have the time, to check over every long-distance call. Yet, a quick audit may reveal some unusual trends, such as the following:

♦ Unusually long telephone calls

♦ Calls that take place outside of working hours

♦ Multiple calls to a certain area unrelated to business

One good way to control this type of fraud is with call accounting software, which is widely available. This type of software not only helps to easily and efficiently distribute telephone expenses between departments, but also serves as a check against fraud and abuse.

Software such as TELEMATE Software's FraudFighter and other products automatically monitor the telephone system to detect unusual patterns that may indicate fraudulent telephone activity.

If you decide to use call accounting and fraud detection software on your network, make sure it includes the following features:

◆ The capability to issue warning messages to an administrator if an unusual pattern is being detected

◆ The capability to be programmed with the company's legitimate calling patterns

◆ The capability to monitor remote sites

Most modern PBXes have a Station Message Detail Reporting (SMDR) plug, into which a call accounting system is connected. The telephone system then sends a record of every call made through the SMDR port into the call accounting system for later review and analysis.

In addition, telephone fraud software should be able to monitor the PBX for SMDR activity. With a little work and ingenuity, a hacker can turn off SMDR and erase all call details. TELEMATE's software monitors the PBX for SMDR activity. If no SMDR output occurs for one hour, the software places a test call and then checks to see if a call record exists. If no record is made, the system sets off an alarm.

Protection Services

According to Bell Atlantic NYNEX Mobile (BANM), the wireless industry loses more than $1.5 million daily to cellular fraud. BANM has taken the lead in offering security systems to its customers by being the first to implement cellular personal identification numbers (PIN), clone-detecting software, and authentication for cellular services.

Using PINs can contribute a great deal to cellular security and eliminate the need to change phone numbers even if a cell phone has been cloned. The PIN strategy requires the cellular user to enter a four-digit PIN after entering the phone number. This way, even if the cell phone is cloned, the thief cannot use it unless he or she also knows the PIN number.

In addition, many cellular phones include automatic authentication. Authentication is superior to the PIN strategy because human error is not possible, and it is significantly easier to use because no PIN needs to be remembered. If this service is available, you should take advantage of it.

In addition, some providers, including Bell Atlantic, have an in-house fraud task force that helps to detect cloning, alert customers, and shut down thieves as quickly as possible. Before contracting for cellular services, check with your provider to see if it offers this type of service.

AT&T Wireless Services also offers similar programs. Its Fraud Protection Feature (FPF) is included free to all customers. Basically a PIN solution, FPF uses a unique seven-digit number that is programmed into the phone's speed dial. The number is dialed once prior to making any calls. However, programming it into the speed dial may also present some security problems if the phone is stolen; you may want to enter this number manually every time you make a call instead.

AT&T's Fraud Management System (FMS) is a type of automatic burglar alarm that is used to identify a cloned telephone. If a phone deviates from its normal activity, it sets off an alarm at an AT&T service center, and an AT&T fraud analyst will investigate. A deviation from normal activity could be any departure from the normal calling pattern, such as calls being made at unusual hours. Part of this investigation involves *Radio Frequency Fingerprinting*, which can identify every cellular phone's unique signal frequency pattern. This information is used to validate any customer attempting to place a call. FMS automatically denies a call made from a phone identified as a clone.

In addition, AT&T's Roaming Authorization service permits the fraud analyst to suspend roaming privileges if he or she suspects that the fraudulent activity is taking place in a certain area. This results in denial of service to the counterfeiter, while still giving the valid customer the capability to use the phone in other areas.

As with some other major providers, AT&T has an interdisciplinary fraud team in every AT&T Wireless Services Region.

Cellular Future

The Personal Communication Services (PCS) phone, a small, pocket-sized phone, looms on the horizon. This innovative design permits both voice and data to be transmitted digitally and has many possibilities for use both as a cellular communication device and as a device for network communications in smaller areas.

Calls made on PCS networks are more difficult to intercept because the system is digital. Some new risks arise, however. For example, the PCS can be used to pinpoint the user's location, which raises all sorts of questions regarding privacy.

AT&T offers digital wireless throughout its national wireless network through the AT&T digital PCS service. Already available in 40 major metropolitan markets, AT&T's PCS service combines voice, messaging, and paging in a single device. Consequently, customers are able to consolidate three separate devices—a pager, a telephone, and a personal messaging system—into a single device.

The digital technology employed in PCS also affords users a great deal more privacy and security, and resistance to cloning. A PIN is often not required, especially in a purely digital system (as opposed to a hybrid analog/digital cellular device).

Pacific Bell's Pure Digital PCS system offers security by digitally encrypting at three separate levels:

◆ **In the removable "smart chip."** After you dial a telephone number, the network's authentication center transmits a randomly generated code that challenges the smart chip's identity. The chip must respond correctly before the PCS network establishes the connection.

♦ **In the Global System for Mobile Communications network.** Before the connection is completed, the call is digitally encrypted to prevent scanners from eavesdropping on the conversation or cloning the telephone number.

♦ **In the telephone.** After the PCS telephone is turned on, users can add an additional level of security and enter a PIN code.

In digital PCS technology, the sender's voice is encoded before transmission, which enhances security.

Internet Telephony

Internet telephony gives users a tool for bypassing long-distance companies, and making long-distance calls over the Internet. This phenomenon is not likely to replace long-distance carriers, but it does present an opportunity to reduce international long-distance bills. The technology was first introduced by VocalTec in 1995, and is remarkably simple. All that is needed is a multimedia PC with a modem, an Internet connection, and special software. Several companies offer the software at low cost. Unfortunately, sound quality varies, systems are not interoperable, and calls are usually not full-duplex.

Internet telephony has been rapidly evolving as a means of bypassing long-distance tolls. For the most part, it is still a curiosity, but it holds tremendous potential. Who wouldn't want to place a call from California to Stockholm, talk for an hour, and then not have to pay a penny? The American Carriers Telecommunication Association, which represents the long-distance carriers, is obviously a bit peeved about the whole thing and is lobbying hard to eliminate this economic threat, and is asking the government to place heavy regulations on Internet telephony or eliminate it completely.

The advantages of Internet telephony, once the technology matures, are many, besides the obvious cost savings. Because the communication is handled by a computer, the possibility of multimedia text, graphics, and audio conversation looms in the future – even videophones are possible. In addition, computer-based answering machines can be much more sophisticated. Answering machine software can route calls, save messages, and create database records from call logs. Unfortunately, the technology is still limited and voice quality is not as good as plain old telephone service (POTS) conversations.

Internet telephony has its own security concerns as well. As with any Internet-based communication session, an Internet telephone conversation is susceptible to hacking or eavesdropping. Most Internet telephone offerings have not yet addressed the security issue in any meaningful way, although encryption software is probably the best approach at present to protect Internet-based telephone conversations. Eavesdropping on an Internet phone conversation could be relatively easy for an intruder, although some Internet phone software offerings do include some protection in the form of encryption.

Encryption is particularly important for unsecured communication channels such as the Internet. Voice communications, as with any type of communication that takes place over the Internet, should be encrypted, so an eavesdropper cannot read (or hear) the information being transmitted. You can find Internet phone encryption in Phil's Pretty Good Software's PGPfone, which also comes with excellent security features.

PGPfone is a freeware product available for either Macintosh or Windows 95/Windows NT platforms. The product relies on speech compression and strong cryptography to give users the capability to have a real-time, secure telephone conversation while using the desktop or notebook computer as the telephone. The software takes the user's voice, digitizes, compresses, and encrypts it, and sends it over a modem to the recipient, who must run the same software. Although the product runs a variety of cryptographic and speech compression protocols, they are all transparent to the users, and the product offers an intuitive, natural user interface that makes it very similar to using a standard telephone. Furthermore, because public-key protocols are used to negotiate keys, secure channels are not needed.

To run this free product, you must have at least a 14.4Kbps modem (but a 28.8Kbps modem is recommended), a 25MHz Macintosh running System 7.1 or a 66MHz Pentium Windows 95/Windows NT machine with the relevant multimedia peripherals.

Both parties negotiate keys using the Diffie-Hellman key exchange protocol, which does not reveal anything to any attacker or wiretapper. However, this protocol enables both parties to establish a common key for encrypting and decrypting the voice conversation.

Summary

In this chapter, we discussed telephone fraud and ways to prevent it. You learned the following:

◆ Cellular telephony brings risks as well as convenience. An attacker with a specialized piece of hardware can capture the cell phone's electronic serial number, program it into another phone, and run up your bill.

◆ Cellular conversations can be overheard. No sensitive information should be discussed on a cell phone, and never give out a credit card number or other critical information on a cell phone.

◆ Telephone fraud costs millions every year, and is more common than most managers think. Call accounting software and fraud detection systems can be deployed to spot unusual trends, fraudulent activity, and theft in long-distance usage.

◆ Internet telephony has risks of its own. A voice conversation running over the public Internet is especially vulnerable to eavesdropping; encryption must be used to protect an Internet conversation if it is of a sensitive nature.

Chapter 16

Securing Your Web Connection

IN THIS CHAPTER

♦ Making your Web site more secure

♦ CGI scripts and their vulnerabilities

♦ Downloadable applets – are they safe?

♦ The vulnerabilities of your Web browser

THE WORLD WIDE WEB has made a tremendous impact on how we do business, how we gather information, and even how we communicate. Along with the Web's rapid growth, however, comes a concern for security. The world is full of people who would misuse the Web to do harm either for personal gain or for no reason at all. Vandals have become more high-tech; no longer do they limit themselves to a can of spray paint; now, they arm themselves with computers and Internet connections.

Your corporate Web page is a window into your business. If you are an astute marketer, you know the great potential this provides. You want new customers to see your marketing material to find out about your products; and you want existing customers to see your technical support material and data on your latest releases.

Macy's store windows are well-known for their attractive displays. When you walk by the store, you are treated to a well-laid-out sample of what's inside. But, looking in through the window won't tell you what's going on in the back office. You would have to break in for that. A Web site is very similar; it gives passersby a glimpse into what the proprietor has to offer. But if it isn't locked up properly, an intruder can break in and gain access to more information than you meant to give. You have to lock up your Web site, just like you have to lock up the doors to the office at night.

Ensuring Secure Web Communications

The Web was designed to be public and open — and designed not with security in mind at all. This design has led to enormous problems in terms of securing machines on the Internet.

When a client contacts a Web site, that client (user) becomes "root" for just a single instant. *Root* is a superuser on a UNIX machine who has the ability to go anywhere on the server. Normally, a user cannot use this power, but a clever hacker can easily trick a Web server into giving him or her root authority.

You can secure communications between a client-side Web browser and the Web server through encryption, typically using either SSL or S-HTTP (described later). Both protocols can be used to secure transmissions while connected to a particular server.

The IETF (Internet Engineering Task Force) HTTP Working Group has made some comments regarding the security threats inherent in HTTP, the protocol commonly used in Web communications. The standards body's concerns include the following:

♦ **Client/session authentication.** HTTP 1.0 does not include a secure method of user authentication.

♦ **Idempotent methods.** Developers of client software should make sure that actions taken by their applications are safe and idempotent. Users of the software should be aware of all actions taken by the software being run. *Idempotence* refers to a condition where two consecutive, identical client requests will return the same responses from the server.

♦ **Abuse of server log information.** Servers are, through a variety of means, capable of collecting information about what sort of information is requested by clients. This information is confidential, and server providers should make sure that logging information is not distributed. If this information is misused, a visitor to a Web site may find himself or herself on several dozen "spam" lists.

Secure Hypertext Transfer Protocol (S-HTTP)

The World Wide Web and the Web browsers used to access documents through the Web depend largely on HyperText Transfer Protocol (HTTP). Because the Web is so easy to use and so widely accepted, many savvy business people have expressed a great deal of interest in using it as a client/server architecture for Web-based applications. Doing that, however, may require authentication and other security measures. In its original form, HTTP does little to support cryptography.

To change this situation, Microsoft collaborated with credit card giants MasterCard and Visa to develop Secure HyperText Transfer Protocol (S-HTTP).

S-HTTP is a message-oriented communications protocol that extends the HTTP protocol. It coexists with HTTP's messaging model and can be easily integrated with HTTP applications.

S-HTTP establishes a secure communications mechanism between an HTTP-based client/server pair. This safeguards commercial transactions by adding the means to establish confidentiality, authenticity, integrity, and nonrepudiability of origin to an HTTP-based transaction. Clients can use S-HTTP to authenticate the server and to encrypt the data transmitted between the client and server. S-HTTP encrypts Web transmissions at the server daemon layer.

Client-side public key certificates are not required, as S-HTTP supports symmetric key-only operation. This enables spontaneous, private transactions without each party needing an established public key.

Unfortunately, neither of the two major browsers (Microsoft Internet Explorer and Netscape Navigator) supports S-HTTP yet, so this extension is still mostly theoretical. Netscape has pledged to support S-HTTP in the future, however, and Microsoft will most likely follow suit. Explorer and Navigator have closely matched each other in power and features, so you can be sure that Microsoft will not allow Netscape to one-up its browser for very long.

An S-HTTP-enabled client can communicate with a non-S-HTTP server, but these transactions will not use the S-HTTP security features. Nonetheless, the communication can still take place.

To create an S-HTTP-based message, you need three inputs:

♦ A cleartext (unencrypted) message, which is an HTTP message or data object. Because the cleartext message can be carried transparently, HTTP can be carried within an S-HTTP wrapper.

♦ The recipient's cryptographic preferences and keying material (material that is exchanged to create a traffic key, and authenticate the computer pair). This can either be stated explicitly by the recipient or set by a default set of preferences.

♦ The sender's cryptographic preferences and keying material.

The sender's and recipient's preferences are integrated during the creation of the S-HTTP message. This integration process may require some intervention on the user's part if, for example, multiple keys are available for signing the message.

Recovering the message involves four inputs as well:

1. The S-HTTP message

2. The recipient's cryptographic preferences and keying material

3. The recipient's current cryptographic preferences and keying material

4. The sender's previously stated cryptographic options

To recover the message, the recipient must read the headers to see which cryptographic transformations were performed and then remove these transformations using the keying material. The recipient can also verify that the enhancements match inputs 2 and 4.

A message can be either signed, authenticated, or encrypted, or processed using any combination of these three methods or none at all. S-HTTP supports multiple key management schemes, including public-key exchange and manually shared secrets. If you use digital signatures, you can attach a certificate to the message or require the recipient to obtain the certificate independently.

S-HTTP verifies the integrity and authenticity of a message by computing a Message Authentication Code (MAC), which is generated as a keyed hash over the document that contains a shared secret. This mechanism does not require public-key cryptography or encryption. In addition, the freshness of transmissions can be guaranteed through a simple challenge–response mechanism.

S-HTTP messages are syntactically the same as HTTP messages, consisting of a request or status line followed by headers and a body. However, the range of headers differs, and the body is cryptographically enhanced.

Secure Sockets Layer (SSL)

Surfing the Web is inherently insecure. Data transmitted between the client and the server is sent clear, which leaves the door open for it to be intercepted. Although an interception does not happen often, it is a possibility, so when confidential information is involved, you need to use some type of security to prevent the occasional theft. This is where the Secure Sockets Layer steps in.

Secure Sockets Layer (SSL) is the most common method of ensuring security on the Web. You can identify pages secured with SSL by looking at its URL: SSL-protected pages will use the prefix *https:* (HTTP secure). SSL-protected pages also sport the solid key icon in the corner of the browser window.

SSL encrypts Web transmissions at the socket layer. Under SSL, the client and server undergo an initialization process to ensure authentication. After this initial "handshake" procedure takes place, any communication that occurs between the server and client will be encrypted.

SSL was developed jointly by Netscape Communications and RSA, and unlike S-HTTP, is already in common use. However, the U.S. government considers SSL to be a munition, as with other strong encryption products, so it cannot be exported outside of the United States.

SSL is much more flexible than S-HTTP and works with any networking protocol. S-HTTP, on the other hand, can be used only with HTTP. Currently, Navigator works with SSL. Microsoft, creator of S-HTTP, has embraced SSL as a standard, which may have a positive impact on the success and acceptance of S-HTTP.

Cookies

When you log on to a Web page, that Web page can make queries about your machine and collect similar information. This is done through a useful and somewhat sneaky tool called a *cookie* or, more formally, a "Persistent Client State HTTP Cookie."

Rumor has it that when Microsoft first released Windows 95, it gave buyers the convenience of registering their purchase online. However, when they did so, the software giant's server searched the customer's hard drive, cataloged its contents, and included that information along with the registration.

The World Wide Web is, by design, a stateless system. That is, when you call up a Web page, the browser does not maintain an active link to the Web server. The server merely delivers the requested file and then moves on to the next request. This stateless existence simplifies Web serving, because the server does not have to keep track of multiple, simultaneous sessions. However, a stateless system cannot configure itself to a user's preferences.

A cookie is a basic text file, transferred between the Web server and the Web client (browser), that tracks where you went on the Web site, how long you stayed in each area, and other bits and pieces of information that marketing departments love. It essentially takes the stateless Web and gives it stateful qualities. All the major browsers support cookies. Used properly, cookies can be used on the server side to gather information about a visitor to a Web site in order to create custom Web pages designed to cater to that visitor's specific browsing patterns.

Although the application of cookies may present the user with some conveniences, many users view their use as an intrusion into privacy. It is possible to make a simple adjustment in Netscape Navigator 3.*x* to deny cookie access. You can easily see whether cookies are being used simply by checking for the existence of the COOKIES.TXT file. This is an ASCII text file and is plainly readable by anyone. You should be aware, however, that a cookie cannot take files from the local hard drive; it can only send the server specific information about the user.

COOKIE TRACKER BUG

Navigator 3.0 suffered from what was known as a "tracker bug." Netscape identified and fixed this bug in Navigator 3.03; Netscape Communicator is not affected by the bug.

This bug lets a rogue Web site operator keep track of where you go on the Web after you leave. It can also permit a malicious Web site operator to see cookie information that has been exchanged between the client and server. That information could be used to create a "spam" list, or worse, for the purpose of espionage. The bug does not, however, let the Web site operator retrieve or erase files from the client's hard disk.

COOKIE BLOCKING

Pretty Good Privacy, Inc.'s PGPcookie.cutter program, available as freeware for non-commercial use and also commercially, enables individuals to filter out Web cookies that are used to collect information about their personal surfing habits. As Phil Zimmerman, founder of PGP, puts it, "The technology to invade your privacy keeps improving, so the technology to protect your privacy should improve as well."

By analyzing the HTML stream, PGPcookie.cutter can prevent information about a user from being captured. It can identify and block cookies as instructed by the user. In addition, blocked access prevents a cookie from returning to its server with information about the individual who is browsing.

PGPcookie.cutter includes the following key features:

◆ The Selective Blocking and Access feature allows the "good" cookies and blocks those that the user deems intrusive.

◆ The Instant Delete feature instantly removes any cookie within a cookie file.

◆ Choice of Privacy Labels enables you to set up multiple levels of trust, including the option to block all cookies, allow only specified cookies, allow all cookies from trusted domains, or allow all cookies.

◆ The Cookie Counter enables you to see the number of cookies that have been blocked by placing the cursor over the cookie icon in the system tray.

Version Control Software

Version control software is usually thought of as a management utility rather than a security tool. This type of utility comes in handy both when producing and revising documents, and generating and updating software applications. Version control software helps maintain control over which version of a document or application is the latest one. In doing so, it ensures that anyone accessing the document or executable in question always has the latest version. For developers, version control software also offers the ability to go back into previous releases to compare code.

In a Web environment, version control keeps track of the enormous number of files that make up a Web site, including Java applets, text files, CGI scripts, WAV files or other multimedia files.

Besides tracking software bugs and text updates, a secondary use for version control software is to maintain security. Say, for example, some rogue developer or practical joker down the hall breaks into your corporate Web site and creatively changes the spelling of the CEO's last name so it resembles profanity. Version control software products that maintain an audit log can be particularly useful for pointing the finger to the culprit's identity.

You'll want to be able to track any unauthorized changes to the corporate Web site, whether or not they're harmful, so you should consider implementing this sort of tool on your network.

Microsoft Proxy Server

Microsoft's Proxy Server software can be used to shield the corporate network from the Internet. Microsoft Proxy Server is an Internet gateway with two services, Web Proxy and WinSock Proxy. Web Proxy complies with the CERN proxy standard and provides proxy services for FTP Read, Gopher, and WWW. It supports UNIX and Macintosh as well as Windows platforms, although UNIX and Macintosh platforms do not receive the same level of support and services. Proxy Server is tightly integrated with the Windows platform.

CERN stands for Conseil Europeen pour la Recherche Nucleaire, and is a nuclear research laboratory located in Geneva, Switzerland. CERN was responsible for initially developing the World Wide Web, which it originally created as a means of sharing research documents on particle physics.

WinSock Proxy intermediates all Windows Sockets applications and protocols by intercepting the Windows Sockets API network calls. Because it is transparent on the application level, almost any application can be proxied, including Telnet, FTP, RealAudio, SMTP, and VDOLive.

Microsoft Proxy Server, however, is a Windows 95- and NT-specific offering. A mixed environment with Macintosh or UNIX clients will not benefit from Proxy Server, although it can be a flexible product for a Microsoft-centric network. Proxy Server supports the CERN proxy standard. Instead of SOCKS support, Proxy Server uses a Winsock proxy service that lets the Windows client run any IP program, including User Datagram Protocol (UDP) services.

Microsoft Windows NT Server's IP forwarding feature may cause some vulnerabilities. Upon installation of NT Server, this feature is not enabled. However, it is not automatically disabled when Proxy Server is installed. Make sure to disable this feature after installing Proxy Server if it has been previously enabled.

Some of the advantages of Proxy Server include the following:

♦ **Dual-homing.** Proxy Server can be dual-homed. Dual-homing establishes a separate network interface for each side of the server and can support a different network protocol on each interface. It can also be configured as a nonrouting device, so IP packets are not arbitrarily passed between connected networks. The dual-homed network could, for example, accommodate an internal network running the NetWare IPX protocol and an external network running TCP/IP. This type of configuration provides an added level of security on the private network, because IPX is not routable through TCP/IP.

♦ **Prevents IP spoofing.** IP spoofing is a technique where an attacker's computer assumes the identity of a computer in the internal network. The attacker's system "spoofs" the IP address of the internal computer to receive information that was intended for that machine. Proxy Server prevents spoofing by prohibiting IP packets with destination addresses not found in the Local Address Table (LAT) from entering through the public interface.

♦ **Prevents external publication of internal data.** Internet Information Server services are started by default when NT Server is started. Proxy Server disables Web publishing on the external network, thereby hiding the internal HTTP data from the outside, through the Enable/Disable Internet Web Publishing feature.

♦ **Prevents access to unauthorized Internet sites.** If your policy restricts employees from visiting Internet sites not related to business, you can enforce it through Proxy Server's Site/Domain Filtering feature.

♦ **Auditability.** The capability to gather information about what users are accessing and what type of data is moving over the network may be critical in a secure environment. Proxy Server offers two levels of security logging: regular and verbose. The regular setting provides adequate information, but the verbose setting provides many more details about any connection or event. Microsoft strongly recommends enabling the logging feature in a secure environment.

♦ **Prohibits unauthorized users.** Two types of user-level authentication are provided to ensure that a user is authorized to access the system. Through either one, Proxy Server authenticates each connection before allowing any request to pass through the proxy. Access control can be enabled or disabled. When enabled, the anonymous login feature will not function unless permission has been expressly set for a particular machine. Basic authentication sends a username and password to Proxy Server in uuencoded format, which is only marginally secure. However, the Windows NT Challenge/Response Authentication (NTCR) method offers a higher level of security, and is required for a C2-compliant system.

♦ **Prevents unauthorized access to services.** Proxy Server can secure outbound and inbound Internet access down to individual users for a specific protocol.

♦ **Limits visibility of internal network addresses on the Internet.** When Proxy Server receives an internal client request, it issues the request to the external network using its external IP address, thereby shielding the internal network addresses from the outside.

♦ **Prevents unauthorized access to cached data.** Proxy Server provides caching for HTTP resources. The cache is checked before any Internet data request is fulfilled. The SSL Not Cached setting prevents any https page from ever being cached, which prevents a user from viewing data that was issued to another user while in secure mode. Furthermore, the User Authentication Resources Not Cached feature, which is enabled by default, prevents any authenticated resources from being stored in cache at any time.

♦ **System detection and probing.** An attacker may use a TCP/IP network protocol port to gather information and attempt to infiltrate the network. You can disable specific ports through the NT Server's Registry and by changing the bindings on the network interface card.

♦ **Secure transmission.** Proxy Server ensures that data sent between Proxy Server and clients is secure.

♦ **Enables SSL tunneling.** Tunneling is enabled by default whenever a user is granted access to the Web proxy.

Security Threats on the Web

Even if you secure your Web connection, potential still exists for compromising your security. The biggest threats are CGI (Common Gateway Interface) scripts and downloadable applets. Usually, the best way to protect yourself against these dangers is to avoid them.

CGI Scripts

Another common way to attack a Web server is through CGI scripts. A CGI script is a small program, usually written to execute a single task on the Web server. CGI scripts are commonly used to enable users to fill out and submit forms on a Web site and perform other convenient tasks.

However, the CGI script itself contains valuable information about the server on which it runs. This information could be valuable to an intruder, if that intruder can get to the script in its text form.

CGI scripts can also be dangerous because they are vulnerable to attack while executing. An attacker can potentially add to the script's instruction, and cause the server to open the door to access that the server would not normally grant. An attacker could misuse CGI scripts to gain broad access to the server, remove or access confidential data from the server, commit acts of vandalism, or even bring the server to a halt. Attackers could use CGI vulnerabilities to cause the server to mail a copy of the password file to themselves.

Because these vulnerabilities exist, all data on the server running the CGI scripts should be backed up and maintained in a separate location. One surprisingly common problem is that some administrators run their Web servers as root. In fact, the Web server must, in most circumstances, start out as root. But, once started, the Web server should give away its root privileges by calling setuid. The Web server's configuration file typically allows the operator to specify what user it should run as. This can be a generic, unprivileged account, or it can be the account of the individual that owns the CGI scripts.

 HTTP servers typically come with a default directory of CGI programs. Delete these programs, or move them to another location. Some vulnerabilities in these default demo scripts have been detected, which may permit anyone to execute any command on your server.

Systems that have a large memory architecture are particularly good for caching disk reads and accommodating repetitive reads of the same file, which is commonly done by Web servers. The large memory disk cache functions well for Web servers using CGI scripts. These scripts remain in memory and do not have to be loaded again and again from disk.

Because of these vulnerabilities, some users prefer to avoid CGI scripts if possible. Although several alternatives to CGI exist (such as Netscape's NSAPI and Microsoft's ISAPI), these solutions are proprietary. By using them, you'll often sacrifice a measure of portability. ISAPI (Internet Server API) is Microsoft's programming interface that exists on Microsoft's Web server, Internet Information Server. Like CGI, ISAPI offers a set of function calls that allows Web pages to invoke programs that are written as DLLs on the server. NSAPI (Netscape API) accomplishes largely the same thing on Netscape's Web server.

Downloadable Applets

A downloadable applet, whether it is Java or ActiveX, can be a frightening thing to a security manager. These applets enable a small computer program to be downloaded along with a Web page. Applets have their good traits — Web pages enabled with these applets are typically much more rich and dynamic than others and can be filled with useful features. But the mere thought of an unknown computer program coming into the network uninvited should send any manager worth his or her salt into convulsions. Most ordinary users are not familiar with some of the destructive things downloadable applets can do – such as siphon off files or even erase a hard drive. Both Java and ActiveX carry some security risks, because they can cause a potentially hostile program to be automatically downloaded into the client system. Fortunately, both Java and ActiveX include features to protect browsers from this type of risk.

The most effective policy regarding these little devils is to block them at the firewall level. In some critical environments containing sensitive data, this policy prevails, and end users are deprived of dancing logos. But at the same time, they may also be deprived of something more meaningful. Java has matured to the point that it is now being used to create some very serious and useful applications.

In the absence of blocking applets at the firewall, the next best thing is to check the digital signatures on the applets to make sure that they have not been tampered with, and are, in fact, coming from an authorized sender.

In addition to Java and ActiveX, browsers may also have plug-ins such as Macromedia's ShockWave. Although it is unlikely that a plug-in from such a major vendor would contain any malicious code, you still must trust it to be harmless and free from security-related bugs. To date, there have been very few reported incidents of damage being done by a hostile Java or ActiveX program, but the potential is definitely out there.

In the future, we can look to antivirus software vendors to provide more sophisticated tools to examine these types of applets and dynamically block them based on authenticity, content, or intended purpose.

Java and ActiveX take different approaches to security. Whereas Microsoft's ActiveX technology relies largely on human judgment and the use of digital signatures, Java relies more on software. Both approaches have their relative advantages, as described in the following sections.

Java

Despite Sun Microsystems' contention that Java was designed to be a secure system, some security managers still feel more comfortable blocking Java at the firewall. While in some situations this may be wise, Sun has indeed done its job in designing Java with built-in security capabilities.

Java's security model, unlike ActiveX, relies on software and is based on the concept of the "sandbox." The Java sandbox is merely an isolated area that surrounds the applet and prevents it from doing damage outside of this one area. Although this presents a very secure model, the restrictions can be too limiting for some applications. With the Java sandbox, a Java applet, for example, is not allowed to access a file. Although sound security reasons exist for not giving a Java applet access to a file, you may want to give Java this capability to create some sort of Web-based data processing application.

A Java-enabled product using digital signatures can overcome this limitation. The digital signature enables the user to decide whether to give a specific Java applet more authority than it would otherwise have. This feature adds more functionality to Java but also introduces the same problem found in ActiveX: the user must decide whether or not the signer of the digital certificate is trustworthy.

Java implements sandboxes through three components: the class loader, the byte-code verifier, and the security manager. Each of these three components plays a role in maintaining the system's integrity. These components ensure that only the correct classes are loaded, and that they are in the proper format. They further ensure that untrusted classes do not execute malicious instructions, and that untrusted classes cannot gain access to a protected system resource.

Furthermore, the Java Protected Domain concept extends the sandbox into the file system. These domains facilitate the use of permissions by the user, or can use a preconfigured default setting. This capability extends Java's fine-grained control by permitting multiple permissions to exist for individual applications. This model, which is built into the Java platform, enables developers to accommodate a fine level of granularity in security policies, and to facilitate independent permissions for individual applets.

Java actually consists of two parts: the Java Virtual Machine and the Java API. Sun Microsystems describes the Virtual Machine as a "soft computer," or a type of abstraction that you implement on top of an existing physical processor. Because of its unique interface and adapters, it can be ported to new operating systems without requiring you to rewrite it. The Java API presents a standard interface for applets, regardless of the underlying operating system. The API, which forms the Java framework for application development, offers a set of basic interfaces in several areas, which can be used by developers to create Java-based applications.

Part of the Java Standard Extension API is the Java Security API, which presents a framework that enables developers to include secure functionality in Java applets. Functions included in this API include cryptography, digital signatures, encryption, and authentication. It also includes support for key management, including a secure database and certificate facilities.

The Java Security API has an abstract layer that is called by the Java applets. This abstract layer then makes calls to Java Security packages that can implement cryptography and other security mechanisms.

The API, because of Java's modular nature, provides for an easily upgradable security system. If a stronger algorithm becomes available, for example, a module can be easily replaced.

Java's runtime security system is built around the SecurityManager class, which serves to monitor all activities that could potentially be a breach of security policy. Each running application can have only one security manager. Once a security manager is installed by the program, it cannot be uninstalled or replaced; this policy is enforced by the Java Virtual Machine. This class functions as a sort of gateway for Java applets. Whenever a Java program attempts to open a socket or write to a file, the Java runtime environment must ask the installed security manager whether the applet has permission to execute the task. A security manager is made by first extending the java.lang.SecurityManager class, and then implementing the methods of that class.

ActiveX

Microsoft's ActiveX technology relies mostly on digital signatures and users' judgment regarding them. Although digital signatures can be quite effective, they also introduce some risks. To understand why this is true, you need to have a firm grasp of how digital signatures work in ActiveX.

An ActiveX program includes a digital signature from the author of the program and can also include digital signatures from others who endorse the program. When your Web browser comes across an ActiveX program, it verifies the digital signature, tells you who signed the program, and asks you whether or not to run it. In this case, the individual user is responsible for making the most appropriate decision.

The problem is that a user may make an inappropriate decision about whom to trust, or may choose to download a program signed by someone with whom he is not familiar. Although it's probably a safe bet to accept a download signed by Microsoft or some other large, well-known vendor, an end user may be tempted by an attractive program offered on Joe's House of Anarchy or some other such Web page. As such, a great deal of discretion is left up to each individual user. And it only takes one wrong choice to spell doom and disaster for your network.

To avoid this situation, you might put in place a security policy dictating that only ActiveX programs from specified, approved individuals may be accepted; however, enforcing such a policy would be impossible. The alternative is to prohibit all ActiveX programs.

Web Browser Vulnerability

Your Web browser, whether you use Netscape Navigator, Microsoft Internet Explorer, Mosaic, or another brand, contains a great deal of information that could be valuable to an attacker. This information can be held in cache files, the history file, or even in your bookmarks. An attacker or "social engineer" can examine these files to learn about the user. These files can contain information about what sites you accessed, what forms you submitted, and more. The attacker can easily use this information about you, the user, to bypass security. This information would also have obvious uses for an individual engaged in industrial espionage.

Take a look at a simple hypertext link. Hypertext links are one of the most convenient parts of the Web. They even tell you whether you have already visited that particular link by changing its color. How does it know to change colors? Because of the history file kept in the browser. Typically, the browser is set to a default of 30 days, which means that someone who can access your history file can see where you went on the Web for the past month.

The bookmark list feature offered by browsers is also a great convenience. Simply by pulling down this list and clicking the site name, you can go directly to that site or even to a particular page. But again, an attacker that gets hold of this bookmark file can also discover what sites you regularly visit. If you bookmark a site that requires a password, the attacker could look in the cache to possibly discover that password.

The cache is also a great convenience and a good way to speed up access time. Whenever you visit a Web page, a copy of the page is stored locally. So if the page is accessed again in the near future, the browser accesses the local copy instead of having to contact the server and download it again.

If an attacker can get to your cache subdirectory, he or she has hit a gold mine. If you recently submitted credit card information over the Web on a form, that form will probably be in the cache. Form submittals, including accesses to pages requiring IDs and passwords, will also be in the cache. The cache itself is held in a subdirectory under the browser's main directory and is fairly obvious. The subdirectory may, by default, be called "cache," depending on the version of the browser.

How can you keep this valuable information away from prying eyes? First, you can hide or protect the subdirectory. Second, you can flush the cache before each run of the program. IBM's Web Explorer for OS/2 does this automatically. One other option is to disable the cache, but that would seriously affect performance.

Search Engine Vulnerabilities

Search engines—great tools of the Web whether attached to the Web site itself or whether separate search sites, such as AltaVista—can present some additional vulnerabilities to a poorly configured Web site. If not set up properly, a Web site may inadvertently contain links to information about system configuration or links to sensitive files.

A Computer Incident Advisory Capability (CIAC) bulletin reports that an attacker may conduct a search for keywords, such as "root" or "passwd," in an attempt to gain valuable information about how to hack your site. Although it doesn't happen often, the attacker may find one of these golden nuggets and then gain entrance into your internal network through the Web.

If you attach a search engine to your Web site, make sure it is located outside the firewall; if internal information must be accessed, do so through a proxy server.

Conduct a search of your Web site to see if these dangerous keywords turn up:

root

passwd

url:etc

link:passwd

url:htaccess

url:htpasswd

If the attacker's search on the key phrase "url:htaccess" is successful, the attacker may find the location of a password file. If the search for "url:htpasswd" is successful, it may return a username and encrypted password that can be cracked by the attacker at his leisure.

Summary

In this chapter, we discussed the following topics:

◆ Decisions to lock up your Web site depend partly on security policy and technology, and partly on marketing. Of course, you want to make your site easy for visitors, particularly if you are trying to sell them something. Just as a department store tries to make things convenient for its customers, a Web site operator also wants to make the Web site convenient to visit. Security must strike a balance: it must secure the site, but must not make it too difficult for visitors to deal with.

◆ Cookies are little text files that a Web server can access to tell what you did when you visited. This type of information can be extremely useful to the marketing department in terms of discovering what are the most popular areas, and what areas may need more visibility. But many users see this as an invasion of privacy, and cookie information can in fact be misused. Cookies can be turned off with a simple software utility.

◆ A CGI script is a small program usually meant to execute a single task on a Web server. CGI scripts are useful for filling out and submitting Web forms. CGI scripts hold information about the server on which they run — information that could be useful to an attacker. The scripts are also dangerous because they can be attacked while running.

◆ A downloadable applet is a small program that is downloaded along with a Web page. Such applets are used to make a Web page more dynamic, but can be used to introduce a mischievous program into the client system.

◆ Java's security model uses the concept of the "sandbox," which isolates the Java applet after it is downloaded so any damage that occurs is limited to one area of the client.

◆ ActiveX's security model relies on digital signatures. These offer good security in the right circumstances, but the security model leaves a lot up to the individual end user, who has to decide whether or not the sender of the ActiveX application is trustworthy.

Chapter 17

Viruses

IN THIS CHAPTER

- ◆ Examining the wide dispersal of viruses
- ◆ How a virus works
- ◆ Keeping viruses out of your network
- ◆ Taking a look at UNIX viruses
- ◆ Examining macro virus threats

A VIRUS CAN TRIGGER a relatively benign prank, such as flashing a political message on a screen, or it can be devastating. It can delete files, insert obscenities into documents, or crash the system. A computer virus, like a biological virus, replicates itself for the purpose of distributing more copies of the virus throughout the body (network).

Viruses have infiltrated almost every operating system in existence, although some more than others. Viruses tend to show up mainly in DOS/Windows. Very few Macintosh and OS/2 viruses exist, and because NetWare servers do not use the DOS file structure, DOS-based viruses cannot affect a NetWare server. The reason that viruses tend to target DOS/Windows systems may be either animosity toward Microsoft or simply because DOS/Windows has the largest installed base – and a virus writer wanting to affect the most people will target the platform that causes the most harm.

For viruses to work well on a UNIX system, the system administrator or superuser must make a mistake – most often, this involves using more privileges than needed to perform routine tasks. As a general rule then, your security policy should dictate that users always be granted the least extent of privileges required to do their jobs. This is one of the best ways to prevent a virus attack.

Virus attacks follow different patterns, although all virus attacks contain some method of self-preservation (propagation, migration, or obscurity). In UNIX systems, the most common type of self-preservation is obscurity. A computer worm typically protects itself from detection by migration, while viruses use propagation. Trojan horses, logic bombs, and time bombs use obscurity to avoid detection.

Similar to a virus is a *Trojan horse*, which is a program that disguises itself as something else that appears to be useful. A Trojan horse is not actually a virus, because it does not duplicate itself. Instead, it tricks the user into executing it by promising something useful, and then executes a malicious sequence of events.

Before you can write a successful security policy to protect your system against some of these viruses, you should know something about the types of viruses that may pose a threat to you.

Types of Viruses

Although thousands of viruses exist, a relatively small handful cause most of the infections that occur. Many viruses contain minor variations of other viruses; this is because when an antivirus program can successfully detect and eradicate one particular virus, the creator of the virus may then alter the design of the virus enough to once again avoid detection. The new virus must then be isolated, studied, and addressed in the next release of the antivirus product. It's a cat-and-mouse game that has no end.

Several different types of viruses exist. A *boot sector* virus is contained in the boot sector and is executed when a user boots from a floppy disk. A *file* virus, on the other hand, lives in files instead of in the boot sector. Merely copying an infected file does not execute the virus.

The most common virus types are:

◆ **Boot sector virus.** These viruses propagate themselves whenever a computer is booted. If booting from an infected floppy, the virus attempts to install itself on the hard drive. When booting from an infected hard drive, the virus attempts to replicate itself onto any unprotected floppies.

◆ **File infected virus.** These viruses attach themselves to executable programs. When the infected executable is executed, the virus copies itself to memory, and attaches itself to any other executable files it can find.

◆ **Polymorphic virus.** These viruses modify themselves every time they move between computers, making them difficult to detect.

◆ **Stealth virus.** These viruses hide themselves to prevent detection.

◆ **Encrypted virus.** These viruses encrypt themselves to avoid detection.

- **Worms.** A worm is not actually a true virus, but a program that runs independently and travels between machines and across network connections. A worm does not change other programs on its own, but may carry a virus with it that may do so.

- **Trojan horse.** A Trojan horse (also not a true virus) embeds malicious code within an otherwise useful program.

- **Time bombs.** A time bomb executes a malicious act at a specific time.

- **Logic bombs.** A logic bomb executes a malicious act upon execution of a specific logical condition.

- **Macro virus.** This newer type of virus takes the form of a macro, which may be unknowingly executed when a routine task is undertaken.

To protect your system from these viruses, you must implement an antivirus plan in your security policy.

Antivirus Security Policy

The presence of ever-larger enterprise networks has made viruses more prevalent than ever before. Although growing networks have empowered end users and given them unparalleled abilities to communicate, these same large networks have made it easier to spread dangerous little programs. A large percentage of all security problems involve viral infections, which can cause anything from a nuisance message that flashes on-screen to unspeakable damage that can bring down the entire system.

The antivirus part of your security policy must go further than merely stating that an antivirus software package should be deployed. In addition to specifying software, the policy must provide strict rules for adhering to antivirus defense guidelines and provide the means to enforce them. End users should not be able to turn off the antivirus mechanism. Policy should also call for the maximum amount of automation, so the antiviral defense does not depend on end users individually executing their antivirus mechanisms.

The policy may also call for the creation of a response team. Individuals on this team would respond to virus emergencies by disinfecting files and attempting to determine the source of the attack. The policy should also state that the latest version of the antivirus software be installed as soon as it becomes available. Still, nearly a third of organizations do not have any formal procedure for tracking computer virus problems.

Furthermore, the policy must address those end users who are a particularly high risk. These may be users who do not intend to introduce viruses to the network but, because of their behavior, often do so. Users who perform frequent data transfers from the outside, whether it is part of their job or not work-related, may fall into this category. High-risk end users may also include those who (contrary to company policy) attempt to bypass antivirus mechanisms.

The policy should also include a clause that prohibits the use of any unauthorized software. End users often bring in their own disks and favorite programs or even computer games. You might think that allowing employees to play computer games during their break times is a human resources decision that has little to do with security policy; how these games are introduced, however, can directly affect security. Employees bringing in disks from home represent a significant threat to security, as these disks may, and often do, contain viruses. In fact, a significant percentage (60 percent) of all virus infections still result from the introduction of an infected disk. Other major sources of viral infections include downloads or e-mail attachments.

The Virus Prevalence Survey

The National Computer Security Association's (NCSA, not to be confused with the National Center for Supercomputing Applications, or the Northern California Songwriters Association) 1997 Virus Prevalence Survey reveals some startling findings. The study, which was conducted to identify the extent of the virus problem in PCs and networks, reveals that the virus problem is growing at an alarming rate. According to the study, 99.33 percent of medium and large organizations in North America have experienced at least one computer virus infection. The study also shows that use of antivirus software has increased by 13 percent from 1996. Despite this increase, however, the annual infection rate is still growing as well, reaching 406 out of 1,000 machines.

The survey notes that users can protect themselves simply by installing a leading antivirus software product and keeping it active, operational, and updated. According to the NCSA survey, fewer than 30 percent of the world's PCs use an updated, full-time antivirus software strategy. If antivirus software were used more rigorously, it could put a serious dent in virus proliferation. Unfortunately, the incidence of virus infections appears to be increasing.

The survey defines a *virus disaster* as an encounter with viruses in which at least 25 PCs, disks, or files are infected by the same virus simultaneously. About a third of all sites surveyed experienced such a disaster within the preceding 14 months. For those sites that did experience disasters, servers were down for an average of 40 minutes, with the longest downtime being 24 hours. In fact, downing the server is not always appropriate in a virus disaster, and the amount of downtime is not the only metric that reflects the seriousness of this problem. A complete recovery took an average of 44 hours and an average of $8,366 in costs.

Protecting Against Viruses

A common belief is that if access rights on the server are set to execute-only, the LAN will be virus-free. Unfortunately, this is more fiction than fact. It is true that if server-based programs are set to execute-only, a virus running on a workstation is unable to infect a server-based executable. However, an infection can still occur if users copy executables to the server or use the LAN to transfer executables between workstations.

A virus protection package should be installed on all workstations and configured to run automatically at least once a day. Plenty of reliable antivirus software products are available on the market. Furthermore, the virus software should be updated periodically. Vendors of antivirus software typically update their databases to reflect the newest viruses. Merely putting in antivirus software and letting it run may not protect against the newest viruses; the administrator must plan to download the updated database periodically.

Some companies have a stash of laptops that are used by several different employees. This practice can be very useful and productive, as well as cost-effective. However, it can also be dangerous. Because the laptops are used by several individuals, probably travel off-premises, and are subjected to a great deal of file activity, they are especially vulnerable to infection. A strict policy should be put in place that scans each laptop's hard drive for viruses every time a user checks in the laptop.

Antivirus software is just a piece of the puzzle in protecting your system against viruses. You can implement different categories of virus protection to protect your system.

Categories of Virus Protection

Three different categories of virus protection exist, although none provides complete protection when used as a single, stand-alone mechanism. These categories are control, inspection, and integrity.

CONTROL

Control has traditionally been the domain of the standards organizations, which deal with issues relating to system access and the ability to move data within the system. However, by themselves, control policies do not make up a complete solution. A virus can potentially gain control over even a B1 (highly secure) system, and the virus can then change permission sets.

Although discretionary access control (DAC) does offer some limited protection, it is inherently weak and can be easily bypassed. Furthermore, DAC is controlled by the end user, who may choose to ignore it. As a result, it is very common to see a site where the majority of files have no DAC protection. Furthermore, many UNIX sites have permission bit settings set at 777, which allows anyone to read, write, execute, or modify the files.

Mandatory access controls (MAC) offer more control than DAC and are more difficult to bypass. However, these controls are also susceptible to penetration. And of course, once a virus gains control over an operator account (root, operator, isso), no type of control can stop it.

INSPECTION

Inspection is often used by antivirus software packages to locate known viruses as well as holes in operating systems. However, these types of tools can only find known viruses; new viruses are being created so rapidly that these tools are nearly useless unless constantly updated. Audit tools and standard virus scanners must know what they are looking for before they can find them.

INTEGRITY

Integrity-based systems go further than inspection systems by detecting changes in the system. Earlier integrity systems were fairly useless soon after they were invented. These early systems used cyclic redundancy check (CRC) values to detect changes. A virus was created shortly afterward that determined the CRC value of the target file, infected it, and then padded the file so the CRC value would be the same, thereby making detection impossible.

A simple virus, once it infects a file, may change that file's modification date; that is, it affects the integrity of the file's parameters. Some users simply view the date of last modification as an indicator of change; however, this date can be easily changed on a UNIX system with a single user command.

An integrity tool must use cryptographic methods to be effective. CyberSoft's CIT integrity tool uses the RSA MD5 cryptographic hash algorithm and can detect even a single bit flip. Furthermore, CIT can detect additions and deletions to the file system. These additions and deletions can indicate a noninfectious attack, such as a Trojan horse.

Detecting and Preventing Viruses

Centralized management of virus protection efforts is critical to a successful defense. Someone, whether the user or administrator, must update antivirus packages frequently to combat the newest viruses; the only way to ensure that these updates take place is through centralized management. Ideally, an enterprise antivirus strategy will focus on preventing infection as opposed to cleaning up an infected file after infection has already occurred. In addition to centralized management and dispersal of updates, a successful enterprise antivirus approach includes a log of all activity and a report that translates the log into an easily readable format.

Many of the earlier viruses were boot sector viruses that often spread through shared floppy disks. The presence of large enterprise networks has made the threat much greater. The Internet itself presents a major threat. End users can unknowingly download files that hold viruses – even some Java or ActiveX applications may contain harmful viruses that can be released on a system. And Internet e-mail systems, which are often capable of attaching formatted documents for delivery over the network, can transmit viruses to hundreds of individuals.

These viruses can attempt to avoid detection in one of several ways. A polymorphic virus, for example, changes its signature every time it is activated. Consequently, an antivirus product that scans for a specific virus signature will not be able to detect it. A stealth virus avoids detection by intercepting interrupt services to send back phony data to virus protection software. Viruses can also avoid detection through encryption. A virus that is delivered from inside an encrypted file cannot be detected by an ordinary antivirus scan.

Although a well-written virus makes every attempt to avoid detection, you may notice a few telltale signs. Although these signs do not absolutely indicate the presence of a virus, the presence of these symptoms indicate that an infection may have occurred. These symptoms include the following:

◆ Increased file length

◆ Delayed program loading

◆ Lower system resources or available memory

◆ Bad sectors on floppy disks or hard drives

◆ Nonstandard error messages

◆ Fluctuations in screen display

An antivirus software system must be able to accommodate multiple methodologies to effectively combat viral infection. Although simpler packages were effective against earlier viruses, virus writers are getting more sophisticated, and the software to combat them must match that sophistication. Five main methods of detecting viruses exist; ideally, the package will support all five:

◆ **Signature scanning.** This method compares a file's content against a database of virus signatures. The signature database must be frequently updated to accommodate new viruses.

◆ **Integrity checking.** This method checks a profile of current files and disk areas against an archived snapshot. Any difference that is detected may indicate a virus. A checksum is a common type of integrity checking, although this may not be effective against the stealth virus.

◆ **Heuristic analysis.** This method uses artificial intelligence to monitor for specific behaviors that a virus might exhibit, such as attempting an unusual task, or trapping a specific interrupt service.

- ◆ **Polymorphic analysis.** A polymorphic virus changes its appearance constantly. This method moves a suspected file to a separate, safe location and executes it to determine whether it displays any virus-like behavior.

- ◆ **Macro virus analysis.** This type of analysis attempts to detect the new strain of macro viruses before they are executed.

The antivirus software's location is critical in an enterprise network. Although placing the software on the desktop may be partially effective, it is best to detect viruses before they reach the desktop whenever possible. Nonetheless, because individual desktop users often download viruses directly from the Internet, placement of antivirus software on the desktop is essential.

Placing the antivirus software at the gateway or firewall level theoretically would prevent any viruses from entering the network. However, this also results in significant performance problems. For a firewall to detect viruses, it has to rebuild every file, store them temporarily, and scan them before sending them to their destinations. Doing so takes a great deal of horsepower.

A proxy server or firewall separates the internal organization from the outside world. Because it is possible and highly likely that a virus will pass over the network to the internal organization, some of the leading proxy servers and firewalls now include virus protection features. According to the NCSA survey, 29.2 percent of e-mail gateways, 24.5 percent of proxy servers, and 29.4 percent of firewalls now include some sort of antivirus protection.

The antivirus software can also be placed at the e-mail server. E-mail messages are a primary source of infection and, because e-mail messages must pass through the server before being sent to the recipient, this is an excellent location for antivirus software. However, the server should not be the only location, because an enterprise network typically has many methods of connectivity. Internet servers and file servers should also be considered points for protection; indeed, anywhere files or databases are kept could potentially be a source of virus problems.

Consequently, a good enterprise antivirus strategy includes antivirus software not only on the desktop, but also in all servers and file archiving systems. The overall management scheme applied to the antivirus software should also simplify its operation and automate as much of it as possible. Updates need to be made automatically and regularly; when updating is left up to individuals at each desktop, the job may not get done. Furthermore, compliance must be mandatory and enforced via software. Ordinary users must not be able to turn off the automated virus protection, and mandatory virus scans must be able to take place.

The enterprise antivirus system must also be able to manage a large domain of nodes as a single entity, and it must be aware of every entry point into the network. A good system design can isolate the infected machine when necessary; that is, when an individual node on the network has been infected, the central control mechanism should be able to terminate that node's network access to avoid having the virus spread throughout the network. Furthermore, alarms are an important part of the software. The administrator should be able to receive an alarm of some sort when a virus appears somewhere on the network. This may take the form of an e-mail message, pager notification, or an automatic printout of a trouble ticket.

Antivirus software has been proven effective in deterring viral attacks. The NCSA survey indicated, however, that six percent of desktop PCs may have antivirus software installed, but the software is not operational. The survey emphasizes the need for a strict policy to make sure that the antivirus software is running on all machines. The survey also showed that 19 percent of desktop PCs have no antivirus software installed at all. Although automatic software distribution mechanisms have made it easier for IS to ensure that the software and periodic updates are disseminated to all machines on the network, many organizations still have numerous free-standing machines scattered throughout the organization, including laptops issued to road warriors. Your policy must ensure that antivirus software be deployed and updated on these machines as well, because they can be a major source of virus infection.

Special Dangers

E-mail gateways, Linux and UNIX viruses, and other factors can pose special dangers to your system. You may need to give these problem areas extra consideration in your security policy.

E-mail Gateways

Viruses and macros can enter your network via e-mail. The recent batch of so-called macro viruses are a major threat because they are not at all like traditional viruses, and can appear in a word-processing document sent over the Internet.

Traditional e-mail is full of holes and security vulnerabilities. Usually, an enterprise should not send highly sensitive information over the Internet. A sensitive message could be subject to a man-in-the-middle attack or other type of hack that could compromise the data. Many enterprises' security policies prohibit sending sensitive information via e-mail or using the Internet for any type of high-value electronic commerce. This is a valid policy statement that has particular importance if no e-mail firewall is implemented.

Particularly with the introduction of macro viruses, carefully monitoring e-mail attachments has become very important. Even before macro viruses, an infected executable file could be sent as an e-mail attachment. Double-clicking it under Windows 95 invokes the program, which then proceeds to deliver its payload. But users send documents as e-mail attachments more often than executable files. Any Word document can host a Word macro virus, and so e-mail attachments have become a major source of macro virus infection. Attached files can be extracted and manually scanned for the macro virus using a leading antivirus package; however, an e-mail gateway that monitors the attachments automatically is a better approach. Because this is a new innovation, e-mail gateways are just now starting to offer this functionality.

An e-mail firewall or gateway overlays the existing e-mail network and resides on the safe side of the firewall. It monitors all inbound and outbound traffic and uses technology such as S/MIME to encrypt messages at the server level before forwarding them on to the end user.

Two of the specialized antivirus products designed for e-mail gateways are Symantec's Norton AntiVirus for Internet Email Gateways and WorldTalk's WorldSecure software. Each product is a type of gateway software that works with a standard SMTP mail server and functions as an extension to the existing mail system. The gateway product serves as the primary e-mail gateway to the network and passes safe messages to the SMTP servers for delivery to end users.

The e-mail firewall or gateway eliminates the security vulnerabilities that are inherently present in an e-mail environment, and uses technology such as encryption, authentication, and virus scanning before passing the e-mail on to the end user. Through these technologies, you can tamperproof your e-mail and guarantee authenticity.

Linux and UNIX Viruses

Linux and UNIX viruses—what? Yes, regrettably they do exist. The concept that UNIX is immune to virus attacks is a dangerous myth. Those who believe that their UNIX systems cannot be attacked are particularly vulnerable, because proper precautions may not have been taken and a strong security policy may not have been implemented.

In fact, a virus-infected file, once it has entered the UNIX system, enjoys the same protection as any other file on the network; and viruses can easily migrate between systems thanks to Network File System (NFS) and other networking technology.

The Bliss virus is the first virus to attack the Linux operating system. McAfee, a popular vendor of antivirus software, first discovered the virus in February 1997. The Linux.Bliss virus is a nonmemory-resident, parasitic virus written in GNU C. It infects the Linux operating system only. The virus searches for executable Linux files and infects them. The virus shifts the file body down, writes itself to the beginning of the file, and appends the following ID text to the end of the file:

```
"Bliss.a": infected by bliss: 00010002:000045e4
"Bliss.b": infected by bliss: 00010004:000048ac
```

The virus lengths are 17892 and 18604 for Bliss.a and Bliss.b. When an infected file is executed, Bliss.a searches for three uninfected files and then infects them. Bliss.b affects more files.

The presence of the virus is particularly important, because many UNIX observers had claimed for years that viruses were not a major concern to UNIX users. Typically, UNIX is difficult to infect, because the virus writer must have administrative privileges to infect a UNIX system – so the only way to infect the system is if administration is lax. According to McAfee virus researchers who discovered the virus, the virus started to spread because Linux users playing computer games over the Internet play the game in Linux's administrator mode (root).

Although UNIX is significantly less susceptible to virus infection than DOS and Windows systems due to UNIX's access control mechanisms, it still behooves the administrator of a UNIX system to install antivirus protection. Although it is difficult for a virus to get through to a UNIX system, it can be done, and you should take steps to prevent such a possibility.

A memo, written by the anonymous author of the Bliss virus, was posted on the Internet. It serves as a startling testimonial that UNIX viruses can, in fact, exist; and people will write them if for no other reason than to prove that point. The memo indicates that Bliss was not intended to be released "into the wild," and although it was not written to be malicious, it may unintentionally cause some destruction.

Such attacks are evidence that a UNIX system is, indeed, susceptible to hostile attacks, despite widespread claims to the contrary. In fact, the first computer viruses were on UNIX systems – these include the notorious Internet Worm, Trojan horses, and logic bombs. Of course, these types of attacks are not unique to UNIX, and can be introduced to any system.

The problem of UNIX viruses is made even more complex because traditional methods used as counterattacks in DOS and other environments are not adequate for the more complicated UNIX operating system. Furthermore, UNIX is by nature open and heterogeneous, which makes it all the more difficult to prevent viruses from attacking.

Computer viruses typically employ some sort of self-preservation technique, which may involve propagation or migration. In UNIX, the most common method of self-preservation is obscurity; that is, the virus program hides using an obscure name and storage location in order to avoid immediate detection.

The most common type of attack against a UNIX system is a Trojan horse or time bomb. A Trojan horse is a program that appears to be something useful or attractive but, in reality, contains a hidden payload that may cause some sort of destruction or mischief to the system.

Trojan horses are easy to create by modifying any source code and adding a payload to it. A popular and simple payload is the "bin remove" payload:

```
/bin/rm -rf / >/dev/null 2>&1
```

This payload attempts to remove all accessible files on the system as a background process, with all messages directed to waste disposal. All files on the system with permission bit settings of octal 777 will be removed, as well as all files owned by the user, the user's group, or anyone else on the system whose files are write-accessible to the user.

Another simple attack is to insert a back door to the system through the *suid bit shell* attack. This is a Trojan horse attack, in which a Trojan horse program is used to copy a shell program to an accessible directory. The shell program is then set with permission bits to enable it to execute with the userid and permission of the attacker. A one-line suid bit shell attack can be created by adding this command to any user's .login or other executable file:

```
cp /bin/sh /tmp/gotu ; chmod 4777 /tmp/gotu
```

An antivirus program with a Trojan horse detector can be effective in detecting these types of attacks.

Not nearly as many antivirus software packages exist for UNIX as exist for DOS and Windows. CyberSoft made the very first UNIX-based antivirus product in 1991. The Vfind product runs on most UNIX systems and provides for all three methods of protection: control, inspection, and integrity.

Vfind offers control by adding the freely available COPS auditing tool, designed by Dan Farmer (the creator of SATAN), and the proprietary Trojan Horse Detector (THD) auditing tool. THD assumes that most Trojan horse attacks use duplicate file names, where the file name of the Trojan is the same as a common UNIX command. The *ls* command, for example, is usually stored in the /usr/bin directory. Most users permit world-read permission on the account control file, so it is a simple thing to discover the search path selected by a given user to search for system commands. If an area that can be written into is in the search path prior to /usr/bin, the Trojaned version of ls can be installed in that directory and executed. THD looks for duplicate file names as well as other known file names used by Trojans.

Vfind provides inspection through a standard virus scanner. The scanner searches for UNIX, DOS, Macintosh, and Amiga viruses on the UNIX system.

The use of UNIX and Linux targeted antivirus software is becoming increasingly important given the likelihood that the incidence of UNIX viral attacks will become more widespread, particularly with the growth of the Internet, which is still primarily UNIX-based.

Heterogeneous Virus Attacks

Non-UNIX PCs attached to a heterogeneous network can be infected with a virus originating from a UNIX server. Although these viruses may be dormant while on the UNIX system, they become harmful when they migrate to the target system. In this case, the UNIX system functions as a dormant carrier for the virus. UNIX servers providing NFS (network file systems) are particularly susceptible to this type of attack because they allow for easy migration of files between systems. This type of problem is referred to as the *Typhoid Mary Syndrome.*

Transplatform virus attacks on UNIX systems are surprisingly common, usually involving a DOS virus that attacks a PC-based UNIX system. The BIOS and processor functions are actually the same for both operating systems, making it easy to design a transplatform virus. The virus can inspect the operating system using only common BIOS calls and then modify its behavior using a simple *if* structure.

Peter Radatti, founder of CyberSoft, claims to have observed a number of non-UNIX PCs attached to heterogeneous networks that were infected with viruses originating from UNIX workstations. This observation formed the impetus for the creation of his Vfind antivirus program.

Radatti's investigation centered on a network containing PCs where a large population of UNIX workstations and servers became infected. The virus was manually attacked on the PCs using virus scanners.

Radatti first became aware of transplatform viruses when investigating an infection of PCs on this heterogeneous network. During the process of removing the viruses from the PCs on the network, the target platform computers were disconnected from the network, and all removable media was checked. After the infected files were identified and removed, the PCs were reattached to the network. However, a few weeks later, the computer virus reinfected the system. Radatti soon discovered that it was the UNIX system that was the source of the PC viruses. Radatti had discovered his "Typhoid Mary."

The easiest way to minimize the possibility of a Typhoid Mary attack is to regulate what types of files can move between platforms. Although it would still be possible to infect a data file because it is not executable, the virus may be less capable of migrating. However, movement of data files such as word processing documents across platforms may also present a danger, as the computer industry experienced with the Word for Windows Concept macro virus (more on this virus in the next section).

Radatti created the Vfind program after encountering the Typhoid Mary Syndrome. The program's design was based on the assumption that a computer virus could migrate between heterogeneous environments and should therefore scan for UNIX viruses as well as DOS, Macintosh, and Amiga viruses.

Vfind scans all types of storage, not just files. Because it is possible to determine what type of storage systems the end user has in addition to the file system, Vfind includes a universal interface for reading all forms of data. The UNIX system itself provides this universal interface in the form of the *dd* command. This command reads and converts into a byte stream any form of storage that the running UNIX system can access. This enables Vfind to investigate any type of storage media.

Macro Viruses

In 1996, the computer industry saw the introduction of a new category of virus — the Word 6.0 macro virus. The macro virus also represents the startling new possibility of viruses to be cross-platform in nature, as we saw in the section on the "Typhoid Mary Syndrome." It also represents the first virus that can infect a system through a nonexecutable file.

A macro is a small set of instructions carried out by a certain program. The macro is usually implemented to automate routine tasks, such as typing in a long address, performing sorts, or manipulating data.

In DOS, macros are carried out through files with the .BAT extension, and are also known as batch files. These files are interpreted, and executed a line at a time to automate tasks. OS/2 has a more advanced batch language called REXX, which can handle more rigorous tasks and is more robust.

Applications such as word processors and spreadsheets often have their own macro language that can be used to automate tasks within that application. As such, their functionality is limited by the services offered by the host application. Word macros carry out tasks that are part of the Microsoft Word environment. However, through middleware such as Object Linking and Embedding (OLE), a macro can be written to affect other running applications. Although it has not been documented, it is theoretically possible for a Word macro virus to affect another running application through this mechanism.

The macro virus affects a system when it executes, and will, unknown to the user, instruct the system to overwrite an existing system macro with another (destructive or mischievous) macro. When Word opens a document that contains an AUTO macro, the system automatically executes it. Word macro viruses usually start with an AUTO macro, which then instructs the system to infect other macros and template files, with the goal of eventually infecting any document opened by the word processor.

The Word macros usually overwrite the FileSaveAs macro in order to gain control over what file format to save documents in, and what macros to include in any saved document. When the File / Save As command is executed, the virus causes the usual dialog box to be displayed to have the user to fill in the file name and other information as normal. Afterward, however, the virus changes the file to a template, and then the macros are included in the document. When a document is exchanged with another system, the other system becomes infected when the document is read.

When a Word session is over, Word automatically saves all global macros in the global macro file (NORMAL.DOT). Then, future Word sessions will infect any document that is opened.

Several Word macro viruses actually exist, although the most well-known is the Concept virus. This was the first one to be widely detected "in the wild." The Concept virus can run on systems operating Microsoft Word for Windows 6.x and 7.x, Word for Macintosh 6.x, and in the Windows 95 and NT environments. The virus spread throughout the world when it was accidentally released on three shipping CD-ROMs. Microsoft itself became an unknowing conduit for the Concept virus when it released the Microsoft Windows 95 Software Compatibility Test CD-ROM and the Microsoft Office 95 and Windows 95 Business Guide CD-ROMs in 1995. In addition, the ServerWare's Snap-On Tools for Windows NT CD-ROM was inadvertently shipped with the virus. ServerWare withdrew it immediately after discovering it, and remastered the CD-ROM.

The National Computer Security Association claims that the Word Concept macro virus is the most common virus since the fall of 1995. This macro virus is growing more rapidly than any previous virus, and infects 49 percent of all sites surveyed by the NCSA. The NCSA claims that at its current growth rate, the Concept virus could triple in incidents during 1997. Four of the top ten reported viruses are macro viruses.

The rapid growth of macro virus infections can be attributed to several factors:

◆ A macro virus can replicate itself using vectors other than disks, including e-mail attachments. While many users do scan disks before introducing them into a new computer, it has not yet become a common practice to scan e-mail attachments.

◆ A macro virus is not immediately noticeable. Users do not notice any change in performance in their computers; the virus is only noticed after the damage has been done. Because it takes longer to deliver its payload, the computer stays infected for a longer period of time, and has a greater opportunity to infect others.

◆ Organizations have not yet revised their policies and procedures, or updated their software to accommodate the macro virus threat.

Shortly after the Concept virus appeared, Microsoft released a free Macro Scanner/Cleaner, and other antivirus software vendors released their own products to accommodate this new threat.

You can easily discover whether your system is infected with Concept. When you first open an infected document, a message box appears with a "1" inside and an "OK" button. A check in the Tools / Macros option will show loaded macros. If Concept is present, the following five macros will appear in the list (the asterisks are part of the macro names):

AAAZFS *

AAAZAO *

AutoOpen

PayLoad *

FileSaveAs

While AutoOpen and FileSaveAs are actually legitimate macro names, be on the lookout for unusual or unfamiliar macro names.

Using the Tools / Macro option to see active macros may not always yield definitive proof that a macro virus is present, however. Some macro viruses intercept the call and show falsified information.

While most of the leading antivirus vendors have added support for detecting macro viruses, some additional measures may be taken to supplement your antivirus product. You can disable AutoOpen macros by invoking a system macro called DisableAutoMacros. This can also be done by executing Word with this command:

```
WINWORD.EXE /mDisableAutoMacros
```

or by setting the Tools / Options menu to prompt before saving NORMAL.DOT. The File Attributes of the file may also be set to read-only. Although a virus can be written to change that setting back, it never hurts to take the extra step.

Depending on the desired level of security, some companies have chosen to take the extreme step of implementing a policy prohibiting e-mail attachments. Although this policy severely cuts down on the incidence of macro viruses, it also causes a great inconvenience for companies such as publishing firms that routinely send documents via e-mail. However, few options exist at this point, and very little in the way of commercial security products can implement security based on Port 25 (Sendmail through a firewall). Although a router or firewall can certainly specify a port for filtering, it cannot examine the contents of each packet, only the header information; as a result, Word macro viruses can easily pass through the firewall undetected.

Summary

In this chapter, we talked about the following:

◆ Viruses have infiltrated every operating system in existence. Despite claims to the contrary, UNIX is not immune to viruses. UNIX has fewer viruses and is more difficult to attack, but attacks do happen, especially when an administrator is lax in enforcing security policy.

◆ The phenomenal growth of networks represents both convenience and security risks. Because so much more is connected now than ever before, more opportunities exist for a virus to spread rapidly.

◆ Viruses can be regulated through a combination of control, integrity, and inspection. An effective antivirus software product incorporates some aspects of all three.

◆ Viruses can be introduced into the network as an e-mail attachment. An e-mail gateway can mitigate this risk by working with an antivirus product and examining all attachments before they are passed on to the mail server.

◆ Heterogeneous virus attacks are possible when a Windows virus is introduced through a UNIX host. While the Windows virus may remain dormant and harmless to the UNIX host, when PC clients access files from the UNIX host through NFS or other access mechanisms, the virus spreads from UNIX to Windows-based PCs – where they can deliver their payload.

◆ The macro virus is the newest, and most rapidly spreading type of virus. It differs from traditional viruses in that its host is not an executable program but a word-processing document.

Chapter 18

Ensuring Secure Electronic Commerce

ELECTRONIC COMMERCE, UNTIL RECENTLY, depended largely on costly, private, value-added networks. Although these networks tend to be highly secure, they do have some drawbacks: they are expensive, they are difficult to implement, and they are proprietary. More recently, electronic commerce has come to be transacted over the Internet. This model is significantly less expensive, and much more open. The problem, however, is that it is much more vulnerable.

The transactions involved in electronic commerce go much further than the actual exchange of cash for goods. Purchase orders, invoices, and other documents must also be exchanged as part of the transaction. *Electronic data interchange* (EDI) is the exchange of electronic messages between computers without human intervention, conforming to a set of agreed-upon standards. These messages may be related to commerce and include invoices, purchase orders, and other documents needed to perform electronic commerce transactions on the Web.

Doing Business on the Web

The World Wide Web presents us with a new medium for doing business. Although Web-based advertising is still minimal, it is growing rapidly. Within the United States, electronic commerce revenues are expected to reach an estimated $150 billion by the year 2000. Merchants are attracted by the prospect of Internet stores because of the Internet's global reach. A *virtual storefront* can be created at minimal cost, giving small start-up companies an opportunity to compete evenly, at least on this level, with large corporations.

To date, not much has been sold directly over the Internet; company Web sites are used primarily to offer information on products and details on how to order through other avenues. This will probably change very soon. As Web-based advertising takes off, companies will need a convenient mechanism that they and customers can use to buy and sell advertised goods. This is where Web-based electronic commerce comes in.

Is it acceptable to send financial information over the Internet? Well, yes and no. We often give out credit card numbers over the phone, but how do we know some yahoo with a listening device isn't sitting in a truck parked outside? We don't. But the chances of that happening are slim, so we consider it to be an acceptable risk. Other risks and potential problems also exist when doing business on the Web. You should plan for secure Web transactions, just as you plan for a secure network.

Planning for Secure Transactions

Web sites implementing electronic commerce are often managed by the marketing department. This group's first priority may not necessarily be implementing security procedures, however. Frequently, in fact, the marketing staff's take on the issue is to use as little security as possible, because they want to make it easy for people to buy goods from their on-site catalog. After all, when you walk into Macy's, do you have to give them a password at the door? However, it is possible for a Web site to be both secure and easy to access. In fact, numerous commodity products are on the market just for this purpose.

Security should be part of the initial design of your Web site, not an after-thought. The level of security that is installed, however, depends largely on what products are being sold and what level of exposure is acceptable.

The most obvious option for a Web commerce site is to place the Web site on a separate server with no connections to the internal network. This prevents an attacker from using the Web server as a jumping-off point to get to other servers. This may be difficult, however, in cases where you may need to access information on back-end databases. For example, a commercial site may want to give customers access to their account information, shipping logs, or inventory data. If this is the case, a proxy server can serve as a go-between for the Web site and the back-end databases.

The simplest approach to secure selling on the Internet is to simply provide a form on which a client enters a credit card number. The form is then encrypted and transmitted. However, this approach offers only minimal security, because the encrypted number could be intercepted and hacked. A more sophisticated but costly solution is to use smart cards.

Potential Problems

You may encounter several problems when preparing for electronic commerce over the Web, but you can also take precautions to avoid problems.

It is theoretically possible for anyone to gain access to your LAN from the Internet — that is, of course, if your LAN has an Internet link. Some companies prefer to isolate the LAN, or at least certain sensitive departmental LANs, making them islands unto themselves. Although this method ensures that no one can get in, it also ensures that no one can get out, which places a big burden on those employees on that LAN. Short of cutting off access, the next best thing is to implement a firewall and an underlying security policy to limit outside access.

Web-based electronic commerce could potentially result in another problem — bandwidth. Of course, if you're getting so many orders that your network gets clogged, you can probably afford bigger pipes! Usually, when a company adds Internet access, it acquires a fractional T1 line. This is usually more than adequate to accommodate employees who need to access the Internet for legitimate business uses. However, adding a Web server to the network may overburden the network — because Web browsers all over the world may be attempting to access that Web server, which is serving out information over that same fractional T1 line.

Two alternatives exist for alleviating this bandwidth problem: either add more bandwidth or use a Web-hosting service. Both are viable options, but the Web-hosting service may be the most practical solution and, in many cases, the less expensive option. This option involves using a third-party service that, for a fee, places your electronic commerce site on its own server and is responsible for its maintenance. The Web-hosting service option also has the added advantage of having your Web site located elsewhere — so if your primary network goes down, your Web site will still operate.

You can host an intranet and an external Web site on the same server, but doing so results in a number of security drawbacks (in addition to the bandwidth problem). If the same server accommodates the internal network and the Web site, an attacker has a lot more ways to get inside. If you choose to run your own Web site instead of using a Web-hosting service, isolating the Web server from the rest of the network is one of the best ways of ensuring that outsiders don't get in where they don't belong. That is, if the Web server is a separate machine, not connected to the intranet or internal network, outsiders will only be able to access what you want them to see. No sensitive material is placed on the Web server — the machine is, in essence, public.

Although software solutions are available that can separate internal and external information on the same server, this setup it is more difficult to administer.

Another frightening specter that can and does occur in such situations relates to the use of hyperlinks. Hyperlinks that are accessible from an external Web page may point to some data on an internal Web page on the same machine. An attacker only needs to find one improperly-placed hyperlink to ease into the internal portion of the network by way of the external Web site. The only solution here is caution, and regular checking of all hyperlinks on your Web site.

Transferring Information

Electronic commerce and EDI require content integrity to be maintained in a secure fashion. That is, both parties involved in the transaction must have some guarantees that the data has not been altered in transit, whether accidentally or maliciously.

The two main methods of sending data over the Internet are FTP and MIME. FTP (File Transfer Protocol) enables trading partners to transfer files over their Internet connections. With FTP, a temporary link is established between two endpoints over multiple nodes on the public Internet. FTP is fast, simple, and readily available. However, using FTP for sensitive financial documents may be risky, particularly because the file transfer may be sent through several diverse Internet routers. As such, some characters may be converted during the session. Another limitation is that you have to know information about the server to which you are being connected ahead of time, so configuration may be different for each trading partner. Furthermore, you cannot use FTP when the recipient is not online.

A security flaw of FTP-based EDI is that FTP has a feature called *port redirection* that could potentially enable an attacker to bypass the firewall. Many Internet-based EDI messages go directly to servers behind the firewall. An FTP server, before it can be used to receive EDI, must have an uploading area. The FTP server that is located behind the firewall can also be a starting point in an attack on other hosts behind the firewall. The problem stems from what could otherwise be a great convenience, that is, the ability to transmit or receive data from any port by giving the ftpd a PORT command different from the one that would ordinarily be issued. Generally speaking, FTP is not suitable for secure EDI. Besides its complexity and the ability to do port redirection, FTP opens two separate TCP channels: one control socket and one socket for data exchange. The control port uses a fixed address, but the data port can be anywhere, a factor that can cause packet filtering problems.

MIME (Multipurpose Internet Mail Extensions) over SMTP as an EDI solution overcomes these limitations. This protocol encodes data, allowing it to be transferred via SMTP without the accidental character conversions that are common with an FTP transfer. Also, the participants do not have to be online at the same time, because the data can be encapsulated in a temporary location until the recipient retrieves it.

Accidental character conversions can and do occur. Another way characters can get modified during the course of an EDI transaction is through outright attack. To guarantee that the information has not been modified, the sender must include some sort of integrity control value. This value is calculated based on the content of the message and an algorithm known as a one-way hash function. The recipient runs the same algorithm and compares the hash value with that of the sent data; if the two values are equal, no tampering occurred. A commonly used hash algorithm is MD5; this is used by most e-mail security programs. The process is fairly transparent to the users, and is implemented in many EDI programs.

Nonrepudiation of origin is also essential in EDI; this guarantees that the message originated from the person claiming to have sent it. Nonrepudiation of origin uses digital signatures and encryption to prevent spoofing — a technique in which an attacker masquerades as a legitimate sender. You can get nonrepudiation of origin by using digital signatures.

You can add more protection by using acknowledgments and audit trails, which guarantee that the data reaches the proper destination in a timely manner. Unfortunately, because the public Internet can pass through any number of nodes over which the sender has no control, the sender can do very little to guarantee delivery over the Internet. You can find out, however, whether a message has been delivered within a certain period of time through a nonrepudiation of receipt. In this technique, a unique identifier is sent with the original message. This identifier is returned by the recipient with an acknowledgment; the sender then reconciles it with the original message. The recipient may also choose to digitally sign the acknowledgment for further verification. Trading partners should agree on a time limit between when a message is sent and an acknowledgment is received; if the acknowledgment is not received within that period of time, the sender should have an automatic resend feature set up to resend the message.

E-mail can also play an integral part in transferring information for electronic commerce. Several mechanisms are available to ensure your e-mail is secure, but few of them have been successfully interoperable. The most widely used are the Secure Multipurpose Internet Mail Extensions (S/MIME) and the Message Security Protocol (MSP).

MSP is used primarily by the Department of Defense as part of its government-wide Defense Message System (DMS) messaging infrastructure and is not compatible with S/MIME. In true government form, the Department of Defense decided it had to have its own specification; in short, MSP is a like the infamous $250 toilet seats. Although MSP is more secure than S/MIME, it is also more inconvenient. For a Defense user to send a secure message to a civilian agency using S/MIME, the message must go through a gateway that temporarily strips off security and reformats the message. This is an obvious point of vulnerability.

But perhaps the Department of Defense has seen the light of day. A proposed initiative would add MSP services to S/MIME, something that would greatly simplify communications between DMS users and S/MIME users. It would also increase the number of e-mail products that could be deployed by government users and the vendors who want to talk to them.

Now in the IETF (Internet Engineering Task Force) draft stage, S/MIME contains several features currently found only in MSP:

- ◆ **Security labels.** These are short labels that can be attached to a message to indicate priority, security clearance, or other information.

- ◆ **Return receipts.** These are used to guarantee that a user received a particular e-mail message.

◆ **Mail list support.** This feature enables a user to off-load encryption processing to a server for a large distribution.

◆ **Key management.** Support for key management techniques other than RSA.

Making Electronic Commerce User Friendly

Any merchant will tell you that if you want to sell something, you have to make it easy for people to buy. That's why we have impulse items at the checkout counter, and grocery stores have special lanes for ten items or less. Buying over the Internet must also be easy – not only in terms of access and browsing, but in terms of paying for the merchandise.

CyberCash Secure Internet Payment Service

In addition to requiring secure credit card transactions, customers may also enjoy using electronic cash for small denomination payments or electronic checks. On the merchant side, the information sent by customers must be able to link with back-end applications, such as inventory and accounting.

CyberCash's Secure Internet Payment Service establishes an innovative online payment system that is remarkably similar to the modern day point-of-sale (POS) paradigm. Most large stores employ an automated POS system, which instantly ties the customer payment at the checkout to back-end systems.

Transactions can be performed in under 20 seconds, and anyone with a credit card can use the system. CyberCash's mechanism is made secure through automatic encryption, using 768-bit public key encryption. The company promises to move to 1,024-bit encryption at a later date.

The primary components of the CyberCash system include the following:

◆ **The CyberCash Wallet.** This is free to consumers and resides on their computers. The Wallet software's installation process binds an existing credit card to a given ID for the purpose of authentication.

◆ **The Secure Merchant Payment System for merchants.** This software resides on the merchant's Web server and interfaces with the customer's CyberCash Wallet software on the front end, and with the gateway server on the back end.

◆ **The CyberCash Gateway Server, which establishes a link to existing financial networks.** The gateway server offers firewall protection, as well as message translation between Internet and financial network protocols.

Here's how a CyberCash credit card transaction works:

1. First, a customer visits the Web-based storefront and selects goods in a virtual "shopping cart." The customer gets pricing information and provides the merchant with information concerning delivery.

2. The merchant's Web server displays the CyberCash PAY button, which initiates the transaction.

3. When the customer clicks this button, the Web server submits an electronic invoice.

4. The customer's CyberCash Wallet automatically opens and has the customer select a payment instrument.

5. A charge payment message, which is encrypted, is sent to the merchant's Web server.

6. The Secure Merchant Payment System receives the message and adds merchant identification information.

7. The payment request is sent to the CyberCash Gateway Server, which decrypts the messages and authenticates the customer and merchant.

8. The gateway sends a message to the bank requesting approval. This message is sent over a private financial network.

9. The bank sends a positive or negative response back to the server, which relays it back to the customer.

10. The server sends the customer a digital receipt to complete the transaction.

The transactions are protected by encryption, which combines DES private-key and 768-bit RSA public-key technology. (The messages between the customer, merchant, and gateway are encrypted by DES technology. The DES key is then encrypted by RSA technology, and appended to the DES-encrypted message.) CyberCash has also been approved for 1024-bit RSA encryption by the U.S. government. CyberCash is also working with the major credit card companies to comply with the Secure Electronic Transaction (SET) standard defined by Visa and MasterCard (covered later in this chapter).

RSA supports the use of digital signatures, which are basically a type of electronic identifier that can be created and encrypted only by the sender's private key but can be read by any public key. CyberCash uses digital signatures to authenticate the senders of messages.

To use the CyberCash mechanism, a merchant must first set up a Web site and then go through a bank to become a certified CyberCash merchant. A merchant's existing bank will probably be able to handle this requirement.

Java Commerce API

Sun Microsystems' Java Commerce API presents another way to purchase goods securely over the Web. The Java Wallet presents a front-end system that customers can use to make purchases. This is similar in theory to the CyberCash Wallet.

The Java Wallet stores personal information about the shopper, payment instruments such as credit cards, and details of all purchase transactions. In addition, it supports two types of signed applets: payment cassettes and service cassettes (a *cassette* is a prebuilt Java applet). A payment cassette is an applet that implements a specific payment protocol, such as SET. The service cassette can be used to implement a value-added service, such as financial analysis. As with CyberCash, the Java Wallet uses strong encryption.

Building on the Java Commerce API is Sun's Electronic Commerce Toolkit, which presents a complete architecture for Java-based electronic commerce. The toolkit includes a Java Wallet, and five separate cassettes for connecting different types of electronic payment methods with transaction handling mechanisms on the back end.

The Netscape Merchant System

The Netscape Merchant System presents a complete infrastructure for setting up online sales (see Figure 18-1). The suite of merchandise management features promotes online shopping and enables merchants to manage their inventory and sales efficiently. Features include product loading and display, merchandising, shopping, order and transaction processing, and secure order delivery. For security, this system takes advantage of the built-in security of the Netscape Enterprise Server.

The system can be operated stand-alone or integrated with existing sales or order-processing systems. The fact that the system is based on industry standards such as SQL, HTML, HTTP, and RSA facilitates integration. The Merchant System includes three components: the Merchant Server, Transaction Server, and Staging Server.

Merchants use the Merchant Server to create, deliver, and update product displays. Think of it as an automated stock boy. It can update pages remotely and also create a product display page automatically using templates. The Transaction Server is used for order and transaction services, including credit card processing and order fulfillment. This is where the security comes in: this module's Internet Credit Card Processor encrypts the shopper's credit card number using public-key encryption, and authorization with the bank card servicer is conducted via a private, leased line. The system supports Secure Sockets Layer (SSL) for secure communications. This encryption technology authenticates the sender, encrypts the message, and verifies message integrity.

The Merchant System offers credit card verification either over a leased line or over the Internet (see Figure 18-2). The Internet option includes SET support, which offers a high degree of security.

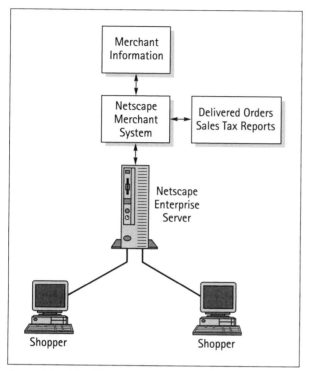

Figure 18-1: The Netscape Merchant System architecture includes everything you need to sell online.

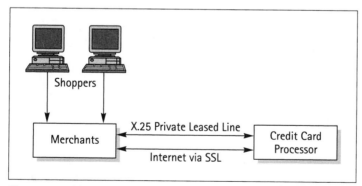

Figure 18-2: Merchants communicate securely with acquirers over the Internet instead of through expensive leased lines.

The Transaction Server module uses several techniques to ensure security. When the customer is ready to process purchases, purchase orders are encrypted at the Transaction Server for transmission to the merchant via secure e-mail. The merchant receives the secure e-mail, decrypts the order, creates an order report, and returns an acknowledgment to the Transaction Server. The Merchant Server's Secure Mail implementation conforms to the S/MIME and Public Key Cryptography Standards (PKCS).

Use of the digital envelope, digital signature, and certificate operations facilitates the secure transmission of the purchase data between the Transaction Server and the merchants. The use of digital certificates in conjunction with the Merchant Server system provides additional reassurance that each party is who he or she claims to be.

The Merchant Server, Transaction Server, and Staging Server applications each require a dedicated machine (see Figure 18-3).

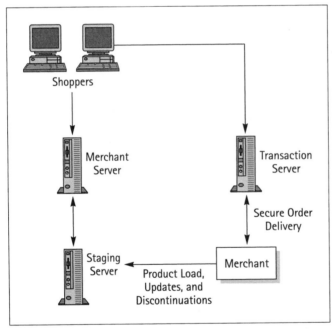

Figure 18-3: The Netscape Merchant System architecture requires dedicated machines for each server.

Note that the Staging Server is an option used for reviewing and updating product displays.

Using Credit Cards on the Internet

For electronic commerce to blossom, a way must exist for consumers to use their credit cards over the Internet. Currently, credit card usage on the Net is still small, but it is likely to grow rapidly, particularly with the introduction of the SET standard.

The Secure Electronic Transaction (SET) standard is a technical specification for securing credit card transactions over the Internet. Developed by credit card giants Visa and MasterCard, SET is based on RSA encryption technology. The specification is open and can be freely used by any developer wanting to create SET-compliant software.

SET takes a step beyond Microsoft's Secure Sockets Layer (SSL). SSL encrypts a credit card number and other information using a 40-bit key. While this type of key can be hacked, it may be adequate for some needs. In addition, while SSL keeps the credit card number and information private while being transmitted, SSL does not address the issue of whether the card is valid, or whether it is owned by the person ordering the merchandise. SET addresses these limitations by using an "electronic wallet" that can identify the user and validate the transaction. An electronic wallet is a type of software application used by the consumer to securely store purchasing information.

SET-based systems have an advantage over other mechanisms, in that SET adds digital certificates that associate the cardholder and merchant with a particular financial institution and the Visa or MasterCard payment system.

MasterCard, along with IBM, has undertaken a pilot project that gives selected MasterCard members the opportunity to take advantage of IBM's CommercePOINT software. CommercePOINT establishes an end-to-end network payment system that enables a user's customers to use a secure environment in which to conduct secure credit card transactions over the Internet.

The CommercePOINT system is one of the first major systems available that displaces the private, value-added networks traditionally used for electronic commerce. CommercePOINT, which uses the SET standard, gives members an early entrance into the electronic commerce market. The alliance is one of several IBM initiatives designed to develop SET-based transactions over networks.

Under the pilot, users and merchants alike will enjoy rapid implementation and turn-key project management. Cardholders will be provided with IBM's digital wallet software, and merchants will use IBM's Net.Commerce merchant server software along with CommercePOINT servers. Banks will use the CommercePOINT acquirer payment gateway for processing merchant transactions conducted over the Internet.

Net.Commerce provides the building blocks for creating a virtual storefront on the Internet. With it, customers are able to browse through an interactive catalog. Security is provided through CommercePOINT's use of digital certificates and other secure payment protocols. Businesses use the IBM World Registry, an IBM-hosted service, or can implement the tools themselves. The IBM Net.Commerce Payment system, based on SET, provides security for credit card transactions.

Through Net.Commerce, merchants can build their own storefront using three components:

◆ **Net.Commerce Merchant Server.** This program manages the interface that is presented to customers, and creates dynamic catalog pages based on customer input.

◆ **Net.Commerce Store Manager.** This program creates an interactive catalog and templates, and tracks marketing statistics.

◆ **Net.Commerce Secure Payments.** This program provides a secure system for credit card authorization.

According to the credit card companies, SET makes using credit cards on the Internet as safe as using them at the corner store. SET-compliant software is only just beginning to appear however, and it will take even more time for financial institutions to create the infrastructure required to support SET technology. When SET becomes more widely accepted, the amount of electronic commerce will most likely surge. Usage of SET will also make it easier for customers to make small "impulse" purchases, a factor that will greatly increase the total amount of money being spent online.

Despite standards such as SET, customers are still nervous about sending a credit card number over the Internet. Whereas SET and other security measures may prevent credit card numbers from being intercepted, theoretically it's still possible for a con artist to set up a phony storefront and simply collect credit card numbers.

A Little Guidance from Uncle Sam

A White House report claims that federal conformance tests would help boost confidence in electronic commerce security tools, although the White House is still trying to balance its own perceived need to access encrypted communications against the industry's need for privacy and confidentiality. According to the report, the proper environment and standards could make the Internet one of the largest categories of trade—and the government wants to avoid undue restrictions to foster growth of this segment of trade. The administration's recommendations for creating a global electronic commerce network focus as much on what the government agrees not to do as it does on what it does agree to do. The purpose of the White House report is to create a framework to allow electronic commerce to flourish on its own by establishing a predictable legal and financial environment. The administration supports an open systems approach and a standard code of conduct for protecting privacy and intellectual property rights.

However, the White House stresses that the market will determine standards, not the government itself. Although the National Institute of Standards and Technology (NIST) may develop test beds and the government will have a significant role as a user of electronic commerce technology, NIST will not create the actual standards, and the report does not advocate any particular technical approach to security.

The Office of Management and Budget (OMB) has also taken a role in promoting privacy on the information superhighway. OMB has issued proposals, based on research undertaken by the NII (National Information Infrastructure) Task Force's Information Policy Committee. The proposals include creating a new regulatory agency and promoting more privacy education programs.

A presidential mandate calls for all federal agencies to use electronic commerce for routine procurements. Complying with the order, however, has proven difficult for most agencies, because of the enormous amount of re-engineering that must take place to convert from a paper-based system to a paperless one.

As per the 1994 Federal Acquisition Streamlining Act, a government-wide Federal Acquisition Network (FACNET) was created. A deadline was set for January 1997 for all federal agencies to comply. FACNET is based on electronic data exchange (EDI), which ultimately enables government agencies and their suppliers to conduct transactions without human intervention.

FACNET, as with any EDI system, allows vendor inventories to be updated automatically. Other tasks, such as invoicing, shipping notices, and material releases, can also be completely automated. A major advantage of this system is that because documents are sent between computers, the data does not have to be rekeyed, thus minimizing the opportunity for human error. Several government agencies have realized some success with EDI, and some have even saved enormous amounts of money. However, many are still finding the technology difficult and costly. EDI systems come with a special type of translation software, which reformats data, and converts it to ANSI X12 EDI format (a common EDI standard that places EDI documents into a common format). On the other end, a mapping package reformats the ANSI data back into its original format.

Smaller government suppliers balk at FACNET because of the expense and the fact that only a small percentage of requests are, at this point, posted to FACNET. As of February 1996, 206 Department of Defense activities were certified Interim FACNET-compliant and could use simplified procedures for soliciting and awarding government contracts. Although the Department of Defense has encountered numerous problems in establishing an electronic commerce infrastructure (primarily the high cost to participating businesses), over 80,000 FACNET-compliant transactions take place every month. In addition, the Defense Information Systems Agency (DISA) has rolled out a more robust infrastructure that supports a higher traffic load, which will in turn enable larger dollar value transactions and more complex contracts to participate in the government's EDI process.

Some government agencies instead turn to the Internet for electronic commerce because of its openness and the capability of more vendors to participate without having to put out a large, upfront expenditure for EDI software.

Another disadvantage of FACNET is that it is designed for a transaction between one agency and one vendor. The Internet, on the other hand, allows a single Web site to serve as a central point of entry for many government suppliers.

The Office of Management and Budget is considering taking another step by embracing the SET protocol.

Summary

This chapter looked at how to establish a secure electronic commerce environment, which allows outsiders to have a look inside your "virtual store." You learned:

♦ Until recently, electronic commerce and EDI depended largely on costly and proprietary value-added networks. The Internet presents an opportunity to open up electronic commerce to many small businesses that would not otherwise be able to afford to implement it.

♦ The external commerce Web site should be hosted on a separate server. While the Web site and the intranet can, in fact, be hosted on the same server, it is unwise to do so because it presents more opportunities for an attacker to break into files.

♦ MIME over SMTP presents a useful solution for EDI over the Internet. While FTP can be used for this purpose, it has several drawbacks.

♦ The SET standard, promoted by credit card giants MasterCard and VISA, holds a great deal of promise in securing Web transactions. Unlike SSL, SET identifies the user and authenticates the transaction, and adds a digital certificate that associates the buyer with a merchant and a specific financial institution.

Chapter 19

Intranets

IN THIS CHAPTER

- ◆ Creating a secure intranet
- ◆ Allowing remote access
- ◆ Using Novell IntranetWare

BRANCH OFFICES HAVE TRADITIONALLY been connected by telephone company services such as X.25, frame relay, or private leased lines. Although these connections are effective solutions and inherently secure, they are also costly. Using the Internet as the corporate backbone (creating an intranet) provides an inexpensive connection alternative, and many large corporations are embracing this strategy.

Although a precise definition of *intranet* is hard to come by, it can generally be defined as an internal network, with or without connection to the public Internet, that uses TCP/IP as the primary transport mechanism and Web-browsing applications as the front end.

Many corporations use Internet technology to support internal operations. For example, it is increasingly common to place internal manuals, employee handbooks, and employee bulletin boards on an internal Web site. This approach is an easy way to get lots of information to employees quickly and presents the most effective way possible to rapidly update data. An employee handbook, for example, may be hundreds of printed pages, and updates are costly to generate. Updating the same handbook on an internal Web site, however, costs practically nothing, and employees get access to the updates immediately through the convenience of the Web browser interface.

The intranet is also used to connect branch offices and telecommuters to corporate headquarters. As such, it creates a sort of all-encompassing WAN based on the public Internet. This allows companies to avoid the expense of remote access equipment and long-distance charges while enjoying the capability of extending the network to virtually anywhere in the world.

Just because the intranet is an internal network doesn't mean that no security problems exist. An attack may come (and often does) from within the organization. In addition, an outside attacker may come in through a hole in the Web server, a loose modem, or any of a hundred mechanisms, and look for a back door to the intranet. Once this occurs, the attacker could gain access to almost anything.

As we saw in Chapter 16, however, TCP/IP is by nature insecure. So how do you create a secure intranet? It can be done, although it depends on what you want out of your intranet and how much connectivity you want to allow. Because its definition is so loose, your intranet can be as secure or insecure as you choose to make it.

Intranet Security

Intranet security can take many forms. As with any type of security, the first step is policy and to think through the different levels of access control — that is, which groups of people will be getting access to what information. In addition to access control, the primary mechanism for bringing security to the intranet is the use of the IPSec standard and a Virtual Private Network (VPN). A VPN enables corporate data to ride piggyback over the Internet in a secure fashion.

IPSec defines protocols for encryption and for adding integrity checks to packets. In addition, several transforms have been proposed. A *transform* is a type of algorithm used to transform an IP packet into an encrypted IP packet that contains an integrity check. The IPSec standard includes a specification for a tunneling mode. Tunneling permits an Internet traffic packet to ride piggyback on top of the Internet by being encapsulated in a valid Internet IP packet. This allows a branch office or remote teleworker to connect to headquarters over the Internet in a secure fashion, as if it were a private connection.

Although IPSec offers encryption and integrity to the intranet, authentication is addressed separately by digital certificates. A digital certificate is typically bound to a public key and authorized by a Certificate Authority (CA), which is a trusted third party.

Several commercial Public Key Infrastructures (PKIs) are available. These permit corporations to deploy an enterprise-wide CA and certificate server. Certificate infrastructures are typically based on X.509, which makes them interoperable. A company deploying its own PKIs from different vendors should be able to cross-recognize each authority. The IETF (Internet Engineering Task Force) is also working on a protocol that would allow CAs to cross-certify one another. Although these certificates are gaining in popularity and functionality, the issue of transporting and using certificates over an intranet still remains. The certificate must be portable and secure. To ensure these qualities, some vendors have created cryptographic tokens that store certificates and their private keys. These can be implemented in the form of a PCMCIA card or smart card.

A firewall can also play an important role in the secure intranet. Although firewalls have traditionally been used to control Internet access, they can also be used in intranets. A firewall can be deployed internally to separate sensitive departments from the rest of the corporation; for example, if the marketing department has sensitive information on its LAN that should not be accessed by the rest of the corporation, you could deploy a firewall in front of that department's LAN.

In an intranet that connects several branch offices, each branch's point of Internet access is also the VPN point of termination. This point is also where the firewall is located; as such, firewall vendors are starting to focus on adding VPN facilities to their product lines.

Internet and intranet servers have differences, but they are minor; they're so similar, in fact, that some servers can serve both purposes. This is not advisable, however – misconfiguring an intranet server can cause the server's documents, which are meant for authorized intranet users only, to be accessible to outsiders via the Internet. Although such misconfigured intranets are unusual, they do exist, and hackers love them.

Remote Access to the Intranet

The latest service that innovative ISPs are offering remote end users is secure access to corporate intranets. It's possible to deploy your own secure remote access solution, as many companies elect to do, but using an ISP's managed remote access connectivity solution is an easy, comparatively inexpensive, and typically secure solution. These services use IP tunneling and encryption technology to enable remote users to dial in to a service center (point of presence, or POP) where users are authenticated. After authentication, an encrypted tunnel is established from the user to the POP over the Internet. At the POP, the user data is decrypted and sent over a dedicated connection to a firewall server at the user's headquarters. Many of the larger ISPs offer secure remote access of this type.

When the intranet is extended to include off-site workers, traveling road warriors, and branch offices, the convenience/security risk trade-off arises: that is, the greater the convenience, the greater the security risk.

Virtual Private Network (VPN) technology can address some of these security concerns. The VPN can take the IP packets and securely transport them over the Internet. An IP packet can be encrypted, encapsulated (or tunneled) inside another IP packet, and then routed securely across the Internet. This can be a particularly effective way of extending a corporate intranet or extranet. This is because it is actually more difficult for an intruder to capture IP packets being routed over the Internet than it is for them to capture IP packets on the corporate LAN. That's because Internet routers typically run secure operating systems and adhere to a rigorous security policy and secure administration procedures.

Authentication, encryption, and integrity must be applied to the VPN. These functions must be applied to every single IP packet; because IP is stateless (as are all Layer 3 protocols), it is impossible to determine whether each IP packet is attached to a given connection. Even in stateful TCP protocols, the connection tracking mechanism still can be spoofed. Authentication and integrity are based on one of two algorithms: Message Digest Version 5 (MD5) or Secure Hash Algorithm (SHA).

Four protocols can be used in a VPN: Layer 2 Forwarding Protocol, Layer 2 Tunneling Protocol, Point-to-Point Tunneling Protocol, and the IP Security (IPSec) protocol. The first three are Layer 2 forwarding protocols. These encapsulate Layer 3 packets such as IP in the Layer 2 PPP before encapsulating them in IP. IPSec, unlike the others, provides the packet-by-packet authentication, integrity, and encryption that is essential for strong security in a VPN. IPSec represents the strongest possibility for VPNs; many commercial vendors of firewalls and intranet software comply with this standard.

F-Secure Virtual Private Network

As an example of a VPN, let's look at DataFellows' F-Secure Virtual Private Network (see Figure 19-1). The product provides the individual in charge of security with the ability to establish secure tunnels between sites, while still allowing access to external sites if needed. It is best used along with a firewall. The device is actually an encrypting router that permits a VPN to be constructed over the Internet with strong cryptographic security.

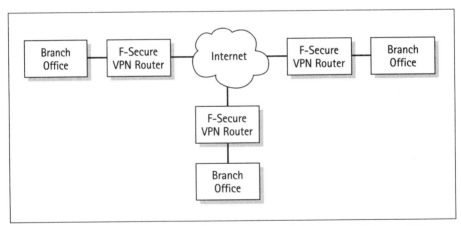

Figure 19-1: A VPN architecture with point-to-point tunnels between all F-Secure VPN routers, forming a fully-connected network

The system runs as a "black box" on any standard Intel hardware and does not need any administration except when a new site is added to the VPN.

F-Secure encrypts TCP/IP packets on the fly for transport over the Internet or an intranet. It works with any installed base of routers and firewalls and uses Triple-DES and Blowfish encryption. It also compresses data, authenticates other encryption servers, and performs distributed key management.

F-Secure VPN is normally placed behind both the corporate firewall and the router. The encryption engine can be installed on a Pentium PC. After some initial key exchange and authentication between F-Secure servers at other sites, the net manager simply removes the keyboard and monitor and the machine becomes a security server. You must then configure the routers to forward all TCP/IP packets destined for encryption to the F-Secure server while all packets traveling to unsecured sites are routed normally. Net managers must also configure one port on their firewall to let encrypted traffic reach the F-Secure server without filtering it.

When it receives a packet, F-Secure VPN compresses and encrypts both the TCP header and the payload. It then encapsulates it in a second packet for tunneling to an F-Secure unit at another site. The software at the destination site decrypts the packet and retrieves the original header before forwarding it to the LAN. By compressing and encrypting simultaneously, F-Secure makes the session even harder to crack and also saves valuable Internet bandwidth.

F-Secure VPN uses the SSH (Secure Shell) protocol, which allows for distributed key management: Rather than storing keys in a central database, which introduces a single target for attacks, F-Secure servers hold their own keys. And they can be configured to change session keys every hour or so to thwart hackers. Key exchange is performed securely using SSH and the public-key algorithm from RSA Data Security, Inc.

Extranets

An *extranet* is even harder to define than an intranet. Generally speaking, it is what occurs when your intranet is extended to the intranets of trading partners or customers.

The biggest risk involved in extending your intranet is that you are allowing others outside your organization into your intranet, although these trading partners or customers probably have different security policies than you do. The best policy regarding extranets is to require those partners to comply with your security policy, or at least the subset of your policy that would apply to them.

Because it involves others outside your organization, setting up the extranet calls for a great deal of coordination. This is usually done through some sort of tunneled access (such as a VPN) that is established between the two intranets over the public Internet.

One of the most important parts of the extranet is the data on your own intranet that you want to provide to your trading partners. For example, customers may gain access to an inventory system or catalog of parts to determine product availability. This level of access may be done by adding the partner to the application's access control list.

But most extranets go much further than offering access to a few databases; some extranets allow partners to share a wide variety of data and applications. As such, it may be beneficial to all parties to adopt a common, Web-based application development environment for the purpose of creating distributed libraries, workflow applications, and messaging. Strong and secure collaboration tools often form the backbone of a large extranet.

At the perimeter of your intranet sits the firewall, which protects your intranet from any harm (or at least some harm) that may come from outside sources. The firewall is an important part of the extranet, in that it can at least keep casual snoops away from sensitive data and limit legitimate users to certain databases. As part of the firewall policy, it is important to determine ahead of time exactly what data and applications should be made available to the trading partners and then to allow them access only to those databases and applications.

Also, before allowing outsiders into your intranet, strong authentication mechanisms must be in place so you can authenticate all transactions. These authentication mechanisms can include digital signatures, secure tokens, or credentials servers. And if the information being transmitted between intranets is sensitive, you should also use encryption. Encryption is part of a VPN, which represents one of the most effective ways of creating an extranet.

Many ISPs offer support for extranets by providing end-to-end security through encrypting and tunneling routers, firewalls, and browsers. Check with your ISP to see what services are available.

Creating an Intranet with Novell IntranetWare

The Novell NetWare 4.11 network operating system contains a selection of Internet and intranet components that gave it the name *IntranetWare*. These added features provide NetWare with a number of Internet features, including more support for TCP/IP and access to the Web and other distributed functions. Previous versions of NetWare required an add-on application before TCP/IP could be used, whereas IntranetWare has this support built in. This software bundle is designed to create an intranet from an existing network infrastructure and allows both IP and IPX to access those intranet resources.

IntranetWare allows for the interconnection of TCP/IP and IPX networks, so all users can access IntranetWare resources on either network. In addition, the bundle includes an IPX/IP gateway, which allows the IPX-based NetWare network to communicate with the TCP/IP network.

Most important for this book, however, an IntranetWare-based intranet adds security through several means; for example, NDS (Novell Directory Services) authentication offers secure access to the server and directories. Additional access controls are included that allow the administrator to control document access. Other security features of Novell NetWare 4.11 include RSA public/private key cryptography and NDS/file system event logging.

One reported security bug in IntranetWare allows it to be hacked: The CGI scripts, which are included with the server, are BASIC programs. The CONVERT.BAS script converts a file to HTML and then sends it to the user. For example,

```
http://www.mycompany.com/scripts/convert.bas?info.txt
```

returns the INFO.TXT file as HTML.

While returning a text file as HTML is quite useful as a way of providing information over the Web, consider the following hack:

```
http://www.mycompany.com/scripts/convert.bas?../../file_on_
  sys_volume
```

This hack yields access to any file on the SYS volume as a text file. This flaw was corrected in NetWare 4.11, although several sites still have this bug.

Summary

In this chapter you learned the following:

- ◆ In the past, branch offices had to be linked through a private leased line, or a service such as X.25 or frame relay. An alternative is to establish a secure, private TCP/IP connection over the public Internet. This is known as an *intranet*.

- ◆ The IPSec specification defines encryption protocols and a tunneling mode. Tunneling enables an encrypted data packet to ride piggyback on top of the Internet securely, by being encapsulated within a valid IP packet.

- ◆ An extranet is what results when the intranets of two or more trading partners are connected for the purpose of conducting business. Extranet security is particularly difficult because it involves divergent security policies and procedures. The best way to approach this challenge is to determine ahead of time which of your own security policies should be adhered to by the trading partner.

Chapter 20

Identifying and Preventing Common Attacks

THE INTERNET HAS BECOME a valuable tool for commerce, business, and academia, and must address the security and privacy concerns of those areas. Private networks are not immune from attack. Even if your corporate network is not attached to the Internet, it can still have a great many vulnerabilities, which may come from an area you least expect.

Types of Attacks

As many different types of attacks exist as do attackers. Those who attack computer networks, whether it be for fun or for profit, constantly seek out new methods while still hammering away at the old ones. Internal attacks and corporate espionage are not only the stuff of spy novels, they are very real and take place every day.

Brute Force Attacks

Forty-bit encryption has long been considered weak and vulnerable to attack. Although the government allows the use of the 56-bit DES encryption standard in certain circumstances, this standard has not proved to be hack-proof either. Government experts had estimated that 56-bit DES encryption would take hundreds of years to crack, but some clever hackers have proven that prediction inaccurate.

An employee of an online commerce provider cracked the standard in 1997, using a program that sought idle time on Internet computers. The program used this unused time to perform massive calculations by farming out algorithms to thousands of computers throughout the Internet over a four-month period. This effort was remarkably exceptional, because it used "unused" CPU time from ordinary computers.

Forty-bit encryption can be cracked in about an hour. Fifty-six bit encryption is 65,000 times more difficult, but as we now know, can still be cracked by an ingenious hacker. On the other hand, 128-bit encryption is considered by most to be impregnable and would require 4.7 trillion billion times as many calculations as would be required to crack 56-bit encryption.

The breaking of 56-bit encryption was undertaken in response to a challenge and a prize of $10,000 offered by RSA Data Security, Inc. The effort linked together tens of thousands of ordinary computers across the U.S. and Canada in a "brute force" attack that tried every possible decryption key.

Denial-of-Service Attacks

The denial-of-service type of attack does not damage data, but instead denies service to users by either clogging the system with a deluge of irrelevant messages or sending disruptive commands to the system.

Denial-of-service attacks have received a lot of attention because of a few recent, high-profile incidents. The United States Department of Agriculture was victim to this type of attack in June 1997, when an unauthorized user broke into the department's system and sent out a deluge of messages to several systems connected to the Internet. The large number of outbound messages overloaded the systems receiving them, causing them to malfunction or crash. The Department of Agriculture had to shut down its systems to stop the unauthorized messages. It took the department three days to restore 70 percent of its systems.

Unfortunately, one can take very few precautions against this type of attack. Denial-of-service is a rather simple type of attack for the hacker to undertake, and it is still a fairly new procedure. Whereas other attacks take advantage of a particular vulnerability or a bug in software, denial-of-service attacks take advantage of the very nature of the Internet itself.

This is a particularly frightening type of attack, and to date, no effective way exists to stop it once it has started, short of shutting down the entire system.

It is interesting to note that denial of service may not even be the result of an aggressive attack. Although it certainly can be carried out by an attacker intent on evil, it can also result from a bug in commercial software. Keeping up with service pack releases can help to minimize the occurrence of bug-related failures.

Since the main method of undertaking a denial-of-service attack is to generate traffic sourced from random IP addresses, it is recommended that you filter traffic destined for the Internet if possible. This filtering involves discarding packets with invalid source IP addresses as they enter the Internet. This procedure does not prevent a denial-of-service attack, but will help others who may be attacked rule out your location as a source of attack. In addition, it prevents individuals from within your organization from undertaking such an attack.

SYN Attacks

Similar to the denial-of-service attack is the *SYN attack*. Recently, this type of attack garnered a lot of attention when an attacker disabled Panix, a large ISP, with a deluge of irrelevant synchronous packets. A SYN attack disrupts the normal communications handshake that occurs between two computers prior to opening a TCP/IP communications port. Normally in this handshake method, one computer sends another computer a synchronous packet (SYN). The second computer then returns an acknowledgment (ACK). The first computer sends back its own ACK, and then communications can begin.

In a SYN attack, however, the attacker's computer does not acknowledge the other computer's ACK, but instead sends the computer a deluge of SYN ACK messages. Computers typically have a default that lets them hold a specified number of SYN ACK messages. When that number has been reached, no one else can initiate a handshake – and no one else can get into the system, thus increasing the possibility that the network may crash.

Internet Security Systems (ISS) is working on a method for combating this attack, which will be included in its RealSecure product. ISS's approach is to establish a real-time attack recognition-and-response system on a separate system in front of the TCP/IP UNIX server connected to the Internet.

ISS's SYN prevention software examines incoming packets to detect a SYN attack pattern. If a SYN flood commences, the software immediately sends the Reset command to the port undergoing the SYN flood and then notifies the administrator of the attack.

IP Spoofing Attacks

Administrators may choose to set up an internal Web site solely for the purpose of transmitting confidential information conveniently and securely. These sites can be set up so that only specified machines can access them, to ensure that only authorized individuals can access the confidential information on the server. Most Web servers include a mechanism to restrict access in this manner.

However, this setup is still vulnerable to attack through IP spoofing. Under this type of attack, one machine disguises itself as another to gain entry to a particular server. This is generally done when an outside computer pretends to be a computer that exists within your network. If your router is not configured to filter out incoming packets whose source address is internal, you are vulnerable to a spoof attack.

Using IP spoofing, an attacker can easily masquerade as an authorized user. Because of this vulnerability, valuable information should not be protected only by the client's identity. Protection based solely on the client's identity should be limited to situations where the host is completely known and trusted. For example, if the network is behind a firewall that filters out outside packets that claim to come from the inside, spoofing cannot occur and any machine claiming to be part of the internal network can be trusted.

A CERT advisory on IP spoofing reports that the CERT Coordination Center has received reports of attacks in which intruders create packets with spoofed source IP addresses. These attacks exploit applications that use authentication based on IP addresses. This exploitation leads to user and possibly root access on the targeted system. After gaining root access, the intruder can take over open terminal and login connections. Furthermore, the attack is possible even if no reply packets reach the intruder.

Once an intruder uses IP spoofing to gain root access, he or she can also use a separate tool not related to IP spoofing to dynamically modify the UNIX kernel. Through this modification, the intruder can then hijack an existing terminal or login connection from any user on the system. After doing so, the intruder can go on to gain access to remote hosts.

By hijacking an existing connection, the intruder can bypass one-time passwords and other authentication measures by tapping into the connection after the authentication has already taken place. The hijacking tool is used primarily on SunOS 4.1.x systems, although the features that make this attack possible are not unique to SunOS.

Certain configurations may be more vulnerable to IP spoofing attacks than others. Some potentially vulnerable configurations include the following:

◆ Routers to external networks that support multiple internal interfaces

◆ Routers with two interfaces that support subnetting on the internal network

◆ Proxy firewalls where the proxy applications use the source IP address for authentication

Now you know what IP spoofing is, but how do you go about protecting your network, particularly one that's especially vulnerable to such attacks?

It is possible to detect IP spoofing. Monitoring packets with a common network monitoring package such as netlog is one simple method. Using this or another commercial monitoring package, check for packets on the external interface that have both source and destination IP addresses in the local domain. If you find such a packet, your network is under attack.

You can also detect IP spoofing by comparing the process accounting logs between systems on the internal network. If a successful IP spoof has occurred, a log entry on the machine that has been spoofed may show a remote access; but on the apparent source machine, no corresponding entry will exist for the remote access.

Detecting an IP spoof through regular use of a monitor is a solid practice, but prevention is also essential. The best approach to preventing IP spoofing is a filtering router that restricts the input to the external interface by not allowing a packet through if it has a source address from the internal network. Furthermore, the filtering router should be configured in the other direction such that no outgoing packet may have a source address different from the internal network. The latter filter will prevent an IP spoofing attack that may be originating from your site. A number of firewall vendors support this feature, including Bay Networks, Cabletron, Cisco, and Livingston.

Web Spoofing Attacks

Web spoofing is a type of man-in-the-middle attack in which the user believes he or she has a secured session with a particular Web server. In reality, however, the user has a secured session with an attacker's server. The user may then be duped into supplying the attacker with passwords, credit card information, and other useful data. The attacker sits between the victim and the Web, thereby making it a man-in-the-middle attack.

To undertake this type of attack, an intruder first compromises a company's Web site (for example, Acme Networks) by using DNS (Domain Name Service) spoofing or by setting up a search engine listing to create an intercept point. DNS spoofing is possible because a DNS server can provide different IP addresses at different times. The DNS for attacker.com, for example, may return a valid IP address for www.attacker.com, or may return a spoofed IP address in order to access another machine. An innocent end user then finds the Acme link on the search engine, clicks it, and is led to a shadow site. The attacker has created an SSL certificate with an authentic-looking domain. The user gets a solid key and then assumes that the transaction will be safe. The attacker then presents a form on the dummy site asking for passwords, credit card information, or other data.

A Web spoof essentially creates a shadow copy of the World Wide Web. A victim's Web accesses are funneled through the attacker's machine, so the attacker can then monitor the victim's activities and steal passwords or account numbers.

This dangerous practice lets the attacker control everything the victim does on the Web, gives the attacker access to any information the victim enters into a Web form, and allows the attacker to cause false data to be sent to other Web servers in the victim's name. This type of attack has been equated to the con in which a criminal sets up a phony ATM machine in a shopping mall. When shoppers enter their PIN numbers, the ATM machine will simply return the card and issue an out-of-order message; but the phony machine has acquired a PIN number. In a Web spoof, a victim visiting a Web page believes that Web page to be legitimate; but in fact, it is a shadow copy of the legitimate page being controlled by the attacker.

Hackers can also use this type of attack for spying; that is, the attacker can be passive and record information about the victim's activities. Another use of the Web spoofing attack is for tampering; that is, the attacker can modify data that travels between the victim and the Web. The attacker could, for example, alter a ship-to address if a victim is placing a product order online.

For example, the attacker will attempt to rewrite the URLs on a Web page, so that they point to the attacker's server instead of a legitimate server. This is a rather simple process where the hacker rewrites a URL on a Web page by adding his own URL to the front of the legitimate URL. For example, assume that a hacker at http://www.badguy.com wants to spoof IDG's web site at http://www.idgbooks.com.

The attacker will add http://www.badguy.com to the front of http://www.idgbooks.com, so the IDG Books URL becomes http://www.badguy.com/http://www.idgbooks.com.

When a victim sees the IDG Books link on a Web site, the victim clicks it, but his or her browser will then request a page from `http://www.badguy.com`, and badguy's server then goes to the Web to retrieve the real document. The IDG Books server sends the page to badguy's server, badguy rewrites the page, and badguy then sends the rewritten page back to the victim.

If the victim submits a form, the data goes to the attacker's server and not the IDG Books server. The attacker's server can then observe or modify data before passing it on to the legitimate server.

When the victim places a request for a page via a secure connection (using Secure Sockets Layer) in a spoofed Web, the page will be delivered, and the indicator (an image of a lock or key) will be turned on. The victim is then lulled into a false sense of security. The victim does indeed have a secure connection, but the secure connection is to `badguy.com`, and not `idgbooks.com`.

What can be done to deter this type of attack? After all, you can see the "bad" address in the URL anyway, right? Yes, but although the attacker's server must show its location to carry out the attack, there are ways the hacker may make the location less noticeable. And more than likely, the attacker is using a stolen machine anyway, so the server location may be of little use. So what do you do?

Three tactics can deter a Web spoof attack. First, disable JavaScript in the browser, so the attacker cannot hide evidence of the attack through a Java program. Second, make sure the browser is configured so that the location line is always visible, and third, make sure that all users pay attention to the URLs being displayed on the location line.

Dictionary Attacks

The Dictionary attack is a simple attack that illustrates the need for carefully chosen passwords. A simple cracker program simply takes all the words from a dictionary file and attempts to gain entry by entering each one as a password. In NetWare, for example, a hack could try to gain entry through four simple steps:

1. The attacker steals the bindery files from a target NetWare server.

2. The attacker runs a cracker program to encrypt all the words from a dictionary file.

3. The cracker program compares the encrypted words to all the encrypted passwords in the NetWare bindery file.

4. When a match is made, the attacker gains a password.

End users often select a common dictionary word as a password. This is a poor practice, and security policy should dictate that passwords should not be words from the dictionary. Instead, they should be a nonsensical combination of letters and numbers and should not reflect any personal information about the user. For example, if your name is Joe Brtszphlk and your birth date is January 5, 1948, don't create a password of jb010548. An attacker with personal information about Joe would easily guess this one.

A variation of the dictionary attack is a brute-force password attack, in which a program attempts all possible combinations of characters until the program finds a password for an account. This time-consuming method can be easily thwarted by activating Intruder Detection on NetWare servers, or a similar option on another network operating system. In NetWare, Intruder Detection, upon detecting a brute-force attack, locks the account to which the attacker is attempting to gain access and makes a log entry of the violation.

The hacker can sidestep Intruder Detection if he or she can somehow gain access to the NetWare bindery files. If the hacker can gain access to the *.OLD files that exist after a BINDFIX procedure, or access the bindery files from a backup tape, the hacker can run a program to extract the encrypted passwords from the files. The hacker can then use the dictionary-cracking program at his or her convenience, without fear of triggering Intruder Detection.

NetWare 4.1.*x* closes some of these vulnerabilities; for security purposes, an upgrade may be in order if you are still running NetWare 3.*x*.

Attack Recognition

Fortunately, some tools exist that you can use to recognize many types of attacks. Having an attack recognition strategy is as important as having a prevention strategy. Because the enterprise has grown so immense and complex, and because the enterprise may be open to trading partners and remote workers in the intranet/extranet paradigm, it must contend with more threats than ever before and with many more ways to penetrate the network. A clever attacker may still be able to get through a network even if it has a good prevention strategy. When this happens, it is important to be able to detect the attack and put a stop to it before it causes widespread damage.

Attack recognition and response software continually monitors network traffic and detects known attack patterns. When it detects one of these patterns, the software automatically executes a predetermined action. This action may include generating a report or long entry, or may include termination of the connection. Ideally, this software should work with other security mechanisms already in place.

An example of attack recognition software is Internet Security Systems' RealSecure, one of the first products available capable of detecting a SYN attack. The software works with existing equipment, such as the firewall. As we discussed in Chapter 12, a firewall is a good first line of defense, but it is only the first line. It should never be considered a complete security solution. Besides the need for other services such as network monitoring, the firewall is often difficult to configure; a single error could leave a hole in security. In addition, the firewall must be constantly updated to reflect the services required by constantly moving end users. Even if properly configured, the firewall can still be penetrated by a clever attacker using an IP spoof attack or by bypassing it completely and gaining access to the network directly through a modem. The need for additional protection above and beyond the firewall is therefore critical.

The attack recognition and response software runs on a network machine located at specific control points throughout the network. These control points may be positions near an Internet router link or near a LAN holding critical data.

The attack detection software uses one of two methods to recognize attacks:

- ◆ **Rule-based approach.** This technique uses a library of known attack patterns. Like antivirus software, a rules-based attack detection package must be frequently updated to reflect new types of attacks.

- ◆ **Statistical-anomaly approach.** This technique assumes that end users, and the networks themselves, exhibit a predictable pattern of behavior. A deviation from this predictable pattern of use indicates a possible attack.

Again, this type of software should be used in conjunction with other security-related hardware, such as firewalls, and software, such as antivirus and security scanning packages. For example, if a security scanner misses a vulnerability that appears only briefly and between scans, the attack recognition software can detect it before it causes any damage.

Ideally, the attack recognition response software should operate in real time, as opposed to merely logging events and generating an audit log for later review. Although an audit log may be a useful analysis tool, it is fairly useless in deterring attacks; its usefulness only extends to analyzing the attack after it has already happened. Another desirable characteristic of the attack recognition package is for it to comply with network management standards, such as SNMP, so it can integrate with other SNMP-compliant network management tools. And lastly, it should be transparent to the end user. As always, security management should be as far removed from individual end users as possible to enable greater control and centralized management as well as rigorous enforcement of security policy.

ISS's RealSecure takes a rules-based approach to attack detection, operating in real time. The package can respond to an attack by:

- ◆ Sending an alert through a console message, e-mail, or pager

- ◆ Logging the event

- ◆ Terminating the connection

- ◆ Initiating a user-supplied script

Ideally, this type of package can become a second line of defense behind the firewall, effectively intercepting an attack that may have penetrated the firewall, or originated from within the firewall.

The software's recognition engine detects low-level IP attacks, including IP spoofing and fragmentation and SYN flooding, as well as high-level attacks, such as those that may emanate from an FTP or Web session. In a large enterprise network, multiple recognition engines should be placed in strategic locations throughout the network.

The security administrator manages the ISS software through a single point of control. This central module is used to configure the software's recognition and response engines and to collect and present events and other data. The central console should display events in real time, including the attacker's keystrokes and a copy of the attacker's screen (see Figure 20-1).

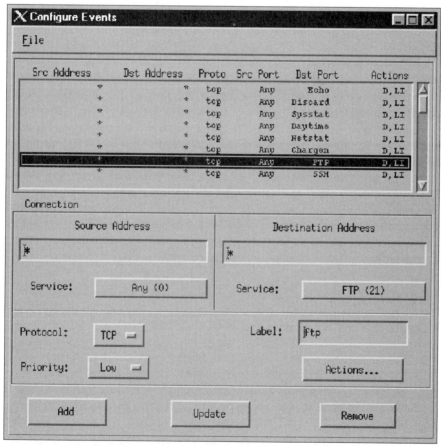

Figure 20-1: The RealSecure administrator's module

Vulnerable External Devices

Microphones, and to a lesser extent video cameras, are becoming standard equipment on modern multimedia PCs and are prevalent in the enterprise network. However, little attention has been given to the security issues that surround the addition of these devices. These devices give us the capability to do video-conferencing, communicate with our PCs through voice control, or even talk on the telephone through the computer. However, they can also be used for dastardly deeds. For example, a shady sort could use the video camera attached to the PC to covertly monitor the area around a PC.

Although it has not been widely reported, the "hot microphone" problem could present a security breach. The hot microphone problem occurs when a speaker does not know the equipment is live and utters inappropriate or private remarks not meant to be heard by others. In the past, the consequences were possible embarrassment, but the presence of microphones and video-conferencing in the workplace now brings this problem into the corporate spy arena.

In addition, computer-based eavesdropping could become a possibility in a networked environment using microphones and video cameras. A clever spy could, for example, configure a computer to record a conversation and then retrieve that recording at a later time, either by using a voice recording device or setting up a real-time monitoring system.

One possibility of addressing the hot microphone issue is to use a Direct Memory Access (DMA) microphone. With this device, audio input is routed into a memory-designated location set up for this express purpose. Anyone who attempts to read the input has to do so through the DMA circuitry – when that person executes a read operation on the memory location, an indicator light goes on.

Some computer microphones have an on/off switch; this is an easy solution that simply enables the user to turn off the switch when not in use. However, many computer microphones are built in and do not have an on/off switch.

Summary

This chapter discussed the following topics:

◆ A common type of attack is when an intruder sends a flood of messages to a server so it is overloaded and unable to respond to any legitimate requests. Utilities and techniques are only just now starting to become available to prevent this type of attack.

◆ A spoof attack is when an attacker masquerades as another user or node in order to gain access to a host. A spoof can be detected through real-time monitoring.

◆ It is important to know how to prevent attacks and how to clean up after an attack has happened. But it is also essential to be able to detect an attack in progress. Attack recognition systems are designed to spot attacks in real time, and give the administrator an opportunity to take action that can stop further harm from taking place.

Chapter 21

Security and TCP/IP Services

IN THIS CHAPTER

◆ Using TCP/IP services

◆ Security flaws of TCP/IP

◆ IPv6: overcoming limitations

◆ TCP wrappers

TRANSMISSION CONTROL PROTOCOL/INTERNET PROTOCOL, or TCP/IP, has an amazing influence on how a mixed-environment network is created. This public domain architecture, developed under the direction of the United States Department of Defense, is inherently open and not associated with any particular hardware platform or vendor. Most computer and network vendors support TCP/IP because it can run over any type of medium. This protocol suite has long been the choice for UNIX networks; more recently, Microsoft started viewing TCP/IP as its protocol of choice for Windows NT networks. Furthermore, IBM has even embraced TCP/IP as an alternative to SNA (Systems Network Architecture) in some circumstances.

Using TCP/IP Services

The TCP/IP suite includes not only the two protocols after which it was named (Transmission Control Protocol and Internet Protocol), but also several lower-level services and utility protocols. Take a closer look at the three core protocols:

◆ **Transmission Control Protocol (TCP).** A connection-oriented protocol used to guarantee end-to-end delivery. TCP is the primary transport for most of the TCP/IP utilities.

◆ **Internet Protocol (IP).** This protocol handles delivery of messages between systems within the same network or on different but interconnected networks. IP handles network-level addresses; it is a network layer protocol that functions as a carrier for transport-level protocols.

◆ **User Datagram Protocol (UDP).** A connectionless protocol that, unlike TCP, does not guarantee end-to-end delivery. UDP is faster than TCP because it does not offer these guarantees and is typically used for real-time, program-to-program applications or other services that require a fast response time.

TCP and UDP are used as a means to transport messages between application-oriented services. These services include:

◆ **Telnet.** This service gives a workstation or host-attached terminal to gain access to a second TCP/IP host system.

◆ **File Transfer Protocol (FTP).** This service facilitates the movement of text and binary files between systems.

◆ **Simple Mail Transfer Protocol (SMTP).** This service facilitates routing of e-mail within a TCP/IP network. SMTP works with a front-end program that handles user e-mail issues such as composing e-mail, reading, forwarding, and filing.

The preceding services comply with the client/server model; that is, a user initiates a service request using client software, and the request is received by server software. Each of these services is assigned a *socket*, which is a logical port associated with TCP or UDP. Programs attach to these sockets in order to communicate with other programs efficiently. Every protocol and service in the TCP/IP suite has a defined socket number; for example, Telnet uses socket 23, FTP uses sockets 20 and 21, and SMTP uses socket 25. Knowing these socket numbers is important to maintaining security and lets the network manager prohibit access to certain services that may present a security risk. See Appendix A for a complete table of socket (port) numbers.

When a client attempts to connect to its corresponding server, it first initiates a TCP or UDP connection to the target system's corresponding socket number. For example, a Telnet client will request a TCP connection to socket 23 on the target system.

Some secure networks do not give access to Telnet or other services because they can be misused to gain access to a system to which a user does not have legitimate access. Barring access to socket 23 at the firewall level prevents a user from using the Telnet service.

TCP/IP has some additional security-related drawbacks, such as the following:

◆ TCP/IP is a bandwidth hog. It uses multiple-character sequences instead of flags, which are used in more bandwidth-sensitive protocols such as SNA or IPX.

◆ It is easy to tap into TCP/IP traffic with a network monitor.

◆ TCP/IP is easy to hack. For example, using Telnet, it is possible to attach to a specific socket CPU and manually type in the protocol.

The preceding list gives just a few examples of the ways TCP/IP is not inherently secure; in fact, it is open to the degree that nothing within the suite really keeps out attackers. Because of these weaknesses, it's important to use a network monitoring program (such as those described in Chapter 8) to keep track of who is accessing TCP/IP servers. You, as the security manager, are responsible for adding security features into the TCP/IP network through firewalls, filters, and other services.

One way to protect a TCP/IP network is to create a Virtual Private Network (VPN) that adds privacy, authentication, and integrity to protect against intruders and to guarantee that messages are not tampered with en route.

IP Names

In a self-contained domain, it is possible to reference a system just using its system name, but in a large network, system names must adhere to the qualified IP name format:

`<hostname>.<domainname>.<type>`

In this format, `<hostname>` refers to the name of a specific system; `<domainname>` refers to the organization to which that system belongs. `<type>` refers to the type of organization, and is usually one of the following:

◆ `.gov` = government body

◆ `.edu` = educational institution

◆ `.com` = commercial institution

◆ `.org` = organization or standards body

When leaving the domain, it is necessary to use the full IP name. The IP address further determines the computers to which a system can connect without requiring a router or gateway. TCP/IP allows two different systems with different network assignments to communicate only through a gateway, even if they are connected to the same physical network.

A TCP/IP gateway can be in the form of a dedicated router, or it can be a computer system that functions as a router. Most UNIX systems, as well as Windows NT, provide a gateway service.

The gateway system, whether it is a router or computer system, keeps a table of network addresses and a record of the physical connections associated with those addresses.

IPv6

The latest version of IP (IPv6) is already being implemented in the networking products of some major vendors. IPv6 attempts to address some of the security-related limitations of IPv4, the existing, 20-year-old protocol.

Implementing IPv6 is no small feat, so much so that some users prefer to stick with IPv4 and the many workarounds invented over the years to overcome its shortcomings. Eventually, however, you will have to face IPv6. The best way to do that is to perform some early testing to identify how and where you can best use IPv6 in the network.

The upgrade offers several new benefits, including new addressing, configuration, and servicing improvements. The best-known change is to the addressing scheme. IPv6 moves from a 32-bit address, which is used in IPv4, to a 128-bit addressing scheme, which dramatically increases the number of devices that can be supported.

One alternative for moving to IPv6 is to use a *network address translator* (NAT), a utility that translates unregistered, internally used IP addresses to legal addresses for use on the Internet. However, the NAT comes with some performance overhead, because it must process all traffic destined for the Internet. As such, you may need to make some modifications to applications. The NAT option is controversial and not recommended.

The addressing problem has been one of the most critical issues facing managers of large internetworks. Some have used multiple Class C addresses to obtain all the addresses they need. These addresses are assigned on demand. However, this means that contiguous subnetworks do not have contiguous IP addresses; consequently, the routing tables must get larger and larger and may create some delays.

You can also migrate to IPv6 through a dual-stack mechanism when linking two sites. *Dual stacks* refers to hosts or routers that are capable of running both IPv4 and IPv6 and using whichever protocol the destination device uses. To do so, the dual stack uses a tunneling mechanism in which IPv6 is tunneled through an IPv4 architecture (see Figure 21-1).

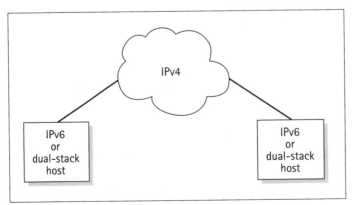

Figure 21-1: IPv6 can be tunneled through IPv4 packets as part of a migration strategy.

This tunneling mechanism can help with a gradual migration, in which a few of the most critical hosts and routers are first upgraded with the IPv6 code. Multiple pockets of IPv6-compliant devices can then be linked through these tunnels over the primary IPv4 configuration.

IPSec

The IP Security Protocol (IPSec) is part of the IPv6 release currently under review by the IETF (Internet Engineering Task Force). IPSec defines encryption, authentication, and key management to ensure that all of the aspects of the VPN (privacy, integrity, authentication, and key management) are addressed. IPSec functions at the network layer of the OSI model and makes sure that all IP data packets have been secured, regardless of the originating application.

IPSec adds an extension header to identify authenticated and encrypted packets. Although this approach is effective, it does add overhead and may even cause a packet to expand beyond the routed network's imposed limit. As a result, the router fragments that packet into two smaller packets, and each packet then needs its own header—thereby increasing the number of packets traveling over the network and increasing network latency. The final IPSec standard may include a compression methodology to mitigate this effect. These precompressed packets are less likely to exceed the imposed packet size limit set by the router. VPNet Technologies offers an IPSec-compatible VPN product line that includes compression.

IPSec addresses many of the security vulnerabilities of TCP/IP. In addition to security, IPSec also promotes interoperability. One problem with TCP/IP is that not all tools are interoperable, locking users into a single provider.

IPSec functions at the IP layer, and can secure anything using UDP or TCP. When IPSec is applied to a firewall, it supports the perimeter security model, where security can be applied to anything that crosses the perimeter. Because IPSec is applied to a firewall, and works independently of workstations and servers, it is ideal for a heterogeneous environment. In addition, because it exists below the transport layer, it is transparent to applications, and you have no need to change desktop software when IPSec is applied to the firewall.

IPSec enables a business to open an encrypted link to a trading partner's network. The link is encrypted after authentication by means of an X.509 digital certificate, at an IPSec-based firewall or gateway.

Unfortunately, the standard, which is primarily concerned with the task of encrypting data between trading partners, is in dispute. The standard is expected to be formally adopted as an IETF standard by early 1998. However, the key management element of the standard, used for exchanging keys over the Internet, is another sticking point for many vendors; two incompatible schemes have been proposed as part of the IPSec specification. That means that not all products will be completely interoperable.

Competing Key Management Schemes

The two competing standards are the Simple Key Management for IP (SKIP), developed by Sun Microsystems, and the Internet Secure Association Key Management Protocol (ISAKMP), developed by the National Security Agency. SKIP is a sessionless protocol for key exchange, whereas ISAKMP uses two-way, stateful communications. Currently, ISAKMP is required for the next version of IP (IPv6), with SKIP as an option. The current version of IP (IPv4), however, lets users select either one.

One drawback of ISAKMP is that it has gone through several revisions (currently it is in its seventh revision). The many versions available means that it may be difficult to determine whether any available ISAKMP-based products are interoperable.

The IETF's IP Security Protocol Working Group was organized to protect the client protocols of IP; specifically, it is responsible for developing a security protocol in the network layer to provide cryptographic security devices that support authentication, integrity, access control, and confidentiality. Anything using UDP or TCP falls under its protection. The protocol formats for the IP Authentication Header and IP Encapsulating Security Payload are independent of the cryptographic algorithm.

Further, the IETF's preliminary goals are to pursue host-to-host security, followed by subnet-to-subnet and host-to-subnet topologies. The working group will also develop protocol and cryptographic techniques to support key management, using the Internet Key Management Protocol (IKMP) as an application layer protocol that is independent of the lower-layer security protocol.

IPSec-compliant firewalls support the perimeter security model, in which strong security is applied to anything that crosses the network perimeter. Traffic within the workgroup, on the other hand, can travel unencumbered. Also, by deploying IPSec at the firewall or router level, it is possible to achieve security in a heterogeneous environment, because it will be independent of individual hosts or clients. Furthermore, an IPSec-compliant firewall is more resistant to tampering, because users cannot change the firewall's configuration.

Because it exists below the transport layer, IPSec is transparent to applications, and no modifications need to be made to software applications. It is also transparent to end users, so you won't have to rely on end users to implement and maintain security.

IPSec uses two headers to provide security: the Authentication Header (AH) and the Encapsulating Security Payload (ESP). The AH provides source authentication and integrity to the IP datagram, and the ESP provides confidentiality.

When two entities wish to communicate, they share a security association made up of cryptographic keys, algorithms, and other details. This association is referenced by a security parameters index (SPI). The AH follows the IPv4 header and contains the SPI.

AUTHENTICATION HEADER

The AH does not provide for confidentiality nor does it prevent someone with a monitor from analyzing your traffic. If you need this type of security on your network, you should use the ESP instead of, or in addition to, the AH.

The AH works by adding authentication information to the IP datagram. This information is calculated based on all the fields in the datagram, including the IP header, other headers, and the user data.

IPSec causes some performance degradation and increased communications latency. The culprit is the calculation of the authentication data that must take place for every IP datagram in the Authentication Header.

Authentication data carried by the AH is calculated using a message digest algorithm (MD5 or SHA-1) that encrypts the message digest or keys the message digest directly. Algorithms with cryptographically strong one-way functions should be used. A conventional checksum is not strong enough to be used with the Authentication Header.

Key management is critical to IP security; however, it is not integrated with the IPSec specification. The IP Authentication Header separates key management from the security protocol mechanisms. The integration of the key management protocol and the security protocol takes place only in the security parameters index (SPI). Because key management is separate from the Authentication Header, it becomes possible to use several different key management mechanisms and you can modify the key management protocol without impacting the security protocol implementation.

ENCAPSULATING SECURITY PAYLOAD

The ESP mechanism adds integrity and confidentiality to IP datagrams. Depending on the algorithm, it may also provide for authentication. It does not provide for nonrepudiation or protection from traffic analysis. ESP works by encrypting data to be protected and then placing this encrypted data in the data portion of the IP Encapsulating Security Payload. The entire IP datagram, or a transport layer segment, can be encrypted, depending on security requirements.

The two different ESP modes are *transport* and *tunnel*. In transport mode, ESP data begins with a transport layer protocol header. In tunnel mode, ESP data contains an IP datagram.

In tunnel mode ESP, the encrypted portions of the ESP store the original IP datagram, and the entire ESP frame is then placed in a datagram with unencrypted IP headers. The data in the unencrypted headers routes the secure datagram between sender and recipient.

In transport mode ESP, the ESP header is placed in the IP datagram just prior to the transport layer protocol header (TCP, UDP, or ICMP). Transport mode enjoys better performance because of the lack of encrypted IP headers and options, as encryption naturally carries a high CPU overhead.

Although IPSec does not present an absolute security solution, it is one more useful component in creating a secure internetwork. The security provided by IPSec depends largely on the strength of the cryptographic algorithms used, the strength of the key being used, and the security of the key management mechanism.

INTEROPERABILITY

In March 1997, interoperability between multivendor security solutions based on IPSec was reached for the first time. A consortium of vendors demonstrated the interoperability of IPSec-based solutions, which now permits secure communications to take place between different vendors' security solutions. Participating vendors included Check Point Software Technologies, Cisco, Entrust Technologies, FTP Software, IRE, Microsoft, Raptor, Timestep Corporation, and Trusted Information Systems.

The proposed key management scheme used by IPSec, known as ISAKMP, permits two parties to rapidly agree on a security association (keys, encryption and authentication algorithms, and other relevant parameters) before communication commences. Because of this key management scheme, any equipment implementing IPSec will be interoperable.

TCP Wrappers

TCP Wrappers is a freely available application that functions similarly to a firewall. You can use it to restrict access and configure it such that only specified user IDs or nodes can execute specified server processes.

TCP Wrappers was developed by Wietse Venema of Eindhoven University of Technology in Eindhoven, Netherlands. Venema worked with Dan Farmer on the now infamous SATAN security program. Check out the following sites for more information:

```
ftp://ftp.win.tue.nl/pub/security/tcp_wrappers.7.6.tar.gz
ftp://cert.org/pub/tools/tcp_wrappers/
```

This application can monitor service requests for FTP, Telnet, *r* commands, and others. It can work on any UNIX system, and you do not need to modify any system files to run it. It works by moving the network services to another location and putting the TCP daemon (tcpd) in its place. It essentially becomes a security layer around the network services (server processes) that are defined in /etc/service. The application does not have a graphical user interface and cannot work with UDP.

Server processes are executed in the file /etc/inetd.conf. Taking the Telnet application as an example, this file should look something like the following before TCP Wrappers is installed:

```
telnet   stream   tcp   nowait   root   \
   /usr/sbin/in.telnetd   in.telnetd
```

After TCP Wrappers is installed, you must modify the /etc/inetd.conf file as follows:

```
telnet    stream    tcp    nowait    root    \
   /usr/sbin/tcpd    /usr/sbin/in.telnetd
```

Inetd then reads the /etc/inetd.conf file to discover what services it needs to support.

When a client requests a service from the TCP Wrappers host, the Internet daemon (inetd) activates tcpd instead of the service that was requested. TCP Wrappers can then monitor and log client information into the syslog configuration file. The TCP daemon checks the host's authority files, determines whether the client has the appropriate authority on the host, and then activates the requested service if allowed. This sequence is transparent to the client user.

After installation, the wrappers are configured to allow different connections via the configuration files /etc/hosts.allow and /etc/hosts.deny. When a daemon/remote client pair matches an entry in the /etc/hosts.allow file, it grants access. When the daemon/remote client pair matches an entry in the /etc/hosts.deny file, it denies access. If these *allow* and *deny* files do not exist, the daemon will be granted access to any host.

The *allow* and *deny* are in the following format:

```
daemon_list : client_list [ : shell_command ]
```

Daemon_list holds a list of daemon process names (ftpd, telnetd, and so on). Client_list is a list of host names, addresses, and patterns.

To follow a generally accepted security policy of "deny everything that is not expressly allowed," you can have TCP Wrappers deny service to all hosts unless explicitly granted by using the following entry in the *allow* file:

```
more /etc/hosts.deny
ALL: ALL
```

In this example, /etc/hosts.deny denies *all* services to *all* hosts, unless they are permitted access by entries in the *allow* file.

For the greatest amount of information, compile with -DPARANOID turned on and set the flag to ON in the makefile. This process offers the greatest level of security and more details about who is accessing your servers and files. Doing so matches hostnames and addresses; if no match can be made, access is denied.

The TCP Wrappers package offers small daemon wrapper programs that are installed without changing existing software or configuration files. The wrappers will report on the name of the client host and of the requested service. The wrappers do not exchange information with either the client or server application. No overhead is imposed on the transmission that takes place between the client and server.

The latest release of TCP Wrappers, version 7.6, strengthens source-routing protection, but includes no other additional new features. The 7.6 patch is actually unnecessary in UNIX systems that can already stop source-routed traffic at the kernel level, such as 4.4BSD, Solaris 2.*x*, and Linux. Older systems, such as SunOS 4, are not able to receive source-routed connections and therefore are not vulnerable to IP spoofing attacks with a source-routed TCP connection.

Most TCP/IP applications are based on the client/server model. Using Telnet as an example, when the Telnet command is executed by a client, a Telnet server process is triggered on the target host. When a client connects to a host, a daemon (inetd) stands by for the connection to be made. Inetd then runs the appropriate server program, and then returns to standby mode where it waits for other connections to be requested.

In TCP Wrappers, inetd runs a tiny wrapper program instead of executing the server program. The wrapper then logs the appropriate information, performs checks, and then goes on to execute the server program. TCP Wrappers may check an access control list (ACL) to determine which clients are allowed or denied access to a given host.

The logging data is sent by default to /var/log/syslog. However, this file is the same place where the Sendmail daemon also logs information, so it may be convenient to change this default so TCP Wrappers data is sent elsewhere. Doing so requires editing the /etc/syslog.conf file by adding the following line,

```
mail.debug ifdef('LOGHOST', /var/log/syslog, @loghost)
```

where *loghost* is defined in the /etc/hosts file. This is set to the name of the current host. If logging to a central host is more desirable (again for the sake of convenience), then amend *loghost* in the /etc/syslog.conf file to *logmaster*. The /etc/hosts file or NIS/NIS+ hosts file is then edited to set the desired central host that the *logmaster* will alias.

Summary

In this chapter, you learned about the following:

◆ Most computer and network vendors support TCP/IP, and it can run over any medium.

◆ TCP is divided into application-oriented services, including FTP, Telnet, and SMTP.

◆ The new IPv6 protocol includes the IPSec (IP Security) specification that overcomes the security limitations of IPv4. IPSec authenticates TCP/IP connections, and adds data confidentiality and integrity to TCP/IP packets. IPSec promotes the concept of virtual private networking, in which branch offices can be connected securely and privately over the Internet.

Part V

Resources

Appendix A

Service Port Numbers

PORTS ARE USED IN TCP to name the ends of logical connections that carry long-term conversations. A service contact port is defined for the purpose of providing services to unknown callers.

The assigned ports range in number from 0 to 1023, and are managed by the IANA (Internet Assigned Numbers Authority). Numbers from 1024 to 65535 are known as *registered port numbers*, and are not controlled by the IANA. On most systems, these numbers can be used by any user process or program executed by an ordinary user.

Every protocol and service in the TCP/IP suite has a defined socket number; for example, Telnet uses socket 23, FTP uses sockets 20 and 21, and SMTP uses socket 25. Knowing these socket numbers is important to maintaining security and enables the network manager to prohibit access to certain services that may present a security risk.

When a client machine attempts to connect to its corresponding server, it first initiates a TCP or UDP connection to the target system's corresponding socket number. For example, a Telnet client requests a TCP connection to socket 23 on the target system.

Some secure networks do not allow access to Telnet or other services because they can be misused to gain access to a system to which a user does not have legitimate access. Barring access to socket 23 at the firewall level, for example, prevents a user from using the Telnet service.

Table A-1 shows the ports used by the server process as its contact port, or "well-known port." For the most part, the same port assignments used for TCP are used with UDP as well.

TABLE A-1 Port Assignments

Service	Port	Protocols	Reference
	0	tcp, udp	Reserved
tcpmux	1	tcp, udp	TCP Port Service Multiplexer
compressnet	2	tcp, udp	Management Utility
compressnet	3	tcp, udp	Compression Process

continued

Table A-1 Port Assignments *(continued)*

Service	Port	Protocols	Reference
#	4	tcp, udp	Unassigned
rje	5	tcp, udp	Remote Job Entry
#	6	tcp, udp	Unassigned
echo	7	tcp, udp	Echo
#	8	tcp, udp	Unassigned
discard	9	tcp, udp	Discard
#	10	tcp, udp	Unassigned
systat	11	tcp, udp	Active Users
#	12	tcp, udp	Unassigned
daytime	13	tcp, udp	Daytime
#	14	tcp, udp	Unassigned
#	15	tcp	Unassigned [was netstat]
#	15	udp	Unassigned
#	16	tcp, udp	Unassigned
qotd	17	tcp, udp	Quote of the Day
msp	18	tcp, udp	Message Send Protocol
chargen	19	tcp, udp	Character Generator
ftp-data	20	tcp, udp	File Transfer [Default Data]
ftp	21	tcp, udp	File Transfer [Control]
#	22	tcp, udp	Unassigned
telnet	23	tcp, udp	Telnet
	24	tcp, udp	Any private mail system
smtp	25	tcp, udp	Simple Mail Transfer Protocol
#	26	tcp, udp	Unassigned
nsw-fe	27	tcp, udp	NSW User System FE

continued

Service	Port	Protocols	Reference
#	28	tcp, udp	Unassigned
msg-icp	29	tcp, udp	MSG ICP
#	30	tcp, udp	Unassigned
msg-auth	31	tcp, udp	MSG Authentication
#	32	tcp, udp	Unassigned
dsp	33	tcp, udp	Display Support Protocol
#	34	tcp, udp	Unassigned
	35	tcp, udp	Any private printer server
#	36	tcp, udp	Unassigned
time	37	tcp, udp	Time
rap	38	tcp, udp	Route Access Protocol
rlp	39	tcp, udp	Resource Location Protocol
#	40	tcp, udp	Unassigned
graphics	41	tcp, udp	Graphics
nameserver	42	tcp, udp	Host Name Server
nicname	43	tcp, udp	Who Is
mpm-flags	44	tcp, udp	MPM FLAGS Protocol
mpm	45	tcp, udp	Message Processing Module [recv]
mpm-snd	46	tcp, udp	MPM [default send]
ni-ftp	47	tcp, udp	NI FTP
auditd	48	tcp, udp	Digital Audit Daemon
login	49	tcp, udp	Login Host Protocol
re-mail-ck	50	tcp, udp	Remote Mail Checking Protocol
la-maint	51	tcp, udp	IMP Logical Address Maintenance
xns-time	52	tcp, udp	XNS Time Protocol
domain	53	tcp, udp	Domain Name Server
xns-ch	54	tcp, udp	XNS Clearinghouse

continued

Table A-1 Port Assignments *(continued)*

Service	Port	Protocols	Reference
isi-gl	55	tcp, udp	ISI Graphics Language
xns-auth	56	tcp, udp	XNS Authentication
	57	tcp, udp	Any private terminal access
xns-mail	58	tcp, udp	XNS Mail
	59	tcp, udp	Any private file service
	60	tcp, udp	Unassigned
ni-mail	61	tcp, udp	NI MAIL
acas	62	tcp, udp	ACA Services
#	63	tcp, udp	Unassigned
covia	64	tcp, udp	Communications Integrator (CI)
tacacs-ds	65	tcp, udp	TACACS-Database Service
sql*net	66	tcp, udp	Oracle SQL*NET
bootps	67	tcp, udp	Bootstrap Protocol Server
bootpc	68	tcp, udp	Bootstrap Protocol Client
tftp	69	tcp, udp	Trivial File Transfer Protocol
gopher	70	tcp, udp	Gopher
netrjs-1	71	tcp, udp	Remote Job Service
netrjs-2	72	tcp, udp	Remote Job Service
netrjs-3	73	tcp, udp	Remote Job Service
netrjs-4	74	tcp, udp	Remote Job Service
	75	tcp, udp	Any private dial-out service
deos	76	tcp, udp	Distributed External Object Store
	77	tcp, udp	Any private RJE service
vettcp	78	tcp, udp	vettcp
finger	79	tcp, udp	Finger

continued

Service	Port	Protocols	Reference
www-http	80	tcp, udp	World Wide Web HTTP
hosts2-ns	81	tcp, udp	HOSTS2 Name Server
xfer	82	tcp, udp	XFER Utility
mit-ml-dev	83	tcp, udp	MIT ML Device
ctf	84	tcp, udp	Common Trace Facility
mit-ml-dev	85	tcp, udp	MIT ML Device
mfcobol	86	tcp, udp	Micro Focus Cobol
	87	tcp, udp	Any private terminal link
kerberos	88	tcp, udp	Kerberos
su-mit-tg	89	tcp, udp	SU/MIT Telnet Gateway
dnsix	90	tcp, udp	DNSIX Security Attribute Token Map
mit-dov	91	tcp, udp	MIT Dover Spooler
npp	92	tcp, udp	Network Printing Protocol
dcp	93	tcp, udp	Device Control Protocol
objcall	94	tcp, udp	Tivoli Object Dispatcher
supdup	95	tcp, udp	SUPDUP
dixie	96	tcp, udp	DIXIE Protocol Specification
swift-rvf	97	tcp, udp	Swift Remote Virtual File Protocol
tacnews	98	tcp, udp	TAC News
metagram	99	tcp, udp	Metagram Relay
newacct	100	tcp	[unauthorized use]
hostname	101	tcp, udp	NIC Host Name Server
iso-tsap	102	tcp, udp	ISO-TSAP
gppitnp	103	tcp, udp	Genesis Point-to-Point Trans Net
acr-nema	104	tcp, udp	ACR-NEMA Digital Imaging and Communication 300
csnet-ns	105	tcp, udp	Mailbox Name Nameserver

continued

Table A-1 Port Assignments *(continued)*

Service	Port	Protocols	Reference
3com-tsmux	106	tcp, udp	3COM-TSMUX
rtelnet	107	tcp, udp	Remote Telnet Service
snagas	108	tcp, udp	SNA Gateway Access Server
pop2	109	tcp, udp	Post Office Protocol – Version 2
pop3	110	tcp, udp	Post Office Protocol – Version 3
sunrpc	111	tcp, udp	SUN Remote Procedure Call
mcidas	112	tcp, udp	McIDAS Data Transmission Protocol
auth	113	tcp, udp	Authentication Service
audionews	114	tcp, udp	Audio News Multicast
sftp	115	tcp, udp	Simple File Transfer Protocol
ansanotify	116	tcp, udp	ANSA REX Notify
uucp-path	117	tcp, udp	UUCP Path Service
sqlserv	118	tcp, udp	SQL Services
nntp	119	tcp, udp	Network News Transfer Protocol
cfdptkt	120	tcp, udp	CFDPTKT
erpc	121	tcp, udp	Encore Expedited Remote Pro.Call
smakynet	122	tcp, udp	SMAKYNET
ntp	123	tcp, udp	Network Time Protocol
ansatrader	124	tcp, udp	ANSA REX Trader
locus-map	125	tcp, udp	Locus PC-Interface Net Map Server
unitary	126	tcp, udp	Unisys Unitary Login
locus-con	127	tcp, udp	Locus PC-Interface Conn Server
gss-xlicen	128	tcp, udp	GSS X License Verification
pwdgen	129	tcp, udp	Password Generator Protocol
cisco-fna	130	tcp, udp	cisco FNATIVE

continued

Service	Port	Protocols	Reference
cisco-tna	131	tcp, udp	cisco TNATIVE
cisco-sys	132	tcp, udp	cisco SYSMAINT
statsrv	133	tcp, udp	Statistics Service
ingres-net	134	tcp, udp	INGRES-NET Service
loc-srv	135	tcp, udp	Location Service
profile	136	tcp, udp	PROFILE Naming System
netbios-ns	137	tcp, udp	NETBIOS Name Service
netbios-dgm	138	tcp, udp	NETBIOS Datagram Service
netbios-ssn	139	tcp, udp	NETBIOS Session Service
emfis-data	140	tcp, udp	EMFIS Data Service
emfis-cntl	141	tcp, udp	EMFIS Control Service
bl-idm	142	tcp, udp	Britton-Lee IDM
imap2	143	tcp, udp	Interim Mail Access Protocol v2
news	144	tcp, udp	NewS
uaac	145	tcp, udp	UAAC Protocol
iso-tp0	146	tcp, udp	ISO-IP0
iso-ip	147	tcp, udp	ISO-IP
cronus	148	tcp, udp	CRONUS-SUPPORT
aed-512	149	tcp, udp	AED 512 Emulation Service
sql-net	150	tcp, udp	SQL-NET
hems	151	tcp, udp	HEMS
bftp	152	tcp, udp	Background File Transfer Program
sgmp	153	tcp, udp	SGMP
netsc-prod	154	tcp, udp	NETSC
netsc-dev	155	tcp, udp	NETSC
sqlsrv	156	tcp, udp	SQL Service

continued

Table A-1 Port Assignments *(continued)*

Service	Port	Protocols	Reference
knet-cmp	157	tcp, udp	KNET/VM Command/Message Protocol
pcmail-srv	158	tcp, udp	PCMail Server
nss-routing	159	tcp, udp	NSS-Routing
sgmp-traps	160	tcp, udp	SGMP-TRAPS
snmp	161	tcp, udp	SNMP
snmptrap	162	tcp, udp	SNMPTRAP
cmip-man	163	tcp, udp	CMIP/TCP Manager
cmip-agent	164	tcp, udp	CMIP/TCP Agent
xns-courier	165	tcp, udp	Xerox
s-net	166	tcp, udp	Sirius Systems
namp	167	tcp, udp	NAMP
rsvd	168	tcp, udp	RSVD
send	169	tcp, udp	SEND
print-srv	170	tcp, udp	Network PostScript
multiplex	171	tcp, udp	Network Innovations Multiplex
cl/1	172	tcp, udp	Network Innovations CL/1
xyplex-mux	173	tcp, udp	Xyplex
mailq	174	tcp, udp	MAILQ
vmnet	175	tcp, udp	VMNET
genrad-mux	176	tcp, udp	GENRAD-MUX
xdmcp	177	tcp, udp	X Display Manager Control Protocol
nextstep	178	tcp	NextStep Window Server
NextStep	178	udp	NextStep Window Server
bgp	179	tcp, udp	Border Gateway Protocol
ris	180	tcp, udp	Intergraph

continued

Service	Port	Protocols	Reference
unify	181	tcp, udp	Unify
audit	182	tcp, udp	Unisys Audit SITP
ocbinder	183	tcp, udp	OCBinder
ocserver	184	tcp, udp	OCServer
remote-kis	185	tcp, udp	Remote-KIS
kis	186	tcp, udp	KIS Protocol
aci	187	tcp, udp	Application Communication Interface
mumps	188	tcp, udp	Plus Five's MUMPS
qft	189	tcp, udp	Queued File Transport
gacp	190	tcp, udp	Gateway Access Control Protocol
prospero	191	tcp, udp	Prospero Directory Service
osu-nms	192	tcp, udp	OSU Network Monitoring System
srmp	193	tcp, udp	Spider Remote Monitoring Protocol
irc	194	tcp, udp	Internet Relay Chat Protocol
dn6-nlm-aud	195	tcp, udp	DNSIX Network Level Module Audit
dn6-smm-red	196	tcp, udp	DNSIX Session Mgt Module Audit Redir
dls	197	tcp, udp	Directory Location Service
dls-mon	198	tcp, udp	Directory Location Service Monitor
smux	199	tcp, udp	SMUX
src	200	tcp, udp	IBM System Resource Controller
at-rtmp	201	tcp, udp	AppleTalk Routing Maintenance
at-nbp	202	tcp, udp	AppleTalk Name Binding
at-3	203	tcp, udp	AppleTalk Unused
at-echo	204	tcp, udp	AppleTalk Echo
at-5	205	tcp, udp	AppleTalk Unused
at-zis	206	tcp, udp	AppleTalk Zone Information

continued

Table A-1 Port Assignments *(continued)*

Service	Port	Protocols	Reference
at-7	207	tcp, udp	AppleTalk Unused
at-8	208	tcp, udp	AppleTalk Unused
tam	209	tcp, udp	Trivial Authenticated Mail Protocol
z39.50	210	tcp, udp	ANSI Z39.50
914c/g	211	tcp, udp	Texas Instruments 914C/G Terminal
anet	212	tcp, udp	ATEXSSTR
ipx	213	tcp, udp	IPX
vmpwscs	214	tcp, udp	VM PWSCS
softpc	215	tcp, udp	Insignia Solutions
atls	216	tcp, udp	Access Technology License Server
dbase	217	tcp, udp	dBASE UNIX
mpp	218	tcp, udp	Netix Message Posting Protocol
uarps	219	tcp, udp	Unisys ARPs
imap3	220	tcp, udp	Interactive Mail Access Protocol v3
fln-spx	221	tcp, udp	Berkeley rlogind with SPX authority
rsh-spx	222	tcp, udp	Berkeley rshd with SPX authority
cdc	223	tcp, udp	Certificate Distribution Center
#	224–241		Reserved
#	242	tcp, udp	Unassigned
sur-meas	243	tcp, udp	Survey Measurement
#	244	tcp, udp	Unassigned
link	245	tcp, udp	LINK
dsp3270	246	tcp, udp	Display Systems Protocol
#	247–255		Reserved
#	256–343		Unassigned

continued

Service	Port	Protocols	Reference
pdap	344	tcp, udp	Prospero Data Access Protocol
pawserv	345	tcp, udp	Perf Analysis Workbench
zserv	346	tcp, udp	Zebra server
fatserv	347	tcp, udp	Fatmen Server
csi-sgwp	348	tcp, udp	Cabletron Management Protocol
#	349–370		Unassigned
clearcase	371	tcp, udp	Clearcase
ulistserv	372	tcp, udp	UNIX Listserv
legent-1	373	tcp, udp	Legent Corporation
legent-2	374	tcp, udp	Legent Corporation
hassle	375	tcp, udp	Hassle
nip	376	tcp, udp	Amiga Envoy Network Inquiry Protocol
tnETOS	377	tcp, udp	NEC Corporation
dsETOS	378	tcp, udp	NEC Corporation
is99c	379	tcp, udp	TIA/EIA/IS-99 modem client
is99s	380	tcp, udp	TIA/EIA/IS-99 modem server
hp-collector	381	tcp, udp	HP performance data collector
hp-managed-node	382	tcp, udp	HP performance data managed node
hp-alarm-mgr	383	tcp, udp	HP performance data alarm manager
arns	384	tcp, udp	A Remote Network Server System
ibm-app	385	tcp, udp	IBM Application
asa	386	tcp, udp	ASA Message Router Object Definition
Asa	386	udp	ASA Message Router Object Definition
Aurp	387	tcp, udp	Appletalk Update-Based Routing Protocol
unidata-ldm	388	tcp, udp	Unidata LDM Version 4
ldap	389	tcp, udp	Lightweight Directory Access Protocol

continued

Table A-1 Port Assignments *(continued)*

Service	Port	Protocols	Reference
uis	390	tcp, udp	UIS
synotics-relay	391	tcp, udp	SynOptics SNMP Relay Port
synotics-broker	392	tcp, udp	SynOptics Port Broker Port
dis	393	tcp, udp	Data Interpretation System
embl-ndt	394	tcp, udp	EMBL Nucleic Data Transfer
netcp	395	tcp, udp	NETscout Control Protocol
netware-ip	396	tcp, udp	Novell NetWare over IP
mptn	397	tcp, udp	Multi-Protocol Transfer Network
Mptn	397	udp	Multi-Protocol Transfer Network
Kryptolan	398	tcp, udp	Kryptolan
kryptolan	398	udp	Kryptolan
#	399	tcp, udp	Unassigned
work-sol	400	tcp, udp	Workstation Solutions
ups	401	tcp, udp	Uninterruptible Power Supply
genie	402	tcp, udp	Genie Protocol
decap	403	tcp, udp	decap
nced	404	tcp, udp	nced
ncld	405	tcp, udp	ncld
imsp	406	tcp, udp	Interactive Mail Support Protocol
timbuktu	407	tcp, udp	Timbuktu
prm-sm	408	tcp, udp	Prospero Resource Manager System Manager
prm-nm	409	tcp, udp	Prospero Resource Manager Node Manager
decladebug	410	tcp, udp	DECLadebug Remote Debug Protocol
rmt	411	tcp, udp	Remote MT Protocol
synoptics-trap	412	tcp, udp	Trap Convention Port

continued

Service	Port	Protocols	Reference
smsp	413	tcp, udp	SMSP
infoseek	414	tcp, udp	InfoSeek
bnet	415	tcp, udp	BNet
silverplatter	416	tcp, udp	Silverplatter
onmux	417	tcp, udp	Onmux
hyper-g	418	tcp, udp	Hyper-G
ariel1	419	tcp, udp	Ariel
smpte	420	tcp, udp	SMPTE
ariel2	421	tcp, udp	Ariel
ariel3	422	tcp, udp	Ariel
opc-job-start	423	tcp, udp	IBM Operations Planning and Control Start
opc-job-track	424	tcp, udp	IBM Operations Planning and Control Track
icad-el	425	tcp, udp	ICAD
smartsdp	426	tcp, udp	smartsdp
svrloc	427	tcp, udp	Server Location
ocs_cmu	428	tcp, udp	OCS_CMU
ocs_amu	429	tcp, udp	OCS_AMU
utmpsd	430	tcp, udp	UTMPSD
utmpcd	431	tcp, udp	UTMPCD
iasd	432	tcp, udp	IASD
nnsp	433	tcp, udp	NNSP
mobileip-agent	434	tcp, udp	MobileIP-Agent
mobilip-mn	435	tcp, udp	MobilIP-MN
dna-cml	436	tcp, udp	DNA-CML
comscm	437	tcp, udp	comscm
dsfgw	438	tcp, udp	dsfgw

continued

Table A-1 Port Assignments *(continued)*

Service	Port	Protocols	Reference
dasp	439	tcp, udp	dasp
sgcp	440	tcp, udp	sgcp
decvms-sysmgt	441	tcp, udp	decvms-sysmgt
cvc_hostd	442	tcp, udp	cvc_hostd
https	443	tcp, udp	https MCom
snpp	444	tcp, udp	Simple Network Paging Protocol
microsoft-ds	445	tcp, udp	Microsoft-DS
ddm-rdb	446	tcp, udp	DDM-RDB
ddm-dfm	447	tcp, udp	DDM-RFM
ddm-byte	448	tcp, udp	DDM-BYTE
as-servermap	449	tcp, udp	AS Server Mapper
tserver	450	tcp, udp	TServer
#	451–511		Unassigned
exec	512	tcp	Remote process execution; authentication performed using passwords and UNIX loppgin names
biff	512	udp	Used by mail system to notify users of new mail received; currently receives messages only from processes on the same machine
login	513	tcp	Remote login a la Telnet; automatic authentication performed based on privileged port numbers and distributed databases which identify "authentication domains"
who	513	udp	Maintains databases showing who's logged in to machines on a local net and the load average of the machine
cmd	514	tcp	Like exec, but automatic authentication is performed as for login server

continued

Service	Port	Protocols	Reference
syslog	514	udp	
printer	515	tcp, udp	Spooler
#	516	tcp, udp	Unassigned
talk	517	tcp, udp	Like tenex link, but across machine – unfortunately, doesn't use link protocol (this is actually just a rendezvous port from which a tcp connection is established)
ntalk	518	tcp, udp	
utime	519	tcp, udp	unixtime
efs	520	tcp	Extended file name server
router	520	udp	Local routing process (on site); uses variant of Xerox NS routing information protocol
#	521–524		Unassigned
timed	525	tcp, udp	timeserver
tempo	526	tcp, udp	newdate
#	527–529		Unassigned
courier	530	tcp, udp	rpc
conference	531	tcp, udp	chat
netnews	532	tcp, udp	readnews
netwall	533	tcp, udp	For emergency broadcasts
#	534–538		Unassigned
apertus-ldp	539	tcp, udp	Apertus Technologies Load Determination
uucp	540	tcp, udp	uucpd
uucp-rlogin	541	tcp, udp	uucp-rlogin
#	542	tcp, udp	Unassigned
klogin	543	tcp, udp	
kshell	544	tcp, udp	krcmd

continued

Table A-1 Port Assignments *(continued)*

Service	Port	Protocols	Reference
#	545–549		Unassigned
new-rwho	550	tcp, udp	new-who
#	551–555		Unassigned
dsf	555	tcp, udp	
remotefs	556	tcp, udp	rfs server
#	557–559		Unassigned
rmonitor	560	tcp, udp	rmonitord
monitor	561	tcp, udp	
chshell	562	tcp, udp	chcmd
#	563	tcp, udp	Unassigned
9pfs	564	tcp, udp	Plan 9 file service
whoami	565	tcp, udp	whoami
#	566–569		Unassigned
meter	570	tcp, udp	demon
meter	571	tcp, udp	udemon
#	572–599		Unassigned
ipcserver	600	tcp, udp	Sun IPC server
nqs	607	tcp, udp	nqs
urm	606	tcp, udp	Cray Unified Resource Manager
sift-uft	608	tcp, udp	Sender-Initiated/Unsolicited File Transfer
npmp-trap	609	tcp, udp	npmp-trap
npmp-local	610	tcp, udp	npmp-local
npmp-gui	611	tcp, udp	npmp-gui
ginad	634	tcp, udp	ginad
mdqs	666	tcp, udp	
doom	666	tcp, udp	doom Id Software

continued

Service	Port	Protocols	Reference
elcsd	704	tcp, udp	errlog copy/server daemon
entrustmanager	709	tcp, udp	EntrustManager
netviewdm1	729	tcp, udp	IBM NetView DM/6000 Server/Client
netviewdm2	730	tcp, udp	IBM NetView DM/6000 send/tcp
netviewdm3	731	tcp, udp	IBM NetView DM/6000 receive/tcp
netgw	741	tcp, udp	netGW
netrcs	742	tcp, udp	Network-Based Revision Control System
flexlm	744	tcp, udp	Flexible License Manager
fujitsu-dev	747	tcp, udp	Fujitsu Device Control
ris-cm	748	tcp, udp	Russell Information Science Calendar Manager
kerberos-adm	749	tcp, udp	Kerberos administration
rfile	750	tcp	
loadav	750	udp	
pump	751	tcp, udp	
qrh	752	tcp, udp	
rrh	753	tcp, udp	
tell	754	tcp, udp	send
nlogin	758	tcp, udp	
con	759	tcp, udp	
ns	760	tcp, udp	
rxe	761	tcp, udp	
quotad	762	tcp, udp	
cycleserv	763	tcp, udp	
omserv	764	tcp, udp	
webster	765	tcp, udp	
phonebook	767	tcp, udp	phone

continued

Table A-1 Port Assignments *(continued)*

Service	Port	Protocols	Reference
vid	769	tcp, udp	
cadlock	770	tcp, udp	
rtip	771	tcp, udp	
cycleserv2	772	tcp, udp	
submit	773	tcp	
notify	773	udp	
rpasswd	774	tcp	
acmaint_dbd	774	udp	
entomb	775	tcp	
acmaint_transd	775	udp	
wpages	776	tcp, udp	
wpgs	780	tcp, udp	
concert	786	tcp, udp	Concert
mdbs_daemon	800	tcp, udp	
device	801	tcp, udp	
xtreelic	996	tcp, udp	Central Point Software
maitrd	997	tcp, udp	
busboy	998	tcp	
puparp	998	udp	
garcon	999	tcp	
applix	999	udp	Applix ac
puprouter	999	tcp, udp	
cadlock	1000	tcp	
ock	1000	udp	
	1023	tcp, udp	Reserved
	1024	tcp, udp	Reserved

Appendix B

Security Standards and Protocols

Secure Hypertext Transfer Protocol (S-HTTP)

The World Wide Web and the browsers used to access documents through the Web rely largely on HyperText Transfer Protocol (HTTP). Because the Web is so easy to use and so widely accepted, many savvy business people have expressed a great deal of interest in using it as a client/server architecture for Web-based applications. Doing that, however, may require authentication and other security measures. In its original form, HTTP does little to support cryptography.

To change this situation, Microsoft collaborated with credit card giants MasterCard and Visa to develop Secure HyperText Transfer Protocol (S-HTTP). S-HTTP is a message-oriented communications protocol that extends the HTTP protocol. It coexists with HTTP's messaging model and can be easily integrated with HTTP applications.

S-HTTP establishes a secure communications mechanism between an HTTP-based client/server pair. This safeguards commercial transactions by adding the means to establish confidentiality, authenticity, integrity, and nonrepudiability of origin to an HTTP-based transaction. Clients can use S-HTTP to authenticate the server and to encrypt the data transmitted between the client and server. S-HTTP encrypts Web transmissions at the server daemon layer.

Client-side public key certificates are not required, as S-HTTP supports symmetric key-only operation. This enables spontaneous, private transactions without each party needing an established public key.

Unfortunately, neither of the two major browsers (Microsoft Internet Explorer and Netscape Navigator) supports S-HTTP yet, so this extension is still mostly theoretical. Netscape has pledged to support S-HTTP in the future, however, and Microsoft will most likely follow suit. Explorer and Navigator have closely matched each other in power and features, so you can be sure that Microsoft will not allow Netscape to one-up its browser for very long.

An S-HTTP-enabled client can communicate with a non-S-HTTP server, but these transactions will not use the S-HTTP security features. Nonetheless, the communication can still take place.

To create an S-HTTP-based message, you need three inputs:

♦ A cleartext (unencrypted) message, which is an HTTP message or data object. Because the cleartext message can be carried transparently, HTTP can be carried within an S-HTTP wrapper.

♦ The recipient's cryptographic preferences and keying material (material that is exchanged to create a traffic key, and authenticate the computer pair). This can either be stated explicitly by the recipient or set by a default set of preferences.

♦ The sender's cryptographic preferences and keying material.

The sender's and recipient's preferences are integrated during the creation of the S-HTTP message. This integration process may require some intervention on the user's part if,. for example, multiple keys are available for signing the message. Recovering the message involves four inputs as well:

1. The S-HTTP message

2. The recipient's cryptographic preferences and keying material

3. The recipient's current cryptographic preferences and keying material

4. The sender's previously stated cryptographic options

To recover the message, the recipient must read the headers to see which cryptographic transformations were performed and then remove these transformations using the keying material. The recipient can also verify that the enhancements match inputs 2 and 4.

A message can be either signed, authenticated, or encrypted, or processed using any combination of these three methods or none at all. S-HTTP supports multiple key management schemes, including public key exchange and manually shared secrets. If you use digital signatures, you can attach a certificate to the message or require the recipient to obtain the certificate independently.

S-HTTP verifies the integrity and authenticity of a message by computing a Message Authentication Code (MAC), which is generated as a keyed hash over the document that contains a shared secret. This mechanism does not require public-key cryptography or encryption. In addition, the freshness of transmissions can be guaranteed through a simple challenge–response mechanism.

S-HTTP messages are syntactically the same as HTTP messages, consisting of a request or status line followed by headers and a body. However, the range of headers differs, and the body is cryptographically enhanced.

Secure Sockets Layer (SSL)

Surfing the Web is inherently insecure. Data transmitted between the client and the server is sent clear, which leaves the door open for it to be intercepted. Although an interception does not happen often, it is a possibility, so when confidential information is involved, you need to use some type of security to prevent the occasional theft. This is where Secure Sockets Layer steps in.

Secure Sockets Layer (SSL) is the most common method of ensuring security on the Web. You can identify pages secured with SSL by the looking at its URL: SSL-protected pages will use the prefix *https:* (HTTP secure). SSL-protected pages also sport the solid key icon in the corner of the browser window.

SSL encrypts Web transmissions at the socket layer. Under SSL, the client and server undergo an initialization process to ensure authentication. After this initial "handshake" procedure takes place, any communication that occurs between the server and client will be encrypted.

SSL was developed jointly by Netscape Communications and RSA, and unlike S-HTTP, is already in common use. However, the U.S. government considers SSL to be a munition, as with other strong encryption products, so it cannot be exported outside the United States.

SSL is much more flexible than S-HTTP and works with any networking protocol. S-HTTP, on the other hand, can be used only with HTTP. Currently, Navigator works with SSL. Microsoft, creator of S-HTTP, has embraced SSL as a standard, which may have a positive impact on the success and acceptance of S-HTTP.

IP Security Protocol (IPSec)

The IP Security Protocol (IPSec) is part of the IPv6 release currently under review by the IETF (Internet Engineering Task Force). IPSec defines encryption, authentication, and key management to ensure that all of the aspects of the VPN (privacy, integrity, authentication, and key management) are addressed. IPSec functions at the network layer of the OSI model and makes sure that all IP data packets have been secured, regardless of the originating application.

IPSec adds an extension header to identify authenticated and encrypted packets. Although this approach is effective, it does add overhead and may even cause a packet to expand beyond the routed network's imposed limit. As a result, the router fragments that packet into two smaller packets, and each packet then needs its own header – thereby increasing the number of packets traveling over the network and increasing network latency. The final IPSec standard may include a compression methodology to mitigate this effect.

IPSec functions at the IP layer, and can secure anything using UDP or TCP. IPSec addresses many of the security vulnerabilities of TCP/IP. In addition to security, IPSec also promotes interoperability. One problem with TCP/IP is that not all tools are interoperable, locking users into a single provider.

When IPSec is applied to a firewall, it supports the perimeter security model, where security can be applied to anything that crosses the perimeter. Because IPSec is applied at the firewall level, and works independently of workstations and servers, it is ideal for a heterogeneous environment. In addition, because it exists below the transport layer, it is transparent to applications, and you have no need to change desktop software when IPSec is applied to the firewall. This makes an

IPSec-compliant firewall more resistant to tampering, because users cannot change the firewall's configuration.

IPSec enables a business to open an encrypted link to a trading partner's network. The link is encrypted after authentication by means of an X.509 digital certificate, at an IPSec-based firewall or gateway. Unfortunately, the standard, primarily concerned with the task of encrypting data between trading partners, is in dispute. The standard is expected to be formally adopted as an IETF standard by early 1998. However, the key management element of the standard, used for exchanging keys over the Internet, is another sticking point for many vendors; two incompatible schemes have been proposed as part of the IPSec specification. That means that not all products will be completely interoperable.

The IETF's IP Security Protocol Working Group was organized to protect the client protocols of IP; specifically, it is responsible for developing a security protocol in the network layer to provide cryptographic security devices that support authentication, integrity, access control, and confidentiality. Anything using UDP or TCP falls under its protection.

IPSec uses two headers to provide security: the Authentication Header (AH) and the Encapsulating Security Payload (ESP). The AH provides source authentication and integrity to the IP datagram, and the ESP provides confidentiality. The protocol formats for the IP Authentication Header and IP Encapsulating Security Payload are independent of the cryptographic algorithm.

When two entities wish to communicate, they share a security association made up of cryptographic keys, algorithms, and other details. This association is referenced by a security parameters index (SPI). The AH follows the IPv4 header and contains the SPI.

Further, the IETF's preliminary goals are to pursue host-to-host security, followed by subnet-to-subnet and host-to-subnet topologies. The working group will also develop protocol and cryptographic techniques to support key management, using the Internet Key Management Protocol (IKMP) as an application layer protocol that is independent of the lower-layer security protocol.

Point-to-Point Tunneling Protocol (PPTP)

For the most part, remote access is achieved by directly dialing into some sort of remote access server. Although this works well enough, it does carry with it some management overhead and a significant amount of long-distance charges. The proliferation of the Internet has the potential to change the nature of remote access. Instead of relying on a large, expensive WAN, remote access can be achieved through the convenient and low-cost interface of the Web browser.

The Point-to-Point Protocol (PPP) is typically used for this remote access because tunneling PPP over the Internet provides a convenient alternative to remote dial-in. However, tunneling PPP over the Internet brings up a number of security issues. The Point-to-Point Tunneling Protocol (PPTP) is an attempt at addressing the security issue, as well as offering multiprotocol support and scalability.

PPTP, originally submitted as a standard by Microsoft and several other vendors, encapsulates multiprotocol PPP inside a modified implementation of GRE V2 (GRE is Generic Routing Encapsulation). PPTP is very similar, if not identical, to Layer 2 Forwarding (L2F), a proposal from Cisco Systems. Because it was designed by Microsoft, PPTP was created to give remote users dial-in access to the corporate network, over the Internet, to Windows NT servers.

Microsoft introduced PPTP in version 4.0 of Windows NT. The company developed the technology along with several remote access server manufacturers, including 3Com, Ascend Communications, and U.S. Robotics. With PPTP, an organization can establish a Virtual Private Network over the Internet. Not only is this less expensive and much simpler than traditional remote access, it also addresses several security concerns typically associated with the Internet. PPTP is able to secure the connection through standard technologies such as the Password Authentication Protocol (PAP) and the Challenge Handshake Authentication Protocol (CHAP). Microsoft plans to submit the PPTP specification to the IETF for ratification as a standard.

An advantage of PPTP and L2F is that it can support multiprotocol access over TCP/IP and also permits multiple users to share a tunnel. Multiprotocol support is especially important in today's mixed environment. Support for IPX, AppleTalk, and NetBEUI enables a wide variety of remote users to securely and safely access the corporate network over TCP/IP. In addition, PPTP will support any type of PPP authentication scheme, which gives the security manager some flexibility in guaranteeing the security of the connection.

PPTP has some limitations, however, and some obstacles also exist with tunneling PPP in general. Most notably, security is a major concern. Again, policy is critical, as are standard security procedures and devices such as firewalls.

Because PPTP supports IP, IPX, NetBIOS and NetBEUI, it should be able to accommodate almost any remote network user. A Virtual Private Network based on PPTP will be compatible with all of Windows NT Server's security provisions. Although it supports PAP, CHAP, and encryption, some ISPs may even offer additional security options, such as caller ID or dialback.

Much of the work is done by the Internet Service Provider. The ISP actually provides the links, and the ISP at the user end may also provide authentication services so that the central site does not have to implement it.

Three computers are involved in the PPTP tunnel: a PPTP client, a network access server, and a PPTP server. If a tunnel is being created between a PPTP client and a PPTP server that are both on the same LAN, however, the network access server is unnecessary. Typically, however, PPTP runs over the Internet. The remote PPTP client relies on an ISP to access a private LAN. The client runs Windows NT or 95, and must actually make two connections to establish the tunnel.

First, the client uses Dial-Up Networking and PPP to connect to an ISP's network access server. After this connection has been made, the client can send and receive data over the Internet. Then the client uses Dial-Up Networking again to make a second logical connection of the PPP connection that was just made. The client sends data over this second connection in the form of IP datagrams. These datagrams hold PPP packets. This second connection creates the VPN to the PPTP server on the private LAN running Windows NT. This connection is what is called the *tunnel*.

Tunneling is a way to send packets to a node on a private network by routing them over a second network, such as the Internet. The second network's routers cannot gain access to the computers on the private network, which makes the tunneled connection more secure. The second network can, however, transmit packets to the PPTP server, which is a sort of middleman computer that is connected both to the private network and the secondary network. Packets are then routed to computers on the private network by way of routers on the secondary network, which know only the address of the PPTP server.

The PPTP server, when it receives a packet from the second network (the Internet), sends that packet through the private network to its destination. When the PPTP server receives the packet from the Internet, it discovers where to send it by examining the encapsulated PPP packet. The PPP packets are encapsulated, encrypted, and compressed into IP datagrams before being sent over the Internet. The IP datagrams are created using a modified version of the GRE (Generic Routing Encapsulation) protocol. The PPTP server then takes the IP datagram apart, retrieves the PPP packet, and decrypts it to learn the destination address.

Creating a secure channel via PPTP actually involves three processes:

- ◆ **PPP connection.** The PPTP client uses PPP to connect to an ISP over a POTS (plain old telephone service) or ISDN line.

- ◆ **PPTP control connection.** Using the connection already established via PPP, a control connection from the PPTP client to a PPTP server on the Internet is created. This connection is made via TCP, and is referred to as the PPTP tunnel.

- ◆ **PPTP data tunneling.** PPTP creates IP datagrams that hold encrypted PPP packets. These packets are then sent through the PPTP tunnel, created in the preceding process, to the PPTP server. The server then disassembles the datagrams, decrypts the packets, and sends them to the destination on the private network.

PPTP offers security through several different means. Windows NT Server's remote access server (RAS) contains several authentication and encryption capabilities; these capabilities are extended to PPTP clients. It is also possible to further protect the PPTP server by configuring it to ignore everything outside of PPTP traffic. It is easy to use PPTP with existing firewalls. PPTP offers the following methods of security:

- ◆ Authentication
- ◆ Access control

- ◆ Data encryption

- ◆ PPTP packet filtering

- ◆ Working with third-party firewalls

AUTHENTICATION

The PPTP tunnel server acts as a sort of gateway to the private network and calls for a standard Windows NT logon with the client entering a username and password. Authentication of the remote clients is accomplished using the same PPP authentication techniques used for any RAS client dialing in directly to a RAS server. This means that all RAS authentication schemes, including Challenge Handshake Authentication Protocol (CHAP), Microsoft Challenge Handshake Authentication Protocol (MS-CHAP), and Password Authentication Protocol (PAP), are all supported on PPTP.

As always, user accounts must be carefully managed to avoid attack. The user accounts of the remote PPTP users reside in the NT Server directory and are controlled by the User Manager for domains. In addition to careful password management, a secure password model is necessary, as is the case with all networks.

ACCESS CONTROL

After the remote user has gained access by passing the authentication procedures, further access to the private network is regulated by the Windows NT security model. Access to any network resource can only be gained if permission has been configured.

DATA ENCRYPTION

PPTP uses the RAS *shared secret* encryption process. Under this model, both ends of the connection share the encryption key. This shared secret is the user password. The encryption key is taken from a hashed password, which is stored on both the client and server. The 40-bit session key is created via the RSA RC4 standard and is used to encrypt all data that is sent over the Internet. It is this encryption that keeps the remote connection secure. As discussed earlier, 40-bit encryption can be hacked and is generally thought to be inadequate. Users in the U.S. can obtain a 128-bit session key through a cryptography pack, although it can be used only inside the U.S.

PPTP PACKET FILTERING

Further protection can be afforded over the tunneled network by enabling PPTP filtering on the PPTP server. Once enabled, the PPTP server accepts and routes only PPTP packets from authenticated users. Consequently, any other packet from any location cannot enter the PPTP server or the private network. Packet filtering therefore ensures that only authorized data can enter or leave the private LAN. This feature can be enabled by using the Protocols tab on the Network option of the Control Panel in Windows NT.

PPTP AND FIREWALLS

PPTP traffic uses TCP port 1723; IP protocol uses ID 47. PPTP can be used with most firewalls and routers by configuring them to allow traffic for TCP port 1723, and protocol 47 to be routed through the firewall or router.

RADIUS AND PPTP

Voluntary tunneling involves the creation of a PPTP tunnel at the request of a user for a specific purpose. Compulsory tunneling, on the other hand, creates a tunnel automatically without any user interaction.

The RADIUS (Remote Authentication Dial-In User Service) protocol is used to authorize dial-up network users. It gives these dial-up users authorization and authentication data to be kept in a central location, instead of having to subject them to manual configuration. This enables the central administration of compulsive tunneling, thereby freeing the users from having to manually configure the tunnel.

With a voluntary tunnel, it is possible to simultaneously open a secure tunnel over the Internet while also accessing other Internet hosts without tunneling. A compulsory tunnel can be created without the end user's consent or knowledge. The compulsory tunnel's termination point is generally on the remote access server (RAS), and traffic coming from the end user's computer is forwarded over the tunnel by RAS.

RADIUS creates additional security by simplifying authorization and by encrypting user passwords that are sent between the client and RADIUS server. RADIUS servers can support several methods of authentication, including PAP, CHAP, UNIX login, or other mechanisms. You have three ways to add user authentication and authorization using compulsory tunnels and RADIUS:

◆ Authenticate and receive authorization once, at the RAS end of the tunnel.

◆ Authenticate once at the RAS end of the tunnel, and then forward the RADIUS reply to the remote end of the tunnel.

◆ Authenticate on both ends of the tunnel.

The remote user dials into RAS and enters a password. RAS then uses RADIUS to check the password and receives information from the RADIUS proxy server, telling it to tunnel the user to a given PPTP server. RAS then opens a tunneled connection to the appropriate PPTP server. The PPTP server then authenticates the user once more and checks the password against the same RADIUS server.

Secure MIME (S/MIME)

S/MIME (Secure MIME) is an open specification for secure electronic messaging. Essentially, S/MIME enables encrypted messages to be exchanged between e-mail programs from different vendors. S/MIME is based on the widely-used Internet MIME standard, which provides a structure for Internet mail messages and extensions.

S/MIME was created to prevent the interception and forgery of e-mail. S/MIME is integrated into several e-mail and messaging products. Digital IDs supporting RSA Data Security's S/MIME protocol include encryption and decryption, authentication, and digital enveloping.

Encryption and authentication have been particularly important in the age of electronic commerce and far-flung offices. Very few e-mail packages, however, have offered encryption until the advent of S/MIME, because of the lack of open security specifications.

S/MIME is based on the Public Key Cryptography Standards (PKCS) that were established by a consortium that included RSA, Microsoft, Lotus, Apple, Novell, Digital Equipment Corporation, Sun Microsystems, and the Massachusetts Institute of Technology in 1991. PKCS is a widely implemented suite of cryptographic standards, and is used to enable developers to independently create secure, interoperable applications.

S/MIME uses a hybrid "digital envelope" approach to security. Bulk message encryption is accomplished with a symmetric cipher, and key exchange is accomplished with a public key algorithm. Digital signatures are also created through the public key algorithm.

S/MIME calls for RSA as the public key algorithm, and recommends DES, Triple-DES, and RC2 for symmetric encryption algorithms. The specification can be used in any e-mail environment, not just the Internet.

RSA submitted the S/MIME specification to the IETF for consideration as an Internet standard, although the IETF has removed it from the standards track, due to questions about RSA's requirement that developers pay a licensing and royalty fee to RSA.

The IETF decision has caused some confusion, because S/MIME has already been implemented in several major products, including Netscape Communications' Communicator 4.0 and Microsoft's Internet Explorer. Despite the IETF's decision, however, vendors continue to pledge support to S/MIME. Time and the marketplace will tell whether or not it will become the de facto standard.

It is possible that the IETF may instead favor an e-mail security specification from Pretty Good Privacy Inc., called Open PGP. Pretty Good Privacy has indicated that it would put the specification in the public domain, and would give the IETF authority over change.

BS 7799

The United Kingdom has taken the first step toward implementing a broad security standard. Great Britain's Department of Trade and Industry introduced a new British Standard in January 1997 (BS 7799), known as the "Code of Practice for Information Security Management." The standard started being enforced by the end of 1997.

BS 7799 introduces a common framework for companies to develop, implement, and measure their security management. BS 7799 includes a recommendation for the development of a business continuity plan, which would promote disaster recovery after an emergency. The code is based on the security practices already in place by some of the country's leading international firms.

Consultants are already in place to audit British companies for BS 7799 compliance. The code may break out of the U.K. eventually, as it is currently under review by ISO for acceptance as an international standard. BS 7799 has received almost universal acceptance in larger companies with more than 10,000 employees.

The National Computing Centre's Information Security Breaches Survey 1996 showed that overall, 47 percent of about 9,500 respondents were aware of BS 7799. One of five had reviewed their own standards against BS 7799, and 50 percent said that they plan to do so.

Interestingly, nearly 80 percent of the respondents reported at least one security breach, and the number of respondents reporting computer-related theft has risen 60 percent since the previous survey, which took place in 1994. The survey also showed an increase in incidents that resulted from user error, up from 23 percent in 1994 to 34 percent in 1996. The latter statistic underscores the need for centralized security management and strict controls over user configuration. The Centre shows the average cost of an incident to be nearly £16,000, with the most expensive incident being a theft worth £750,000.

We often learn our lessons too late, after an attack has already occurred. The Centre's survey confirms this fact by reporting that in 56 percent of reported incidents, corporate security standards were amended or new measures were implemented after the incident.

The United States National Institute for Standards and Technology (NIST) has no corollary to BS 7799, but does offer some general advice for security. NIST's Minimal Security Functional Requirements for Multi-User Operational Systems highlights eight major security functions that are important to any secure system:

◆ Identification and authentication

◆ Access control

◆ Accountability

◆ Audit trails

◆ Object reuse

◆ Accuracy

◆ Reliability

◆ Data exchange

Although implementation of a standard may not eliminate attacks and security breaches completely, adhering to standards will minimize the impact of a breach and reduce the number of attacks that are possible due to poor security.

Appendix C

Secure Shell Program

THE SECURE SHELL (SSH) program, which is freely available, replaces the rlogin, rsh, rcp, and rdist commands with a more secure version that adds authentication and encryption mechanisms to provide for greater security. You can also use it to replace Telnet in most circumstances.

You can find the program at any of these locations:

- ◆ sunsite.unc.edu:/pub/packages/security/ssh

- ◆ ftp.gw.com:/pub/unix/ssh

- ◆ ftp.net.ohio-state.edu:/pub/security/ssh

- ◆ ftp.neosoft.com:/pub/security

- ◆ ftp://ftp.cs.hut.fi/pub/ssh/

SSH is based on the RSA public-key cryptographic system. Public-key cryptography uses a key pair, whereby the sender performs encryption with one key and the recipient uses a second but mathematically related key to decrypt the information. Although the encryption key is made public, the decryption key is secret. The RSA system is used for performing authentication and for securely exchanging the cryptographic session key. A symmetric cryptographic system is used for encrypting the actual session – this can be DES, Triple-DES, IDEA, or Blowfish.

The server program must run as root on the server machine, because the server program must change to an arbitrary user ID. In addition, the server must be able to create a privileged TCP/IP port. Furthermore, the client program must also run as root if .rhosts authentication is used, because the client program will have to create a privileged port and because the client host key is stored in a file that can only be read by root. Root privileges can be revoked after the privileged port has been created and after the host key has been read.

Without SSH, you have no way to protect data transmitted between an X server and a client running on a remote machine. You can use SSH to run X11 applications securely, without needing the cooperation of the vendors of the X server or related application. SSH does this by creating a fake display on the server and forwarding X11 requests over the secure channel.

SSH is available for several UNIX implementations, including:

- ◆ 386BSD 0.1; i386
- ◆ AIX 3.2.5, 4.1, 4.2; RS6000, PowerPC
- ◆ BSD 4.4; several platforms
- ◆ BSD/OS 1.1, 2.0.1; i486
- ◆ BSD/386 1.1; i386
- ◆ BSDI 2.1; x86 (using gnu make)
- ◆ ConvexOS 10.1; Convex
- ◆ Digital UNIX 4.0, 4.0A, 4.0B; Alpha
- ◆ DGUX 5.4R2.10; DGUX
- ◆ FreeBSD 1.x, 2.x; Pentium
- ◆ HP-UX 7.x, 9.x, 10.0; HPPA
- ◆ IRIX 5.2, 5.3; SGI Indy
- ◆ IRIX 6.0.1; Mips-R8000
- ◆ Linux 1.2.x, 2.0.x, Slackware 2.x, 3.x, RedHat 2.1, 3.0; i486, Sparc
- ◆ Linux 3.0.3, 4.0; Alpha
- ◆ Linux/Mach3, Macintosh (PowerPC)
- ◆ Linux/m68k (1.2.x, 2.0.x, 2.1.x)
- ◆ Mach3; Mips
- ◆ Mach3/Lites; i386
- ◆ Machten 2.2VM (m68k); Macintosh
- ◆ NCR UNIX 3.00; NCR S40
- ◆ NetBSD 1.0A, 1.1, 1.2; Pentium, Sparc, Mac68k, Alpha
- ◆ OpenBSD 2.0; x86.
- ◆ NextSTEP 3.3; 68040
- ◆ OSF/1 3.0, 3.2, 3.2; Alpha
- ◆ Sequent Dynix/ptx 3.2.0 V2.1.0; i386
- ◆ SCO UNIX; i386 (client only)

- SINIX 5.42; Mips R4000

- Solaris 2.3, 2.4, 2.5; Sparc, i386

- Sony NEWS-OS 3.3 (BSD 4.3); m68k

- SunOS 4.1.1, 4.1.2, 4.1.3, 4.1.4; Sparc, Sun3

- SysV 4.x; several platforms

- Ultrix 4.1; Mips

- Unicos 8.0.3; Cray C90

Commercial versions are also available for Windows and Macintosh; free versions are available for OS/2.

SSH consists of the following:

- **SSH** – a client program (slogin)

- **SSHD** – a server daemon

- **SCP** – a secure copy (equivalent to rcp)

- **SSH-ADD** – add key to the authentication agent

- **SSH-AGENT** – authentication agent

- **SSH-KEYGEN** – RSA key generator

When installing SSH, you have three choices:

1. Replace the existing r commands with the SSH implementation. With this installation, you have to move the standard commands to a separate directory.

2. Install the executables in a separate directory, with the names rlogin, rsh, and rcp.

3. Install the executables using their real SSH names (slogin, ssh, and scp).

The latter is the simplest installation and can be done simply by running configure with no options.

The server is installed with other daemon programs and starts upon booting. Clients that want to use SSH will connect to the SSH daemon (sshd), although this is a stand-alone daemon and cannot be run from inetd.

In most cases, the default configuration is adequate. The two configuration files are ssh_config – for the client ssh and sshd_config – for the server SSHD.

If needed, you can edit the defaults. Table C-1 describes the keywords.

TABLE C-1 Configuration Keywords

Keyword	Default	Description
Compression yes/no	no	Determines if compression is used for the connection.
Compression level 1-9	6	Level of compression: 1 is fastest but yields the least compression; 9 is slowest but yields the best compression.
FallBackToRsh yes/no	yes	In the event a secure connection cannot be established, unsecure connections may be attempted. This feature should be disabled in a highly secure system.
KeepAlive yes/no	yes	Determines whether TCP KeepAlive messages can be used. If set to yes, it is possible to detect network outages and automatically close connections. KeepAlive should be used to make sure that server programs know if the other end of the connection is rebooted.
User account	local account	Specify the remote account name. Add this to avoid having to use the -l option when issuing commands.

The host's private key is stored in /etc/ssh_host_key. This file is readable by root. The public key, which is readable by anyone, is stored in /etc/ssh_host_key.pub. Every user's home directory also has a .ssh subdirectory.

SSH can tunnel additional TCP connections through its protocol. The SSH session is always encrypted, so any connection sent through the SSH connection will also be encrypted. Any TCP connection can be encapsulated using tunneling.

You can use SSH to log in to another computer, execute commands on a remote machine, and transfer files between machines. Its features include the following:

◆ Strong authentication

◆ Automatic encryption of communications, protecting against spoofing and hijacking

◆ X11 connection forwarding for secure X11 sessions

◆ Arbitrary TCP/IP ports that can be redirected over the encrypted channel bidirectionally

- ◆ Client-side RSA for authenticating the server before every connection, thereby preventing Trojan horse and man-in-the-middle attacks; server-side RSA authenticates the client before accepting the .rhosts or /etc/hosts.equiv authentication

- ◆ An authentication agent in the user's workstation that holds that user's RSA authentication keys

SSH works by listening for connections on port 22. This port has been officially registered for SSH. The key used for encrypting the session key is regenerated hourly, and the old keys are deleted. This key is never stored on disk.

Client and server are connected via a TCP/IP socket used for bidirectional communication. The connection is initiated by the client; the server listens on a port and waits for connections.

Upon connection, the server sends the client its version identification string. The client parses the server's identification and then returns its own identification. This process ensures that the connection has the correct port and states the protocol version number and software version. If either the client or server cannot understand the other side's version, the connection is terminated.

After this protocol identification process, the client and server move to a packet-based binary protocol. The server sends its host key, server key, and other data to the client. The client generates a 256-bit session key, encrypts it using RSA, and then sends an encrypted session key, specified cipher type, and other data to the server. Both sides then enable encryption, and the server transmits an encrypted confirmation to the client. The client then issues an authentication.

SSH supports a number of encryption mechanisms. During the initialization process, the server sends information concerning what encryption mechanisms it will support and the client selects one. Table C-2 lists the supported encryption mechanisms.

TABLE C-2 SSH-Supported Encryption Mechanisms

Encryption Mechanism	Code
No Encryption	SSH_CIPHER_NONE 0
IDEA in CFB mode	SSH_CIPHER_IDEA 1
DES in CBC mode	SSH_CIPHER_DES 2
Triple-DES in CBC mode	SSH_CIPHER_3DES 3
An experimental stream cipher	SSH_CIPHER_TSS 4
RC4	SSH_CIPHER_RC4 5

The server listens for connections on TCP/IP port 22. The client may connect from any port, but if the client wishes to use .rhosts or /etc/hosts.equiv authentication, it must use a privileged port (less than 1024).

After authentication and during the interactive portion of the session, data written by the command running on the server is sent to stdin or stderr on the client; input from stdin on the client is forwarded to the program on the server. The exchange is asynchronous. No acknowledgments are made because TCP/IP already provides for a reliable transport and SSH protects against spoofing. Either side can disconnect by sending SSH_MSG_DISCONNECT or by closing the connection.

The server may send the following messages:

- SSH_SMSG_STDOUT_DATA represents data written to stdout by the program running on the server. The data is passed as a string argument. The client writes this data to stdout.

- SSH_SMSG_STDERR_DATA represents data written to stderr by the program running on the server. The data is passed as a string argument. The client writes this data to stderr. (Note that if the program is running on a tty, it is not possible to separate stdout and stderr data, and all data will be sent as stdout data.)

- SSH_SMSG_EXITSTATUS indicates that the shell or command has exited. Exit status is passed as an integer argument. This message causes the interactive session to terminate.

- SSH_SMSG_AGENT_OPEN indicates that someone on the server side is requesting a connection to the authentication agent. The server-side channel number is passed as an argument. The client must respond with either SSH_CHANNEL_OPEN_CONFIRMATION or SSH_CHANNEL_OPEN_FAILURE.

- SSH_SMSG_X11_OPEN indicates that a connection has been made to the X11 socket on the server side and should be forwarded to the real X server. An integer argument indicates the channel number allocated for this connection on the server side. The client should send back either SSH_MSG_CHANNEL_OPEN_CONFIRMATION or SSH_MSG_CHANNEL_OPEN_FAILURE with the same server-side channel number.

- SSH_MSG_PORT_OPEN indicates that a connection has been made to a port on the server side for which forwarding has been requested. Arguments are server-side channel number, host name to connect to, and port to connect to. The client should send back either SSH_MSG_CHANNEL_OPEN_CONFIRMATION or SSH_MSG_CHANNEL_OPEN_FAILURE with the same server-side channel number.

◆ SSH_MSG_CHANNEL_OPEN_CONFIRMATION is a message sent by the server to indicate that it has opened a connection as requested in a previous message. The first argument indicates the client-side channel number, and the second argument is the channel number that the server has allocated for this connection.

◆ SSH_MSG_CHANNEL_OPEN_FAILURE indicates that the server failed to open a connection as requested in a previous message. The client-side channel number is passed as an argument. The client closes the descriptor associated with the channel and frees the channel.

◆ SSH_MSG_CHANNEL_DATA is a packet that contains data for a channel from the server. The first argument is the client-side channel number, and the second argument (a string) is the data.

◆ SSH_MSG_CHANNEL_CLOSE indicates that whoever was in the other end of the channel has closed it. The argument is the client-side channel number. The client lets all buffered data in the channel drain and, when ready, closes the socket, frees the channel, and sends the server a SSH_MSG_CHANNEL_CLOSE_CONFIRMATION message for the channel.

◆ SSH_MSG_CHANNEL_CLOSE_CONFIRMATION indicates that a channel previously closed by the client has now been closed on the server side as well. The argument indicates the client channel number. The client frees the channel.

Messages sent by the client include the following:

◆ SSH_CMSG_STDIN_DATA represents the data that will be sent as input to the program running on the server. The data is passed as a string.

◆ SSH_CMSG_EOF indicates that the client has encountered EOF (an end of file flag) while reading standard input. The server allows any buffered input data to drain and then closes the input to the program.

◆ SSH_CMSG_WINDOW_SIZE indicates that window size on the client has been changed. The server updates the window size of the tty and causes SIGWINCH (a UNIX window resize signal) to be sent to the program. The new window size is passed as four integer arguments: row, col, xpixel, ypixel.

◆ SSH_MSG_PORT_OPEN indicates that a connection has been made to a port on the client side for which forwarding has been requested. Arguments are client-side channel number, host name to connect to, and port to connect to. The server should send back either SSH_MSG_CHANNEL_OPEN_CONFIRMATION or SSH_MSG_CHANNEL_OPEN_FAILURE with the same client-side channel number.

- SSH_MSG_CHANNEL_OPEN_CONFIRMATION indicates that the client has opened a connection as requested in a previous message. The first argument indicates the server-side channel number, and the second argument is the channel number that the client has allocated for this connection.

- SSH_MSG_CHANNEL_OPEN_FAILURE indicates that the client failed to open a connection as requested in a previous message. The server-side channel number is passed as an argument. The server closes the descriptor associated with the channel and frees the channel.

- SSH_MSG_CHANNEL_DATA is a packet that contains data for a channel from the client. The first argument is the server-side channel number, and the second argument (a string) is the data.

- SSH_MSG_CHANNEL_CLOSE indicates that whoever was at the other end of the channel has closed it. The argument is the server channel number. The server allows buffered data to drain and, when ready, closes the socket, frees the channel, and sends the client a SSH_MSG_CHANNEL_CLOSE_CONFIRMATION message for the channel.

- SSH_MSG_CHANNEL_CLOSE_CONFIRMATION indicates that a channel previously closed by the server has now been closed on the client side as well. The argument indicates the server channel number. The server frees the channel.

If an unsupported message is sent during interactive mode, the connection is terminated with SSH_MSG_DISCONNECT and an error message.

Appendix D

Sample Security Policy

As you saw in Part I, the security policy document is the first and most important step toward creating a secure environment. The policy document itself does not usually specify products or detailed strategies, but rather, presents a high-level view from which a more detailed strategy can be fashioned.

Your security policy may be only a few pages long or it may stretch to a hundred pages long, depending on the level of granularity required and the size and scope of your network. Although it may take your security policy committee several weeks or months to create a final security policy document, one alternative is to use a "canned" policy, such as those that are available from Baseline Software Inc. (http://www.baselinesoft.com).

The policy should include at least the basics: details on passwords, access levels, physical security, Internet threats, viruses, and response. Following is a sample skeleton policy that addresses these basic items and more.

Sample Policy

1. Network Passwords

   1.a Default passwords. If an operating system or other software package comes installed with a default password, that password shall be changed immediately after installation.

   1.b Password choices. Passwords shall not consist of proper names, birth dates, or dictionary words. The password shall be at least six characters long, and at least two of those characters shall be numeric.

   1.c Changing passwords. All passwords shall be changed every month.

   1.d Guest passwords. Guests (contractors, consultants, or interns) shall follow the same rules for passwords. The network administrator shall terminate the guest's password immediately when it is no longer required.

   1.e Sharing passwords. Passwords shall not be shared under any circumstances.

   1.f Conspicuous posting. Passwords shall not be posted in any conspicuous location (such as on a note stuck to the monitor, or in a desk drawer).

2. Access Levels

   2.a Data classification. All electronic files shall be labeled or flagged such that access to the file can be allowed or denied automatically, based on that file's access classification.

   2.b Personnel classification. Each individual who has access to the network shall be given a classification that limits his or her access to files and programs. If, for the purpose of a special project, an individual requires access beyond what is normally granted to that person, that special access shall be granted only for the duration of the project.

3. Physical Security

   3.a Computer room. The central computer room, which may contain servers, mainframes, and IS personnel, shall be locked at all times. Only authorized personnel shall be granted entry. Furthermore, no sign shall be placed on the door that indicates the room's contents.

   3.b Main work area. The main work area shall be locked, with access granted to all employees and authorized individuals via "smart cards."

   3.c Reception area. The reception area shall be policed by the receptionist. Anyone claiming to be a service person must have a work order signed by an employee. The employee shall be called by the receptionist before the service person is granted access.

   3.d Portable devices. Small computing devices, such as laptops, portable printers, and so forth, shall be physically locked with a secure cable to prevent their theft. Employees who travel with company laptops shall cooperate with the system administrator to make regular backups of data contained on the laptop.

4. Response to Violation

   4.a Internal security breach. Internal security breaches that are unintentional will be met with instruction on proper procedure. Intentional violations will be met with a reprimand, reassignment, or termination, depending on the severity and frequency of the infraction.

   4.b External security breach. If an external security breach occurs, a response team shall be convened to determine the source of the break-in. If the seriousness of the event warrants it, law enforcement authorities shall be contacted.

5. Internet

   5.a Monitoring. A monitoring program shall be employed to indicate whether any employee is spending an undue amount of time on unproductive Internet activities (such as visiting Web sites not related to work).

5.b Web server. The Webmaster shall be the only person authorized to upload files onto the company Web server. Documents placed on the public Web server must not contain any hyperlinks to internal documents. If an internal document must be made public, it should be replicated and placed on the Web server.

5.c Firewall. A firewall shall be implemented for the purpose of network security.

6. **Viruses**

   6.a Physical prevention. No employee shall be allowed to load any software that has not been checked for viruses and approved by IS.

   6.b Software prevention. A commercial antivirus program shall be deployed throughout the network at the desktop, server, and firewall level. The program shall be updated as often as is recommended by the vendor.

7. **Encryption**

   Sensitive documents must be encrypted before transmitting them via e-mail.

8. **Fax**

   No sensitive documents shall be sent via fax unless the recipient fax machine is known to be secure.

9. **Termination**

   If an employee must be terminated, his or her network access shall be disabled prior to giving him or her notice of termination. The employee will be escorted out of the building after notice has been given.

10. **Backup of Data**

    All data shall be backed up periodically. Backup shall not be the responsibility of each employee; instead, it shall be carried out centrally by the administrator. Backup media shall be kept off-site.

11. **Destruction of Media**

    If storage media must be discarded for any reason, it must be determined first by the security manager whether the data on the media contains any sensitive data. Nonsensitive data may simply be erased before discarding. Any media containing sensitive data should be either destroyed, degaussed, or thoroughly cleansed according to data remanance procedures.

12. **Background Checks**

    Potential hires shall undergo a thorough background check before employment is offered.

13. Security Personnel

The position of Security Manager shall be established. This individual will head an interdepartmental security team for the purpose of reviewing and establishing security procedures. The Security Manager shall have the authority to implement necessary procedures and procure the equipment necessary to carry them out. The Security Manager shall also have the authority to mandate security-related procedures for employees.

14. Disaster Plan

The Security Manager and the interdepartmental security team shall create a Disaster Plan, which will include specifications for off-site backup, hot-site and cold-site operations, alternative methods of communication, and acquisition of supplies. The Disaster Plan shall set as its goal at least 50 percent restoration of operations within 24 hours.

15. Audit/Review

At least once a year, the interdepartmental security team shall conduct a thorough review of all corporate security systems.

Appendix E

Products and Vendors

ABSOLUTE SOFTWARE CORP.

Absolute's CompuTrace computer tracing system, described in Chapter 13, combats computer theft with a unique stealth technology that automatically calls into the CompuTrace monitoring center every week. If a PC is reported stolen, the CompuTrace software informs the monitoring center where it is calling from as soon as it is plugged into a phone line. Absolute's Theft Recovery Officer then reports the location to the owner and law enforcement authorities.

Absolute Software Corp.
1212 West Broadway, Suite 304
Vancouver, BC, Canada V6H 3V1

Voice: 604-730-9851
Fax: 604-730-2621
Web: http://www.absolute.com

ADIC

ADIC provides storage solutions and automated tape storage libraries for client/server networks. Products are available with 4mm (DAT), 8mm, and DLT drive technology, and are supported by all major suppliers of backup and HSM (hierarchical storage management) software products and all major operating systems.

ADIC
10201 Willow Road
Redmond, WA 98052

Voice: 206-881-8004
Fax: 206-881-2296
Web: http://www.adic.com/products/hndsfree.html

AVENTAIL

Aventail MobileVPN and Aventail PartnerVPN use a *directed* VPN (Virtual Private Network) model as opposed to the traditional, open-ended tunnel model to achieve a greater level of security. The directed model provides directional control of information across the VPN, encrypts data, and offers user-based authentication.

Aventail
117 South Main Street, Fourth Floor
Seattle, WA 98104

Voice: 206-777-5600 or 888-762-5785
Fax: 206-777-5656
Web: http://www.aventail.com

AXENT TECHNOLOGIES, INC.

AXENT provides the OmniGuard suite of enterprise-wide information security solutions for distributed computing environments. OmniGuard provides enhanced data confidentiality, access control, user administration, and intrusion detection across the Internet and intranets, for UNIX, Windows environments, NetWare, and midrange systems.

AXENT Technologies, Inc.
2400 Research Boulevard
Rockville, MD 20850

E-mail: info@axent.com
Web: http://www.axent.com

BASELINE SOFTWARE INC.

Baseline's Information Security Policies Made Easy is a collection of over 840 prewritten security policies that organizations can use as their own in-house policy documents. The product is delivered in hardcopy book, CD-ROM, and floppy disk, and is written by security expert Charles Cresson Wood.

Baseline Software Inc.
P.O. Box 1219
Sausalito, CA 94966-1219

Voice: 415-332-7763
Fax: 415-332-8032
E-mail: info@baselinesoft.com
Web: http://www.baselinesoft.com

CHEYENNE, A DIVISION OF COMPUTER ASSOCIATES, INC.

Computer Associates, owner of Cheyenne Software, continues to offer Cheyenne's InocuLAN antivirus product, a copy of which is included with this book's CD-ROM. InocuLAN's unique features include Real-Time Cure, Universal Manager, Virus Wall, Virus Quarantine, Hands-Free updates, extensive alerting options, support for Windows NT 4.0, and virus protection for Internet downloads and e-mail attachments. InocuLAN is certified by the NCSA (National Computer Security Association) to detect 100 percent of viruses in the wild.

Cheyenne
One Computer Associates Plaza
Islandia, NY 11788

Voice: 516-342-5224 or 800-243-9462
Web: http://www.cheyenne.com

CISCO SYSTEMS, INC.

Cisco's line of firewalls accommodate networks of any size. The Cisco Centri firewall provides small- to medium-size businesses with a security solution that is tightly integrated with Windows NT and easy to set up and administer. Cisco's PIX firewall series delivers high security and fast performance to corporate networks. Unlike typical CPU-intensive proxy servers that perform extensive processing on each data packet, the Cisco PIX firewalls use a non-UNIX, secure, real-time, embedded system for greater performance.

Cisco Systems, Inc.
170 West Tasman Drive
San Jose, CA 95134

Voice: 408-526-4000 or 800-553-NETS
Fax: 408-526-4100
Web: http://www.cisco.com

DIGITAL SECURED NETWORKS TECHNOLOGY, INC.

Digital Secured Networks' NetFortress encryption device requires no configuration, and provides a method for sending confidential information over the Internet. You can also use the device to create secure Virtual Private Networks over the Internet.

Digital Secured Networks Technology, Inc.
2701 N. Rocky Point Dr., #650
Tampa, FL 33607

Voice: 813-288-7388
Fax: 813-288-7389
Web: http://www.dsnt.com

ENTRUST TECHNOLOGIES, INC.

Entrust by Entrust Technologies, Inc. (formerly Nortel Secure Networks) is a file-signing and encryption package. The client interface is highly intuitive, and the product centralizes key management and balances administrative roles.

Entrust Technologies, Inc.
2323 North Central Expressway, Suite 360
Richardson, TX 75080

Voice: 972-994-8000
Fax: 972-994-8005
E-mail: entrust@entrust.com
Web: http://www.entrust.com

FINJAN, INC.

Finjan's line of Java and ActiveX security products includes SurfinGate, a corporate-level Java security solution for protecting the corporate network from harmful Java applets that could otherwise enter in through the Internet. SurfinGate inspects all Java content at the gateway, creates a unique identifier for each applet on the fly, and compares the applet byte code and behavior to user-defined security parameters.

Finjan, Inc.
2620 Augustine Drive, Suite 250
Santa Clara, CA 95054

Voice: 408-727-8120
Fax: 408-727-8528
Web: http://www.finjan.com

FORTRES GRAND CORP.

The Windows-based Fortres 101 product protects boot process, desktop settings and arrangement, and the file system. Users can block or control access, prevent execution from floppies, and prevent users from downloading programs.

Fortres Grand Corp.
P.O. Box 888
Plymouth, IN 46563

Voice: 800-331-0372
Fax: 800-882-4381
Web: http://www.fortres.com

GLOBAL DATA SECURITY

Global Data Security's LANauditor automatically maintains a detailed inventory of the hardware and software installed on each file server and workstation on a network. LANauditor supports several commonly used network and client operating systems and complies with the Desktop Management Interface (DMI) standard.

Global Data Security
3990 Ruffin Rd.
San Diego, CA 92123

Voice: 800-809-4629 or 619-874-7500
Fax: 619-874-7520
E-mail: info@sd.gdsecurity.com
Web: http://www.gdsecurity.com

HAYSTACK LABS

See Trusted Information Systems.

INNOVATIVE SECURITY PRODUCTS

ISP provides a wide variety of security hardware and software that focuses on prevention of physical theft. The company offers a selection of lid locks, drive locks, cables, and other hardware devices designed to help secure computers and peripherals.

Innovative Security Products
P.O. Box 8682
Prairie Village, KS 66208

Voice: 913-385-2002
Fax: 913-642-9546
E-mail: sales@wesecure.com
Web: http://www.isecure.com

INTERNET SECURITY SYSTEMS, INC.

Internet Security Systems offers a family of adaptive security products. RealSecure is an automated, real-time attack recognition and response system for your network. System Security Scanner (S3) enables system administrators to proactively seek out internal system vulnerabilities, and ISS's Internet Scanner Toolset can conduct network vulnerability analysis and decision support.

Internet Security Systems, Inc.
41 Perimeter Center, Suite 660
Atlanta, GA 30346

Voice: 770-395-0150
Fax: 770-395-1972
Web: http://www.iss.net

KANSMEN CORPORATION

You can use Kansmen's LittleBrother Pro to restrict network users from unproductive activities, such as visiting Internet sites not related to work. The monitoring program reviews the activities of internal users, and can generate instant reports in graphical or text format.

Kansmen Corporation
546 Valley Way
Milpitas, CA 95035

Voice: 408-263-9881
Fax: 408-263-9883
E-mail: info@kansmen.com, sales@kansmen.com
Web: http://www.kansmen.com

LEGATO SYSTEMS, INC.

Legato's NetWorker is an enterprise storage management solution that takes advantage of existing resources. The scaleable family of products provides for backup and recovery, archive and retrieval, and file migration for networks of all sizes.

Legato Systems, Inc.
3210 Porter Dr.
Palo Alto, CA 94304

Voice: 650-812-6000
Fax: 650-812-6032
Web: http://www.legato.com

MIROS INC.

Miros' TrueFace CyberWatch product uses face recognition technology to restrict access to sensitive data. The hardware portion of the product, a small video camera, takes pictures of each user and stores them in a database. Anyone who attempts to use the system is then "seen" by the camera, and the user's image is compared to the database to determine whether or not access is allowed.

Miros Inc.
572 Washington St., Suite 18
Wellesley, MA 02181

Voice: 781-235-0330
Fax: 781-235-0720
Web: http://www.miros.com

NORTEL SECURE NETWORKS
See Entrust Technologies, Inc.

ON TECHNOLOGY
ON Technology's ON Guard overcomes the complexities of UNIX. ON Technology uses its own secure, special-purpose operating system, Secure32OS, designed specifically for firewalls.

ON Technology
One Cambridge Center
Cambridge, MA 02142

Voice: 617-374-1400
Fax: 617-374-1433
Web: http://www.on.com

PC GUARDIAN
In addition to antitheft physical security devices such as cables and computer hardware locks, PC Guardian offers a selection of encryption software and access control solutions.

PC Guardian
1133 E. Francisco Blvd.
San Rafael, CA 94901

Voice: 415-459-0190 or 800-288-8126
Fax: 415-459-1162
Web: http://www.pcguardian.com

PRETTY GOOD PRIVACY, INC.
Pretty Good Privacy (PGP) is a leader in digital encryption products that enable secure digital communication and storage for both individuals and businesses. PGP's family of encryption products includes all forms of digital information: e-mail, data, telephony, fax, image, and video.

Pretty Good Privacy, Inc.
2121 S. El Camino Real, Suite 902
San Mateo, CA 94403

Voice: 650-572-0430
Fax: 650-572-1932
Web: http://www.pgp.com

RSA DATA SECURITY, INC.
RSA's encryption technology is embedded in Microsoft Windows, Netscape Navigator, Intuit's Quicken, Lotus Notes, and hundreds of other products. RSA Data Security offers a wide variety of toolkits that enable software and hardware developers to incorporate encryption technologies into their products.

RSA Data Security, Inc.
100 Marine Parkway, Suite 500
Redwood City, CA 94065-1031

Voice: 650-595-8782
Fax: 650-595-1873
Web: http://www.rsa.com

SEATTLE SOFTWARE LABS, INC.
See WatchGuard Technologies, Inc.

SOFTWARE.COM
Software.com's Post.Office is a POP3/SMTP mail server with integrated list manager for the Internet community as well as corporate intranets. Post.Office offers a secure alternative to existing tools such as Sendmail and smail. This messaging server is based entirely on the open standards of the Internet, ensuring maximum compatibility with other systems.

Software.com
525 Anacapa Street
Santa Barbara, CA 93101-1603

Voice: 805-882-2470
Fax: 805-882-2473
Web: http://www.software.com/

TELEMATE SOFTWARE, INC.
TELEMATE Software, Inc. develops an integrated telemanagement solution that includes call accounting, facilities management, and toll-fraud detection.

TELEMATE Software, Inc.
4250 Perimeter Park South, Suite 200
Atlanta, GA 30341-1201

Voice: 770-936-3700
Fax: 770-936-3710
E-mail: info@telemate.com
Web: http://www.telemate.com

TRUSTED INFORMATION SYSTEMS

Trusted Information Systems has acquired Haystack Labs, provider of the WebStalker Pro Web server security monitoring tool. WebStalker Pro detects and responds to a variety of security incidents, including illegal logins and illegal file access. It also controls access to the Web server by monitoring access by FTP, Telnet, login, rexec, rlogin, and rsh.

Trusted Information Systems
10713 RR 620 North, Suite 512
Austin, TX 78726

Voice: 512-918-3555
Fax: 512-918-1265
Web: http://www.tis.com

VERISIGN, INC.

VeriSign is a major provider of digital authentication services and products for electronic commerce and other forms of secure communications. VeriSign's services and products fall into three lines of business: digital ID services, private-label certificate services, and certificate management products.

VeriSign, Inc.
1390 Shorebird Way
Mountain View, CA 94043

Voice: 650-961-7500
Fax: 650-961-7300
Web: http://www.verisign.com

WATCHGUARD TECHNOLOGIES, INC.

WatchGuard Security System by WatchGuard Technologies (formerly Seattle Software Labs, Inc.) consists of two components: the Firebox (hardware) and Security Management System (software). The Firebox is a firewall that runs transparent proxies and a dynamic stateful packet filter to control the flow of IP-based information. The "all-in-one" firewall and network security management system provides security for both intranets and the Internet, easy setup and usage, and strong reporting capabilities.

WatchGuard Technologies, Inc.
316 Occidental Ave. South, Suite 300
Seattle, WA 98104

Voice: 206-521-8340
Fax: 206-521-8341
Web: http://www.watchguard.com

Appendix F

About the CD-ROM

THE COMPANION **CD-ROM** CONTAINS two leading programs that will significantly enhance your network's security: Trusted Information System's (formerly Haystack Labs) WebStalker Pro monitoring software and Cheyenne Software's CA-InocuLAN enterprise antivirus system. The CD-ROM also contains Internet Explorer 4.

The CD is organized into the following subdirectories:

- ◆ ILANNW – CA-InocuLAN for NetWare
- ◆ ILANNT – CA-InocuLAN for Windows NT
- ◆ WSNT – WebStalker for Windows NT
- ◆ WSAIX – WebStalker for AIX
- ◆ WSSOL – WebStalker for Solaris
- ◆ Internet Explorer 4 – Internet Explorer 4

WebStalker Pro

WebStalker continually monitors Web sites and detects the following:

- ◆ Unauthorized users logging into the Web site
- ◆ Users illegally becoming administrator
- ◆ Hackers using your Web site as a jump-point for moving to other sensitive machines within your network that may contain sensitive information
- ◆ Vandalism of your Web site
- ◆ Illegal shut-down of the Web server
- ◆ Attempts to tamper with the WebStalker program

WebStalker takes immediate action when it detects a violation. In addition to recording all violations in a log file, WebStalker also notifies the security manager of any incident via e-mail or pager. You can also configure WebStalker to shun users who create security problems by preventing them from logging in for a specified period of time. For immediate response, WebStalker sends an SNMP trap to your network management system, and can terminate the offender's system process and prevent the offender from logging in again.

WebStalker will work with all major network management systems, including NetView, OpenView, and SunNet Manager.

Versions are included on the CD-ROM for Windows NT, Solaris, and AIX. To install WebStalker for Solaris or AIX, refer to INSTALL.TXT for installation instructions. To install Web Stalker for Windows NT, double-click SETUP.EXE and follow the instructions. For more information, consult the WebStalker Web site at http:// www.tis.com.

CA-InocuLAN

Cheyenne's CA-InocuLAN provides enterprise-wide protection from viruses. Provided here for both Windows NT and NetWare environments, InocuLAN can protect desktops, servers, messaging systems, and more. Taking an enterprise approach to virus protection is essential. This approach includes centralized control, automated virus signature updates, and support for multiple platforms.

The required key codes for InocuLAN are as follows:

NetWare	CIXXE-W14CM-X19XC-J71JE
Windows 95	LYKX1-X14C1-XC9HM-17HRK
Windows NT	CMMXG-X14CM-XC9HC-J7CZC
Windows NT Workstation	IIWXG-X14CE-XW9HC-17MHL

InocuLAN provides a single installation process that permits you to install the InocuLAN Windows Manager Windows interface, DOS Manager menu-driven interface, InocuLAN Server NLM, and Alert NLM. InocuLAN for Windows Manager is the Windows interface; InocuLAN for DOS Manager is the menu-driven interface; InocuLAN Server NLM is installed on a file server and provides the manager with the ability to administer InocuLAN from the server console; and Alert NLM is a notification system that sends alert messages through a variety of methods. Windows Manager and DOS Manager can be installed on the workstation or on the server.

You must have supervisor or equivalent rights on a server before installing InocuLAN or Alert. For NetWare 3.*x* users, InocuLAN will not create a user object. The program is file-based. If a user object exists, it will be preserved to maintain notification compatibility with InocuLAN 3.0. If you are using NetWare 4.*x*, the user object added is CHEY_VSVR_servername. In order to keep the IPX internal network address constant, load it from the AUTOEXEC.NCF file. You should use the following statement:

```
ipx internal net nnnnnn
```

To install from within Windows, insert the CD-ROM into the drive, choose Run from the File menu in the Windows Program Manager and, in the text box, type the appropriate subdirectory (ILANNT or ILANNW) and \SETUP:

\ILANNT\SETUP

or

\ILANNW\SETUP

Then click OK. The InocuLAN setup program loads, and the license screen appears.

Internet Explorer 4

To install Internet Explorer 4, you'll find the setup file in the Internet Explorer 4.0 folder. Double-click the .EXE file for the browser and follow the directions.

Glossary

access   The ability of information to flow between a subject and an object.

ANSI   American National Standards Institute. The standards body responsible for data communications and terminal standards.

ASCII   American Standard Code for Information Interchange. A seven-bit coding mechanism that matches text characters with numeric values to allow data to be exchanged between communications devices.

asymmetric cipher   A public key cipher.

attack   A method of breaking the integrity of a cipher.

audit trail   A record that is usually generated electronically, and provides documentation that can be used to trace transactions and other occurrences.

authenticate   The process of establishing whether an individual claiming an identity is really that individual.

authentication   Assurance that a message has not been modified during transit.

autokey   A cipher whose key is generated by message data.

bandwidth   A value of a communications channel that shows how much information can be sent in a given time period. Usually expressed in bits per second (bps).

bit   The smallest unit of electronic information.

block   A quantity of data, usually measured in bits, that is treated as a single unit.

block cipher   A cipher under which data must be accumulated before ciphering is completed.

Brown Book   The Department of Defense Guide to Understanding Trusted Facility Management. This document explores issues involved in creating and maintaining a trusted facility.

break   The result of an attack; that is, when an intruder compromises the integrity of a cipher.

block size   The amount of data contained in a block.

brute force attack   A type of attack under which every possible combination (such as in passwords) is attempted.

byte   Eight bits.

Certification Authority (CA)   An entity that distributes public and private key pairs.

channel   An information transfer path.

cipher   A security method designed to hide data content by acting on individual bits, without regard to the semantics of the actual content.

ciphering   Using a cipher.

ciphertext   What results after enciphering takes place. Ciphering contains the same data as plaintext, although the plaintext is hidden and is difficult or impossible to recover without a key.

codebook attack   A type of attack where the intruder attempts to create a codebook of all possible transformations between plaintext and ciphertext under a single key.

conventional cipher   A secret key cipher.

cookie   Properly known as a "persistent client state HTTP cookie." A text file, transferred between the Web server and the Web client (browser), that tracks where you went on the Web site, how long you stayed in each area, and other information.

covert channel   A channel that permits a process to transfer information in such a way that the system's security policy is being violated.

CRC   Cyclic redundancy check. An error-checking hash mechanism.

cryptanalyst   An individual who attacks (breaks) ciphers.

cryptographer   A creator of ciphers.

cryptographic mechanism   The process of enciphering and deciphering.

cryptography   The science of transforming data into an alternate format that hides the original information. Cryptography renders a message unintelligible to anyone who intercepts it.

cryptology   The study of steganography, cryptography, and cryptanalysis.

data integrity   The state of data when it has not been compromised or altered in any way.

data remanence   The residual data that may be left over on storage media after it has been erased.

decipher   The process of uncovering the data hidden within ciphertext.

decryption   The process of extracting data that has been hidden by encryption.

degaussing   The process of demagnetizing electronic storage media in order to erase its contents.

demilitarized zone (DMZ)   A perimeter network that adds an extra layer of protection, by establishing a server network that exists between the protected network and the external network (the Internet). The term is named after the zone that separates North and South Korea, a sort of political "no-man's land."

denial–of–service attack   A type of computer attack that denies service to users by either clogging the system with a deluge of irrelevant messages or sending disruptive commands to the system.

DES   Data Encryption Standard. A 64-bit block cipher with a 56-bit key.

Desktop Management Interface   A standard that establishes a common, standard interface for different management applications.

digital certificate   A password-protected and encrypted file that contains identification information about its holder. It includes a *public key*, which is used to verify the sender's digital signature, and a unique *private key*. Exchanging keys and certificates allows two parties to verify each other's identities before communicating.

discretionary access control   A method of limiting access to objects based on the identity of subjects, or groups of subjects. Typically, an individual with a certain level of access can pass permission on to another subject, unless doing so is restricted by mandatory access control.

domain   Those objects to which a subject has access.

encipher   The process of transforming plaintext data into ciphertext.

encryption   The process of hiding plaintext data with a cipher or code.

exclusive–OR   XOR. A Boolean logic function.

firewall   A device and accompanying software that filters packets based on header information, destination, or other parameters.

gateway   A type of firewall, router, or other device that is deployed in an internal WAN. The gateway blocks the transmission of certain types of traffic.

granularity   The relative degree of detail to which any mechanism or process can be adjusted.

hash   The process of creating a fixed value from arbitrary data, such that if the arbitrary data (such as an e-mail message) is altered, the hash value also changes.

hierarchical storage management   A system of migrating infrequently used files to a hierarchy of less expensive, offline storage media.

IDEA   International Data Encryption Algorithm. A secret key block cipher, used in Pretty Good Privacy (PGP). IDEA uses a 64-bit block and a 128-bit key.

inheritance   When an object acquires the rights and properties of another object.

Internetwork   Multiple networks connected by a router, bridge, or gateway.

intranet   A private, TCP/IP-based network that uses Internet technology, but is not accessible to the public.

key   A secret value used to protect data. Keys may be used to protect files and restrict access.

keyspace   The number of keys supported by a cipher.

least privilege   A policy concept that grants every subject only those privileges required to carry out his or her tasks.

macro virus   A small set of instructions that is carried out by a certain program. A legitimate macro is usually implemented to automate routine tasks, such as typing in a long address, performing text sorts, or manipulating data. A macro virus implements destructive or mischievous tasks.

man-in-the-middle attack   A type of attack that takes advantage of the store-and-forward mechanism used by insecure networks such as the Internet. In this type of attack, an attacker places himself between two parties and intercepts messages before transferring them on to their intended destination.

mandatory access control   A method of limiting access to objects based on flags or labels contained by the objects, and each subject's stated authorization to access different types of objects.

message digest   A value (or hash) that is calculated based on arbitrary data.

message key   An encrypted key that is transported with the original message. The message key, once deciphered, is then used to decipher the full message.

object   An entity that contains or receives information, such as a record, block, file, or directory.

Open Platform for Secure Enterprise Connectivity (OPSEC)   A platform for integrating and managing enterprise security through an open and extensible management framework. OPSEC includes a series of published APIs, supports industry-standard protocols, and offers a high-level scripting language.

Orange Book   The Department of Defense Trusted Computer System Evaluation Criteria. This document presents a method for evaluating the security controls of a data processing system.

OSI reference model   A networking reference model that divides communications into seven connected layers, each of which builds on the functions of the one below it.

Layer 7: Application Layer

Layer 6: Presentation Layer

Layer 5: Session Layer

Layer 4: Transport Layer

Layer 3: Network Layer

Layer 2: Data Link Layer

Layer 1: Physical Layer

packet snarfing   Also know as *eavesdropping*. When a host sets its network interface on promiscuous mode and copies the packets that pass by for later analysis.

padding   Meaningless data added to the start or end of messages. Padding is used to hide the length of the message, or to add volume to a data structure that requires a fixed size.

password   A secret character string used for authentication.

PGP   Pretty Good Privacy. A public key cipher mechanism that uses the RSA and IDEA ciphers. RSA is first employed to transfer a random key, then IDEA is employed to encrypt the actual message.

plaintext   The original message, in unencrypted, readable form.

public key cipher   An asymmetric cipher that uses one key to encipher a message, and a second key to decipher the ciphertext. The first key (used to encipher the message) can be exposed, and is known as the *public key*. The second key is secret, and is known as the *private key*.

RAID   Redundant Array of Independent Disks. A cluster of disks used to back up data onto multiple drives.

read access   Permission to read information.

Red Book   The Department of Defense Trusted Network Interpretation Environments Guideline. This document provides network administrators with insights into maintaining a trusted network environment.

router   An intelligent device used to send data packets to various destinations throughout the network.

RSA   A public key algorithm (named for Rivest/Shamir/Adelman).

secret key cipher   A symmetric cipher, where the same key is used to encipher a message and to decipher the ciphertext.

Secure HyperText Transfer Protocol (S-HTTP)   A message-oriented communications protocol that extends the HTTP protocol. It coexists with HTTP's messaging model and can be easily integrated with HTTP applications.

security policy   A document that sets out rules and practices that regulate how an organization manages and protects its information.

security testing   The process of determining whether a security feature or process is implemented as designed and adequate for its intended purpose.

Sendmail   An e-mail transport mechanism used in the UNIX operating system and on the Internet.

sensitive information   Information that requires a high level of protection.

Simple Network Management Protocol (SNMP)   A core service of the TCP/IP protocol suite. It provides a framework for systems to report problems, configuration information, and performance data to a central network management site.

snarfing   *See* packet snarfing.

spoofing   A type of attack in which one computer disguises itself as another in order to gain access to a system.

steganography   A method of cryptology that hides the existence of a message.

strength   The relative ability of a cipher to hide its message.

subject   An entity, such as a person or process, that causes information to move between objects.

substitution   A basic type of encryption that replaces one symbol with a corresponding symbol.

symmetric cipher   A secret key cipher.

Telnet   A terminal emulation protocol and part of the TCP/IP suite that permits a user to remotely log on to a second computer.

Triple-DES   A block cipher in which DES is executed three times.

trustee   A user or group of users who have specific access rights to work with a particular directory, file, or object.

Trojan horse   A type of computer program that performs an ostensibly useful function, but contains a hidden function that compromises the host system's security.

Virtual LAN (VLAN)   A network configuration in which frames are broadcast within the VLAN, and routed between VLANs. The broadcast domain can be made up of devices connected to a single port on a switch, users on multiple ports on a single switch, or users attached to multiple ports on different switches.

write access   Permission to write to an object.

XOR   Exclusive-OR. A Boolean logic function.

Index

my2cents.idgbooks.com

Register This Book — And Win!

Visit **http://my2cents.idgbooks.com** to register this book and we'll automatically enter you in our fantastic monthly prize giveaway. It's also your opportunity to give us feedback: let us know what you thought of this book and how you would like to see other topics covered.

Discover IDG Books Online!

The IDG Books Online Web site is your online resource for tackling technology — at home and at the office. Frequently updated, the IDG Books Online Web site features exclusive software, insider information, online books, and live events!

10 Productive & Career-Enhancing Things You Can Do at www.idgbooks.com

- Nab source code for your own programming projects.

- Download software.

- Read Web exclusives: special articles and book excerpts by IDG Books Worldwide authors.

- Take advantage of resources to help you advance your career as a Novell or Microsoft professional.

- Buy IDG Books Worldwide titles or find a convenient bookstore that carries them.

- Register your book and win a prize.

- Chat live online with authors.

- Sign up for regular e-mail updates about our latest books.

- Suggest a book you'd like to read or write.

- Give us your 2¢ about our books and about our Web site.

You say you're not on the Web yet? It's easy to get started with IDG Books' *Discover the Internet,* available at local retailers everywhere.

IDG BOOKS WORLDWIDE, INC.
END-USER LICENSE AGREEMENT

READ THIS. You should carefully read these terms and conditions before opening the software packet(s) included with this book ("Book"). This is a license agreement ("Agreement") between you and IDG Books Worldwide, Inc. ("IDGB"). By opening the accompanying software packet(s), you acknowledge that you have read and accept the following terms and conditions. If you do not agree and do not want to be bound by such terms and conditions, promptly return the Book and the unopened software packet(s) to the place you obtained them for a full refund.

1. **License Grant.** IDGB grants to you (either an individual or entity) a nonexclusive license to use one copy of the enclosed software program(s) (collectively, the "Software") solely for your own personal or business purposes on a single computer (whether a standard computer or a workstation component of a multiuser network). The Software is in use on a computer when it is loaded into temporary memory (RAM) or installed into permanent memory (hard disk, CD-ROM, or other storage device). IDGB reserves all rights not expressly granted herein.

2. **Ownership.** IDGB is the owner of all right, title, and interest, including copyright, in and to the compilation of the Software recorded on the disk(s) or CD-ROM ("Software Media"). Copyright to the individual programs recorded on the Software Media is owned by the author or other authorized copyright owner of each program. Ownership of the Software and all proprietary rights relating thereto remain with IDGB and its licensers.

3. **Restrictions on Use and Transfer.**

    (a) You may only (i) make one copy of the Software for backup or archival purposes, or (ii) transfer the Software to a single hard disk, provided that you keep the original for backup or archival purposes. You may not (i) rent or lease the Software, (ii) copy or reproduce the Software through a LAN or other network system or through any computer subscriber system or bulletin-board system, or (iii) modify, adapt, or create derivative works based on the Software.

    (b) You may not reverse engineer, decompile, or disassemble the Software. You may transfer the Software and user documentation on a permanent basis, provided that the transferee agrees to accept the terms and conditions of this Agreement and you retain no copies. If the Software is an update or has been updated, any transfer must include the most recent update and all prior versions.

4. **Restrictions on Use of Individual Programs.** You must follow the individual requirements and restrictions detailed for each individual program in Appendix F, "About the CD-ROM," of this Book. These limitations are also contained in the individual license agreements recorded on the Software Media. These limitations may include a requirement that after using the program for a specified period of time, the user must pay a registration fee or discontinue use. By opening the Software packet(s), you will be agreeing to abide by the licenses and restrictions for these individual programs that are detailed in Appendix F, "About the CD-ROM," and on the Software Media. None of the material on this Software Media or listed in this Book may ever be redistributed, in original or modified form, for commercial purposes.

5. **Limited Warranty.**

   (a) IDGB warrants that the Software and Software Media are free from defects in materials and workmanship under normal use for a period of sixty (60) days from the date of purchase of this Book. If IDGB receives notification within the warranty period of defects in materials or workmanship, IDGB will replace the defective Software Media.

   (b) IDGB AND THE AUTHOR OF THE BOOK DISCLAIM ALL OTHER WARRANTIES, EXPRESS OR IMPLIED, INCLUDING WITHOUT LIMITATION IMPLIED WARRANTIES OF MERCHANTABILITY AND FITNESS FOR A PARTICULAR PURPOSE, WITH RESPECT TO THE SOFTWARE, THE PROGRAMS, THE SOURCE CODE CONTAINED THEREIN, AND/OR THE TECHNIQUES DESCRIBED IN THIS BOOK. IDGB DOES NOT WARRANT THAT THE FUNCTIONS CONTAINED IN THE SOFTWARE WILL MEET YOUR REQUIREMENTS OR THAT THE OPERATION OF THE SOFTWARE WILL BE ERROR FREE.

   (c) This limited warranty gives you specific legal rights, and you may have other rights that vary from jurisdiction to jurisdiction.

6. **Remedies.**

   (a) IDGB's entire liability and your exclusive remedy for defects in materials and workmanship shall be limited to replacement of the Software Media, which may be returned to IDGB with a copy of your receipt at the following address: Software Media Fulfillment Department, Attn.: Network Security in a Mixed Environment, IDG Books Worldwide, Inc., 7260 Shadeland Station, Ste. 100, Indianapolis, IN 46256, or call 1-800-762-2974. Please allow three to four weeks for delivery. This Limited Warranty is void if failure of the Software Media has resulted from accident, abuse, or misapplication. Any replacement Software Media will be warranted for the remainder of the original warranty period or thirty (30) days, whichever is longer.

(b) In no event shall IDGB or the author be liable for any damages whatsoever (including without limitation damages for loss of business profits, business interruption, loss of business information, or any other pecuniary loss) arising from the use of or inability to use the Book or the Software, even if IDGB has been advised of the possibility of such damages.

(c) Because some jurisdictions do not allow the exclusion or limitation of liability for consequential or incidental damages, the above limitation or exclusion may not apply to you.

7. U.S. Government Restricted Rights. Use, duplication, or disclosure of the Software by the U.S. Government is subject to restrictions stated in paragraph (c)(1)(ii) of the Rights in Technical Data and Computer Software clause of DFARS 252.227-7013, and in subparagraphs (a) through (d) of the Commercial Computer – Restricted Rights clause at FAR 52.227-19, and in similar clauses in the NASA FAR supplement, when applicable.

8. General. This Agreement constitutes the entire understanding of the parties and revokes and supersedes all prior agreements, oral or written, between them and may not be modified or amended except in a writing signed by both parties hereto that specifically refers to this Agreement. This Agreement shall take precedence over any other documents that may be in conflict herewith. If any one or more provisions contained in this Agreement are held by any court or tribunal to be invalid, illegal, or otherwise unenforceable, each and every other provision shall remain in full force and effect.

Installation Instructions

THE COMPANION CD-ROM CONTAINS two leading programs that will significantly enhance your network's security: Trusted Information System's (formerly Haystack Labs) WebStalker Pro monitoring software and Cheyenne Software's CA-InocuLAN enterprise antivirus system. The CD-ROM also contains Internet Explorer 4.

To install WebStalker for Solaris or AIX, refer to INSTALL.TXT for installation instructions. To install WebStalker for Windows NT, double-click SETUP.EXE and follow the instructions. For more information, consult the WebStalker Web site at http://www.tis.com.

To install CA-InocuLAN from within Windows, insert the CD-ROM into the drive, choose Run from the File menu in the Windows Program Manager and, in the text box, type the appropriate subdirectory (ILANNT or ILANNW) and \SETUP:

\ILANNT\SETUP

or

\ILANNW\SETUP

Then click OK. The InocuLAN setup program loads, and the license screen appears. The required key codes for InocuLAN are as follows:

NetWare	CIXXE-W14CM-X19XC-J71JE
Windows 95	LYKX1-X14C1-XC9HM-17HRK
Windows NT	CMMXG-X14CM-XC9HC-J7CZC
Windows NT Workstation	IIWXG-X14CE-XW9HC-17MHL

To install Internet Explorer 4, you'll find the setup file in the Internet Explorer 4.0 folder. Double-click the .EXE file for the browser and follow the directions.